Lucian's

The Ass

An Intermediate Greek Reader

Greek text with running vocabulary and commentary

Evan Hayes
and
Stephen Nimis

Lucian's *Lucius, or The Ass*: An Intermediate Greek Reader
Greek text with Running Vocabulary and Commentary

First Edition

© 2012 by Evan Hayes and Stephen Nimis

Revised October 2012

The Greek text is based on the edition of C. Jacobitz, published by Teubner in
1907.

ISBN-13: 978-0-9832228-2-8
ISBN-10: 0983222827

Published by Faenum Publishing, Ltd.
Cover Design: Evan Hayes

Fonts: Gentium (Open Font License)
         GFS Porson (Open Font License)

nimissa@muohio.edu
hayesee@muohio.edu

Table of Contents

Acknowledgments

The idea for this project grew out of work that we, the authors, did with support from Miami University's Undergraduate Summer Scholars Program, for which we thank Martha Weber and the Office of Advanced Research and Scholarship. The Miami University College of Arts and Science's Dean's Scholar Program allowed us to continue work on the project and for this we are grateful to the Office of the Dean, particularly to Phyllis Callahan and Nancy Arthur for their continued interest and words of encouragement.

Work on the series, of which this volume is a part, was generously funded by the Joanna Jackson Goldman Memorial Prize through the Honors Program at Miami University. We owe a great deal to Carolyn Haynes, and the 2010 Honors & Scholars Program Advisory Committee for their interest and confidence in the project.

The technical aspects of the project were made possible through the invaluable advice and support of Bill Hayes, Christopher Kuo, and Daniel Meyers. The equipment and staff of Miami University's Interactive Language Resource Center were a great help along the way. We are also indebted to the Perseus Project, especially Gregory Crane and Bridget Almas, for their technical help and resources.

We owe special thanks to Carolyn DeWitt and Kristie Fernberg, whose administrative support, patience, and good humor were essential for the completion of this manuscript.

We also profited greatly from advice and help on the POD process from Geoffrey Steadman. We are grateful to Joel Relihan for a number of corrections that appear in this revised version. All responsibility for errors, however, rests with the authors themselves.

φιλτάτῳ καὶ ἐξοχώτατῳ
Alex Robbins

Introduction

The aim of this book is to make Pseudo-Lucian's *Lucius, or The Ass* accessible to intermediate students of Greek. The running vocabulary and commentary are meant to provide everything necessary to read each page. The commentary is primarily grammatical, explaining subordinate clauses, conditions etc., and parsing unusual verb forms. The page by page vocabularies gloss all but the most common words. We have endeavored to make these glossaries as useful as possible without becoming fulsome. A glossary of all words occurring three or more times in the text can be found as an appendix in the back, but it is our hope that most readers will not need to use this appendix often. There is also a list of verbs occurring in the text that have unusual forms in the back of the book. Brief explanations of allusions and proper names are given, but this is not primarily a literary commentary.

The Ass is a great intermediate Greek text. The narrative is fast-paced and funny, and the language is fairly simple and easy to follow. The reputation of the story has suffered at the hands of critics due in part to an unfavorable comparison to its more famous Latin relative, Apuleius' *The Golden Ass*. These two narratives share some similarities too close to be accidental, and their complex relationship will be discussed below. But irrespective of that comparison, *The Ass* is an unpretentious satirical text that tells a funny story in a casual and light-hearted manner. There is little moralizing or didacticism in the story, although modern audiences will no doubt find the mistreatment of animals and other fellow humans by many characters in the story appalling. The story is told entirely from the perspective of the main character, Lucius, who is turned into an ass by magic. Unlike the Lucius of Apuleius's version of the story, also narrated in the first person , this Lucius does not seem to achieve any religious or philosophical illumination from his adventures. The final episode is a funny twist of events completely in tune with the tenor of the rest of the novel. There is a hilarious love-making episode with lots of double-entendre, and other episodes that portray the doings of various low-life characters who are rarely present in ancient literature at all. Thieves, religious charlatans, witches, millers, servants, soldiers and bakers all find a place in this strange story of chance and magic.

As mentioned above, *The Ass* and Apuleius' *The Golden Ass* have numerous striking similarities in plot and expression. There appears to have been another longer Greek version of the story known as the *Metamorphoses*, which is now lost; and the most common theory is that Pseudo-Lucian's version is an epitome of this longer work. Apuleius' Latin version, which Apuleius explicitly states is based on a Greek story, is also generally thought to be a translation of this earlier Greek *Metamorphoses*. Thus, the similarities between Apuleius and Pseudo-Lucian are to be accounted for by their lost common source. In our text, we have provided samples of parallels from Apuleius' Latin text in an appendix, choosing the most salient examples, so that the reader can get an idea of the similarities. Finally, although the majority opinion is that *The Ass* is not an authentic work of Lucian, we cannot be completely certain on this matter either.

An excellent and balanced survey of the question of sources can be found in H. J. Mason, "Greek and Latin Versions of the Ass-Story, *Aufstieg und Niedergang der römische Welt* II 34.2 (Berlin-New York: 1994), 1665-1707.

A side-by-side comparison of the stories is provided by T. van Thiel, *Der Eselroman*: Vol II, Synoptische Ausgabe. *Zetemeta* 54.2 (Munich, 1972).

Arguing for Lucianic authorship is G. Anderson, "Studies in Lucian's Comic Fiction," *Mnemosyne Supplementband* 43 (Leiden, 1976).

How to use this book:

The presentation assumes the reader has a basic acquaintance with Greek grammar. Generally, particles have not been included in the page-by-page glossaries, along with other common nouns and adjectives. If necessary, all of these words can be found in the glossary at the end. Verbs, being a special problem in Greek, have been treated more fully. A simple and more generic dictionary entry is given in the glossary on each page, with a more specific meaning provided in the commentary below if necessary. We have also included a list of verbs with unusual forms and their principal parts as an appendix, which should be useful in identifying the dictionary form of verbs. A good strategy for attacking a text like this is to read a section of the Greek to get as much out of it as possible, then to look at the glossary below for unrecognized vocabulary items, and lastly to consult the commentary. The fuller glossary at the end of the book can be a last resort.

In translating expressions we have sought to provide an English version that reproduces the grammatical relationships as much as possible, producing in many cases awkward expressions (sometimes called "translationese"). Good idiomatic translations are available for this text, but the translations in the commentary are meant to provide explanations of how the Greek works.

The Greek text is based on the edition of C. Jacobitz (Leipzig, 1907), which is in the public domain and is available in digitized form on the Bibliotheca Augustana (www.hs-augsburg.de/~harsch/augustana.html). We have made a few minor changes to make the text more readable. This is not a scholarly text; for that the reader is referred to the edition of MacLeod in the Oxford Classical Texts.

The images used throughout the text are taken from *Apuleio Volgare*, tr. Matteo Maria Boiardo. Venice, 1518.

An Important Disclaimer:

This volume is a self-published "Print on Demand" (POD) book, and it has not been vetted or edited in the usual way by publishing professionals. There are sure to be some factual and typographical errors in the text, for which we apologize in advance. The volume is also available only through online distributors, since each book is printed only when ordered online. However, this publishing channel and format also account for the low price of the book; and it is a simple matter to make changes to the pdf file when they come to our attention. For this reason, any corrections or suggestions for improvement are welcome and will be addressed as quickly as possible in future versions of the text.

Evan Hayes
hayesee@muohio.edu

Stephen Nimis
nimissa@muohio.edu

Evan Hayes is a recent graduate in Classics and Philosophy at Miami University and the 2011 Joanna Jackson Goldman Scholar.

Stephen Nimis is a Professor of Classics at Miami University.

Abbreviations

abs.	absolute	inf.	infinitive
acc.	accusative	m.	masculine
act.	active	n.	neuter
adj.	adjective	nom.	nominative
adv.	adverb	obj.	object
ao.	aorist	opt.	optative
app.	appositive	part.	participle
comp.	comparative	pas.	passive
cond.	condition	perf.	perfect
dat.	dative	pl.	plural
dep.	deponent	plupf.	pluperfect
dir. obj.	direct object	pred.	predicate
f.	feminine	prep.	preposition
fut.	future	pr.	present
gen.	genitive	pron.	pronoun
imp.	imperative	reflex.	reflexive
impf.	imperfect	rel.	relative
imper.	impersonal	seq.	sequence
ind. com.	indirect command	sg.	singular
ind. obj.	indirect object	subj.	subject
ind. quest.	indirect question	superl.	superlative
ind. st.	indirect statement	voc.	vocative
indic.	indicative		

Λουκιανοῦ

Λούκιος ἢ Ὄνος

Lucian's

Lucius, or The Ass

ΛΟΥΚΙΟΣ Η ΟΝΟΣ

Lucius sets out for Hypata in Thessaly on business.

[1.] Ἀπῄειν ποτὲ ἐς Θετταλίαν· ἦν δέ μοι πατρικόν τι συμβόλαιον ἐκεῖ πρὸς ἄνθρωπον ἐπιχώριον· ἵππος δέ με κατῆγε καὶ τὰ σκεύη καὶ θεράπων ἠκολούθει εἷς. ἐπορευόμην οὖν τὴν προκειμένην ὁδόν· καί πως ἔτυχον καὶ ἄλλοι ἀπιόντες ἐς Ὕπατα πόλιν τῆς Θετταλίας, ἐκεῖθεν ὄντες· καὶ ἁλῶν ἐκοινωνοῦμεν, καὶ οὕτως ἐκείνην τὴν ἀργαλέαν ὁδὸν ἀνύσαντες πλησίον ἤδη τῆς πόλεως ἦμεν, κἀγὼ ἠρόμην τοὺς Θετταλοὺς εἴπερ ἐπίστανται ἄνδρα οἰκοῦντα ἐς τὰ Ὕπατα,

---

ἀκολουθέω: to follow
ἀλή, ἡ: salt
ἀνήρ, ἀνδρός, ὁ: a man
ἀνύω: to effect, achieve, complete
ἀπέρχομαι: to go away, depart
ἀργαλέος, -α, -ον: painful, troublous, difficult
εἴπερ: if indeed
ἐκεῖθεν: from that place
ἐπίσταμαι: to know, be acquainted with
ἐπιχώριος, -α, -ον: of or from a place, native
ἔρομαι: to ask, enquire
θεράπων, -οντος, ὁ: a servant, attendant
Θετταλία, ἡ: Thessaly
Θετταλός, ὁ: a Thessalian
ἵζω: to make to sit, seat, place
ἵππος, ὁ: a horse

κατάγω: to lead down, bring down
κοινωνέω: to have in common, share
ὁδός, ἡ: a way, path, road
οἰκέω: to inhabit, live in
πατρικός, -ή, -όν: of one's father, paternal, hereditary
πλήσιος, -α, -ον: near, close to (+ *gen.*)
πόλις, -εως, ἡ: a city
πορεύομαι: to be carried, go, walk
ποτέ: at one time, once upon a time
πρόκειμαι: to be set before one, propose, prescribe
πως: in some way, somehow
σκεύη, τά: possessions, belongings
συμβόλαιον, τό: a contract, engagement, transaction
τυγχάνω: to hit, happen upon, befall
Ὕπατα, ἡ: Hypata

ἀπῄειν: impf. of ἀπο-ἔρχομαι, "I was going"
κατῆγε: impf. of κατα-ἄγω, "was conveying me"
ἠκολούθει: impf. of ἀκολούθω, "was following"
ἔτυχον: ao. of τυγχάνω, "others happened to be" + part.
ἀπιόντες: pr. part. of ἀπο-ἔρχομαι after ἔτυχον, "departing toward"
ἐκεῖθεν ὄντες: "being from there"
ἁλῶν ἐκοινωνοῦμεν: "we shared salt" i.e. ate together
ἀνύσαντες: ao. part., "thus having finished"
ἦμεν: impf. of εἰμί, "we were"
κἀγὼ: (= καὶ ἐγὼ)
ἠρόμην: ao. of ἐρωτάω, "I asked"
εἴπερ ἐπίστανται: ind. quest., "whether they knew"

Ἵππαρχον τοὔνομα. γράμματα δὲ αὐτῷ ἐκόμιζον οἴκοθεν, ὥστε οἰκῆσαι παρ' αὐτῷ. οἱ δὲ εἰδέναι τὸν Ἵππαρχον τοῦτον ἔλεγον καὶ ὅπῃ τῆς πόλεως οἰκεῖ καὶ ὅτι ἀργύριον ἱκανὸν ἔχει καὶ ὅτι μίαν θεράπαιναν τρέφει καὶ τὴν αὐτοῦ γαμετὴν μόνας· ἔστι γὰρ φιλαργυρώτατος δεινῶς.

He arrives at the home of Hipparchus. (cf. Ap. Met. 1.22, p. 151)

ἐπεὶ δὲ πλησίον τῆς πόλεως ἐγεγόνειμεν, κῆπός τις ἦν καὶ ἔνδον οἰκίδιον ἀνεκτόν, ἔνθα ὁ Ἵππαρχος ᾤκει. [2.] οἱ μὲν οὖν ἀσπασάμενοί με ᾤχοντο, ἐγὼ δὲ κόπτω προσελθὼν τὴν

ἀνεκτός, -ή, -όν: bearable, sufferable, tolerable
ἀργύριον, τό: silver, money
ἀσπάζομαι: to welcome, bid farewell
γαμετή, ἡ: a married woman, wife
γράμμα, -ατος, τό: something written, a letter
δεινός, -ή, -όν: fearful, terrible, dreadful
εἷς, μία, ἕν: one
ἔνδον: in, within
ἔνθα: there
θεράπαινα, ἡ: a female slave, handmaid
ἱκανός, -ή, -όν: sufficient, considerable, adequate
Ἵππαρχος, ὁ: Hipparchus
κῆπος, ὁ: a garden, orchard

κομίζω: to carry, convey
κόπτω: to strike, hit, knock
λέγω: to speak, say
μόνος, -η, -ον: alone, only
οἶδα: to know
οἰκέω: to inhabit, live
οἰκίδιον, τό: a small house, cottage
οἴκοθεν: from one's house, from home
οἴχομαι: to be gone, leave
ὄνομα, -ατος, τό: a name
ὅπῃ: by which way, where
πλήσιος, -α, -ον: near, close to (+ *gen.*)
πόλις, -εως, ἡ: a city
προσέρχομαι: to go up
τρέφω: to raise, maintain, support
φιλάργυρος, -ον: fond of money, miserly

τοὔνομα: (= τὸ ὄνομα)
ὥστε οἰκῆσαι: ao. inf. in result clause "so that I could lodge with him"
οἱ δὲ: "and they"
εἰδέναι: ao. inf. of ὁράω in ind. st. after ἔλεγον, "that they knew him"
ὅπῃ ... οἰκεῖ: ind. quest. after ἔλεγον, "and where he lived"
καὶ ὅτι ἔχει: "and that he had"
καὶ ὅτι τρέφει: "and that he kept"
μόνας: agreeing collectively with θεράπαιναν and γαμετὴν, "only one handmaid and his wife"
ἔστι γὰρ: Note the casual shift from indirect to direct speech.
ἐγεγόνειμεν: plupf., "when we had become"
οἱ μὲν: "while they"
ἀσπασάμενοί: ao. part. of ἀσπάζω, "having bid farewell"

θύραν, καὶ μόλις μὲν καὶ βραδέως, ὑπήκουσε δ' οὖν γυνή, εἶτα καὶ προῆλθεν. ἐγὼ μὲν ἠρόμην εἰ ἔνδον εἴη Ἵππαρχος: «Ἔνδον,» ἔφη: «σὺ δὲ τίς ἢ τί βουλόμενος πυνθάνῃ;»

«Γράμματα ἥκω κομίζων αὐτῷ παρὰ Δεκριανοῦ τοῦ Πατρέως σοφιστοῦ.»

βούλομαι: to will, wish
βραδύς, -εῖα, -ύ: slow
γράμμα, -ατος, τό: something written, a letter
γυνή, γυναικός, ἡ: a woman, wife
Δεκριανὸς, ὁ: Decrianus
εἶτα: then, next
ἔνδον: in, within, at home
ἔρομαι: to ask, enquire

ἥκω: to have come, be present
θύρα, ἡ: a door
κομίζω: to carry, convey
μόλις: scarcely
προέρχομαι: to come forward, advance
πυνθάνομαι: to learn
σοφιστής, -οῦ, ὁ: a sophist, teacher
ὑπακούω: to listen, attend, answer (a knock)

ᾤχοντο: impf. of οἴχομαι, "they went"
προσελθὼν: ao. part. of προς-έρχομαι, "having approached"
μόλις βραδέως: "hardly a short time"
ὑπήκουσε: ao. ὑπο-ἀκούω, "answered the door"
προῆλθεν: ao. προ-έρχομαι, "she came forward"
ἠρόμην: ao. of ἐρωτάω, "I asked"
εἰ ἔνδον εἴη: opt. in ind. quest. in sec. sequence, "whether he was inside"
τί βουλόμενος: "wishing what"
πυνθάνῃ: 2 s. mid. πυνθάνομαι, "do you inquire"

Note the different meanings of the word αὐτός:

1.) Without the definite article

   a.) The nominative forms of the word are always intensive (= Latin *ipse*): αὐτός: "he himself," αὐτοί, "they themselves"; φιλῶ ὥσπερ οὖς ἔτεκον αὐτή: "I love him just like those I *myself* bore"

   b.) The other cases of the word are the unemphatic third person pronouns: him, them, etc. γράμματα δὲ αὐτῷ ἐκόμιζον οἴκοθεν: "I was bringing letters from home *to him*" μετ' αὐτοῦ: "with *him*." This is the most common use of the word in the *Onos*.

2.) With the definite article

   a.) In predicative position, it is also intensive (= Latin *ipse*): τὸν ἄνδρα αὐτόν "the man *himself*"; τῶν σπλάγχνων αὐτῶν ἅπτομαι: "I touch *the very* innards"

   b.) In attributive position or with no noun it means "the same": τὸν αὐτόν ἄνδρα: "the same man"; ἴσως ἐμοὶ τὰ αὐτὰ νοήσας "perhaps thinking *the same things* as I"

«Μεῖνόν με,» ἔφη, «αὐτοῦ,» καὶ τὴν θύραν συγκλείσασα
ᾤχετο εἴσω πάλιν· καί ποτε ἐξελθοῦσα κελεύει ἡμᾶς εἰσελθεῖν.
κἀγὼ δὲ παρελθὼν εἴσω ἀσπάζομαι αὐτὸν καὶ τὰ γράμματα
ἐπέδωκα.

Entering the house he finds Hipparchus and his wife at dinner.

ἔτυχε δὲ ἐν ἀρχῇ δείπνου ὢν καὶ κατέκειτο ἐπὶ
κλινιδίου στενοῦ, γυνὴ δὲ αὐτοῦ καθῆστο πλησίον, καὶ τράπεζα
μηδὲν ἔχουσα παρέκειτο. ὁ δὲ ἐπειδὴ τοῖς γράμμασιν ἐνέτυχεν,
«Ἀλλ᾽ ὁ μὲν φίλτατος ἐμοί,» ἔφη, «καὶ τῶν Ἑλλήνων
ἐξοχώτατος Δεκριανὸς εὖ ποιεῖ καὶ θαρρῶν πέμπει παρ᾽ ἐμοὶ

ἀρχή, ἡ: a beginning, origin
ἀσπάζομαι: to welcome, greet
γράμμα, -ατος, τό: a letter
γυνή, γυναικός, ἡ: a woman, wife
δεῖπνον, τό: dinner
Δεκριανὸς, ὁ: Decrianus
εἰσέρχομαι: to go in, enter
εἴσω: to within, inside
Ἕλλην: Greek
ἐντυγχάνω: to fall in with, read
ἐξέρχομαι: to go or come out
ἔξοχος, -ον: standing out
ἐπιδίδωμι: to give, hand over
εὖ: well
θαρσέω: to have courage, be bold
θύρα, ἡ: a door
κάθημαι: to be seated

κατάκειμαι: to lie down
κελεύω: to urge, bid, command
κλινίδιον, τό: a couch
μένω: to stay, remain, await
οἴχομαι: to be gone, leave
πάλιν: back, again
παράκειμαι: to lie beside
παρέρχομαι: to go by, beside or past, to
    pass by, pass
πέμπω: to send, dispatch
πλήσιος, -α, -ον: near, close to (+ gen.)
στενός, -ή, -όν: narrow, strait
συγκλείω: to shut
τράπεζα, -ης, ἡ: a table
τυγχάνω: to hit, happen upon
φίλτατος, -η, -ον: dearest

μεῖνόν: ao. imper., "wait for me"
συγκλείσασα: ao. part. f. nom., "having locked"
ἐξελθοῦσα: ao. part., "having come out"
εἰσελθεῖν: ao. inf. in ind. com. after κελεύει, "she ordered us to enter"
κἀγὼ: (= καὶ ἐγὼ)
παρελθὼν: ao. part. of παρα-ἔρχομαι, "having entered"
ἐπέδωκα: ao. of ἐπι-δίδωμι, "I handed to him"
ἔτυχε...ὢν: "he happened to be"
ἔτυχεν: ao. of τυγχάνω
καθῆστο: impf. of κατα-ἦμαι, "his wife *sat me down*"
μηδὲν ἔχουσα: "having nothing"
ἐνέτυχεν: ao. of ἐν-τυγχάνω, "he read" + dat.
θαρρῶν: pr. part. used adverbially, "bravely"

τοὺς ἑταίρους τοὺς ἑαυτοῦ· τὸ δὲ οἰκίδιον τὸ ἐμὸν ὁρᾷς, ὦ
Λούκιε, ὡς ἔστι μικρὸν μέν, ἀλλὰ εὐγνωμον τὸν οἰκοῦντα
ἐνεγκεῖν· ποιήσεις δὲ αὐτὸ σὺ μεγάλην οἰκίαν ἀνεξικάκως
οἰκήσας.» καὶ καλεῖ τὴν παιδίσκην, «Ὦ Παλαίστρα, δὸς τῷ
ἑταίρῳ κοιτῶνα καὶ κατάθες λαβοῦσα εἴ τι κομίζει σκεῦος,
εἶτα πέμπε αὐτὸν εἰς βαλανεῖον· οὐχὶ γὰρ μετρίαν ἐλήλυθεν
ὁδόν.»

ἀνεξίκακος, -ον: enduring, tolerant
βαλανεῖον, τό: a bath
δίδωμι: to give
ἑταῖρος, ὁ: a comrade, companion
εὐγνώμων, -ον: of good feeling,
   kindhearted, considerate
καλέω: to call, summon
κοιτών, -ῶνος, ὁ: a bed-chamber
κομίζω: to take care of, convey
Λούκιος, ὁ: Lucius
μέτριος, -α, -ον: measured, moderate

ὁδός, ἡ: a way, path, road
οἰκέω: to inhabit, live
οἰκία, ἡ: a building, house
οἰκίδιον, τό: a small house, cottage
παιδίσκη, ἡ: a young girl, maiden
Παλαίστρα, ἡ: Palaestra
πέμπω: to send, dispatch
ποιέω: to make, do
σκεύη, τά: possessions, belongings
τίθημι: to set, put, place
φέρω: to bear, carry, offer

ἐνεγκεῖν: ao. inf. of **φέρω**: epexegetic inf. explaining **εὐγνωμον**, "glad *to provide*
  for"
οἰκήσας: ao. part. used instrumentally, "by inhabiting"
δὸς: ao. imper. of **δίδωμι**, "give!"
κατάθες: ao. imper. of **κατα-τίθημι**, "deposit!"
λαβοῦσα: ao. part. of **λαμβάνω**, "having taken it, deposit it"
εἴ τι κομίζει σκεῦος: "if he has any baggage" i.e. "whatever baggage he has"
ἐλήλυθεν: perf. of **ἔρχομαι**, "he has come"

The Conjugation of ἔρχομαι

Among irregular verbs in *The Ass*, **ἔρχομαι** ("to go/come") deserves
special attention. It has forms from three different verbs. The bold forms are
preferred to their alternatives.

Stem	Present	Pr. Part.	Future	Aorist	Perfect
ἐρχ-	**ἔρχομαι**	ἐρχόμενος	ἔρξομαι		
ἐλθ-			ἐλεύσομαι	**ἦλθον**	ἐλήλουθα
ι-, ει-		**ἰων**	**εἰμι**		

The rest of the present system is also based on the ι- stem:

    ἰῶ (subj.)   ἴθι (imper.)
    ἴοιμι (opt.)   ἦα (impf.)
    ἰέναι (inf.)

After the servant Palaestra shows him his room, Lucius is invited to dine with Hipparchus.

[3.] ταῦτα εἰπόντος τὸ παιδισκάριον ἡ Παλαίστρα ἄγει
με καὶ δείκνυσί μοι κάλλιστον οἰκημάτιον: καί, «Σὺ μέν,» ἔφη,
«ἐπὶ ταύτης τῆς κλίνης κοιμήσῃ, τῷ δὲ παιδί σου σκιμπόδιον
αὐτοῦ παραθήσω καὶ προσκεφάλαιον ἐπιθήσω.» ταῦτα
εἰπούσης ἡμεῖς ἀπήειμεν λουσόμενοι δόντες αὐτῇ κριθιδίων
τιμὴν εἰς τὸν ἵππον: ἡ δὲ πάντα ἔφερε λαβοῦσα εἴσω καὶ
κατέθηκεν. ἡμεῖς δὲ λουσάμενοι ἀναστρέψαντες εἴσω εὐθὺς
παρήλθομεν, καὶ ὁ Ἵππαρχός με δεξιωσάμενος ἐκέλευε

ἄγω: to lead, convey, bring	κοιμάω: to lay down, put to sleep
ἀναστρέφω: to turn back	κριθίδιον, τό: barley
ἀπέρχομαι: to go away, depart	λούω: to wash
δείκνυμι: to show, display, exhibit	οἰκημάτιον, τό: a little room
δεξιόομαι: to welcome, greet	παιδισκάριον, τό: a little maiden
δίδωμι: to give	παῖς, παιδός, ὁ: a slave, boy
εἴσω: to within, inside	Παλαίστρα, ἡ: Palaestra
ἐπιτίθημι: to place upon	παρατίθημι: to place beside
Ἵππαρχος, ὁ: Hipparchus	παρέρχομαι: to go by, pass by
ἵππος, ὁ: a horse	προσκεφάλαιον, τό: a pillow
κατατίθημι: to put down	σκιμπόδιον, τό: a small pallet
κελεύω: to bid, command, order	τιμή, ἡ: value, price, compensation
κλίνη, ἡ: a bed	φέρω: to bear, carry

εἰπόντος (sc. μου): ao. part. in gen. abs., "him having spoken"
κοιμήσῃ: fut. of κοιμίζω, "you will sleep"
παραθήσω: fut. of παρα-τίθημι, "I will set beside for" + dat.
αὐτοῦ: "here"
ἐπιθήσω: fut. of τίθημι, "I will set down"
εἰπούσης (sc. αὐτῆς): ao. part. in gen abs., "she having said these things"
ἀπήειμεν: impf. of ἀπο-έρχομαι, "we went away"
λουσόμενοι: fut. part. showing purpose, "in order to wash"
δόντες: ao. part. of δίδωμι, "having given"
ἡ δὲ: "and she"
λαβοῦσα: ao. part. of λαμβάνω, "having taken"
κατέθηκεν: ao. of κατα-τίθημι, "she stored it"
λουσάμενοι: ao. part., "having washed"
παρήλθομεν: ao. of παρα-έρχομαι, "we returned"
δεξιωσάμενος: ao. part of δεξιόομαι, "having greeted us"

Defective Verbs

The principal parts of some verbs come from completely different words. Sometimes there are more than one form for a specific tense, in which case one will usually be preferred. Here are some important examples*:

Present	Future	Aorist	Perfect	Aorist Pas.	Meaning
ἔρχομαι					to go
	ἐλεύσομαι	ἦλθον	ἐλήλουθα		
	εἶμι				
λέγω	λέξω	ἔλεξα	λέλεγμαι	ἐλέχθην	to speak
	ἐρέω		εἴρηκα		
		εἶπον			
φέρω	οἴσω	ἤνεγκον	ἐνήνοχα	ἠνέχθην	to carry
αἱρέω	αἱρήσω	εἷλον	ᾕρηκα	ᾑρέθην	to take
ὁράω			ἑώρακα		to see
	ὄψομαι				
	εἴσομαι	εἶδον	οἶδα		to see/know
τρέχω	δραμοῦμαι	ἔδραμον	δεδράμηκα		to run
ἐσθίω	ἔδομαι	ἔφαγον	ἐδήδοκα	ἠδέσθην	to eat

* NB: The shading indicates the preferred form where multiple forms exist.

συνανακλίνεσθαι μετ᾿ αὐτοῦ. τὸ δὲ δεῖπνον οὐ σφόδρα λιτόν: ὁ δὲ οἶνος ἡδὺς καὶ παλαιὸς ἦν. ἐπεὶ δὲ ἐδεδειπνήκειμεν, πότος ἦν καὶ λόγος οἷος ἐπὶ δείπνου ξένου, καὶ οὕτω τὴν ἑσπέραν ἐκείνην πότῳ δόντες ἐκοιμήθημεν.

The next day Lucius tells Hipparchus his plans, keeping secret his wish to witness some kind of magic.

τῇ δ᾿ ὑστεραίᾳ ὁ Ἵππαρχος ἤρετό με, τίς μὲν ἔσται ἡ νῦν μοι ὁδὸς καὶ εἰ πάσαις ταῖς ἡμέραις αὐτοῦ προσμενῶ.

«Ἄπειμι μέν,» ἔφην, «εἰς Λάρισσαν, ἔοικα δὲ ἐνταῦθα διατρίψειν τριῶν ἢ πέντε ἡμερῶν.» [4.] ἀλλὰ τοῦτο μὲν ἦν

ἀπέρχομαι: to go away, depart
δειπνέω: to take a meal, eat dinner
δεῖπνον, τό: a meal, dinner
διατρίβω: to spend time
δίδωμι: to give
ἐνθάδε: here, in this place
ἔοικα: to seem (good)
ἔρομαι: to ask, enquire
ἑσπέρα, ἡ: evening
ἡδύς, -εῖα, -ύ: sweet, pleasant
ἡμέρα, ἡ: a day
κοιμάω: to lay down, put to sleep
λιτός, -ή, -όν: simple, inexpensive, frugal

λόγος: a word, conversation
ξένος, ὁ: a foreigner, guest
ὁδός, ἡ: a way, road, journey
οἶνος, ὁ: wine
οἷος, -α, -ον: such as
παλαιός, -ά, -όν: old
πέντε: five
πότος, ὁ: a drink, drinking
προσμένω: to stay through, remain longer
σφόδρα: very, exceedingly
τρεῖς: three
ὑστεραῖος, -α, -ον: the next day

συνανακλίνεσθαι: pr. inf. of συν-ανα-κλίνομαι in ind. com. after ἐκέλευε, "he ordered us to recline"
ἐδεδειπνήκειμεν: plupf. of δείπνω, "after we had supped"
τὴν ἑσπέραν: acc. of duration, "for that night"
δόντες: ao. part. of δίδωμι, "having given ourselves to" + dat.
ἐκοιμήθημεν: ao. pas. of κομάω, "we were put to bed"
ἤρετό: ao. of ἐρωτάω, "he asked"
τίς μὲν ἔσται: Note the more vivid form of indirect question retaining the mood of the original question "what my road will be."
εἰ ... προσμενῶ: fut. of προσ-μείνω, "whether I will remain"
ἄπειμι: fut. of ἀπο-ἔρχομαι, "I will depart"
ἔοικα: pf., "I am likely to" + inf.
διατρίψειν: fut. inf. δια-τρίβω, "to spend (time)"

σκῆψις. ἐπεθύμουν δὲ σφόδρα μείνας ἐνταῦθα ἐξευρεῖν τινα τῶν μαγεύειν ἐπισταμένων γυναικῶν καὶ θεάσασθαί τι παράδοξον, ἢ πετόμενον ἄνθρωπον ἢ λιθούμενον. καὶ τῷ ἔρωτι τῆς θέας ταύτης δοὺς ἐμαυτὸν περιῄειν τὴν πόλιν, ἀπορῶν μὲν τῆς ἀρχῆς τοῦ ζητήματος, ὅμως δὲ περιῄειν:

He meets a kinswoman, Abroia, who invites him to stay with her.

κἂν τούτῳ γυναῖκα ὁρῶ προσιοῦσαν ἔτι νέαν, εὐπορουμένην, ὅσον ἦν ἐκ τῆς ὁδοῦ συμβαλεῖν: ἱμάτια γὰρ ἀνθινὰ καὶ παῖδες συχνοὶ καὶ χρυσίον περιττόν. ὡς δὲ πλησιαίτερον γίνομαι, προσαγορεύει με ἡ γυνή, καὶ ἀμείβομαι

ἀμείβω: to exchange, respond
ἄνθινος, -η, -ον: of or like flowers, blooming, fresh
ἀπορέω: to be without, lack
ἀρχή, ἡ: a beginning, origin, first cause
γυνή, γυναικός, ἡ: a woman, wife
δίδωμι: to give
ἐξευρίσκω: to find out, discover
ἐπιθυμέω: to set one's heart upon, desire
ἐπίσταμαι: to know
ἔρως, -ωτος, ὁ: love, desire
εὐπορέω: to prosper, thrive, be well off
ζήτημα, -ατος, τό: a search
θέα, ἡ: a seeing, view, sight
θεάομαι: to look on, view, behold
ἱμάτιον τό: an outer garment, a cloak
λιθόω: to turn to stone
μαγεύω: to practice magic
μένω: to stay, remain

νέος, νέα, νέον: young, youthful
ὁδός, ἡ: a way, path, street
ὁράω: to see
παῖς, παιδός, ὁ: a slave, boy
παράδοξος, -ον: incredible, paradoxical
περιέρχομαι: to go around, wander
περισσός, -ή, -όν: too much, prodigious
πέτομαι: to fly
πλήσιος, -α, -ον: near, close to (+ *gen.*)
πόλις, -εως, ἡ: a city
προσαγορεύω: to address, greet
προσέρχομαι: to approach
σκῆψις, -εως, ἡ: a pretext, excuse, pretense
συμβάλλω: to throw together, infer
συχνός, -ή, -όν: great, many
σφόδρα: very, exceedingly
χρυσίον, τό: a piece of gold, jewelry

μείνας: ao. part. of μένω, "by remaining"
ἐξευρεῖν: ao. inf. of ἐξ-ευρίσκω after ἐπεθύμουν, "I desired *to discover*"
ἐπισταμένων: pr. part. gen. of ἐπίσταμαι, "some one *of those knowing*" + inf.
θεάσασθαί: ao. inf. of θεάομαι after ἐπεθύμουν, "and *to see*"
δοὺς: ao. part. of δίδωμι, "having given myself to" + dat.
περιῄειν: impf. of περι-ἔρχομαι, "I wandered around"
κἂν (= καὶ ἐν) τούτῳ (sc. χρόνῳ): "meanwhile"
προσιοῦσαν: pr. part. of προς-ἔρχομαι, "a woman approaching"
συμβαλεῖν: ao. inf. of συν-βάλλω after ἦν, "so far as it was possible *to calculate*"

αὐτῇ ὁμοίως, καὶ φησίν, «Ἐγὼ Ἀβροιά εἰμι, εἴ τινα τῆς σῆς μητρὸς φίλην ἀκούεις, καὶ ὑμᾶς δὲ τοὺς ἐξ ἐκείνης γενομένους φιλῶ ὥσπερ οὓς ἔτεκον αὐτή· τί οὖν οὐχὶ παρ' ἐμοὶ καταλύεις, ὦ τέκνον;»

«Ἀλλὰ σοὶ μέν,» ἔφην, «πολλὴ χάρις, αἰδοῦμαι δὲ οὐδὲν ἀνδρὶ φίλῳ ἐγκαλῶν ἔπειτα φεύγων τὴν ἐκείνου οἰκίαν· ἀλλὰ τῇ γνώμῃ, ὦ φιλτάτη, κατάγομαι παρὰ σοί.»

«Ποῖ δέ,» ἔφη, «καὶ κατάγῃ;»

«Παρὰ Ἱππάρχῳ.»

«Τῷ φιλαργύρῳ;» ἔφη.

«Μηδαμῶς,» εἶπον, «ὦ μῆτερ, τοῦτο εἴπῃς. λαμπρὸς γὰρ καὶ πολυτελὴς γέγονεν εἰς ἐμέ, ὥστε καὶ ἐγκαλέσαι ἄν τις τῇ τρυφῇ.

Ἀβροιά, ἡ: Abroea
αἰδέομαι: to be ashamed to do
ἀκούω: to hear
ἀνήρ, ἀνδρός, ὁ: a man
γνώμη, ἡ: thought, intention
ἐγκαλέω: to call in, accuse, charge with (+ dat.)
ἔπειτα: thereupon
κατάγομαι: to lodge, stay
καταλύω: to put down, lodge with (+ gen.)
λαμπρός, -ά, -όν: bright, magnificent
μηδαμῶς: in no way, not at all
μήτηρ, μήτερος, ἡ: a mother
οἰκία, ἡ: a building, house

ὅμοιος, -α, -ον: like, similar
πολυτελής, -ές: lavish, extravagant
τέκνον, τό: a child
τίκτω: to bear, give birth
τρυφή, ἡ: softness, luxuriousness, wantonness
φεύγω: to flee, run away
φιλάργυρος, -ον: fond of money, miserly
φιλέω: to love, regard with affection
φίλη, ἡ: a friend
φίλος, -η, -ον: beloved, dear
φίλτατος, -η, -ον: dearest
χάρις, -ιτος, ἡ: favor, grace

γενομένους: ao. part. of γίγνομαι, "those descended from" + gen.
ἔτεκον: ao. of τέκνω, "just as those whom I bore"
οὐδὲν ἐγκαλῶν: pr. part. of ἐν-καλέω, "having no quarrel with" + dat.
φεύγων: after αἰδοῦμαι, "I am ashamed to flee"
τῇ γνώμῃ: dat., "I stay with you in thought"
κατάγῃ: pr. 2 s. mid. of κατα-άγω, "where do you stay?"
μηδαμῶς ... εἴπῃς: ao. subj. in prohibition, "never say"
γέγονεν: perf. of γίγνομαι, "he has been"
ὥστε ἐγκαλέσαι ἄν τις: result clause with the inf. representing a potential opt. with ἄν, "so that someone might accuse him of" + dat.
ἐγκαλέσαι: ao. inf. of ἐν-καλέω

12

Abroia then warns Lucius that Hipparchus' wife is a witch.

ἡ δὲ μειδιάσασα καί με τῆς χειρὸς λαβομένη ἄγει
ἀπωτέρω καὶ λέγει πρὸς ἐμέ, «Φυλάττου μοι,» ἔφη, «τὴν
Ἱππάρχου γυναῖκα πάσῃ μηχανῇ· μάγος γάρ ἐστι δεινὴ καὶ
μάχλος καὶ πᾶσι τοῖς νέοις ἐπιβάλλει τὸν ὀφθαλμόν· καὶ εἰ μή
τις ὑπαχούσῃ αὐτῇ, τοῦτον τῇ τέχνῃ ἀμύνεται, καὶ πολλοὺς
μετεμόρφωσεν εἰς ζῷα, τοὺς δὲ τέλεον ἀπώλεσε· σὺ δὲ καὶ
νέος εἶ, τέκνον, καὶ καλός, ὥστε εὐθὺς ἀρέσαι γυναικί, καὶ
ξένος, πρᾶγμα εὐκαταφρόνητον.»

ἄγω: to lead to convey, bring
ἀμύνω: to keep off, mid. to take revenge
ἀπόλλυμι: to destroy, kill, slay
ἀπωτέρω: further off
ἀρέσκω: to please, satisfy
γυνή, γυναικός, ἡ: a woman, wife
δεινός, -ή, -όν: fearful, terrible
ἐπιβάλλω: to throw or cast upon
εὐκαταφρόνητος, -ον: easily despised,
    contemptible
ζῷον, τό: an animal
λέγω: to say
μάγος ὁ: a magician, sorcerer
μάχλος, -ον: lewd, lustful

μειδιάω: to smile, laugh
μεταμορφόω: to transform
μηχανή, ἡ: an instrument, contrivance,
    trick
νέος, νέα, νέον: young, youthful
ξένος, ὁ: a foreigner, stranger
ὀφθαλμός, ὁ: an eye
πρᾶγμα, -ατος, τό: a deed, act, matter
τέκνον, τό: a child
τέχνη, ἡ: art, skill, craft
ὑπακούω: to listen, attend
φυλάττω: to keep watch , keep guard
χείρ, χειρός, ἡ: a hand

ἡ δὲ μειδιάσασα: ao. part., "but she, with a smile"
λαβομένη: ao. part. of λαμβάνω, "having taken my hand"
φυλάττου μοι: pr. imper. mid., "watch out for my sake!"
εἰ μή τις ὑπακούσῃ: ao. subj. in fut. more vivid cond., "if someone does not obey"
μετεμόρφωσεν: ao. of μετα-μορφόω, "she has transformed"
ἀπώλεσε: ao. of ἀπο-όλλυμι, "she destroyed"
ὥστε ἀρέσαι: result clause with ao. inf. of ἀρέσκω, "so that you are pleasing to" +
    dat.

Upon making this discovery, Lucius resolves to seek the aid of the servant Palaestra to witness some magic.

[5.] ἐγὼ δὲ πυθόμενος ὅτι τὸ πάλαι μοι ζητούμενον οἴκοι παρ᾽ ἐμοὶ κάθηται, προσεῖχον οὐδὲν αὐτῇ ἔτι. ὡς δέ ποτε ἀφείθην, ἀπῄειν οἴκαδε λαλῶν πρὸς ἐμαυτὸν ἐν τῇ ὁδῷ, Ἄγε δὴ σὺ ὁ φάσκων ἐπιθυμεῖν ταύτης τῆς παραδόξου θέας, ἔγειρέ μοι σεαυτὸν καὶ τέχνην εὕρισκε σοφήν, ᾗ τεύξῃ τούτων ὧν ἐρᾷς, καὶ ἐπὶ τὴν θεράπαιναν τὴν Παλαίστραν ἤδη ἀποδύου — τῆς γὰρ γυναικὸς τοῦ ξένου καὶ φίλου πόρρω ἵστασο — κἀπὶ

ἄγε: come! come on!
ἀπέρχομαι: to go away, depart
ἀποδύομαι: to strip down, strip naked
ἀφίημι: to send forth, discharge
ἐγείρω: to wake up, rouse
ἐπιθυμέω: to set one's heart upon, desire greatly
ἐράω: to love, desire
εὑρίσκω: to find
ζητέω: to seek, search for
θέα, ἡ: a looking at, sight, view
θεράπαινα, ἡ: a female slave, handmaid
κάθημαι: to sit, abide
λαλέω: to talk
ξένος, -η, -ον: foreign, strange

ὁδός, ἡ: a way, path, street
οἴκαδε: to one's home, home, homewards
οἴκοι: at home, in the house
πάλαι: long ago
Παλαίστρα, ἡ: Palaestra
παράδοξος, -ον: incredible, paradoxical
πόρρω: forwards, onwards, further
προσέχω: to hold to, offer
πυνθάνομαι: to learn
σοφός, -ή, -όν: skilled
τέχνη, ἡ: art, skill, craft
τυγχάνω: to hit
φάσκω: to say, affirm, assert
φίλος, -η, -ον: beloved, dear

πυθόμενος: ao. part. of πυνθάνω, "having learned"
ὅτι … κάθηται: ind. st. after πυθόμενος, "that it was abiding"
τὸ πάλαι: "for a long time"
προσεῖχον: impf. of προσ-έχω, "I paid attention to" + dat.
ἀφείθην: ao. pas. of ἀπο-ΐημι, "when I got away from"
ἀπῄειν: impf. of ἀπο-ἔρχομαι, "I went"
ὁ φάσκων: "you who are claiming" + inf.
θέας: gen. after ἐπιθυμεῖν
ἔγειρε: imper., "arouse yourself!"
ᾗ τεύξῃ: fut. of τυγχάνω, "by which you will gain" + gen.
ὧν ἐρᾷς: "which you desire" ὧν is attracted into the case of its antecedent (instead of accusative)
ἀποδύου: mid. imper., "strip yourself (for a wrestling match)"
πόρρω ἵστασο: pr. imper. of ἵστημι, "stand away from" + gen.
κἀπὶ (= καὶ ἐπὶ) ταύτης: "rolling over that one (i.e. Palaestra)"

ταύτης κυλιόμενος καὶ γυμναζόμενος καὶ ταύτῃ
συμπλεκόμενος εὖ ἴσθι ὡς ῥαδίως γνώσῃ· δοῦλοι γὰρ τὰ
δεσποτῶν ἐπίστανται καὶ καλὰ καὶ αἰσχρά.

*Upon returning home, he discovers Palaestra alone and the two exchange
amorous barbs, planning a rendezvous after the masters are asleep.*

καὶ ταῦτα λέγων πρὸς ἐμαυτὸν εἰσῄειν οἴκαδε. τὸν μὲν
οὖν Ἵππαρχον οὐ κατέλαβον ἐν τῇ οἰκίᾳ οὐδὲ τὴν ἐκείνου
γυναῖκα, ἡ δὲ Παλαίστρα τῇ ἑστίᾳ παρήδρευε δεῖπνον ἡμῖν
εὐτρεπίζουσα. [6.] κἀγὼ εὐθὺς ἔνθεν ἑλών, «Ὡς εὐρύθμως,»
ἔφην, «ὦ καλὴ Παλαίστρα, τὴν πυγὴν τῇ χύτρᾳ ὁμοῦ
συμπεριφέρεις καὶ κλίνεις. ἡ δὲ ὀσφὺς ἡμῖν ὑγρῶς ἐπικινεῖται.
μακάριος ὅστις ἐνταῦθα ἐνεβάψατο.»

αἱρέω: to take up, grasp
αἰσχρός, -ά, -όν: shameful, low, ugly
γιγνώσκω: to know
γυμνάζω: to train naked, train in gymnastic exercise
γυνή, γυναικός, ἡ: woman, wife
δεῖπνον, τό: dinner
δοῦλος, ὁ: a slave
εἰσέρχομαι: to go into, enter
ἐμβάπτω: to dip in
ἔνθεν: thence
ἐπικινέω: to move
ἐπίσταμαι: to know
ἑστία, ἡ: the hearth, fire
εὔρυθμος, -ον: rhythmical
εὐτρεπίζω, -ιῶ: to make ready, prepare
κᾶλον, τό: wood
καταλαμβάνω: to seize upon, lay hold of

κλίνω: to tilt, slope
κυλίω: to roll along
μακάριος, -α, -ον: blessed, happy
οἶδα: to know
οἴκαδε: to one's home, homewards
οἰκία, ἡ: a house, home
ὁμοῦ: together
ὀσφύς, ἡ: loins, waist
Παλαίστρα, ἡ: Palaestra
παρεδρεύω: to frequent, attend
πυγή, -ῆς, ἡ: buttocks
ῥάδιος, -α, -ον: easy, ready
συμπεριφέρω: to carry around x (acc.) along with y (dat.)
συμπλέκω: to twine or plait together
ὑγρός, -ά, -όν: wet, running, fluid
χύτρα, ἡ: a pot

ὡς ῥᾳδίως γνώσῃ: fut. of γιγνώσκω in ind. st. after ἴσθι, "know well that you will easily discover"
τὰ δεσποτῶν: "the affairs of their masters"
εἰσῄειν: impf. of εἰς-ἔρχομαι, "I went"
οὐ κατέλαβον: ao. of κατα-λαμβάνω, "I did not overtake"
παρήδρευε: impf. of παρεδρεύω, "was busy at" + dat.
ἔνθεν ἑλών: an epic phrase "picking up from there"
ἑλών: ao. part. of αἱρέω
ἐνεβάψατο: ao. of ἐν-βάπτω, "whoever *has dipped in*"

ἡ δὲ – σφόδρα γὰρ ἦν ἰταμὸν καὶ χαρίτων μεστὸν τὸ
κοράσιον – «Φεύγοις ἄν,» εἶπεν, «ὦ νεανίσκε, εἴ γε νοῦν ἔχοις
καὶ ζῆν ἐθέλοις, ὡς πολλοῦ πυρὸς καὶ κνίσης μεστά: ἢν γὰρ
αὐτοῦ μόνον ἅψῃ, τραῦμα ἔχων πυρίκαυτον αὐτοῦ μοι
παρεδρεύσει, θεραπεύσει δέ σε οὐδεὶς ἀλλ' οὐδὲ θεὸς ἰατρός,

ἅπτω: to fasten, (*mid.*) to touch
ἐθέλω: to will, wish
ζάω: to live
θεραπεύω: to heal
ἰατρός, ὁ: a healer, physician
ἰταμός, -ή, -όν: hasty, eager
κνῖσα, -ης, ἡ: smoke
κοράσιον, τό: a little girl, maiden
μεστός, -ή, -όν: filled, full of (+ *gen.*)
μόνος, -η, -ον: alone, only

νεανίσκος, ὁ: a youth, young man
παρεδρεύω: to frequent, attend
πῦρ, πυρός, τό: fire
πυρίκαυστος, ον: inflamed, caused by
   burning
σφόδρα: very, exceedingly
τραῦμα, -ατος, τό: a wound, hurt
φεύγω: to flee, run away
χάρις, -ιτος, ἡ: favor, grace

φεύγοις ἄν ... εἴ γε ἔχοις καὶ ἐθέλοις: pr. opt. in future less vivid condition "you
   would flee if you had sense and wished to live"
ἢν ἅψῃ ... παρεδρεύσει: ao. subj. and fut. in fut. more vivid cond., "if you only
   touch it, you will serve"
ἅψῃ: ao. subj. of ἅπτω
ἀλλ' οὐδὲ: "not even a divine healer"

Future Conditions

Note the difference between the future less vivid and future more vivid
conditions. The future less vivid indicates a future action as merely a **possibility**;
the future more vivid indicates a future action as a **probability**.

less vivid: εἰ plus optative in the protasis, ἄν plus the optative in the apodosis;
   translate "If he were to (or if he should)..., then he would..."
      φεύγοις ἄν, εἴ γε νοῦν ἔχοις καὶ ζῆν ἐθέλοις
      "you would flee if you should have sense and should wish
      to live"

more vivid: ἐάν (Attic contraction = ἢν) plus subjunctive in the protasis, future
   indicative in the apodosis; translate "if he does..., then he will...."
      ἢν γὰρ αὐτοῦ μόνον ἅψῃ, παρεδρεύσει
      "for if you only touch it, you will serve"

An imperative can substitute for the future indicative of the apodosis.

      ἐὰν δὲ χαλᾶται, μετάθες
      "if there is a slackening, change position!"

ἀλλ᾽ ἡ κατακαύσασά σε μόνη ἐγώ, καὶ τὸ παραδοξότατον, ἐγὼ
μέν σε ποιήσω πλέον ποθεῖν, καὶ τῆς ἀπὸ τῆς θεραπείας
ὀδύνης ἀρδόμενος ἀεὶ ἀνθέξῃ καὶ οὐδὲ λίθοις βαλλόμενος τὴν
γλυκεῖαν ὀδύνην φεύξῃ. τί γελᾷς; ἀκριβῆ βλέπεις
ἀνθρωπομάγειρον. οὐ γὰρ μόνα ταῦτα φαῦλα ἐδώδιμα
σκευάζω, ἀλλ᾽ ἤδη τὸ μέγα τοῦτο καὶ καλόν, τὸν ἄνθρωπον,
οἶδα ἔγωγε καὶ σφάττειν καὶ δέρειν καὶ κατακόπτειν, ἥδιστα
δὲ τῶν σπλάγχνων αὐτῶν καὶ τῆς καρδίας ἅπτομαι.»

ἀεί: always, for ever	κατακαίω: to burn
ἀκριβής, -ές: exact, accurate, precise	κατακόπτω: to cut up, cut in pieces
ἀνθρωπομάγειρος, ὁ: a cook of human flesh	λίθος, -ου, ὁ: a stone
ἀντέχω: to cling	μόνος, -η, -ον: alone, only
ἅπτω: to fasten, (*mid.*) to touch (+ *gen.*)	ὀδύνη, ἡ: pain
ἄρδω: to water	οἶδα: to know
βάλλω: to throw, hurl, pelt	παράδοξος, -ον: incredible, paradoxical, strange
βλέπω: to see	πλεών, -ον: more
γελάω: to laugh	ποθέω: to long for, yearn after
γλυκύς, -εῖα, -ύ: sweet	ποιέω: to make
δέρω: to skin, flay	σκευάζω: to prepare, make ready
ἐδώδιμος, -η, -ον: eatable	σπλάγχνον, τό: the inner parts
ἡδύς, -εῖα, -ύ: sweet, pleasant	σφάζω: to slay, slaughter
θεραπεία, ἡ: a treatment	φαῦλος, -η, -ον: easy, slight
καρδία, ἡ: the heart	φεύγω: to flee, run away

ἡ **κατακαύσασα**: ao. part., "only the one who burnt you"
σε ποθεῖν: "I will cause you to desire"
ἀπὸ τῆς θεραπείας: "the pain *from the treatment*"
ἀρδόμενος: pr. pas. part. after **ἀνέξῃ**, "to being treated for" + gen.
ἀνθέξῃ: fut. of **ἀνα-ἔχω**, "you will continue to submit" + part.
οὐδὲ βαλλόμενος: pr. pas. part., "not even if being pelted"
φεύξῃ: fut. of **φεύγω**, "nor will you escape"
σφάττειν καὶ δέρειν καὶ κατακόπτειν: pr. inf. after **οἶδα**, "I know how to slaughter etc."
ἥδιστα: "with the greatest delight"
ἅπτομαι: pr. mid., "I fasten on" + gen.

«Τοῦτο μὲν ὀρθῶς,» ἔφην, «λέγεις: καὶ γὰρ ἐμὲ
πόρρωθεν καὶ μηδὲ ἐγγὺς ὄντα οὐ κατακαύματι μὰ Δί' ἀλλὰ
ὅλῳ ἐμπρησμῷ ἐπέθηκας, καὶ διὰ τῶν ὀμμάτων τῶν ἐμῶν τὸ
σὸν μὴ φαινόμενον πῦρ κάτω ἐς τὰ σπλάγχνα τἀμὰ ῥίψασα
φρύγεις, καὶ ταῦτα οὐδὲν ἀδικοῦντα: ὥστε πρὸς θεῶν ἴασαί με
ταύταις αἷς λέγεις αὐτὴ ταῖς πικραῖς καὶ ἡδείαις θεραπείαις,
καί με ἤδη ἀπεσφαγμένον λαβοῦσα δεῖρε, ὅπως αὐτὴ θέλεις.»

ἀδικέω: to do wrong
ἀποσφάζω: to cut the throat, slaughter
δέρω: to skin, flay
ἐγγύς: near, close
ἐθέλω: to will, wish
ἐμπρησμός, ὁ: a burning down, conflagration
ἐπιτίθημι: to lay, put or place upon
ἡδύς, -εῖα, -ύ: sweet, pleasant
θεραπεία, ἡ: a treatment
ἰάομαι: to heal, cure
κατάκαυμα, -ατος, τό: a burn

κάτω: down, downwards
λέγω: to speak, say
ὅλος, -η, -ον: whole, entire, complete
ὄμμα, -ατος, τό: an eye
ὀρθός, -ή, -όν: straight, correct
πικρός, -ά, -όν: pointed, sharp, bitter
πρόσωθεν: from afar
πῦρ, πυρός, τό: fire
ῥίπτω: to throw, cast
σπλάγχνον, τό: the inner parts
φαίνω: to show
φρύγω: to roast

μηδὲ ἐγγὺς ὄντα: "(me) not being near"
οὐ...ἀλλὰ: "not only...but"
ἐπέθηκας: ao. of ἐπι-τίθημι, "you have set upon me with" + dat. of means
μὴ φαινόμενον πῦρ: "your invisible fire"
ῥίψασα: ao. part. of ῥίπτω, "having hurled your fire"
ταῦτα: n. pl. acc. of resp., "for such things"
ἀδικοῦντα (sc. **με**): "me who is wronging not at all"
ἴασαι: ao. imper. mid. of ἰάομαι, "heal me!"
αἷς λέγεις: "of which you speak" the rel. pron. is attracted into the case of its antecedent ταύταις θεραπείαις
ἀπεσφαγμένον: perf. part. of ἀπο-σφάττω, "me already *slaughtered*"
λαβοῦσα: ao. part. of λαμβάνω, "having taken"
ὅπως αὐτὴ θέλεις: "however you yourself wish"

18

ἡ δὲ μέγα καὶ ἥδιστον ἐκ τούτου ἀνακαγχάσασα ἐμὴ τὸ λοιπὸν
ἦν, καὶ συνέκειτο ἡμῖν, ὅπως, ἐπειδὰν κατακοιμίσῃ τοὺς
δεσπότας, ἔλθῃ εἴσω παρ' ἐμὲ καὶ καθευδήσῃ.

ἀνακαγχάζω: to burst out laughing   καθεύδω: to lie down, sleep
δεσπότης, -ου, ὁ: a master, lord   κατακοιμίζω: to put to bed
εἴσω: to within, into   λοιπός, -ή, -όν: remaining, the rest
ἐπειδάν: whenever   σύγκειμαι: to lie together, be agreed
ἡδύς, -εῖα, -ύ: sweet, pleasant

ἀνακαγχάσασα: ao. part. of ἀνα-καγκάζω, "having burst out laughing"
ἐμὴ...ἦν: "she was mine"
συνέκειτο: impf., "it was agreed"
ἐπειδὰν κατακοιμίσῃ: gen. temp. clause, "whenever she put to bed"
κατακοιμίσῃ: ao. subj. of κατακοιμίζω
ὅπως ... ἔλθῃ ... καθευδήσῃ: ind. jussive subjunctives expressive purpose after
    συνέκειτο, "it was agreed *that she should come and sleep with*"
ἔλθῃ: ao. subj. of ἔρχομαι
καθευδήσῃ: ao. subj. of καθεύδω

General Conditions and Temporal Clauses

Present general conditions use **ἄν** + the subjunctive in the protasis, as do present
general temporal clauses.
    ἐὰν ποτε παύῃ, βαίνομεν: "if ever he stops, we go."
    ἐπειδὰν ποτε παύῃ, βαίνομεν: "whenever he stops, we go."

Past general conditions use the optative (no **ἄν**) in the protasis, as do past general
temporal clauses.
    εἰ ποτε παύοι, ἐβαίνομεν: "If ever he stopped, we went."
    ἐπειδή παύοι, ἐβαίνομεν: "whenever he stopped, we went."

Examples from the *Onos*:
    ἐπειδὰν κατακοιμίσῃ τοὺς δεσπότας "when (whenever that might be) she
      put her masters to sleep"
    ἐπὰν γυναῖκα ἴδῃ "whenever he sees a woman"
    εἰ δέ μοι περιπῖπτον ἴδοι τὸ φορτίον ... τοῦτο μὲν οὐδέποτε εἰργάσατο
      "If ever he saw the load tipping ... this he never did"
    εἰ ποτε χωρίον εἴη τῆς ὁδοῦ τραχὺ "If ever the stretch of road was harsh"
    εἰ δέ ποτε καὶ συνελάσειέ με ταῖς ἵπποις ... ἀπωλλύμην "If ever he drove
      me out with the horses ... I would die."

For the use of potential **ἄν** in past general clauses, see p. 70.

Upon retiring to his room, Lucius finds everything ready for a tryst.

[7.] κἀπειδὴ ἀφίκετό ποτε ὁ Ἵππαρχος, λουσάμενοι ἐδειπνοῦμεν καὶ πότος ἦν συχνὸς ἡμῶν ὁμιλούντων: εἶτα τοῦ ὕπνου καταψευσάμενος ἀνίσταμαι καὶ ἔργῳ ἀπῄειν ἔνθα ᾤκουν. πάντα δὲ τὰ ἔνδον εὖ παρεσκεύαστο: τῷ μὲν παιδὶ ἔξω ὑπέστρωτο, τράπεζα δὲ τῇ κλίνῃ παρειστήκει ποτήριον ἔχουσα: καὶ οἶνος αὐτοῦ παρέκειτο καὶ ὕδωρ ἕτοιμον καὶ ψυχρὸν καὶ θερμόν. πᾶσα δὲ ἦν αὕτη τῆς Παλαίστρας παρασκευή. τῶν δὲ στρωμάτων ῥόδα πολλὰ κατεπέπαστο, τὰ

ἀνίστημι: to make to stand up, raise up
ἀπέρχομαι: to go away, depart
ἀφικνέομαι: to arrive
δειπνέω: to take a meal, have dinner
ἔνδον: in, within
ἔνθα: there
ἔξω: out, outside
ἔργον, τό: a deed, work, act
ἕτοιμος, -ον: at hand, ready, prepared
θερμός, -ή, -όν: hot, warm
καταπάσσω: to sprinkle, strew
καταψεύδομαι: to speak falsely of, lie about (+ gen.)
κλίνη, ἡ: a bed
λούω: to wash
οἰκέω: to inhabit, occupy
οἶνος, ὁ: wine

ὁμιλέω: to be in company with
παῖς, παιδός, ὁ: a slave, boy
Παλαίστρα, ἡ: Palaestra
παράκειμαι: to lie beside
παρασκευάζω: to get ready, prepare
παρασκευή, ἡ: preparation
παρίστημι: to place beside
ποτήριον, τό: a cup
πότος, ὁ: a drink, drinking
ῥόδον, τό: a rose
στρῶμα, -ατος, τό: bedding
συχνός, -ή, -όν: much, long
τράπεζα, -ης, ἡ: a table
ὕδωρ, ὕδατος, τό: water
ὕπνος, ὁ: sleep, slumber
ὑποστόρνυμι: to lay under, make a bed
ψυχρός, -ά, -όν: cold, chill

ἀφίκετό: ao. of ἀφικνέομαι, "he arrived"
λουσάμενοι; ao. part. mid., "having bathed"
ἡμῶν ὁμιλούντων: gen. abs., "while we talked"
καταψευσάμενος: ao. part. of κατα-ψευζω, "having pretended" + gen.
ἀπῄειν: impf. of ἀπο-ἔρχομαι, "I went"
ᾤκουν: impf. of οἰκέω, "where I was abiding"
παρεσκεύαστο: plpf. pas. of παρα-σκευάζω, "had been prepared"
ὑπέστρωτο: plpf. pas.of ὑπο-στόρνυμι, "(bedding) had been made up for" + dat.
παρειστήκει: plpf. of παρα-ἵστημι, "was standing next to"
ποτήριον ἔχουσα: "holding a wine-cup"
κατεπέπαστο: plpf. of κατα-πετάννυμι, "had been spread out on" + gen.

μὲν οὕτω γυμνὰ καθ' αὑτά, τὰ δὲ λελυμένα, τὰ δὲ στεφάνοις συμπεπλεγμένα. κἀγὼ τὸ συμπόσιον εὑρὼν ἕτοιμον ἔμενον τὸν συμπότην.

Palaestra joins Lucius and tells him to get ready for a wrestling match with her.

[8.] ἡ δὲ ἐπειδὴ κατέκλινε τὴν δέσποιναν, σπουδῇ παρ' ἐμὲ ἧκε, καὶ ἦν εὐφροσύνη τὸν οἶνον ἡμῶν καὶ τὰ φιλήματα προπινόντων ἀλλήλοις. ὡς δὲ τῷ ποτῷ παρεσκευάσαμεν ἑαυτοὺς εὖ πρὸς τὴν νύκτα, λέγει πρός με ἡ Παλαίστρα: «Τοῦτο μὲν πάντως δεῖ σε μνημονεύειν, ὦ νεανίσκε, ὅτι εἰς Παλαίστραν ἐμπέπτωκας, καὶ χρή σε νῦν ἐπιδεῖξαι εἰ γέγονας ἐν τοῖς ἐφήβοις γοργὸς καὶ παλαίσματα πολλὰ ἔμαθές ποτε.»

γοργός, -ή, -όν: fierce, terrible
γυμνός, -ή, -όν: naked, unclad
δέσποινα, ἡ: the mistress, lady of the house
ἐμπίτνω: fall upon
ἐπιδείκνυμι: to show, exhibit
ἕτοιμος, -ον: at hand, ready, prepared
εὑρίσκω: to find
εὐφροσύνη, ἡ: mirth, merriment
ἔφηβος, ὁ: one arrived at puberty
ἥκω: to have come, be present
κατακλίνω: to lay down, put to bed
λέγω: to say
λύω: to loose, separate
μένω: to stay, remain, await
μνημονεύω: to call to mind, remember

νύξ, νυκτός, ἡ: night
οἶνος, ὁ: wine
πάλαισμα, -ατος, τό: a wrestling move
Παλαίστρα, ἡ: Palaestra
πάντως: altogether
παρασκευάζω: to get ready, prepare
ποτόν, τό: a drink
προπίνω: to drink before
σπουδή, ἡ: haste, speed
στέφανος, ὁ: a garland
συμπλέκω: to twine together
συμπόσιον, τό: a drinking-party, symposium
συμπότης, -ου, ὁ: a fellow-drinker
φίλημα, -ατος, τό: a kiss
χρή: it is necessary

καθ' αὑτά: "according to themselves," i.e. "naturally "
τὰ δὲ λελυμένα: pf. part. pas., "some having been plucked"
συμπεπλεγμένα: pf. part. of συμ-πλέκω, "some having been weaved"
εὑρών: ao. part. of εὑρίσκω, "having found"
κατέκλινε: ao. of κατα-κλίνω, "after she had caused to lie down"
ἧκε: impf. of ἥκω
ἡμῶν ... προπινόντων: gen. abs., "as we proffered to each other"
δεῖ σε μνημονεύειν: "it is necessary that you remember"
ἐμπέπτωκας: perf. of ἐμ-πίπτω, "you have fallen in with"
ἐπιδεῖξαι: ao. inf. of ἐπι-δείκνυμι with χρή, "it is necessary that you show"
εἰ γέγονας: perf. of γίγνομαι in ind. quest., "whether you have become"
ἔμαθές: ao. of μανθάνω, "whether you learned"

«Ἀλλ' οὐκ ἂν ἴδοις φεύγοντά με τὸν ἔλεγχον τοῦτον· ὥστε ἀπόδυσαι, καὶ ἤδη παλαίωμεν.»

ἡ δέ, «Οὕτως,» ἔφη, «ὡς ἐγὼ θέλω, παράσχου μοι τὴν ἐπίδειξιν· ἐγὼ μὲν νόμῳ διδασκάλου καὶ ἐπιστάτου τὰ ὀνόματα τῶν παλαισμάτων ὧν ἐθέλω εὑροῦσα ἐρῶ, σὺ δὲ ἔτοιμος γίνου ἐς τὸ ὑπακούειν καὶ ποιεῖν πᾶν τὸ κελευόμενον.»

«Ἀλλ' ἐπίταττε,» ἔφην, «καὶ σκόπει ὅπως εὐχερῶς καὶ ὑγρῶς τὰ παλαίσματα καὶ εὐτόνως ἔσται.»

ἀποδύνω: to strip off
διδάσκαλος, ὁ: a teacher, master
ἐθέλω: to will, wish
ἔλεγχος, ὁ: a test, trial
ἐπίδειξις, -εως, ἡ: a demonstration
ἐπιστάτης, -ου, ὁ: an attendant, supervisor
ἐπιτάττω: to enjoin, order
ἕτοιμος, -ον: at hand, ready, prepared
εὔτονος, -ον: well-strung, vigorous
εὐχερής, -ές: easily handled, easy

κελεύω: to bid, command, order
νόμος, ὁ: a custom, law
ὄνομα, -ατος, τό: a name
πάλαισμα, -ατος, τό: a wrestling move
παλαίω: to wrestle
παρέχω: to furnish, provide, supply
σκοπέω: to look at, behold
ὑγρός, -ά, -όν: wet, running, fluid
ὑπακούω: to listen, obey
φεύγω: to flee, run away

οὐκ ἂν ἴδοις: pot. opt. of ὁράω, "you won't be able to see"
ἀπόδυσαι: ao. imper. mid. of ἀπο-δύω, "so strip yourself!"
παλαίωμεν: jussive pr. subj., "let us wrestle"
παράσχου: ao. imper. mid. of παρα-ἔχω, "present to me!"
ὧν ἐθέλω: "that I wish," the rel. pron. is attracted into the case of its antecedent παλαισμάτων
εὑροῦσα: ao. part. of εὑρίσκω, "having found"
ἐρῶ: fut. of λέγω, "I will say"
γίνου: pr. imper., "become ready"
ἐς τὸ ὑπακούειν: art. inf., "for the obeying"
ὅπως ἔσται: future after the imperative σκόπει, "see how easy the holds will be"

Palaestra directs their lovemaking and Lucius happily complies.

[9.] ἡ δὲ ἀποδυσαμένη τὴν ἐσθῆτα καὶ στᾶσα ὅλη γυμνὴ ἔνθεν ἤρξατο ἐπιτάττειν, «Ὦ μειράκιον, ἔκδυσαι καὶ ἀλειψάμενος ἔνθεν ἐκ τοῦ μύρου συμπλέκου τῷ ἀνταγωνιστῇ· δύο μηρῶν σπάσας κλῖνον ὑπτίαν, ἔπειτα ἀνώτερος ὑποβάλων διὰ μηρῶν καὶ διαστείλας αἰώρει καὶ τεῖνε ἄνω τὰ σκέλη, καὶ χαλάσας καὶ στήσας κολλῶ αὐτῷ καὶ παρεισελθὼν βάλε καὶ

αἰωρέω: to lift up, raise
ἀλείφω: to anoint (with oil)
ἀνταγωνιστής, -οῦ, ὁ: an opponent, competitor, rival
ἄνω: upwards
ἀνώτερος, -α, -ον: higher, above
ἀποδύνω: to strip off
ἄρχω: to begin
βάλλω: to throw, thrust
γυμνός, -ή, -όν: naked, unclad
διαστέλλω: to part, open up
δύο: two
ἐκδύω: to take off, strip off
ἔνθεν: there, then
ἐπιτάττω: to order
ἐσθής, -ῆτος, ἡ: dress, clothing
ἵστημι: to make to stand

κλίνω: to lean, lay down
κολλάω: to glue, cement
μειράκιον, τό: a boy, lad, stripling
μηρός, ὁ: a thigh
μύρον, τό: an unguent, sweet oil
ὅλος, -η, -ον: whole, entire, complete
παρεισέρχομαι: to come in beside, be inserted
σκέλος, -εος, τό: the leg
σπάω: to draw, pull out
στάζω: to drop, let fall, shed
συμπλέκω: to twine together, grapple
τείνω: to stretch
ὑποβάλλω: to throw under
ὕπτιος, -α, -ον: backward, on one's back
χαλάω: to slacken, loosen

στᾶσα: ao. part. of ἵστημι, "standing"
ἤρξατο: ao. of ἄρχομαι + inf.
ἔκδυσαι: ao. imper. of ἐκ-δύω, "strip!"
ἀλειψάμενος: ao. part. mid. of ἀλείφω, "having oiled yourself"
συμπλέκου: pr. imper. mid., "embrace!" + dat.
σπάσας: ao. part. of σπάω, "having pulled" + gen.
κλῖνον: ao. imper., "cause me to lie prone!"
ὑποβάλων: ao. part. of ὑποβάλλω, "having struck"
διαστείλας: ao. part. of δια-στέλλω, "having separated"
αἰώρει: pr. imper. of αἰωρέω, "hover (above)"
χαλάσας: ao. part. of χαλάζω, "having let fall"
στήσας: ao. part. of ἵστημι, "setting upon"
κολλῶ: ao. imper. mid. of κολλάω, "glue yourself to" + dat.
παρεισελθών: ao. part. of παρα-εἰς-ἔρχομαι, "having inserted yourself"
βάλε: ao. imper. of βάλλω, "strike!"

πρώσας νύσσε ἤδη πανταχοῦ ἕως πονέσῃ, καὶ ἡ ὀσφὺς
ἰσχυέτω, εἶτα ἐξελκύσας κατὰ πλάτος διὰ βουβῶνος δῆξον, καὶ
πάλιν συνώθει εἰς τὸν τοῖχον, εἶτα τύπτε· ἐπειδὰν δὲ χάλασμα

βουβών, -ῶνος, ὁ: the groin	πανταχοῦ: everywhere
δάκνω: to bite	πλάτος, ὁ: breadth, width
ἐξέλκω: to draw out, withdraw	πονέω: to labor, suffer
ἐπειδάν: whenever	προωθέω: to push forward
ἕως: until, till	συνωθέω: to force one's way in
ἰσχύω: to be strong	τοῖχος, ὁ: a wall
νύσσω: to prick, stab	τύπτω: to beat, strike
ὀσφῦς, ἡ: loins	χάλασμα, -ατος, τό: a relaxation, a gap
πάλιν: back, again	

πρώσας: ao. part. of προ-ωθέω, "having thrust forward"
νύσσε: pr. imper., "pierce!"
ἕως πονέσῃ: ao. subj. of πονέω, "until you wear yourself out"
ἰσχυέτω: 3 s. pr. imper., "let your loins be strong"
ἐξελκύσας: ao. part. of ἐξ-έλκύω, "having drawn out"
κατὰ πλάτος: "widely"
δῆξον: ao. imp. of δάκνω, "bite!"
συνώθει: pr. imper., "force your way in!"
ἐπειδὰν ἴδῃς: ao. subj. in indef. clause, "when you see (whenever that may be)"

Love and War

The love-making scene of Lucius and Palaestra is filled with double
entendres involving military and wrestling metaphors. The name Παλαίστρα
means "wrestling place"; a παλαίσμα is a wrestling throw or move; a
παλαιστὴς is a wrestler or suitor. Here are some other technical terms:

ἀλειψάμενος: rubbing with oil was a preliminary to wrestling and
   lovemaking
ἅμμα: a knot, hence a "clinch" in wrestling, also a maiden's girdle
ἀνακλάω: "bend back" in wrestling
ἀπολέλυσαι: to be released from a hold in wrestling; to be released from
   military service
ἄφες (ἀφίημι): release, send forth, yield; disband an army
βαθύνω: to deepen or hollow out something, to deepen a phalanx
ἐμβάλλω: to strike into, to make an inroad or an invasion
ἐπιβὰς: to "mount" a four-legged creature, to mount a chariot, to attack
παρεμβολὴ: an insertion, an insertion of men in ranks, an encampment, to
   trip someone in wrestling
συμπλέκω: "embrace" used of a wrestler's hold and a lover's embrace
συντρέχω: run together so as to meet in battle, encounter
χάλασμα: gap in the line of battle
χαλάω: to loosen one's grip; to unstring a bow, to become slack
ψιλὸν: bare or open territory or light-armed troops

ἴδῃς, τότ' ἤδη ἐπιβὰς ἄμμα κατ' ἰξύος δήσας σύνεχε, καὶ πειρῶ μὴ σπεύδειν, ἀλλ' ὀλίγον διακαρτερήσας σύντρεχε. ἤδη ἀπολέλυσαι.»

Palaestra orders even more positions and maneuvers.

[10.] κἀγὼ ἐπειδὴ ῥᾳδίως πάντα ὑπήκουσα καὶ εἰς τέλος ἡμῖν ἔληξε τὰ παλαίσματα, λέγω πρὸς τὴν Παλαίστραν ἅμα ἐπιγελάσας, «Ὦ διδάσκαλε, ὁρᾷς μὲν ὅπως εὐχερῶς καὶ εὐηκόως πεπάλαισταί μοι, σκόπει δέ, μὴ οὐκ ἐν κόσμῳ τὰ παλαίσματα ὑποβάλλῃς: ἄλλα γὰρ ἐξ ἄλλων ἐπιτάττεις.»

ἄμμα, -ατος, τό: anything tied, a knot, clinch
ἀπολύω: to release, dismiss
διακαρτερέω: to endure to the end, last out
διδάσκαλος, ὁ: a teacher, master
ἐπιβαίνω: to go upon
ἐπιγελάω: to laugh approvingly
ἐπιτάττω: to put upon, place after
εὐήκοος, -ον: hearing well, obedient
εὐχερής, -ές: easily handled, easy, ready
ἰξύς, -ύος, ἡ: the waist
κόσμος, ὁ: order
λέγω: to speak, say
λήγω: to stay, abate, cease

ὀλίγος, -η, -ον: few, little, small
πάλαισμα, -ατος, τό: a bout of wrestling
Παλαίστρα, ἡ: Palaestra
παλαίω: to wrestle
πειράω: to attempt, endeavor, try
ῥάδιος, -α, -ον: easy, ready
σκοπέω: to look after, take care
σπεύδω: to hasten, hurry
συνέχω: to hold together
συντρέχω: to run together with, coincide
τέλος, -εος, τό: fulfillment, completion, end
ὑπακούω: to listen, obey
ὑποβάλλω: to throw under, suggest

ἐπιβὰς: ao. part. of ἐπι-βαίνω, "having mounted"
δήσας: ao. part., " having bound"
σύνεχε: pr. imper., " hold tight!"
πειρῶ: ao. imper. of πειράω, "try not to hurry"
διακαρτερήσας: ao. part., "by bearing patiently"
σύντρεχε: pr. imper., "pace yourself with"
ἀπολέλυσαι: perf. 2 s. of ἀπο-λύω, "already *you are released*"
ὑπήκουσα: ao. of ὑπο-ἀκούω, "I obeyed"
ἔληξε: ao. of λήγω, "ceased"
ἐπιγελάσας: ao. of ἐπι-γελάω, "at the same time with a laugh"
ὅπως πεπάλαισται: perf. of παλάιω in ind. quest. after ὁρᾷς, "you see *how easily it was wrestled*"
μὴ οὐκ ... ὑποβάλλῃς: pr. subj. in obj. clause after verb of caution with the imperative σκόπει, "watch out *lest you suggest* holds indecorously"

ἡ δὲ ἐπὶ κόρρης πλήξασά με, «Ὡς φλύαρον,» ἔφη, «παρέλαβον τὸν μαθητήν. σκόπει οὖν μὴ πληγὰς ἔτι πλείους λάβῃς ἄλλα καὶ οὐ τὰ ἐπιταττόμενα παλαίων.»

καὶ ταῦτα εἰποῦσα ἐπανίσταται καὶ θεραπεύσασα ἑαυτήν, «Νῦν,» ἔφη, «δείξεις εἴπερ νέος εἶ καὶ εὔτονος παλαιστὴς καὶ εἰ ἐπίστασαι παλαίειν καὶ ποιεῖν τὰ ἀπὸ γονατίου.»

καὶ πεσοῦσα ἐπὶ τοῦ λέχους ἐς γόνυ, «Ἄγε δὴ σὺ ὁ παλαιστής, ἔχεις τὰ μέσα, ὥστε τινάξας ὀξεῖαν ἐπίπρωσον καὶ

ἄγε: come! come on!
γονάτιον, τό: the knee
γόνυ, τό: the knee
δείκνυμι: to show, display, exhibit
ἐπανίστημι: to set up again
ἐπιπρωθέω: to push forward (upon)
ἐπιτάττω: to order
εὔτονος, -ον: well-strung, vigorous
ἐφίστημι: to set or place upon
θεραπεύω: to treat, take care of
κόρρη, ἡ: face, jaw
λαμβάνω: to take, receive
λέχος, -εος, τό: a bed
μαθητής, -οῦ, ὁ: a learner, pupil

μέσος, -η, -ον: middle, in the middle
νέος, νέα, νέον: young, youthful
ὀξύς, -εῖα, -ύ: sharp, keen
παλαιστής, ὁ: a wrestler
παλαίω: to wrestle
παραλαμβάνω: to take up, take on
πίπτω: to fall, fall down
πληγή, ἡ: a blow, stroke
πλήττω: to strike, hit
σκοπέω: to look after, take care
τινάττω: to shake, brandish
φλύαρος, ὁ: one who talks nonsense, a babbler

πλήξασά: ao. part. of πλήττω, "having slapped me"
παρέλαβον: ao. of παρα-λαμβάνω, "I have taken as a pupil"
μὴ λάβῃς: after σκόπει, "watch out lest you receive more blows"
λάβῃς: ao. subj. of λαμβάνω
ἄλλα (sc. παλαίσματα) καὶ οὐ τὰ: "others and not the ones ordered"
παλαίων: pr. part. used instrumentally, "by throwing holds"
εἰποῦσα: ao. part. of λέγω, "having said"
ἐπανίσταται: pr. mid. of ἐπι-ἀνα-ἵστημι, "she rises up"
θεραπεύσασα: ao. part., "having ministered to herself"
δείξεις: fut. of δείκνυμι, "you will show"
εἴπερ νέος εἶ: ind. quest., "whether you are young"
εἰ ἐπίστασαι: "whether you know how to" + inf.
πεσοῦσα: ao. part. of πίπτω, "having dropped down"
τινάξας: ao. part. of τινάσσω: "having brandished"
ἐπίπρωσον: ao. imper. of ἐπι-προ-ὠθέω, "push forward upon!"

βάθυνον. ψιλὸν ὁρᾷς αὐτοῦ παρακείμενον, τούτῳ χρῆσαι·
πρῶτον δὲ κατὰ λόγον, ὡς ἄμμα σφίγγε, εἶτα ἀνακλάσας
ἔμβαλλε καὶ σύνεχε καὶ μὴ δίδου διάστημα. ἐὰν δὲ χαλᾶται,
θᾶττον ἐπάρας ἀνώτερον μετάθες καὶ κρούσας κῦψον καὶ
σκόπει ὅπως μὴ ἀνασπάσῃς θᾶττον ἢ κελευσθῇς, ἀλλὰ δὴ
κυρτώσας πολὺ αὐτὸν ὕφελκε, καὶ ὑποβαλὼν κάτω αὖθις τὴν

ἄμμα, -ατος, τό: anything tied, a knot, clinch
ἀνακλάω: to bend back
ἀνασπάω: to pull back, withdraw
ἀνώτερος, -α, -ον: higher
αὖθις: back, back again
βαθύνω: to sink deep
διάστημα, -ατος, τό: an interval, gap, space between
δίδωμι: to give
ἐμβάλλω: to throw in, strike inside
ἐπαίρω: to lift up, raise
θάττων, -ον: quicker, swifter
κάτω: down, downwards
κελεύω: to bid, command, order

κινέω: to move
κρούω: to strike
κύπτω: to bend forward, stoop down
κυρτόω: to curve into an arch
μετατίθημι: to place among
παράκειμαι: to lie before
παρεμβολή, ἡ: an insertion
σκοπέω: to look after, take care
συνέχω: to secure
σφίγγω: to bind tight, bind fast
ὑποβάλλω: to throw down, put under
ὑφέλκω: to withdraw
χαλάω: to slacken, loosen
χράομαι: to use, make use of (+ *dat.*)
ψιλός, -ή, -όν: bare, uncovered, open

βάθυνον: ao. imper., "drive deeply!"
χρῆσαι: ao. imper. mid. of χράομαι, "make use of it!" + dat.
ἀνακλάσας: ao. part. of ἀνα-κλάω, "having bent (me) back"
μὴ δίδου: pr. imper. mid., "don't allow!"
ἐὰν χαλᾶται: pr. subj. of χαλάω in fut. more vivid cond., "if there is slackening"
ἐπάρας: ao. part. of ἐπαίρω, "having raised up"
μετάθες: ao. imper. of μετα-τίθημι, "change position!"
κρούσας: ao. part., "having struck"
κῦψον: ao. imper. of κύπτω, "bend forward!"
μὴ ἀνασπάσῃς: after σκόπει, "see to it *that you do not pull back*"
ἀνασπάσῃς: ao. subj. of ἀνα-σπάζω
θᾶττον ἢ: "faster than you are commanded"
κελευσθῇς: ao. pas. subj. of κελεύω
κυρτώσας: ao. part. of κυρτόω, "having made curved (your member) a great deal"
ὑποβαλὼν: ao. part. of ὑπο-βάλλω, "striking downward"

παρεμβολὴν σύνεχε καὶ κινοῦ, εἶτα ἄφες αὐτόν· πέπτωκε γὰρ καὶ λέλυται καὶ ὕδωρ ὅλος ἔστι σοι ὁ ἀνταγωνιστής.»

ἐγὼ δὲ ἤδη μέγα ἀναγελῶν, Ἐθέλω, ἔφην, καὶ αὐτός, ὦ διδάσκαλε, παλαίσματα ὀλίγ' ἄττα ἐπιτάξαι, σὺ δὲ ὑπάκουσον ἐπαναστᾶσα καὶ κάθισον, εἶτα δοῦσα κατὰ χειρὸς πάραψαι τὸ λοιπὸν καὶ καταμάττου, καί με πρὸς τοῦ Ἡρακλέους περιλαβοῦσα ἤδη κοίμισον.

ἀναγελάω: to laugh loud
ἀνταγωνιστής, -οῦ, ὁ: an opponent, competitor, rival
ἀφίημι: to send forth, discharge
διδάσκαλος, ὁ: a teacher, master
δίδωμι: to give
ἐθέλω: to will, wish
ἐπανίστημι: to set up again
ἐπιτάττω: to order
Ἡρακλέης, ὁ: Heracles
καθίζω: to make to sit down, seat
καταμάττω: wipe off
κοιμίζω: to put to sleep

λοιπός, -ή, -όν: remaining, the rest
λύω: to loose
ὀλίγος, -η, -ον: few, little, small
ὅλος, -η, -ον: whole, entire, complete
πάλαισμα, -ατος, τό: a wrestling move, hold
παράπτω: to apply
περιλαμβάνω: to seize around, embrace
πίπτω: to fall
ὕδωρ, ὕδατος, τό: water
ὑπακούω: to listen, obey
χείρ, χειρός, ἡ: a hand

σύνεχε: pr. imper., "keep secure your infiltration!"
κινοῦ: pr. imper. of κινέω, "keep moving!"
ἄφες: ao. imper. of ἀπο-ἵημι, "yield!"
πέπτωκε: perf. of πίπτω, "for (your member) has fallen"
ὕδωρ ὅλος ἔστι: "is all wet"
ὀλίγ' ἄττα: "some holds"
ἐπιτάξαι: ao. inf. of ἐπι-τάττω after ἐθέλω, "I wish to *prescribe*"
ὑπάκουσον: ao. imper. of ὑπο-ἀκούω, "obey!"
ἐπαναστᾶσα: ao. part. of ἐπι-ανα-ἵστημι, "having got up"
κάθισον: ao. imper. of καθίζω, "sit down!"
δοῦσα κατὰ χειρὸς: ao. part. of δίδωμι, having given (water) for the hands"
πάραψαι: ao. inf. of purpose of παρα-ἄπτω, "in order to apply"
καταμάττου: pr. imper., "wipe off!"
περιλαβοῦσα: ao. part. of περιλαμβάνω, "having embraced me"
κοίμισον: ao. imper. of κοιμίζω, "put me to bed"

The Ass

After their frolicking is over, Lucius asks to witness some magic.

[11.] Ἐν τοιαύταις ἡδοναῖς καὶ παιδιαῖς παλαισμάτων ἀγωνιζόμενοι νυκτερινοὺς ἀγῶνας ἐστεφανούμεθα, καὶ ἦν πολλὴ μὲν ἐν τούτῳ τρυφή· ὥστε τῆς εἰς τὴν Λάρισσαν ὁδοῦ παντάπασιν ἐπιλελήσμην. καί ποτε ἐπὶ νοῦν μοι ἦλθε τὸ μαθεῖν ὧν ἕνεκα ἤθλουν, καὶ φημὶ πρὸς αὐτήν, «Ὦ φιλτάτη, δεῖξόν μοι μαγγανεύουσαν ἢ μεταμορφουμένην τὴν δέσποιναν· πάλαι γὰρ τῆς παραδόξου ταύτης θέας ἐπιθυμῶ. μᾶλλον δ᾽ εἴ τι σὺ οἶδας, αὐτὴ μαγγάνευσον, ὥστε φανῆναί μοι ἄλλην ἐξ

ἀγών, -ου, ὁ: a competition
ἀγωνίζομαι: to contend for a prize
ἀθλέω: to contend, practice athletics
δείκνυμι: to show, display, exhibit
δέσποινα, ἡ: a mistress, lady of the house
ἕνεκα: on account of, for the sake of (+ gen.)
ἐπιθυμέω: to set one's heart upon, desire greatly
ἡδονή, ἡ: delight, enjoyment, pleasure
θέα, ἡ: a seeing, view, sight
λανθάνω: to escape notice
μαγγανεύω: to use charms, practice magic
μανθάνω: to learn
μεταμορφόω: to transform

νοῦς, νοῦ, ὁ: a mind
νυκτερινός, -ή, -όν: by night, nightly
ὁδός, ἡ: a way, path, journey
οἶδα: to know
παιδία, ἡ: childish play
πάλαι: long ago, for a long time
πάλαισμα, -ατος, τό: a wrestling match
παντάπασι: altogether, wholly
παράδοξος, -ον: incredible, strange
στεφανόω: to crown, wreath
τοιοῦτος, -αύτη, -οῦτο: such as this
τρυφή, ἡ: softness, luxuriousness, wantonness
φαίνομαι: to appear, seem
φίλτατος, -η, -ον: dearest

ἐστεφανούμεθα: impf. mid., "we were crowning ourselves (as victors)"
ὥστε ... ἐπιλελήσμην: pf. ind. in clause showing actual result, "so that I forgot" + gen.
ἐπιλελήσμην: pf. mid. of ἐπι-λανθάνω
ἦλθε: ao. of ἔρχομαι
τὸ μαθεῖν: ao. inf. of μανθάνω the subject of ἦλθε, "the learning came"
ὧν ἕνεκα: "on account of which"
ἤθλουν: impf. of ἀθλέω, "I was contending"
δεῖξόν: ao. imper. of δείκνυμι, "show me!"
μαγγανεύουσαν ἢ μεταμορφουμένην: pr. part. acc. s., "using charms or changing shape"
μᾶλλον δὲ: "but better yet"
μαγγάνευσον: ao. imper. of μαγγανεύω, "you yourself use magic!"
ὥστε φανῆναί: inf. in result clause, "so that another appearance be shown to me"
φανῆναί: ao. pas. inf. of φαίνω
ἄλλην ἐξ ἄλλης: "one after another"

ἄλλης ὄψιν. οἶμαι δὲ καὶ σὲ οὐκ ἀπείρως τῆσδε τῆς τέχνης
ἔχειν· τοῦτο δὲ οὐ παρ' ἑτέρου μαθών, ἀλλὰ παρὰ τῆς ἐμαυτοῦ
ψυχῆς λαβὼν οἶδα, ἐπεί με τὸν πάλαι ἀδαμάντινον, ὡς ἔλεγον
αἱ γυναῖκες, ἐς μηδεμίαν γυναῖκα τὰ ὄμματα ταῦτα ἐρωτικῶς

ἀδαμάντινος, -η, -ον: adamant
ἄπειρος, -ον: unacquainted with,
   inexperienced
γυνή, γυναικός, ἡ: a woman
ἔλεγος, ὁ: a song of mourning, a lament
ἐρωτικός, -ή, -όν: amatory
λέγω: to say
μανθάνω: to learn

μηδείς: and not one
οἶδα: to know
οἴομαι: to suppose, think, imagine
ὄμμα, -ατος, τό: an eye
πάλαι: long ago, for a long time
τέχνη, ἡ: art, skill, craft
ψυχή, ἡ: soul

σὲ ... ἔχειν: ind. st. after οἶμαι, "I suppose that you are"
τοῦτο...οἶδα: "this (that Palaestra practices magic) I know"
μαθών: ao. part. of μανθάνω, "by having learned this"
λαβὼν: ao. part. of λαμβάνω, "but rather by having received it"

Indirect Statement: accusative + infinitive

     In this construction the finite verb of direct speech is changed to an
infinitive of the same tense of the direct speech. The subject of the verb in direct
speech becomes accusative *unless the subject of the indirect speech is the same as the
subject of the main verb.* In that case the subject will be nominative if expressed.

Direct speech:	"He is coming" ἔρχεται
Indirect speech:	She thinks that he is coming. νομίζει αὐτὸν ἔρχεσθαι.
but	He thinks he (himself) is coming νομίζει (αὐτὸς) ἔρχεσθαι

Examples from the *Onos*:
  ἐγὼ δὲ κράτιστον εἶναι ἔγνων ἐλθεῖν: "I decided *that it would be best to go.*"
  οἶμαι δὲ καὶ σὲ οὐκ ἀπείρως ἔχειν: "I suppose *that you are not inexperienced.*"
  ᾤοντο γὰρ ἄνθρωπον εἶναι τὸν ἐωνημένον: "they supposed *that what they
    had purchased was a man*"
  οἱ δὲ εἰδέναι τὸν Ἵππαρχον τοῦτον ἔλεγον: "and they said *that they knew
    this Hipparchus*"

ποτε ἐκτείναντα συλλαβοῦσα τῇ τέχνῃ ταύτῃ αἰχμάλωτον ἔχεις ἐρωτικῷ πολέμῳ ψυχαγωγοῦσα.»

Palaestra protests she knows nothing of magic, but promises to arrange for Lucius to see her mistress.

ἡ δὲ Παλαίστρα, «Παῦσαι,» φησί, «προσπαίζων. τίς γὰρ ᾠδὴ δύναται μαγεῦσαι τὸν ἔρωτα, ὄντα τῆς τέχνης κύριον; ἐγὼ δέ, ὦ φίλτατε, τούτων μὲν οἶδα οὐδὲν μὰ τὴν κεφαλὴν τὴν σὴν καὶ τήνδε τὴν μακαρίαν εὐνήν· οὐδὲ γὰρ γράμματα ἔμαθον, καὶ ἡ δέσποινα βάσκανος οὖσα τυγχάνει εἰς τὴν αὐτῆς τέχνην· εἰ δέ μοι καιρὸς ἐπιτρέψοι πειράσομαι

αἰχμάλωτος, -ον: taken prisoner, held captive
βάσκανος, -ον: envious, jealous
γράμμα, -ατος, τό: a letter
δέσποινα, ἡ: a mistress, lady of the house
δύναμαι: to be able, capable
ἐκτείνω: to stretch out, cast
ἐπιτρέπω: to turn towards
ἔρως, -ωτος, ὁ: love
ἐρωτικός, -ή, -όν: amatory
εὐνή, ἡ: a bed
καιρός, ὁ: the proper time
κεφαλή, ἡ: a head
κύριος, ὁ: a lord, master
μά: (swearing) by (+ acc.)

μαγεύω: to conjure, achieve through magic
μακάριος, -α, -ον: blessed, happy
μανθάνω: to learn
οἶδα: to know
Παλαίστρα, ἡ: Palaestra
παύομαι: to cease, stop
πειράω: to attempt, endeavor, try
πόλεμος, ὁ: a fight, war
προσπαίζω: to play, joke
συλλαμβάνω: to collect, gather together
τέχνη, ἡ: art, skill, craft
τυγχάνω: to hit, happen upon, befall
φίλτατος, -η, -ον: dearest
ψυχαγωγέω: to lead the soul, beguile
ᾠδή, ἡ: a song, incantation

ἐκτείναντα: ao. part. of ἐκ-τείνω, "(me) who have directed these eyes"
συλλαβοῦσα: ao. part. of συν-λαμβάνω, "(you) having captured me with" + dat.
αἰχμάλωτον ἔχεις: "you hold me prisoner"
ψυχαγωγοῦσα: pr. part., "by beguiling with" + dat.
παῦσαι: ao. mid. imper. of παύω, "cease!" + part.
μαγεῦσαι: ao. inf. after δύναται, "what spell can *bewitch*"
ὄντα: "since he is the master"
ἔμαθον: ao. of μανθάνω, "not even *did I learn*"
οὖσα τυγχάνει: "she happens to be"
εἰ ... ἐπιτρέψοι: ao. opt. of ἐπι-τρέπω in fut. less vivid cond., "if the occasion should permit me"
πειράσομαι: fut. of πειράω + inf., "I will try." Note the more vivid apodosis.

31

παρασχεῖν σοι τὸ ἰδεῖν μεταμορφουμένην τὴν κεκτημένην.»
καὶ τότε μὲν ἐπὶ τούτοις ἐκοιμήθημεν.

A few days later Palaestra informs Lucius that her mistress intends to become a bird by magic.

[12.] ἡμέραις δὲ ὕστερον οὐ πολλαῖς ἀγγέλλει πρός με ἡ
Παλαίστρα ὡς ἡ δέσποινα αὐτῆς μέλλοι ὄρνις γενομένη
πέτεσθαι πρὸς τὸν ἐρώμενον.

κἀγώ, «Νῦν,» ἔφην, «ὁ καιρός, ὦ Παλαίστρα, τῆς εἰς
ἐμὲ χάριτος, ᾗ νῦν ἔχεις τὸν σαυτῆς ἱκέτην ἀναπαῦσαι
πολυχρονίου ἐπιθυμίας.»

«Θάρρει,» ἔφη.

ἀγγέλλω: to bear a message, report	**κοιμάω**: to put to sleep
ἀναπαύω: to make to cease, stop	**κτάομαι**: to get, gain, acquire
δέσποινα, ἡ: a mistress, lady of the house	**μέλλω**: to be about to, be going to
ἐπιθυμία, ἡ: desire, yearning, longing	**μεταμορφόω**: to transform
ἐράω: to love	**ὄρνις, ὄρνιθος, ὁ**: a bird
ἡμέρα, ἡ: a day	**Παλαίστρα, ἡ**: Palaestra
θαρρέω: to take courage	**παρέχω**: to furnish, provide, supply
ἱκέτης, -ου, ὁ: one who comes to seek protection, a suppliant	**πέτομαι**: to fly
ἱκνέομαι: to come	**πολυχρόνιος, -ον**: long-existing
καιρός, ὁ: the proper time	**ὕστερος, -α, -ον**: later
	χάρις, -ιτος, ἡ: favor, grace

παρασχεῖν: ao. inf. of **παρα-έχω**
τὸ ἰδεῖν: art. inf., "the seeing"
κεκτημένην: perf. part. of **κτάομαι**, "the one who owns," i.e. the mistress
ἐκοιμήθημεν: ao. pas. of **κοιμάω**, "we put ourselves to bed"
ἡμέραις: dat. of deg. of diff., "later by a few days"
ὡς ... μέλλοι: opt. in implied ind. st. after **ἀγγέλλει** (pres.), "she indicates to me that her mistress was about to" + inf. The opt. is used instead of the subj. even though the verb is a (vivid) present because the narration is still logically in the past.
γενομένη: ao. part. of **γίγνομαι**, "once she had become"
πέτεσθαι: pr. inf. mid. of **πέτομαι** after **μέλλοι**, "to fly"
τὸν ἐρώμενον: pr. part., "her beloved"
ᾗ νῦν ἔχεις: "by which you now are able to" + inf.
ἀναπαῦσαι: ao. inf. of **ἀνα-παύω**, "to release from" + gen.

κἀπειδὴ ἑσπέρα ἦν, ἄγει με λαβοῦσα πρὸς τὴν θύραν
τοῦ δωματίου, ἔνθα ἐκεῖνοι ἐκάθευδον, καὶ κελεύει με
προσάγειν ὀπῇ τινι τῆς θύρας λεπτῇ καὶ σκοπεῖν τὰ γινόμενα
ἔνδον. ὁρῶ οὖν τὴν μὲν γυναῖκα ἀποδυομένην. εἶτα γυμνὴ τῷ
λύχνῳ προσελθοῦσα καὶ χόνδρους δύο λαβοῦσα τὸν μὲν
λιβανωτὸν τῷ πυρὶ τοῦ λύχνου ἐπέθηκε καὶ στᾶσα πολλὰ τοῦ
λύχνου κατελάλησεν· εἶτα κιβώτιον ἁδρὸν ἀνοίξασα, πάνυ
πολλὰς ἔχον πυξίδας ἐν αὐτῷ, ἔνθεν ἀναιρεῖται καὶ προφέρει

ἄγω: to lead or carry, to convey, bring
ἁδρός, -ά, -όν: thick, large
ἀναιρέω: to take up, raise
ἀνοίγνυμι: to open
ἀποδύνω: to strip off, undress
γυμνός, -ή, -όν: naked, unclad
δύο: two
δωμάτιον, τό: a bedchamber
ἔνδον: in, within
ἔνθα: there
ἐπιτίθημι: to place upon
ἑσπέρα, ἡ: evening
θύρα, ἡ: a door
καθεύδω: to sleep
καταλαλέω: to talk loudly

κελεύω: to bid, command, order
κιβώτιον, τό: a chest
λεπτός, -ή, -όν: little, slight
λιβανωτός, ὁ: frankincense
λύχνος, ὁ: a lamp
ὀπή, ἡ: an opening, hole, crack
προσάγω: to bring to
προσέρχομαι: to go to
προφέρω: to bring forth
πυξίς, -ίδος, ἡ: a box
πῦρ, πυρός, τό: fire
σκοπέω: to look at
στάζω: to drop, let fall, shed
χόνδρος, ὁ: a grain

θάρρει: pr. imper., "be brave!"
λαβοῦσα: ao. part. of **λαμβάνω**, "having taken me"
προσάγειν, σκοπεῖν: pr. inf. in ind. com. after **κελεύει**, "she orders me to
approach and to look"
προσελθοῦσα: ao. part. of **προσ-έρχομαι**, "having approached" + dat.
λαβοῦσα: ao. part. of **λαμβάνω**, "having taken"
ἐπέθηκε: ao. of **ἐπι-τίθημι**, "she placed it on"
στᾶσα: ao. part. of **ἵστημι**, "standing"
κατελάλησεν: ao. of **κατα-λαλέω**, "she spoke many things"
ἀνοίξασα: ao. part. of **ἀνα-οίγνυμι**, "having opened"
ἔχον: pr. part. acc. s. n. agreeing with **κιβώτιον**, "a box *containing*"

μίαν: ἡ δὲ εἶχεν ἐμβεβλημένον ὅ τι μὲν οὐκ οἶδα, τῆς δὲ ὄψεως αὐτῆς ἕνεκα ἔλαιον αὐτὸ ἐδόκουν εἶναι. ἐκ τούτου λαβοῦσα χρίεται ὅλη, ἀπὸ τῶν ὀνύχων ἀρξαμένη τῶν κάτω, καὶ ἄφνω πτερὰ ἐκφύεται αὐτῇ, καὶ ἡ ῥὶν κερατίνη καὶ γρυπὴ ἐγένετο,

καὶ τἆλλα δὲ ὅσα ὀρνίθων κτήματα καὶ σύμβολα πάντα εἶχε: καὶ ἦν ἄλλο οὐδὲν ἢ κόραξ νυκτερινός. ἐπεὶ δὲ εἶδεν ἑαυτὴν ἐπτερωμένην,

---

ἄρχω: to begin
ἄφνω: suddenly
γρυπός, -ή, -όν: hooked, curved
εἷς, μία, ἕν: one
ἐκφύω: to grow out
ἔλαιον, τό: olive-oil
ἐμβάλλω: to throw in, put in
ἕνεκα: on account of, for the sake of (+ gen.)
κάτω: down, downwards
κεράτινος, -η, -ον: of horn
κόραξ, -ακος, ὁ: a crow

κτῆμα, -ατος, τό: a possession, attribute
νυκτερινός, -ή, -όν: of night, nightly
οἶδα: to know
ὅλος, -η, -ον: whole, entire, complete
ὄνυξ, -υχος, ὁ: a nail
ὄρνις, ὄρνιθος, ὁ: a bird
ὄψις, -εως, ἡ: look, appearance, aspect
πτερόν, τό: feathers
πτερόω: to feather, give feathers or wings
ῥίς, ῥινός, ἡ: a nose
σύμβολον, τό: a sign, mark
χρίω: to anoint

ἐν αὐτῷ: "within itself"
εἶχεν ἐμβεβλημένον: plpf. periphrastic, "she had put into it"
ἐμβεβλημένον: pf. part. of ἐν-βάλλω
ὅ τι μὲν οὐκ οἶδα: the whole clause is the object of ἐμβεβλημένον, "I do not know what"
αὐτὸ ἐδόκουν εἶναι: "I thought it to be"
λαβοῦσα: ao. part. of λαμβάνω, "having taken"
ὅλη: "completely"
ἀρξαμένη: ao. part. of ἄρχω, "having begun"
ῥὶν: acc. of resp., "with respect to her nose"
ἐγένετο: ao. of γίγνομαι, "she became"
εἶχε: impf. of ἔχω, "she began acquiring"
ἄλλο οὐδὲν ἢ: "she was nothing other than"
ἐπτερωμένην: perf. part. of πτερόω in ind. st. after εἶδεν, "she saw that she had become feathered"

κρώξασα δεινὸν καὶ οἷον ἐκεῖνο οἱ κόρακες, ἀναστᾶσα ᾤχετο πετομένη διὰ τῆς θυρίδος.

Lucius is astonished at the sight and immediately asks Palaestra to transform him into a bird too. (cf. Ap. Met. III.25, p.154)

[13.] ἐγὼ δὲ ὄναρ ἐκεῖνο οἰόμενος ὁρᾶν τοῖς δακτύλοις τῶν ἑαυτοῦ βλεφάρων ἡπτόμην, οὐ πιστεύων τοῖς ἐμαυτοῦ ὀφθαλμοῖς οὔθ᾽ ὅτι βλέπουσιν οὔθ᾽ ὅτι ἐγρηγόρασιν. ὡς δὲ μόλις καὶ βραδέως ἐπείσθην ὅτι μὴ καθεύδω, ἐδεόμην τότε τῆς Παλαίστρας πτερῶσαι κἀμὲ καὶ χρίσασαν ἐξ ἐκείνου τοῦ φαρμάκου ἐᾶσαι πέτεσθαί με: ἠβουλόμην γὰρ πείρᾳ μαθεῖν εἰ

ἀνίστημι: to make to stand up, raise up	μανθάνω: to learn
ἅπτω: to touch	μόλις: scarcely
βλέπω: to see	οἴομαι: to suppose, think, imagine
βλέφαρον, τό: an eyelid	οἴχομαι: to be gone, leave
βούλομαι: to will, wish	ὄναρ, τό: a dream
βραδύς, -εῖα, -ύ: slow	ὀφθαλμός, ὁ: the eye
δάκτυλος, ὁ: a finger	Παλαίστρα, ἡ: Palaestra
δεινός, -ή, -όν: fearful, terrible	πείθω: to prevail upon, persuade
δέομαι: to need, ask	πεῖρα, -ας, ἡ: a trial, attempt, experiment
ἐγείρω: to awaken, wake up	πέτομαι: to fly
θυρίς, -ίδος, ἡ: a window	πιστεύω: to trust, believe (+ dat.)
καθεύδω: to sleep	πτερόω: to feather, give feathers or wings
κόραξ, -ακος, ὁ: a crow	φάρμακον, τό: a drug, medicine
κρώζω: to crow	χρίω: to anoint

κρώξασα: ao. part. of κρώζω, "having crowed"
καὶ οἷον ἐκεῖνο: "a terrible sound *just like that one* crows make"
ἀναστᾶσα: ao. part. of ἀνα-ἵστημι, "arising"
ᾤχετο: impf. of οἴχομαι, "she went"
ὁρᾶν: pr. inf. after οἰόμενος, "supposing *that I was seeing*"
ἡπτόμην: impf. mid. of ἅπτω, "I kept touching my own" + gen.
ὅτι βλέπουσιν: ind. st. after πιστεύων, "believing neither *that they were seeing...*"
ὅτι ἐγρηγόρασιν: "...nor that they were awake"
ἐγρηγόρασιν: perf. of ἐγείρω
ἐπείσθην: ao. pas. of πείθω, "I was persuaded"
πτερῶσαι: ao. inf. of πτερόω after ἐδεόμην, "I begged her *to befeather me*"
χρίσασαν: ao. part. acc. s. f. modifying the acc. subj. of πτερῶσαι and ἐᾶσαι, "by anointing me"
ἐᾶσαι: ao. inf. after ἐδεόμην, "to allow me" + inf.

Indirect Statement: ὅτι or ὡς + the indicative

Verbs that take the accusative + infinitive construction of indirect statement (see p. 30), can also take ὅτι or ὡς + the indicative. In this construction ὅτι or ὡς is just like the English word "that." The only changes from direct speech are changes to the person and number of the verb and subject.

Direct speech: "I am coming"
                                  ἔρχομαι

Indirect speech: I say that I am coming.
                                  λέγω ὅτι ἔρχομαι.
                                  He said that he was coming.
                                  εἶπε ὅτι ἔρχεται.

Examples from the *Onos*:
ἔλεγον ὅτι ἀργύριον ἱκανὸν ἔχει καὶ ὅτι μίαν θεράπαιναν τρέφει:
    "They said *that he had* sufficient money and *that he kept* a single servant."
οὐ πιστεύων τοῖς ἐμαυτοῦ ὀφθαλμοῖς οὔθ' ὅτι βλέπουσιν οὔθ' ὅτι
    ἐγρηγόρασιν: "not believing my own eyes, that *they were seeing* nor that
    they were awake."

Indirect questions are introduced by the direct or indirect form of interrogative words and follow the same rules as indirect speech introduced by ὅτι + the indicative.

Direct question: "Where is the fool going?"
                                  ποῖ ὁ μῶρος βαίνει;

Indirect question: He asked where the fool was going.
                                  ἤρετο ὅποι ὁ μῶρος βαίνει.

Example from the *Onos*:
ἠβουλόμην γὰρ πείρᾳ μαθεῖν εἰ ὄρνις ἔσομαι: "For I wished to see
    whether I would be a bird"

Note that in English the tense of the verb in indirect discourse or question changes depending on the tense of the main verb, but that in Greek the verb in indirect discourse retains the tense of the original statement or question. Compare the translations of ὅτι ἔρχομαι and ὅτι ἔρχεται in the examples above.

The verbs in indirect statement or question can also be changed to the corresponding tense of the optative in secondary sequence. See p. 85.

μεταμορφωθεὶς ἐκ τοῦ ἀνθρώπου καὶ τὴν ψυχὴν ὄρνις ἔσομαι.
ἡ δὲ τὸ δωμάτιον ὑπανοίξασα κομίζει τὴν πυξίδα.

When Palaestra produces the magic ointment, Lucius applies it, but turns into an ass instead of a bird.

ἐγὼ δὲ σπεύδων ἤδη ἀποδύσας χρίω ὅλον ἐμαυτόν, καὶ
ὄρνις μὲν οὐ γίνομαι ὁ δυστυχής, ἀλλά μοι οὐρὰ ὄπισθεν
ἐξῆλθε, καὶ οἱ δάκτυλοι πάντες ᾤχοντο οὐκ οἶδ' ὅποι· ὄνυχας
δὲ τοὺς πάντας τέσσαρας εἶχον, καὶ τούτους οὐδὲν ἄλλο ἢ
ὁπλάς, καί μοι αἱ χεῖρες καὶ οἱ πόδες κτήνους πόδες ἐγένοντο,
καὶ τὰ ὦτα δὲ μακρὰ καὶ τὸ πρόσωπον μέγα. ἐπεὶ δὲ κύκλῳ

δάκτυλος, ὁ: a finger
δυστυχής, -ές: unlucky, unfortunate
δωμάτιον, τό: a bedchamber
ἐξέρχομαι: to come out
κομίζω: to take care of, convey
κτῆνος, -εος, τό: a beast
κύκλος, ὁ: a ring, circle
μακρός, -ά, -όν: long
μεταμορφόω: to transform
οἶδα: to know
οἴχομαι: to be gone, leave
ὅλος, -η, -ον: whole, entire, complete
ὄνυξ, -υχος, ὁ: a nail
ὄπισθεν: behind, at the back

ὁπλή, ἡ: a hoof
ὅποι: to which place, whither
ὄρνις, ὄρνιθος, ὁ: a bird
οὐρά, ἡ: the tail
οὖς, ὠτός, τό: an ear
πούς, ποδός, ὁ: a foot
πρόσωπον, τό: a face
πυξίς, -ίδος, ἡ: a box
σπεύδω: to hasten, quicken
τέσσαρες, -ων: four
ὑπανοίγω: to open secretly
χείρ, χειρός, ἡ: a hand
χρίω: to anoint
ψυχή, ἡ: soul, life

μαθεῖν: ao. inf. of μανθάνω, "to learn"
μεταμορφωθεὶς: ao. part. pas. of μετα-μορφόω, "having been transformed"
εἰ ... ἔσομαι: fut. in ind. quest., "whether I would be"
τὴν ψυχὴν: acc. of resp., "in mind"
ὑπανοίξασα: ao. part. of ὑπο-ανα-οίγνυμι, "having opened up"
ἀποδύσας: ao. part., "having stripped"
ἐξῆλθε: ao. of ἐξ-έρχομαι, "came out from behind"
οὐκ οἶδα ὅποι: "I know not whither"
εἶχον: impf., "I was getting"
οὐδὲν ἄλλο ἢ: "nothing other than"

περιεσκόπουν, αὐτὸν ἑώρων ὄνον, φωνὴν δὲ ἀνθρώπου ἐς τὸ μέμψασθαι τὴν Παλαίστραν οὐκέτι εἶχον. τὸ δὲ χεῖλος ἐκτείνας κάτω καὶ αὐτῷ δὴ τῷ σχήματι ὡς ὄνος ὑποβλέπων ᾐτιώμην αὐτήν, ὅση δύναμις, ὄνος ἀντὶ ὄρνιθος γενόμενος.

Palaestra curses her error, but assures Lucius she will cure him in the morning by providing him roses to eat.

[14.] ἡ δὲ ἀμφοτέραις ταῖς χερσὶν τυψαμένη τὸ πρόσωπον, «Τάλαινα,» εἶπεν, «ἐγώ, μέγα εἴργασμαι κακόν: σπεύσασα γὰρ ἥμαρτον ἐν τῇ

αἰτιάομαι: to charge, accuse, blame
ἁμαρτάνω: to miss, mistake
ἀμφότερος, -α, -ον: each, both
ἀντί: instead of (+ gen.)
δύναμις, -εως, ἡ: power, ability
ἐκτείνω: to stretch out
ἐργάζομαι: to work, bring about
κακός, -ή, -όν: bad
κάτω: down, downwards
μέμφομαι: to blame, censure
ὄνος, ὁ: an ass
ὁράω: to see
ὄρνις, ὄρνιθος , ὁ: a bird
οὐκέτι: no more, no longer

Παλαίστρα, ἡ: Palaestra
περισκοπέω: to look round
πρόσωπον, τό: a face
σπεύδω: to hasten, hurry
σχῆμα, -ατος, τό: form, figure, appearance
τάλας, τάλαινα, τάλαν: suffering, wretched
τύπτω: to beat, strike
ὑποβλέπω: to look up
φωνή, ἡ: a sound, voice
χεῖλος, -εος, τό: a lip
χείρ, χειρός, ἡ: a hand

ἐγένοντο: ao. of γίγνομαι, "became"
περιεσκόπουν: impf. of περι-σκοπέω, "when I began looking around"
ἑώρων: impf. of ὁράω, "I saw"
ἐς τὸ μέμψασθαι: ao. inf. art. of μέμφομαι, "for the blaming"
οὐκέτι εἶχον: "I no longer had"
ἐκτείνας: ao. part. nom. s. of ἐκ-τείνω, "by extending down my lip"
αὐτῷ δὴ τῷ σχήματι: "with mien and all"
ὡς ὄνος ὑποβλέπων: "looking up at her as an ass does"
ᾐτιώμην: impf. of αἰτιάομαι, "I accused"
γενόμενος: ao. part. of γίγνομαι after ᾐτιώμην, "because I had become"
τυψαμένη: ao. part. mid. of τύπτω, "having struck her face"
εἴργασμαι: perf. of ἐργάζω, "I have done"
σπεύσασα: ao. part. of σπεύδω, "by my haste"

ὁμοιότητι τῶν πυξίδων καὶ ἄλλην ἔλαβον οὐχὶ τὴν τὰ πτερὰ
φύουσαν. ἀλλὰ θάρρει μοι, ὦ φίλτατε: ῥᾴστη γὰρ ἡ τούτου
θεραπεία: ῥόδα γὰρ μόνα εἰ φάγοις, ἀποδύσῃ μὲν αὐτίκα τὸ
κτῆνος, τὸν δὲ ἐραστήν μοι τὸν ἐμὸν αὖθις ἀποδώσεις. ἀλλά
μοι, φίλτατε, τὴν μίαν νύκτα ταύτην ὑπόμεινον ἐν τῷ ὄνῳ,
ὄρθρου δὲ δραμοῦσα οἴσω σοι ῥόδα καὶ φαγὼν ἰαθήσῃ.» ταῦτα
εἶπε καταψηλαφήσασά μου τὰ ὦτα καὶ τὸ λοιπὸν δέρμα.

ἀποδίδωμι: to give back, restore, return
ἀποδύνω: to strip off, shed
αὖθις: back, again
αὐτίκα: straightway, at once
δέρμα, -ατος, τό: skin, hide
εἷς, μία, ἕν: one
ἐραστής, -οῦ, ὁ: a lover
ἐσθίω: to eat
θαρρέω: to take courage
θεραπεία, ἡ: a treatment, cure
ἰάομαι: to heal, cure
καταψηλαφάω: to caress, touch lightly
κτῆνος, -εος, τό: a beast
λοιπός, -ή, -όν: remaining, the rest
μόνος, -η, -ον: alone, only

νύξ, νυκτός, ἡ: night
ὁμοιότης, -ητος, ἡ: a likeness, resemblance
ὄνος, ὁ: an ass
ὄρθρος, ὁ: daybreak, dawn
οὖς, ὠτός, τό: an ear
πτερόν, τό: feathers
πυξίς, -ίδος, ἡ: a box
ῥᾴδιος, -α, -ον: easy, ready
ῥόδον, τό: a rose
τρέχω: to run
ὑπομένω: to stay, remain
φέρω: to bear, carry, bring
φίλτατος, -η, -ον: dearest, most beloved
φύω: to bring forth, produce

ἥμαρτον: ao. of **ἁμαρτάνω**, "I made a mistake"
ἔλαβον: ao. of **λαμβάνω**, "I took"
φύουσαν: pr. part. acc. s. f., "not (the box) *producing* feathers"
θάρρει: pr. imper., "be brave!"
ῥᾴστη: superlative of **ῥᾴδιος**, "very easy"
εἰ φάγοις: opt. in fut. less vivid protasis, "if you were to eat"
φάγοις: ao. opt. of **ἐσθίω**
ἀποδύσῃ, ἀποδώσεις: fut. indic. in fut. more vivid apodosis, "you will shed and you will return"
ἀποδώσεις: fut. of **ἀπο-δίδωμι**
νύκτα: acc. of duration "for one night"
ὑπόμεινον: ao. imper. of **ὑπο-μένω**, "wait!"
δραμοῦσα: ao. part. of **τρέχω**, "having run out"
οἴσω: fut. of **φέρω**, "I will bring"
φαγὼν: ao. part. of **ἐσθίω**, "by eating"
ἰαθήσῃ: ao. pas. of **ἰάομαι**, "you will be cured"

Lucian

Lucius must spend the night with the other animals, who refuse to share their food.

[15.] ἐγὼ δὲ τὰ μὲν ἄλλα ὄνος ἤμην, τὰς δὲ φρένας καὶ τὸν νοῦν ἄνθρωπος ἐκεῖνος ὁ Λούκιος, δίχα τῆς φωνῆς. πολλὰ οὖν κατ' ἐμαυτὸν μεμψάμενος τὴν Παλαίστραν ἐπὶ τῇ ἁμαρτίᾳ δακὼν τὸ χεῖλος ἀπῄειν ἔνθα ἠπιστάμην ἑστῶτα τὸν ἐμαυτοῦ ἵππον καὶ ἄλλον ἀληθινὸν ὄνον τὸν Ἱππάρχου. οἱ δὲ αἰσθόμενοί με εἴσω παριόντα, δείσαντες μὴ τοῦ χόρτου κοινωνὸς αὐτοῖς ἐπεισέρχομαι, τὰ ὦτα κατακλίναντες ἕτοιμοι

αἰσθάνομαι: to perceive, notice , see
ἀληθινός, -ή, -όν: genuine, real
ἁμαρτία, ἡ: a failure, mistake
ἀπέρχομαι: to go away, depart
δάκνω: to bite
δείδω: to fear
δίχα: apart from, without (+ gen.)
εἴδομαι: to be visible, appear
εἴσω: to within, into
ἔνθα: there
ἐπεισέρχομαι: to come in besides
ἐπίσταμαι: to know
ἕτοιμος, -ον: ready, prepared

ἵππος, ὁ: a horse, mare
ἵστημι: to make to stand
κατακλίνω: to lay down
κοινωνός, ὁ: a companion, partner
μέμφομαι: to blame, censure
νοῦς, νοῦ, ὁ: a mind
οὖς, ὠτός, τό: an ear
παρέρχομαι: to come along side, arrive
φρήν, φρενός, ἡ: a thought
φωνή, ἡ: a voice
χεῖλος, -εος, τό: a lip
χόρτος, ὁ: feed, hay

καταψηλαφήσασα: ao. part., "having touched lightly"
τὰ μὲν ἄλλα ... τὰς δὲ φρένας: acc. of resp., "in other things, but in mind"
ἤμην: impf. of εἰμι, "I was"
δίχα: "except for" + gen.
κατ' ἐμαυτὸν: "to myself"
μεμψάμενος: ao. part. of μέμφομαι, having blamed"
δακὼν: ao. part. of δάκνω, " having bit"
ἀπῄειν: impf. of ἀπο-ἔρχομαι, "I went out"
ἑστῶτα: perf. part. acc. s. of ἵστημι in ind. st. after ἠπιστάμην, "where I knew my horse *was standing*"
αἰσθόμενοι: ao. part. of αἰσθάνομαι, "having perceived"
παριόντα: pr. part. acc. s. of παρα-ἔρχομαι in ind. st. after αἰσθόμενοι, "that I was arriving"
δείσαντες: ao. part. of δείδω, "they being afraid"
μὴ ... ἐπεισέρχομαι: pr. ind. in a clause of fearing where the subj. would be expected, "afraid that I was coming in after" + gen.

40

ἦσαν τοῖς ποσὶν ἀμύνειν τῇ γαστρί· κἀγὼ συνεὶς πορρωτέρω
ποι τῆς φάτνης ἀποχωρήσας ἑστὼς ἐγέλων, ὁ δέ μοι γέλως
ὀγκηθμὸς ἦν. ταῦτα δ' ἄρ' ἐνενόουν πρὸς ἐμαυτόν· «Ὦ τῆς

ἀμύνω: to ward off, defend
ἀποχωρέω: to go away from
γαστήρ, γαστρός, ἡ: the belly, stomach
γελάω: to laugh
γέλως, ὁ: laughter
ἐννοέω: to have in one's thoughts, think, reflect

ἵστημι: to make to stand
ὀγκηθμός, ὁ: braying
πούς, ποδός, ὁ: a foot
πρόσω: forwards, further
συνίημι: to put together, understand
φάτνη, ἡ: a manger, feeding-trough

κατακλίναντες: ao. part. of **κατα-κλινω**, "having laid back their ears"
ἀμύνειν: epexegetic inf. after **ἕτοιμοι**, "ready to defend" + dat.
συνεὶς: ao. part. of **συν-ἵημι**, " I having understood"
πορρωτέρω ποι: "somewhat further"
ἀποχωρήσας: ao. part. of **ἀπο-χωρέω**, "having stepped away from" + gen.
ἑστὼς: perf. part. of **ἵστημι**, "having stood"

Indirect Statement: accusative + participle

   Some verbs take the accusative + participle construction for indirect speech instead of accusative + infinitive. If the subject of the participle is the same as the subject of the main clause, the nominative is used instead of the accusative (if it is expressed) and the participle will agree with it. No matter which construction is used, translate indirect statement into English with "that" plus a finite verb.

Direct speech:	"He is coming"
	ἔρχεται
Indirect speech:	She knows that he is coming.
	γιγνώσκει αὐτὸν ἐρχόμενον.
but	
	He knows he (himself) is coming
	γιγνώσκει (αὐτὸς) ἐρχόμενος.

Examples from the *Onos*:
   ἀπῄειν ἔνθα ἠπιστάμην ἑστῶτα τὸν ἐμαυτοῦ ἵππον: "I returned where I knew *that the horse was standing*"
   ἠγνόουν δὲ οὐκ εἰς δέον δεδιώς: "I failed to recognize *that I was afraid*"
   κἀγὼ τὴν τύχην ὁρῶν μοι προσμειδιῶσαν: "and I, seeing *that fate was smiling* on me"

ἀκαίρου ταύτης περιεργίας. τί δέ, εἰ λύκος παρεισέλθοι ἢ ἄλλο τι θηρίον; κινδυνεύεταί μοι μηδὲν κακὸν πεποιηκότι διαφθαρῆναι.» ταῦτα ἐννοῶν ἠγνόουν ὁ δυστυχὴς τὸ μέλλον κακόν.

In the dead of night thieves break in and rob the place.

[16.] ἐπεὶ γὰρ ἦν ἤδη νὺξ βαθεῖα καὶ σιωπὴ πολλὴ καὶ ὕπνος ὁ γλυκύς, ψοφεῖ μὲν ἔξωθεν ὁ τοῖχος ὡς διορυττόμενος, καὶ διωρύττετό γε, καὶ ὀπὴ ἤδη ἐγεγόνει ἄνθρωπον δέξασθαι δυναμένη, καὶ εὐθὺς ἄνθρωπος ταύτῃ παρῄει καὶ ἄλλος

ἀγνοέω: not to know, be ignorant
ἄκαιρος, -ον: ill-timed, inopportune
βαθύς, -εῖα, -ύ: deep
γλυκύς, -εῖα, -ύ: sweet
δέχομαι: to take, accept, receive
διαφθείρω: to destroy
διορύσσω: to dig through
δύναμαι: to be able, capable
δυστυχής, -ές: unlucky, unfortunate
ἐννοέω: to have in one's thoughts, think, reflect
ἔξωθεν: from without
θηρίον, τό: a wild animal

κακός, -ή, -όν: bad
κινδυνεύω: to be in danger
λύκος, ὁ: a wolf
μέλλω: to be about to, be going to
νύξ, νυκτός, ἡ: night
ὀπή, ἡ: an opening, hole
παρεισέρχομαι: to come in secretly
παρέρχομαι: to go through
περιεργία, ἡ: curiosity
ποιέω: to make, do
σιωπή, ἡ: silence
τοῖχος, ὁ: a wall
ὕπνος, ὁ: sleep, slumber
ψοφέω: to make a noise, sound

ἐνενόουν: impf. of ἐν-νοέω, "I was pondering"
εἰ … παρεισέλθοι: ao. opt. in fut. less vivid cond., "if a wolf were to enter." The apodosis is τί δέ, "what would happen then?"
παρεισέλθοι: ao. opt. of παρα-εἰς-ἔρχομαι
πεποιηκότι: perf. part dat. s. of ποιέω, "to me not *having done*"
διαφθαρῆναι: ao. inf. of διαφθείρω after κινδυνεύεται, "there is a risk to me to be destroyed"
ἠγνόουν: impf. of ἀγνοέω, "I was ignorant"
μέλλον: pr. part. n. s. modifying κακόν, "the coming evil"
ὡς διορυττόμενος: pr. part., "as though someone was digging through." ὡς here indicates an imputed motive.
διωρύττετό γε: impf. of δια-ὀρύττω, "and indeed someone was digging through"
ἐγεγόνει … δυναμένη: "the opening had become sufficient" + inf.
ἐγεγόνει: plpf. of γίγνομαι
δέξασθαι: ao. inf. of δέχομαι, "to receive"
παρῄει: impf. of παρα-ἔρχομαι, "was passing through"

ὁμοίως, καὶ πολλοὶ ἔνδον ἦσαν καὶ πάντες εἶχον ξίφη. εἶτα καταδήσαντες ἔνδον ἐν τοῖς δωματίοις τὸν Ἵππαρχον καὶ τὴν Παλαίστραν καὶ τὸν ἐμὸν οἰκέτην ἀδεῶς ἤδη τὴν οἰκίαν ἐκένουν τά τε χρήματα καὶ τὰ ἱμάτια καὶ τὰ σκεύη κομίζοντες ἔξω. ὡς δὲ οὐδὲν ἄλλο ἔνδον κατελείπετο, λαβόντες ἐμέ τε καὶ τὸν ἄλλον ὄνον καὶ τὸν ἵππον ἐπέσαξαν, ἔπειτα ὅσα ἐβάστασαν, ἐπικατέδησαν ἡμῖν.

They load up the animals with loot and drive them over a rough road.

καὶ οὕτως μέγα ἄχθος φέροντας ἡμᾶς ξύλοις παίοντες ἤλαυνον εἰς τὸ ὄρος ἀτρίπτῳ ὁδῷ φεύγειν πειρώμενοι. τὰ μὲν

ἀδεής, -ές: without fear, with impunity
ἄτριπτος, -ον: not worn, unused
ἄχθος, -εος, τό: a weight, burden, load
βαστάζω: to lift up, carry off
δωμάτιον: a bed-chamber
ἐλαύνω: to drive
ἔνδον: in, within
ἔξω: out
ἐπισάττω: to load down
ἱμάτιον, τό: an outer garment, clothing
ἵππος, ὁ: a horse, mare
καταδέω: to bind down, tie up
καταλιμπάνω: to leave behind
κενόω: to empty out
κομίζω: to take care of, carry

ξίφος, -εος, τό: a sword
ξύλον, τό: a piece of wood, stick
ὁδός, ἡ: a way, path, road
οἰκέτης, -ου, ὁ: a house-slave, servant
οἰκία, ἡ: a house
ὅμοιος, -α, -ον: like, similar
ὄρος, -εος, τό: a mountain, hill
παίω: to strike, hit
Παλαίστρα, ἡ: Palaestra
πειράω: to attempt, endeavor, try
σκεύη, τά: possessions, belongings
φέρω: to bear, carry
φεύγω: to flee, run away
χρῆμα, -ατος, τό: a thing that one uses, money

εἶχον: impf., "all were holding"
καταδήσαντες: ao. part. of κατα-δέω, "having bound"
ἐκένουν: impf., "they began emptying"
κατελείπετο: impf. pas. of κατα-λείπω, "was left behind"
λαβόντες: ao. part of λαμβάνω, "having taken"
ἐπέσαξαν: ao. of ἐπι-σάττω, "they loaded up"
ὅσα ἐβάστασαν: ao., "whatever they had carried off"
ἐπικατέδησαν: ao. of ἐπι-κατα-δέω, "they tied down upon us"
ἤλαυνον: impf. of ἐλαύνω, "they were driving"
ὡς … πειρώμενοι: pr. part. of πειράομαι, "trying (I suppose) to" + inf.

οὖν ἄλλα κτήνη οὐκ ἔχω εἰπεῖν ὅ τι ἔπασχεν, ἐγὼ δὲ ἀνυπόδητος ἀσυνήθης ἀπιὼν πέτραις ὀξείαις ἐπιβαίνων, τοσαῦτα σκεύη φέρων ἀπωλλύμην. καὶ πολλάκις προσέπταιον, καὶ οὐκ ἦν ἐξὸν καταπεσεῖν, καὶ εὐθὺς ἄλλος ὄπισθεν κατὰ

τῶν μηρῶν ἔπαιεν ξύλῳ. ἐπεὶ δὲ πολλάκις Ὦ Καῖσαρ ἀναβοῆσαι ἐπεθύμουν, οὐδὲν ἄλλο ἢ ὠγκώμην, καὶ τὸ μὲν ὦ μέγιστον καὶ εὐφωνότατον ἐβόων, τὸ δὲ Καῖσαρ οὐκ ἐπηκολούθει. ἀλλὰ μὴν καὶ δι'

ἀναβοάω: to shout, cry out
ἀνυπόδητος, -ον: unshod, barefoot
ἀπέρχομαι: to go away, depart
ἀπόλλυμι: to destroy, kill
ἀσυνήθης, -ες, -εος: unaccustomed, inexperienced
βοάω: to cry, shout
ἐπακολουθέω: to follow after
ἐπιβαίνω: to go upon
ἐπιθυμέω: to set one's heart upon, desire greatly
εὔφωνος, -ον: loud voiced
Καῖσαρ, -αρος, ὁ: Caesar
καταπίπτω: to fall down

κτῆνος, -εος, τό: a beast
μηρός, ὁ: a thigh, rump
ξύλον, τό: wood, a stick
ὀγκάομαι: to bray
ὀξύς, -εῖα, -ύ: sharp
ὄπισθεν: behind, at the back
παίω: to strike, hit
πάσχω: to experience, suffer
πέτρα, ἡ: a rock
πολλάκις: many times, often
προσπταίω: to stumble
σκεύη, τά: possessions, belongings
τοσοῦτος, -αύτη, -οῦτο: so large, so great
φέρω: to bear, carry

οὐκ ἔχω εἰπεῖν: "I cannot say"
ὅ τι ἔπασχεν: object of εἰπεῖν, "what they were suffering"
ἀπιών: pr. part. of ἀπο-έρχομαι, "departing"
πέτραις ὀξείαις: dat. after ἐπι-βαίνω, "stepping on sharp rocks"
ἀπωλλύμην: impf. of ἀπ-όλλυμι, "I was being killed"
προσέπταιον: impf. of προσ-πταίω, "I would strike against"
οὐκ ἦν ἐξὸν: pr. part. n. s. of ἐξ-ειμι in periphrastic expression, "it was not permitted" + inf.
καταπεσεῖν: ao. inf. of κατα-πίπτω, "to fall down"
ἀναβοῆσαι: ao. inf. of ἀνα-βοάω after ἐπεθύμουν, "I wished to shout out"
ὠγκώμην: impf. of ὀγκάομαι, "I would bray"
ἐβόων: impf., "I would try to shout"
ἐπηκολούθει: impf. of ἐπι-ἀκολούθω, "the 'Caesar' would not follow"

αὐτὸ τοῦτο ἐτυπτόμην ὡς προδιδοὺς αὐτοὺς τῷ ὀγκηθμῷ.
μαθὼν οὖν ὅτι ἄλλως ἐβόων, ἔγνων σιγῇ προϊέναι καὶ
κερδαίνειν τὸ μὴ παίεσθαι.

They arrive at a mountain retreat, where the thieves rest a while.

[17.] ἐπὶ τούτῳ ἡμέρα τε ἤδη ἦν, καὶ ἡμεῖς ὄρη πολλὰ
ἀναβεβήκειμεν, καὶ στόματα δὲ ἡμῶν δεσμῷ ἐπείχετο, ὡς μὴ
περιβοσκόμενοι τὴν ὁδὸν ἐς τὸ ἄριστον ἀναλίσκοιμεν· ὥστε ἐς
τὴν τότε καὶ ἔμεινα ὄνος. ἐπεὶ δὲ ἦν αὐτὸ τὸ μέσον τῆς
ἡμέρας, καταλύομεν εἴς τινα ἔπαυλιν συνήθων ἐκείνοις

ἄλλως: in another way or manner
ἀναβαίνω: to go up, climb
ἀναλίσκω: to waste time
ἄριστον, τό: breakfast
βοάω: to cry aloud, to shout
γιγνώσκω: to know
δεσμός, ὁ: a band, bond
ἔπαυλις, -εως, ἡ: a farmhouse
ἡμέρα, ἡ: a day
καταλύω: to put down, lodge
κερδαίνω: to gain, earn
μανθάνω: to learn
μένω: to stay, remain

μέσος, -η, -ον: middle, in the middle
ὀγκηθμός, ὁ: braying
ὁδός, ἡ: a way, path, road
ὄρος, -εος, τό: a mountain, hill
παίω: to strike, hit
περιβόσκω: to feed around
προδίδωμι: to give away, betray
προέρχομαι: to go forward, advance
σιγή, ἡ: silence
στόμα, τό: the mouth
συνήθης, -ες: living with, acquainted
τύπτω: to beat, strike

ἀλλὰ μὴν καὶ: to indicate something indisputable, "but indeed even for this"
ἐτυπτόμην: impf. pas. of τύπτω, "I was beaten"
ὡς προδιδοὺς: pr. part. of προ-δίδωμι, "since (I suppose) I would betray"
μαθὼν: ao. part. of μανθάνω, "having learned"
ἄλλως: "uselessly"
ἔγνων: ao. of γιγνώσκω, "I decided to" + inf.
προϊέναι: pr. inf. of προ-ἔρχομαι after ἔγνων, "I decided *to proceed*"
τὸ μὴ παίεσθαι: art. pas. inf., obj. of κερδαίνειν, "the not being beaten"
ἐπὶ τούτῳ (sc. χρόνῳ): "meanwhile"
ἀναβεβήκειμεν: plpf. of ἀνα-βαίνω, "we had climbed"
ἐπείχετο: impf. pas. of ἐπι-ἔχω, "our mouths *were held*"
μὴ ... ἀναλίσκοιμεν: pr. opt. in neg. purpose clause, "lest we waste time." The
    preceding ὡς indicates that this is an imputed purpose.
περιβοσκόμενοι: pr. part., "by grazing"
ὥστε ἔμεινα: result clause with definite result, "so that I remained"
ἐς τὴν τότε (sc. ἡμέραν): "for that day"
ἔμεινα: ao. of μένω

ἀνθρώπων, ὅσον ἦν ἐκ τῶν γινομένων σκοπεῖν· καὶ γὰρ φιλήμασιν ἠσπάζοντο ἀλλήλους καὶ καταλύειν ἐκέλευον αὐτοὺς οἱ ἐν τῇ ἐπαύλει καὶ παρέθηκαν ἄριστον καὶ τοῖς κτήνεσιν ἡμῖν παρέβαλον κριθία. καὶ οἱ μὲν ἠρίστων, ἐγὼ δὲ ἐπείνων μὲν κακῶς· ἀλλ᾽ ἐπειδὴ οὔπω τότε κριθὰς ὠμὰς ἠριστήκειν, ἐσκοπούμην ὅ τι καὶ καταφάγοιμι.

Lucius sees a vegetable garden and makes his way there to eat.

ὁρῶ δὲ κῆπον αὐτοῦ ὀπίσω τῆς αὐλῆς, καὶ εἶχε λάχανα πολλὰ καὶ καλὰ καὶ ῥόδα ὑπὲρ αὐτῶν ἐφαίνετο· κἀγὼ λαθὼν πάντας τοὺς ἔνδον ἀσχολουμένους περὶ τὸ ἄριστον ἔρχομαι

ἀριστάω: to take breakfast
ἄριστον, τό: breakfast
ἀσπάζομαι: to welcome, greet
ἀσχολέω: to engage, occupy
αὐλή, ἡ: a courtyard
ἔνδον: in, within
ἔπαυλις, -εως, ἡ: a farmhouse
κακός, -ή, -όν: bad
καταλύω: to put down, lodge
κατεσθίω: to eat up, devour
κελεύω: to bid, command, order
κῆπος, ὁ: a garden, orchard
κριθή, ἡ: barley

κριθίον, τό: barley
κτῆνος, -εος, τό: a beast, animal
λανθάνω: to escape notice, be unseen
λάχανον, -ου, τό: vegetables, greens
ὀπίσω: back, behind
παραβάλλω: to throw beside or by
παρατίθημι: to place before
πεινάω: to be hungry
ῥόδον, τό: a rose
σκοπέω: to look at, consider
φαίνομαι: to appear, seem
φίλημα, -ατος, τό: a kiss, embrace
ὠμός, -ή, -όν: raw

ὅσον ἦν: "so far as it was possible" + inf.
αὐτοὺς: "them (the robbers)" acc. subj. of **καταλύειν**
οἱ ἐν τῇ ἐπαύλει: *"those in the farmhouse* ordered them to lodge"
παρέθηκαν: ao. of **παρα-τίθημι**, "they placed before them"
παρέβαλον: ao. of **παρα-λαμβάνω**, "they threw before" + dat.
ἠρίστων: impf. of **ἀριστάω**, "they were eating breakfast"
ἐπείνων: impf. of **πεινάω**, "but I was hungry"
ἠριστήκειν: plpf. of **ἀριστάω**, "not ever had I eaten"
ὅ τι καταφάγοιμι: an ind. deliberative quest. changed to the opt. after
    ἐσκοπούμην, "what I might eat"
καταφάγοιμι: ao. opt. of **κατα-ἐσθίω**
λαθὼν: ao. part. of **λανθάνω**, "escaping the notice of all those "
τοῦτο μὲν ... τοῦτο δὲ: , "partly for this... partly for that"

ἐπὶ τὸν κῆπον, τοῦτο μὲν ὠμῶν λαχάνων ἐμπλησθησόμενος,
τοῦτο δὲ τῶν ῥόδων ἕνεκα· ἐλογιζόμην γὰρ ὅτι δῆθεν φαγὼν
τῶν ἀνθέων πάλιν ἄνθρωπος ἔσομαι. εἶτα ἐμβὰς εἰς τὸν κῆπον
θριδάκων μὲν καὶ ῥαφανίδων καὶ σελίνων, ὅσα ὠμὰ ἐσθίει
ἄνθρωπος, ἐνεπλήσθην, τὰ δὲ ῥόδα ἐκεῖνα οὐκ ἦν ῥόδα
ἀληθινά, τὰ δ' ἦν ἐκ τῆς ἀγρίας δάφνης φυόμενα· ῥοδοδάφνην
αὐτὰ καλοῦσιν ἄνθρωποι, κακὸν ἄριστον ὄνῳ τοῦτο παντὶ καὶ
ἵππῳ· φασὶ γὰρ τὸν φαγόντα ἀποθνήσκειν αὐτίκα.

ἄγριος, -α, -ον: of the field, wild
ἀληθινός, -ή, -όν: true, genuine
ἄνθος, ὁ: a blossom, flower
ἄνθρωπος, ὁ: a man
ἀποθνήσκω: to die
ἄριστον, τό: breakfast
αὐτίκα: straightway, at once
δάφνη, ἡ: laurel
ἐμβαίνω: to step in, walk into
ἐμπίμπλημι: to fill up
ἐμπλέω: to fill up (+ gen.)
ἕνεκα: on account of, for the sake of (+
    gen.)
ἐσθίω: to eat

θρίδαξ, -ακος, ἡ: lettuce
ἵππος, ὁ: a horse, mare
κακός, -ή, -όν: bad
καλέω: to call
κῆπος, ὁ: a garden, orchard
λάχανον, -ου, τό: vegetables, greens
λογίζομαι: to count, reckon, think
πάλιν: back, again
ῥαφανίς, -ίδος, ἡ: a radish
ῥοδοδάφνη, ἡ: rose-laurel
ῥόδον, τό: a rose
σέλινον, τό: parsley
φύω: to grow, produce
ὠμός, -ή, -όν: raw

ἐμπλησθησόμενος: fut. pas. part. of ἐν-πίμπλημι expressing purpose, "in order
    to fill myself with" + gen.
ὅτι δῆθεν: "that surely" (with the implication it was not true)
φαγὼν: ao. part. of ἐσθίω, "by eating"
ἔσομαι: fut. of εἰμί, "that I would be"
ἐμβὰς: ao. part. of ἐν-βαίνω, "having stepped into"
ὅσα ἐσθίει: "whatever a man eats raw"
ἐνεπλήσθην: ao. part. pas. of ἐν-πίμπλημι, "I filled myself" + gen.
ἦν … φυόμενα: pr. part. in periphrastic expression, "they were growing"
κακὸν ἄριστον: "a bad breakfast"
τὸν φαγόντα ἀποθνήσκειν: ind. st. after φασὶ, "they say that the one eating dies
    immediately"
φαγόντα: ao. part. of ἐσθίω

The gardener catches Lucius and begins beating him. Lucius tries to escape.

[18.] ἐν τούτῳ ὁ κηπουρὸς αἰσθόμενος καὶ ξύλον
ἁρπάσας, εἰσελθὼν εἰς τὸν κῆπον καὶ τὸν πολέμιον ἰδὼν καὶ
τῶν λαχάνων τὸν ὄλεθρον, ὥσπερ τις δυνάστης μισοπόνηρος
κλέπτην λαβών οὕτω με συνέκοψε τῷ ξύλῳ, μήτε πλευρῶν
φεισάμενος μήτε μηρῶν, καὶ μὴν καὶ τὰ ὦτά μου κατέκλασεν
καὶ τὸ πρόσωπον συνέτριψεν. ἐγὼ δὲ οὐκέτ᾽ ἀνεχόμενος
ἀπολακτίσας ἀμφοτέροις καὶ καταβαλὼν ὕπτιον ἐπὶ τῶν
λαχάνων ἔφευγον ἄνω ἐς τὸ ὄρος.

αἰσθάνομαι: to perceive, notice , see, hear
ἀμφότερος, -α, -ον: each, both
ἀνέχω: to hold up, bear, endure
ἄνω: upwards
ἀπολακτίζω: to kick off, kick back
ἁρπάζω: to snatch up, seize
δυνάστης, -ου, ὁ: a lord, master
εἰσέρχομαι: to go into, enter
καταβάλλω: to throw down, overthrow
κατακλάω: to break down, crush
κῆπος, ὁ: a garden, orchard
κηπουρός, ὁ: a gardener
κλέπτης, -ου, ὁ: a thief
λάχανον, -ου, τό: vegetables, greens

μηρός, ὁ: a thigh, haunch
μισοπόνηρος, -ον: hostile
ξύλον, τό: a piece of wood, stick
ὄλεθρος, ὁ: ruin, destruction
ὄρος, -εος, τό: a mountain, hill
οὖς, ὠτός, τό: an ear
πλευρόν, τό: a rib
πολέμιος, -α, -ον: of war, hostile, enemy
πρόσωπον, τό: a face
συγκόπτω: to beat up, thrash
συντρίβω: to grind, beat to a pulp
ὕπτιος, -α, -ον: backward, on one's back
φείδομαι: to spare
φεύγω: to flee, run away

αἰσθόμενος: ao. part. of αἰσθάνομαι, "having perceived"
ἁρπάσας: ao. part. of ἁρπάζω, "having snatched"
εἰσελθὼν: ao. part. of εἰσ-έρχομαι, "having entered"
ἰδὼν: ao. part. of ὁράω, "having seen"
ὥσπερ...οὕτω: "just as...just so"
λαβών: ao. part. of λαμβάνω, "who has caught"
συνέκοψε: ao. of συν-κόπτω, "he thrashed soundly"
φεισάμενος: ao. part. mid. of φείδω, "sparing neither" + gen.
καὶ μὴν καὶ: "furthermore," indicating a climax
κατέκλασεν: ao. of κατα-κλάω, "he crushed"
συνέτριψεν: ao. of συν-τρίβω, "he shattered"
ἀνεχόμενος: pr. part. of ἀνα-έχω, "no longer enduring"
ἀπολακτίσας: ao. part. of ἀπο-λακτίζω, "having kicked off"
ἀμφοτέροις: dat., "with both (feet)"
καταβαλὼν: ao. part. of κατα-λαμβάνω, "having cast him down"

The dogs are called out and Lucius returns reluctantly to captivity.

ὁ δὲ ἐπειδὴ εἶδε δρόμῳ ἀπιόντα, ἀνέκραγε λῦσαι τοὺς κύνας ἐπ' ἐμοί· οἱ δὲ κύνες πολλοί τε ἦσαν καὶ μεγάλοι καὶ ἄρκτοις μάχεσθαι ἱκανοί. ἔγνων ὅτι δὴ διασπάσονταί με οὗτοι λαβόντες, καὶ ὀλίγον ἐκπεριελθὼν ἔκρινα τοῦτο δὴ τὸ τοῦ λόγου,

παλινδρομῆσαι μᾶλλον ἢ κακῶς δραμεῖν.

ὀπίσω οὖν ἀπῄειν καὶ εἴσειμι αὖθις εἰς τὴν ἔπαυλιν. οἱ δὲ τοὺς μὲν κύνας δρόμῳ ἐπιφερομένους ἐδέξαντο καὶ κατέδησαν, ἐμὲ

ἀνακράζω: to cry out
ἀπέρχομαι: to go away, depart
ἄρκτος, ἡ: a bear
αὖθις: back, again
γιγνώσκω: to know
δέχομαι: to take, accept
διασπάω: to tear apart
δρόμος, ὁ: a course, running
εἰσέρχομαι: to go into, enter
ἐκπεριέρχομαι: to go around
ἔπαυλις, -εως, ἡ: a farmhouse
ἐπιφέρω: to set upon, attack

ἱκανός, -ή, -όν: befitting, sufficing, capable
κακός, -ή, -όν: bad
καταδέω: to bind fast, tie up
κρίνω: to choose
κύων, ὁ: a dog
λύω: to loose
μάχομαι: to fight
ὀλίγος, -η, -ον: few, little, small
ὀπίσω: backwards, back
παλινδρομέω: to run back
τρέχω: to run

εἶδε: ao. of ὁράω, "he saw"
ἀπιόντα: pr. part. acc. s. of ἀπο-ἔρχομαι, "(me) departing"
ἀνέκραγε: ao. of ἀνα-κράζω, "he shouted" + inf.
λῦσαι: ao. inf. of λύω in ind. com. after ἀνέκραγε, "to release"
μάχεσθαι: expexegetic inf. after ἱκανοί, "able *to fight with*" + dat.
ἔγνων: ao. of γιγνώσκω, "I realized"
διασπάσονταί: fut. of δια-σπάω in ind. st., "that these would tear asunder"
λαβόντες: ao. part. of λαμβάνω, "once they got hold of me"
ὀλίγον: acc. of duration, "for a little (time)"
ἐκπεριελθὼν: ao. part. of ἐκ-περι-ἔρχομαι, "having gone round and round"
ἔκρινα: ao. of κρίνω, "I decided"
τοῦτο δὴ τὸ τοῦ λόγου: "according to just this (part) of the saying," i.e. "according to the saying..." What follows is an iambic dimeter.
παλινδρομῆσαι: ao. inf. of παλινδρομέω, "to run back"
δραμεῖν: ao. inf. of τρέχω, "*to run amuck*"
ἀπῄειν: impf. of ἀπο-ἔρχομαι, "I went back"
εἴσειμι: fut. of εἰσ-ἔρχομαι expressing intent, "I am about to enter"
ἐπιφερομένους: "who were setting upon me in a rush"
ἐδέξαντο: ao. of δέχομαι, "they received the dogs back"

δὲ παίοντες οὐ πρότερον ἀφῆκαν πρὶν ἢ ὑπὸ τῆς ὀδύνης πάντα τὰ λάχανα κάτωθεν ἐξεμέσαι.

Back on the road again, Lucius contemplates feigning death, but the treatment of one of his fellow pack animals changes his mind.

[19.] καὶ μὴν ὅτε ὁδοιπορεῖν ὥρα ἦν, τὰ βαρύτατα τῶν κλεμμάτων καὶ τὰ πλεῖστα ἐμοὶ ἐπέθηκαν· κἀκεῖθεν τότε οὕτως ἐξελαύνομεν. ἐπεὶ δὲ ἀπηγόρευον ἤδη παιόμενός τε καὶ τῷ φορτίῳ ἀχθόμενος καὶ τὰς ὁπλὰς ἐκ τῆς ὁδοῦ

ἀπαγορεύω: to give up, grow weary
ἀφίημι: to send forth, discharge
ἄχθομαι: to be loaded down
βαρύς, -εῖα, -ύ: heavy
ἐκεῖθεν: from that place, thence
ἐξελαύνω: to drive out, ride out
ἐξεμέω: to expel, disgorge
ἐπιτίθημι: to lay upon, burden
κάτωθεν: from below, from behind
κλέμμα, -ατος, τό: a theft, loot
λάχανον, -ου, τό: vegetables, greens

ὁδοιπορέω: to travel, walk
ὁδός, ἡ: a way, path, road
ὀδύνη, ἡ: pain
ὁπλή, ἡ: a hoof
ὅτε: when
παίω: to strike, hit
πλεῖστος, -η, -ον: most, largest
πρίν: before
πρότερος, -α, -ον: before, earlier
φορτίον, τό: a load, burden
ὥρα, -ας, ἡ: period, season, time

κατέδησαν: ao. of κατα-δέω, "they bound them"
ἐμὲ δὲ: "but as for me"
ἀφῆκαν: ao. of ἀπο-ἵημι, "they did not leave off" + part.
πρὶν ἢ ... ἐξεμέσαι: ao. inf., "before I disgorged"
ὁδοιπορεῖν: epexegetic inf. after ὥρα ἦν, "it was time *to travel*"
ἐπέθηκαν: ao. of ἐπι-τίθημι, "they loaded on me"
κἀκεῖθεν: (= καὶ ἐκεῖθεν) "and from there"
ἀπηγόρευον: impf., "I was exhausted from" + part.

ἐκτετριμμένος, ἔγνων αὐτοῦ καταπεσεῖν καὶ μηδ' ἂν
ἀποσφάττωσί με ταῖς πληγαῖς ἀναστῆναί ποτε, τοῦτο ἐλπίσας
μέγα μοι ὄφελος ἔσεσθαι ἐκ τοῦ βουλεύματος: ᾠήθην γὰρ ὅτι
πάντως ἡττώμενοι τὰ μὲν ἐμὰ σκεύη διανεμοῦσι τῷ τε ἵππῳ
καὶ τῷ ἡμιόνῳ, ἐμὲ δὲ αὐτοῦ ἐάσουσι κεῖσθαι τοῖς λύκοις.
ἀλλά τις δαίμων βάσκανος συνεὶς τῶν ἐμῶν βουλευμάτων ἐς
τοὐναντίον περιήνεγκεν: ὁ γὰρ ἕτερος ὄνος ἴσως ἐμοὶ τὰ αὐτὰ

ἀνίστημι: to make to stand up, raise up
ἀποσφάζω: to slaughter
βάσκανος, -ον: envious, malicious
βούλευμα, -ατος, τό: a purpose, design, plan
γιγνώσκω: to know
δαίμων, -ονος, ὁ: divine spirit, god
διανέμω: to distribute, apportion
ἐκτρίβω: to rub out, wear out
ἐλπίζω: to hope for
ἐναντίος, -α, -ον: opposite
ἡμίονος, ἡ: a mule

ἡττάομαι: to give way, yield
ἵππος, ὁ: a horse, mare
καταπίπτω: to fall down, drop down
κεῖμαι: to be laid
λύκος, ὁ: a wolf
οἴομαι: to suppose, think, imagine
ὄφελος, τό: an advantage, help
περιφέρω: to carry around, turn around
πληγή, ἡ: a blow, stroke
σκεύη, τά: possessions, belongings
συνίημι: to bring together, understand

ἐκτετριμμένος: perf. part. mid. of **ἐκ-τρίβω** with **ἀπηγόρευον**, "I was exhausted *from having worn out my hooves*"
ἔγνων: ao. of **γιγνώσκω**, "I decided to" + inf.
αὐτοῦ: "in that very spot"
καταπεσεῖν: ao. inf. of **κατα-πίπτω**, "to fall down"
καὶ μηδε … ἀναστῆναι: also after **ἔγνων**, "and not to arise"
ἀναστῆναι: ao. inf. of **ἀνα-ἵστημι**
ἂν ἀποσφάττωσι: pr. subj. in fut. more vivid protasis, "even if they slay me"
ἐλπίσας: ao. part., "with the hope" + fut. inf.
ἔσεσθαι: fut. of **εἰμι** after **ἐλπίσας**, "that this would be"
ᾠήθην: ao. pas. of **οἴομαι**, "I thought"
ἡττώμενοι: pr. pas. part., "being defeated"
ὅτι … διανεμοῦσι: fut., "that they would distribute to" + dat.
ἐάσουσι: fut., "and that they would allow" + inf.
αὐτοῦ κεῖσθαι: "to lie in that spot"
τοῖς λύκοις: dat. of advantage, "for the wolves"
συνεὶς: ao. part. of **συν-ἵημι**, "having understood" + gen.
ἐς τοὐναντίον: (= τὸ ἐναντίον) "to the opposite (opinion)"
περιήνεγκεν: ao. of **περι-φέρω**, "brought (me) about"

νοήσας πίπτει ἐν τῇ ὁδῷ. οἱ δὲ τα μὲν πρῶτα ξύλῳ παίοντες ἀναστῆναι τὸν ἄθλιον ἐκέλευον, ὡς δὲ οὐδὲν ὑπήκουε ταῖς πληγαῖς, λαβόντες αὐτὸν οἱ μὲν τῶν ὤτων, οἱ δὲ τῆς οὐρᾶς ἀνεγείρειν ἐπειρῶντο· ὡς δὲ οὐδὲν ἤννον, ἔκειτο δὲ ὥσπερ λίθος ἐν τῇ ὁδῷ ἀπηγορευκώς, λογισάμενοι ἐν ἀλλήλοις ὅτι δὴ μάτην πονοῦσι καὶ τὸν χρόνον τῆς φυγῆς ἀναλίσκουσιν ὄνῳ νεκρῷ παρεδρεύοντες, τὰ μὲν σκεύη πάντα ὅσα ἐκόμιζεν

ἄθλιος, -α, -ον: struggling, unhappy, wretched	ξύλον, τό: a piece of wood, stick
ἀναλίσκω: to use up, spend, waste	ὁδός, ἡ: a way, path, road
ἀνεγείρω: to rouse	οὐρά, ἡ: the tail
ἀνίστημι: to make to stand up, raise up	οὖς, ὠτός, τό: an ear
ἀνύω: to effect, achieve, accomplish	παίω: strike, hit
ἀπαγορεύω: to give up, grow weary	παρεδρεύω: to attend, tend to
κεῖμαι: to be laid	πειράω: to attempt, endeavor, try
κελεύω: to urge, command, order	πίπτω: to fall, fall down
κομίζω: to take care of, carry	πληγή, ἡ: a blow, stroke
λίθος, -ου, ὁ: a stone	πονέω: to work hard, suffer, toil
λογίζομαι: to count, reckon, think	πρῶτος, -η, -ον: first
μάτην: in vain, fruitlessly	σκεύη, τά: possessions, belongings
νεκρός, -ά, -όν: dead	ὑπακούω: to listen, obey
νοέω: to think, intend	φυγή, ἡ: flight
	χρόνος, ὁ: time

νοήσας: ao. part. of **νοέω**, "having thought of the same thing"

τα πρῶτα: "at first"

ἀναστῆναι: ao. inf. of **ἀνα-ἴστημι** in ind. com. after **ἐκέλευον**, "they ordered him to stand up"

οὐδὲν ὑπήκουε: impf. of **ὑπο-ἀκούω**, "since he wasn't heeding" + dat.

λαβόντες: ao. part. of **λαμβάνω**, "taking hold of him by the" + gen.

οἱ μὲν ... οἱ δὲ: "some ... others"

ἐπειρῶντο: impf., "they kept trying to" + inf.

ἤννον: impf. of **ἀνύω**, "they were accomplishing"

ἀπηγορευκώς: perf. part. of **ἀπο-ἀγορεύω**, "having become exhausted"

λογισάμενοι ὅτι: ao. part., "having calculated that"

παρεδρεύοντες: pr. part. after **ἀναλίσκουσιν**, "that they were wasting time attending to" + dat.

ὅσα ἐκόμιζεν: "whatever he was carrying"

ἐκεῖνος διανέμουσιν ἐμοί τε καὶ τῷ ἵππῳ, τὸν δὲ ἄθλιον κοινωνὸν καὶ τῆς αἰχμαλωσίας καὶ τῆς ἀχθοφορίας λαβόντες τῷ ξίφει ὑποτέμνουσιν ἐκ τῶν σκελῶν καὶ σπαίροντα ἔτι ὠθοῦσιν ἐς τὸν κρημνόν. ὁ δὲ ἀπῄει κάτω τὸν θάνατον ὀρχούμενος.

Continuing on they arrive at a hideout where an old woman prepares dinner for the thieves.

[20.] ἐγὼ δὲ ὁρῶν ἐν τῷ συνοδοιπόρῳ τῶν ἐμῶν βουλευμάτων τὸ τέλος, ἔγνων φέρειν εὐγενῶς τὰ ἐν ποσὶ καὶ προθύμως περιπατεῖν, ἐλπίδας ἔχων πάντως ποτὲ ἐμπεσεῖσθαι εἰς τὰ ῥόδα κἀκ τούτων εἰς ἐμαυτὸν ἀνασωθήσεσθαι: καὶ τῶν λῃστῶν δὲ ἤκουον ὡς οὐκ εἴη ἔτι πολὺ τῆς ὁδοῦ λοιπὸν καὶ

ἄθλιος, -α, -ον: struggling, unhappy, wretched
αἰχμαλωσία, ἡ: captivity
ἀκούω: to hear
ἀνασῴζω: recover what is lost, rescue
ἀπέρχομαι: to go away, depart
ἀχθοφορία, ἡ: the bearing of burdens
βούλευμα, -ατος, τό: a purpose, design, plan
γιγνώσκω: to know
διανέμω: to distribute, apportion
ἐλπίς, -ίδος, ἡ: hope, expectation
ἐμπίτνω: fall upon
εὐγενής, -ές: well-born, brave
θάνατος, ὁ: death
ἵππος, ὁ: a horse, mare
κάτω: down, downwards
κοινωνός, ὁ: a companion, partner

κρημνός, ὁ: an overhang, cliff
λῃστής, -οῦ, ὁ: a robber, plunderer
λοιπός, -ή, -όν: remaining, the rest
ξίφος, -εος, τό: a sword
ὁδός, ἡ: a way, path, journey
ὀρχέομαι: to dance
περιπατέω: to walk about, go around
πούς, ποδός, ὁ: a foot
πρόθυμος, -ον: ready, willing, eager
ῥόδον, τό: a rose
σκέλος, -εος, τό: a leg
σπαίρω: to gasp, pant
συνοδοίπορος, ὁ: a fellow traveler
τέλος, -εος, τό: the fulfillment, completion, end
ὑποτέμνω: to cut from under
φέρω: to bear, carry, endure
ὠθέω: to thrust, push, shove

τὸν δὲ ἄθλιον κοινωνὸν: "my wretched companion in" + gen.
λαβόντες αὐτὸν: ao. part. of λαμβάνω, "having seized him"
σπαίροντα ἔτι: pr. part. acc. s., "still quivering"
ἀπῄει: impf. of ἀπο-ἔρχομαι, "he went down"
ὀρχούμενος: pr. part. of ὀρχέομαι, "dancing"
ἔγνων: ao. of γιγνώσκω, "I decided to" + inf.
τὰ ἐν ποσὶ: "the things at my feet"
ἐμπεσεῖσθαι: fut. inf. of ἐν-πίπτω after ἐλπίδας, "having hopes to fall upon"
ἀνασωθήσεσθαι: fut. pas. inf. of ἀνα-σῴζω also after ἐλπίδας, "to be saved"
ὡς οὐκ εἴη: opt. in ind. st. in sec. seq. after ἤκουον, "I heard that there was not"

ὅτι καταμενοῦσιν ἔνθα καταλύσουσιν· ὥστε ταῦτα πάντα δρόμῳ ἐκομίζομεν, καὶ πρὸ τῆς ἑσπέρας ἤλθομεν εἰς τὰ οἰκεῖα. γραῦς δὲ γυνὴ ἔνδον καθῆστο, καὶ πῦρ πολὺ ἐκαίετο. οἱ δὲ πάντα ἐκεῖνα ἅπερ ἐτυγχάνομεν ἡμεῖς κομίζοντες, εἴσω κατέθηκαν. εἶτα ἤροντο τὴν γραῦν, Διὰ τί οὕτως καθέζῃ καὶ οὐ παρασκευάζεις ἄριστον;

«Ἀλλὰ πάντα,» εἶπεν ἡ γραῦς, «εὐτρεπῆ ὑμῖν, ἄρτοι πολλοί, οἴνου παλαιοῦ πίθοι, καὶ τὰ κρέα δὲ ὑμῖν τὰ ἄγρια σκευάσασα ἔχω.» οἱ δὲ τὴν γραῦν ἐπαινέσαντες, ἀποδυσάμενοι

ἄγριος, -α, -ον: wild
ἀποδύνω: to strip off
ἄριστον, τό: a meal, breakfast
ἄρτος, ὁ: a loaf of bread
γραῦς, γραός, ἡ: an old woman
γυνή, γυναικός, ἡ: a woman, wife
δρόμος, ὁ: a course, running
εἴσω: to within, inside
ἔνθα: there
ἐπαινέω: to approve, applaud, commend
ἐρωτάω: to ask, enquire
ἑσπέρα, ἡ: evening
εὐτρεπής, -ές: ready
Ζεύς, Διός, ὁ: Zeus
καθέζομαι: to remain seated
κάθημαι: to be seated

καίω: to light, kindle
καταλύω: to put down, lodge
καταμένω: to stay behind, remain
κατατίθημι: to put up, store
κομίζω: to take care of, carry
κρέας, τό: flesh, meat
οἰκεῖος, -α, -ον: of the house, domestic
οἶνος, ὁ: wine
παλαιός, -ά, -όν: old
παρασκευάζω: to get ready, prepare
πίθος, ὁ: a wine-jar
πρό: before
πῦρ, πυρός, τό: fire
σκευάζω: to prepare, make ready
τυγχάνω: to hit, happen upon

ὅτι καταμενοῦσιν: fut., "and that they would remain"
καταλύσουσιν: fut., "where they would lodge"
δρόμῳ: dat. of manner, "at a run"
ἤλθομεν: ao. of ἔρχομαι "we arrived'
καθῆστο: plpf. of κατα-ἧμαι "was seated"
ἐτυγχάνομεν: impf., "which we happened to be..." + part.
κατέθηκαν: ao. of κατα-τίθημι, "they deposited"
ἤροντο: ao. of ἐρωτάω, "they asked"
τὰ κρέα τὰ ἄγρια: "wild game"
σκευάσασα ἔχω: ao. part. of σκεύω in periphrastic constr., "I have prepared"
ἐπαινέσαντες: ao. part. of ἐπαινέω, "having praised"

ἠλείφοντο πρὸς τὸ πῦρ καὶ λέβητος ἔνδον ὕδωρ θερμὸν ἔχοντος ἀρυσάμενοι ἔνθεν καὶ καταχεάμενοι αὐτοσχεδίῳ τῷ λουτρῷ ἐχρήσαντο.

A band of youths arrive with spoils. Lucius is guarded while the thieves go out on a mission.

[21.] εἶτα ὀλίγῳ ὕστερον ἦκον νεανίσκοι πολλοὶ κομίζοντες πλεῖστα ὅσα χρυσᾶ καὶ ἀργυρᾶ καὶ ἱμάτια καὶ κόσμον γυναικεῖον καὶ ἀνδρεῖον πολύν. ἐκοινώνουν δὲ οὗτοι ἀλλήλοις: καὶ ἐπειδὴ ταῦτα ἔνδον κατέθεντο, ὁμοίως ἐλούσαντο καὶ οὗτοι. λοιπὸν μετὰ τοῦτο ἦν ἄριστον δαψιλὲς καὶ λόγος πολὺς ἐν τῷ συμποσίῳ τῶν ἀνδροφόνων. ἡ δὲ γραῦς

ἀλείφω: to anoint with oil
ἀνδρεῖος, -α, -ον: of or for a man
ἀνδροφόνος, -ον: murderous
ἀργύρεος, -ᾶ, -οῦν: silver, of silver
ἄριστον, τό: a meal, breakfast
ἀρύω: to draw
αὐτοσχέδιος, -α, -ον: offhand, improvised
γραῦς, γραός, ἡ: an old woman
γυναικεῖος, -α, -ον: of or for a woman
δαψιλής, -ές: abundant, plentiful
ἥκω: to have come, be present
θερμός, -ή, -όν: hot, warm
ἱμάτιον τό: an outer garment, a cloak
κατατίθημι: to put up, store
καταχέω: to pour down upon, pour over
κοινωνέω: to have in common, share

κομίζω: to take care of, carry
κόσμος, ὁ: fashion, ornament, decoration
λέβης, -ητος, ὁ: a kettle, caldron
λοιπός, -ή, -όν: remaining, the rest
λουτρόν, τό: a bath
λούω: to wash
ὀλίγος, -η, -ον: few, little, small
ὅμοιος, -α, -ον: like, similar
πλεῖστος, -η, -ον: most, largest
πῦρ, πυρός, τό: fire
συμπόσιον, τό: a drinking-party, symposium
ὕδωρ, ὕδατος, τό: water
ὕστερος, -α, -ον: later, afterward
χράομαι: to use, enjoy (+ dat.)
χρύσεος, -η, -ον: golden, of gold

ἠλείφοντο: impf., "they anointed themselves"
λέβητος ... ἔχοντος: gen. abs., "the kettle holding"
ἀρυσάμενοι ἔνθεν: ao. part. of ἀρύω, "having drawn (water) from there"
καταχεάμενοι: ao. part. mid. of κατα-χέω, "having poured it over themselves"
ἐχρήσαντο: ao. of χράομαι, "they made use of" + dat.
ὀλίγῳ: dat. of degree of difference, "later *by a little*"
ἦκον: impf., "they began arriving"
ὅσα: "such as gold, etc."
κατέθεντο: ao. of κατα-τίθημι, "they deposited"
λοιπὸν: acc. of duration of time, "for the remaining time after this"

ἐμοὶ καὶ τῷ ἵππῳ κριθὰς παρέθηκεν· ἀλλ' ἐκεῖνος μὲν σπουδῇ τὰς κριθὰς κατέπινε δεδιώς, οἷα εἰκός, ἐμὲ τὸν συνάριστον. ἐγὼ δὲ ἐπειδὰν ἴδοιμι τὴν γραῦν ἐξιοῦσαν τῶν ἔνδον ἄρτον ἤσθιον. τῇ δὲ ὑστεραίᾳ καταλιπόντες τῇ γραίᾳ νεανίσκον ἕνα οἱ λοιποὶ πάντες ἔξω ἐπὶ τὸ ἔργον ἀπήεσαν. ἐγὼ δὲ ἔστενον ἐμαυτὸν καὶ τὴν ἀκριβῆ φρουράν· τῆς μὲν γὰρ γραὸς καταφρονῆσαι ἦν μοι καὶ φυγεῖν ἐκ τῶν ἐκείνης ὀμμάτων δυνατόν, ὁ δὲ νεανίσκος μέγας τε ἦν καὶ φοβερὸν ἔβλεπε, καὶ τὸ ξίφος ἀεὶ ἔφερεν καὶ τὴν θύραν ἀεὶ ἐπῆγε.

ἀεί: always, for ever
ἀκριβής, -ές: exact, accurate, precise
ἀπέρχομαι: to go away, depart
ἄρτος, ὁ: a loaf of bread
βλέπω: to see
γραῖα, ἡ: an old woman
γραῦς, γραός, ἡ: an old woman
δυνατός, -ή, -όν: strong, mighty, able
εἷς, μία, ἕν: one
ἐξέρχομαι: to go out
ἔξω: out
ἐπειδάν: whenever
ἔργον, τό: a deed, work
ἐσθίω: to eat
θύρα, ἡ: a door
ἵππος, ὁ: a horse, mare
καταλείπω: to leave behind
καταπίνω: to gulp down

καταφρονέω: to think down upon
κριθή, ἡ: barley
λοιπός, -ή, -όν: remaining, the rest
νεανίσκος, ὁ: a youth, young man
ξίφος, -εος, τό: a sword
ὄμμα, -ατος, τό: an eye
παρατίθημι: to place before
πήγνυμι: to fasten
σπουδή, ἡ: haste, speed
στένω: to moan, sigh, groan
συνάριστος, ὁ: a meal companion
ὑστεραῖος, -α, -ον: on the day after, the next day
φέρω: to bear, carry
φεύγω: to flee, run away
φοβερός, -ά, -όν: fearful
φρουρά, ἡ: a watch, guard

παρέθηκεν: ao. of παρα-τίθημι, "she placed before us"
κατέπινε: impf., "they were gulping down"
δεδιώς: perf. part., "fearing"
οἷα εἰκός: "so it seems"
ἐπειδὰν ἴδοιμι: opt. in gen. temp. clause, "whenever I could see, I would eat." The ἄν in ἐπειδὰν is potential.
ἐξιοῦσαν: pr. part. of ἐξ-έρχομαι, "the woman exiting"
ἤσθιον: impf. of ἐσθίω
καταλιπόντες: ao. part. of κατα-λείπω, "leaving behind with" + dat.
ἀπήεσαν: impf. of ἀπο-έρχομαι, "the rest departed"
ἔστενον: impf., "I kept groaning"
καταφρονῆσαι: ao. inf. after ἦν δυνατόν, "it was possible to dismiss"
φυγεῖν: ao. inf. of φεύγω, "to escape"
ἔβλεπεν: impf., "he kept watching"
ἐπῆγε: impf. of πήγνυμι, "he kept closed"

Three days later the thieves return with a young maiden as captive.

[22.] τρισὶ δὲ ὕστερον ἡμέραις μεσούσης σχεδὸν τῆς νυκτὸς ἀναστρέφουσιν οἱ λησταί, χρυσίον μὲν οὐδὲ ἀργύριον οὐδὲ ἄλλο οὐδὲν κομίζοντες, μόνην δὲ παρθένον ὡραίαν, σφόδρα καλήν, κλάουσαν καὶ κατεσπαραγμένην τὴν ἐσθῆτα καὶ τὴν κόμην· καὶ καταθέμενοι αὐτὴν ἔνδον ἐπὶ τῶν στιβάδων θαρρεῖν ἐκέλευον καὶ τὴν γραῦν ἐκέλευον ἀεὶ ἔνδον μένειν καὶ τὴν παῖδα ἐν φρουρᾷ ἔχειν. ἡ δὲ παῖς οὔτε ἐμφαγεῖν τι ἤθελεν οὔτε πιεῖν, ἀλλὰ πάντα ἔκλαε καὶ τὴν κόμην τὴν αὑτῆς

ἀεί: always, for ever
ἀναστρέφω: to turn back, return
ἀργύριον, τό: a piece of silver
γραῦς, γραός, ἡ: an old woman
ἐθέλω: to will, wish
ἐσθής, -ῆτος, ἡ: dress, clothing
ἐσθίω: to eat
ἡμέρα, ἡ: a day
θαρρέω: to take courage
κατασπαράττω: to tear to pieces
κατατίθημι: to put down
κελεύω: to bid, command, order
κλάω: to break, tear
κόμη, ἡ: hair
κομίζω: to take care of, carry
λῃστής, -οῦ, ὁ: a robber

μένω: to stay, remain
μεσόω: to be in the middle of (+ *gen.*)
μόνος, -η, -ον: alone, only
νύξ, νυκτός, ἡ: night
παῖς, παιδός, ἡ: child, girl
παρθένος, ἡ: a maiden, girl
πίνω: to drink
στιβάς, -άδος, ἡ: a bed of straw
σφόδρα: very, exceedingly
σχεδόν: close, near
τρεῖς: three
ὕστερος, -α, -ον: later, afterward
φρουρά, ἡ: a watch, guard
χρυσίον, τό: a piece of gold
ὡραῖος, -α, -ον: youthful, ripe

τρισὶ ἡμέραις: dat. of degree of difference, "later by three days"
μεσούσης τῆς νυκτός: the genitive indicates a less definite time, "near the middle of the night"
κατεσπαραγμένην: perf. part. mid. of κατα-σπαράττω modifying παρθένον, "having torn"
ἐσθῆτα, κόμην: acc. of respect
καταθέμενοι: ao. part. of κατα-τίθημι, "having deposited her"
θαρρεῖν: pr. inf. after ἐκέλευον, "they ordered her to take heart"
ἐν φρουρᾷ: "under watch"
ἐμφαγεῖν … πιεῖν: ao. inf. of ἐν-ἐσθίω and πίνω after ἤθελεν, "she wished neither to eat nor to drink"
τὴν αὑτῆς: "her own"

57

ἐσπάραττεν· ὥστε καὶ αὐτὸς πλησίον ἑστὼς παρὰ τῇ φάτνῃ
συνέκλαιον ἐκείνῃ τῇ καλῇ παρθένῳ.

They set out to rob a stranger who has been sighted.

ἐν δὲ τούτῳ οἱ λῃσταὶ ἔξω ἐν τῷ προδόμῳ ἐδείπνουν.
πρὸς ἡμέραν δὲ τῶν σκοπῶν τις τῶν τὰς ὁδοὺς φρουρεῖν
εἰληχότων ἔρχεται ἀγγέλλων ὅτι ξένος ταύτῃ παριέναι μέλλοι
καὶ πολὺν πλοῦτον κομίζοι. οἱ δὲ οὕτως ὡς εἶχον ἀναστάντες
καὶ ὁπλισάμενοι κἀμὲ καὶ τὸν ἵππον ἐπισάξαντες ἤλαυνον.

ἀγγέλλω: to bear a message, report	ξένος, ὁ: a foreigner, stranger
ἀνίστημι: to make to stand up, raise up	ὁδός, ἡ: a way, path, road
δειπνέω: to dine, eat dinner	ὁπλίζω: to make ready
ἐλαύνω: to drive, set moving	παρέρχομαι: to go by, pass
ἔξω: out	παρθένος, ἡ: a maiden, girl
ἐπισάττω: to pile a load upon, burden	πίμπλημι: to fill
ἡμέρα, ἡ: a day	πλοῦτος, ὁ: riches, wealth
ἵππος, ὁ: a horse	πρόδομος, ὁ: vestibule, entryway
ἵστημι: to make to stand	σκοπός, ὁ: one that watches, a lookout
κομίζω: to take care of, carry	σπαράττω: to tear, rend
λαγχάνω: to obtain by lot	συγκλαίω: to weep with
λῃστής, -οῦ, ὁ: a robber	φάτνη, ἡ: a manger
μέλλω: to be about to, be going to	φρουρέω: to keep watch, guard

ὥστε ... συνέκλαιον: impf. indic. in result clause indicating actual result, "so that I
myself started crying"
ἑστώς: perf. part. of ἵστημι, "standing nearby"
ἐν δὲ τούτῳ (sc. χρόνῳ): "meanwhile"
εἰληχότων: perf. part. gen. pl. of λαγχάνω agreeing with σκοπῶν, "of the
lookouts chosen to" + inf.
ὅτι ... μέλλοι ... κομίζοι: pr. opt. in ind. st. in sec. seq. (even though the verb is the
(vivid) pr. tense), "that a stranger was about to ... and was bringing"
ταύτῃ: "in this place"
παριέναι: pr. inf. with μέλλοι, "to pass by"
ὡς εἶχον: "just as they were"
ἀναστάντες: ao. part. of ἀνα-ίστημι, "standing up"
ἐπισάξαντες: ao. part. of ἐπι-σάττω, "having piled on"

ἐγὼ δὲ ὁ δυστυχὴς ἐπιστάμενος ἐπὶ μάχην καὶ πόλεμον
ἐξελαύνεσθαι ὀκνηρῶς προήειν, ἔνθεν ἐπαιόμην τῷ ξύλῳ
ἐπειγομένων αὐτῶν. ἐπεὶ δὲ ἤκομεν ἐς τὴν ὁδὸν ἔνθα ὁ ξένος
παρελάσειν ἔμελλεν, συμπεσόντες οἱ λησταὶ τοῖς ὀχήμασιν
αὐτόν τε καὶ τοὺς ἐκείνου θεράποντας ἀπέκτειναν, καὶ ὅσα ἦν
τιμιώτατα ἐξελόντες τῷ ἵππῳ κἀμοὶ ἐπέθηκαν, τὰ δὲ ἕτερα
τῶν σκευῶν αὐτοῦ ἐν τῇ ὕλῃ ἔκρυψαν.

ἀποκτείνω: to kill, slay
δυστυχής, -ές: unlucky, unfortunate
ἐξαιρέω: to take out, remove
ἐξελαύνω: to drive out
ἐπείγω: to urge on, hasten
ἐπίσταμαι: to know
ἐπιτίθημι: to place upon
ἥκω: to have come
θεράπων, -οντος, ὁ: an attendant, servant
ἵππος, ὁ: a horse, mare
κρύπτω: to hide, cover
λῃστής, -οῦ, ὁ: a robber, plunderer
μάχη, ἡ: battle, fight
μέλλω: to be going to, be about to

ξένος, ὁ: a foreigner, stranger
ξύλον, τό: a piece of wood, stick
ὁδός, ἡ: a way, path, road
ὀκνηρός, -ά, -όν: shrinking, hesitating, timid
ὄχημα, -ατος, τό: a carriage, cart
παίω: to strike, hit
παρελαύνω: to drive past
πόλεμος, ὁ: battle, war
προέρχομαι: to go forth
σκεύη, τά: possessions, belongings
συμπίπτω: to fall together, attack
τίμιος, -ον: valued, valuable
ὕλη, ἡ: a forest

ἐξελαύνεσθαι: pr. pas. inf. after ἐπιστάμενος, "understanding *that I was being driven*"
προήειν: impf. of προ-έρχομαι, "I was advancing timidly"
ἔνθεν: "for which reason"
ἐπειγομένων: pr. part. gen. pl. in gen. abs., "them being in a hurry"
παρελάσειν: fut. inf. of παρα-ελαύνω after ἔμελλεν, "he was about *to drive past*"
συμπεσόντες: ao. part of συν-πίπτω, "having fallen upon" + dat.
ἀπέκτειναν: ao. of ἀπο-κτείνω, "they killed"
ἐξελόντες: ao. part. of ἐξ-αιρέω, "having extracted"
ἐπέθηκαν: ao. of ἐπι-τίθημι, "they placed upon" + dat.
ἔκρυψαν: ao. of κρύπτω, "they hid"

On the way back Lucius injures his foot.

ἔπειτα ἤλαυνον ἡμᾶς οὕτως ὀπίσω, κἀγὼ ἐπειγόμενος
καὶ τῷ ξύλῳ τυπτόμενος κρούω τὴν ὁπλὴν περὶ πέτραν ὀξεῖαν
καί μοι ἀπὸ τῆς πληγῆς γίνεται τραῦμα ἀλγεινόν: καὶ
χωλεύων ἔνθεν τὸ λοιπὸν τῆς ὁδοῦ ἐβάδιζον. οἱ δὲ πρὸς
ἀλλήλους ἔλεγον, «Τί γὰρ ἡμῖν δοκεῖ τρέφειν τὸν ὄνον τοῦτον
πάντα καταπίπτοντα; ῥίψωμεν αὐτὸν ἀπὸ τοῦ κρημνοῦ οἰωνὸν
οὐκ ἀγαθόν.» «Ναί,» φησίν, «ῥίψωμεν αὐτὸν καθαρισμὸν τοῦ
στρατοῦ ἐσόμενον.» καὶ οἱ μὲν συνετάττοντο ἐπ᾽ ἐμέ: ἐγὼ δὲ
ἀκούων ταῦτα τῷ τραύματι λοιπὸν ὡς ἀλλοτρίῳ ἐπέβαινον: ὁ
γάρ τοῦ θανάτου με φόβος ἀναίσθητον τῆς ὀδύνης ἔθηκεν.

ἀγαθός, -ή, -όν: good
ἀκούω: to hear
ἀλγεινός, -ή, -όν: painful, grievous
ἀλλότριος, -α, -ον: of or belonging to
 another
ἀναίσθητος, -ον: unfeeling, without sense
 of (+ *gen.*)
βαδίζω: to go, walk
ἐλαύνω: to drive, set moving
ἐπείγω: to hasten
ἔπειτα: thereupon
ἐπιβαίνω: to go on
θάνατος, ὁ: death
καθαρισμός, ὁ: a cleansing, purification
καταπίπτω: to fall down
κρημνός, ὁ: an overhang, cliff
κρούω: to strike
λέγω: to say
λοιπός, -ή, -όν: remaining, the rest

ξύλον, τό: a piece of wood, stick
ὁδός, ἡ: a way, path, journey
ὀδύνη, ἡ: pain
οἰωνός, ὁ: an omen, token
ὀξύς, -εῖα, -ύ: sharp, keen
ὀπίσω: backwards, back
ὁπλή, ἡ: a hoof
πέτρα, ἡ: a rock
πληγή, ἡ: a blow, stroke
ῥίπτω: to throw, cast, hurl
στρατός, ὁ: an army, troop
συντάττω: to draw up, form a battle line
τίθημι: to set, put, place
τραῦμα, -ατος, τό: a wound, injury
τρέφω: to raise, care for
τύπτω: to beat, hit
φόβος, ὁ: fear
χωλεύω: to be lame, limp

τὸ λοιπὸν: acc. of duration, "for the rest of the journey"
δοκεῖ: "why is it a good idea to" + inf.
ῥίψωμεν: ao. subj. jussive of **ῥίπτω**, "let's throw"
ἐσόμενον: fut. part. of **εἰμι** showing purpose, "in order to be"
λοιπὸν: "for the rest (of the journey)"
ὡς ἀλλοτρίῳ: agreeing with **τραύματι**, "as though the wound of another"
ἔθηκεν: ao. of **τίθημι**, "made me insensible of" + gen.

The thieves consider killing the lame Lucius.

[23.] ἐπεὶ δὲ ἤλθομεν εἴσω ἔνθα κατελύομεν, τὰ μὲν σκεύη τῶν ἡμετέρων ὤμων ἀφελόντες εὖ κατέθηκαν, αὐτοὶ δὲ ἀναπεσόντες ἐδείπνουν. καὶ ἐπειδὴ νὺξ ἦν, ἀπῄεσαν ὡς τὰ λοιπὰ τῶν σκευῶν ἀνασῶσαι. «Τὸν δὲ ἄθλιον τοῦτον ὄνον,» ἔφη τις αὐτῶν, «τί ἐπάγομεν ἄχρηστον ἐκ τῆς ὁπλῆς; τῶν δὲ σκευῶν ἃ μὲν ἡμεῖς οἴσομεν, ἃ δὲ καὶ ὁ ἵππος.» καὶ ἀπῄεσαν τὸν ἵππον ἄγοντες. νὺξ δὲ ἦν λαμπροτάτη ἐκ τῆς σελήνης. κἀγὼ τότε πρὸς ἐμαυτὸν εἶπον, «Ἄθλιε, τί μένεις ἔτι ἐνταῦθα;

ἄγω: to lead
ἄθλιος, -α, -ον: struggling, unhappy, wretched
ἀναπίπτω: to fall back
ἀνασῴζω: to recover, rescue
ἀπέρχομαι: to go away, depart
ἀφαιρέω: to take from, take away from
ἄχρηστος, -ον: useless, unserviceable
δειπνέω: to take a meal, dine
ἐπάγω: to lead on, bring
ἡμέτερος, -α, -ον: our
ἵππος, ὁ: a horse, mare

καταλύω: to put down, lodge
κατατίθημι: to place down, store
λαμπρός, -ά, -όν: bright, radiant
λοιπός, -ή, -όν: remaining, the rest
μένω: to stay, remain
νύξ, νυκτός, ἡ: night
ὄνος, ὁ: an ass
ὁπλή, ἡ: a hoof
σελήνη, ἡ: the moon
σκεύη, τά: possessions, belongings
φέρω: to bear, carry
ὦμος, ὁ: a shoulder

ἤλθομεν: ao., "we came"
ἀφελόντες: ao. part. of ἀπο-αιρέω, "having discarded from" + gen.
κατέθηκαν: ao. of κατα-τίθημι, "they deposited carefully"
ἀναπεσόντες: ao. part. of ἀνα-πίπτω, "having reclined"
ἀπῄεσαν: impf. of ἀπο-ἔρχομαι, "they departed"
ὡς ἀνασῶσαι: ao. inf. of ἀνα-σῴζω, "in order (I suppose) to recover"
ἐκ τῆς ὁπλῆς: "because of his hoof"
τῶν δὲ σκευῶν ἃ μὲν: "of the gear, some..."
οἴσομεν: fut. of φέρω, "we will carry"
ἃ δὲ: "(of the gear) the rest..."
ἀπῄεσαν: impf. of ἀπο-ἔρχομαι, "they departed"

γῦπές σε καὶ γυπῶν τέκνα δειπνήσουσιν. οὐκ ἀκούεις οἷα περὶ
σοῦ ἐβουλεύσαντο; θέλεις τῷ κρημνῷ περιπεσεῖν; νὺξ μὲν αὕτη
καὶ σελήνη πολλή: οἱ δὲ οἴχονται ἀπιόντες: φυγῇ σῷζε σαυτὸν
ἀπὸ δεσποτῶν ἀνδροφόνων.»

Lucius realizes he is not securely tied and decides to escape.

    ταῦτα πρὸς ἐμαυτὸν ἐννοούμενος ὁρῶ ὅτι οὐδὲ
προσεδεδέμην οὐδενί, ἀλλά με ὁ σύρων ἐν ταῖς ὁδοῖς ἱμὰς
παρεκρέματο. τοῦτό με καὶ παρώξυνεν ὡς μάλιστα ἐς τὴν
φυγήν, καὶ δρόμῳ ἐξιὼν ἀπῄειν. ἡ δὲ γραῦς, ἐπεὶ εἶδεν

ἀκούω: to hear
ἀνδροφόνος, -ον: murderous
ἀπέρχομαι: to go away, depart
βουλεύω: to take counsel, plan
γραῦς, γραός, ἡ: an old woman
γύψ, ἡ: a vulture
δειπνέω: to take a meal, eat for dinner
δεσπότης, -ου, ὁ: a master, lord
δρόμος, ὁ: a course, running, race
ἐθέλω: to will, wish
ἐννοέω: to think, consider, reflect
ἐξέρχομαι: to go out, leave
ἱμάς, ὁ: a leather strap

κρημνός, ὁ: an overhang, cliff
νύξ, νυκτός, ἡ: night
ὁδός, ἡ: a way, path, road
οἴχομαι: to be gone, leave
παρακρεμάννυμι: to hang beside
παροξύνω: to urge, spur on
περιπίπτω: to fall in with, encounter
προσδέω: need besides
σελήνη, ἡ: the moon
σύρω: to draw, drag
σῴζω: to save
τέκνον, τό: a child, offspring
φυγή, ἡ: flight

δειπνήσουσιν: fut., "will devour you"
οἷα ... ἐβουλεύσαντο: "do you hear *what sort of things they plotted* for you"
περιπεσεῖν: ao. inf. of περι-πίπτω, "do you wish *to fall over*" + dat.
ἀπιόντες: pr. part. of ἀπο-ἔρχομαι, "departing"
ὅτι προσεδεδέμην: perf. pas. of προσ-δέω, "I see *that I have been bound*"
οὐδενί: dat. of means, "by nothing"
παρώξυνεν: impf. of παρα-οξύνω, "this urged me on"
ὡς μάλιστα: "as much as possible"
ἐξιὼν: pr. part. of ἐξ-ἔρχομαι, "exiting at a run"
ἀπῄειν: impf. of ἀπο-ἔρχομαι, "I departed"
ἀποδιδράσκειν: epexegetic inf. after ἔτοιμον, "ready *to run*"
ἄξιον ... εἶναι: ind. st. after εἰπὼν, "saying that (it) was worthy of" + gen.
τὸ ὑπὸ γραίας ἁλῶναι: ao. inf. of ἁλίσκομαι. The art. inf. phrase is the acc. subj.
    of εἶναι, "the being captured by an old woman"
ἔσυρον: impf., "I dragged her along"
ἡ δὲ: "but she" (the old woman)

ἀποδιδράσκειν ἕτοιμον, λαμβάνεταί με ἐκ τῆς οὐρᾶς καὶ εἴχετο. ἐγὼ δὲ ἄξιον κρημνοῦ καὶ θανάτων ἄλλων εἰπὼν εἶναι τὸ ὑπὸ γραίας ἁλῶναι, ἔσυρον αὐτήν, ἡ δὲ μάλ' ἀνέκραγεν ἔνδοθεν τὴν παρθένον τὴν αἰχμάλωτον:

The captive girl leaps on his back to escape with him.

ἡ δὲ προελθοῦσα καὶ ἰδοῦσα γραῦν δίκην Δίρκης ἐξ ὄνου ἡμμένην τολμᾷ τόλμημα γενναῖον καὶ ἄξιον ἀπονενοημένου νεανίσκου: ἀναπηδᾷ γὰρ εἰς ἐμέ, καὶ ἐπικαθίσασά μοι ἤλαυνεν: κἀγὼ τῷ τε ἔρωτι τῆς φυγῆς καὶ τῇ τῆς κόρης σπουδῇ ἔφυγον

αἰχμάλωτος, -ον: captive, taken prisoner
ἁλίσκομαι: to be taken, be captured
ἀνακράζω: to cry out
ἀναπηδάω: to leap up, jump on
ἄξιος, -ία, -ον: worthy, deserving (+ gen.)
ἀποδιδράσκω: to run away, escape
ἀπονοέομαι: to have lost all sense
ἅπτω: to touch, fasten upon
γενναῖος, -α, -ον: noble
γραῦς, γραός, ἡ: an old woman
δική, ἡ: justice, law, custom
ἐλαύνω: to drive, set moving
ἐπικαθίζω: to set upon
ἔρως, -ωτος, ὁ: love, desire
ἕτοιμος, -ον: at hand, ready, prepared

θάνατος, ὁ: death
κόρη, ἡ: a maiden, girl
κρημνός, ὁ: an overhang, cliff
νεάνισκος, ὁ: a youth, young man
ὄνος, ὁ: an ass
οὐρά, ἡ: the tail
παρθένος, ἡ: a maiden, girl
προέρχομαι: to go forward
σπουδή, ἡ: haste, speed, eagerness
σύρω: to drag
τολμάω: to take heart, dare
τόλμημα, -ατος, τό: an adventure, deed of daring
φεύγω: to flee, run away
φυγή, ἡ: flight

ἀνέκραγεν: ao. of ἀνα-κράζω, "she shouted to" + acc.
ἡ δὲ: "but she (the maiden)"
προελθοῦσα: ao. part. of προ-έρχομαι, "she coming forth"
ἰδοῦσα: ao. part., "and seeing"
δίκην Δίρκης: "in the manner of Dirce"
Δίρκην: The Theban Dirce was dragged to death by a bull as punishment.
ἡμμένην: perf. mid. part. of ἅπτω, "having fastened herself"
τόλμημα: internal accusative with τολμᾷ, "she dares *a bold act*"
ἀπονενοημένου: perf. part. of ἀπο-νοέω, "worthy *of a senseless youth*"
ἐπικαθίσασα: ao. part. of ἐπι-καθίζω, "having sat on me"
τῷ ἔρωτι: dat. of cause, "for love of" + gen.
σπουδῇ: dat. of manner, "hastily"
ἔφυγον: ao. of φεύγω, "I fled"

ἵππου δρόμῳ· ἡ δὲ γραῦς ὀπίσω ἀπελέλειπτο. ἡ δὲ παρθένος τοῖς μὲν θεοῖς ηὔχετο σῶσαι αὐτὴν τῇ φυγῇ· πρὸς δὲ ἐμέ, «Ἤν με,» ἔφη, «κομίσῃς πρὸς τὸν πατέρα, ὦ καλὲ σύ, ἐλεύθερον μέν σε παντὸς ἔργου ἀφήσω, κριθῶν δὲ μέδιμνος ἔσται σοι ἐφ᾽ ἑκάστης ἡμέρας τὸ ἄριστον.»

ἐγὼ δὲ καὶ τοὺς φονεῖς τοὺς ἐμαυτοῦ φευξόμενος καὶ πολλὴν ἐπικουρίαν καὶ θεραπείαν ἐκ τῆς ἀνασωθείσης ἐμοὶ κόρης ἐλπίζων ἔθεον τοῦ τραύματος ἀμελήσας.

ἀμελέω: to have no care for
ἀνασῴζω: to recover, rescue
ἀπολείπω: to leave behind
ἄριστον, τό: breakfast
ἀφίημι: to send forth, discharge
γραῦς, γραός, ἡ: an old woman
δρόμος, ὁ: a course, running
ἕκαστος, -η, -ον: every, each
ἐλεύθερος, -α, -ον: free
ἐλπίζω: to hope
ἐπικουρία, ἡ: aid, help
ἔργον, τό: a deed, work
εὔχομαι: to pray
ἡμέρα, ἡ: a day
θεός, ὁ: a god

θεραπεία, ἡ: a treatment, cure
θέω: to run
ἵππος, ὁ: a horse, mare
κομίζω: to take care of, carry
κόρη, ἡ: a maiden, girl
κριθή, ἡ: barley
μέδιμνος, ὁ: a corn-measure, bushel
ὀπίσω: backwards, behind
παρθένος, ἡ: a maiden, girl
πατήρ, ὁ: a father
σῴζω: to save
τραῦμα, -ατος, τό: a wound, injury
φεύγω: to flee, run away
φονεύς, -έως, ὁ: a murderer
φυγή, ἡ: flight

ἵππου δρόμῳ: dat. of manner, "*with the pace* of a horse"
ἀπελέλειπτο: plpf. pas. of ἀπο-λείπω, "she was left behind"
ηὔχετο: impf., "began praying to" + dat.
σῶσαι: ao. inf. of σῴζω after ηὔχετο, "to save"
ἤν ... κομίσῃς: ao. subj. of κομίζω in fut. more vivid condition, "if you bring me"
ἀφήσω: fut. of ἀπο-ἵημι in fut. more vivid condition, "I will release you from" + gen.
ἔσται: fut. of εἰμι in fut. more vivid condition, "and there will be"
τὸ ἄριστον: acc. of resp., "for breakfast"
φευξόμενος: fut. part. indicating purpose, "in order to flee"
ἀνασωθείσης: ao. pas. part. of ἀνα-σῴζω modifying κόρης, "from the girl once she was saved"
ἔθεον: impf., "I rushed on"
ἀμελήσας: ao. part. of ἀμελέω "not heeding" + gen.

They are recaptured by the thieves, who return them to the hideout. (cf. Ap. Met. VI.30, p. 156)

[24.] ἐπεὶ δὲ ἥκομεν ἔνθα ἐσχίζετο τριπλῆ ὁδός, οἱ πολέμιοι ἡμᾶς καταλαμβάνουσιν ἀναστρέφοντες καὶ πόρρωθεν εὐθὺς πρὸς τὴν σελήνην ἔγνωσαν τοὺς δυστυχεῖς αἰχμαλώτους καὶ προσδραμόντες λαμβάνονταί μου καὶ λέγουσιν, «Ὦ καλὴ κἀγαθὴ σὺ παρθένος, ποῖ βαδίζεις ἀωρίᾳ, ταλαίπωρε; οὐδὲ τὰ δαιμόνια δέδοικας; ἀλλὰ δεῦρο ἴθι πρὸς ἡμᾶς, ἡμεῖς σε τοῖς οἰκείοις ἀποδώσομεν,» σαρδώνιον γελῶντες ἔλεγον, κἀμὲ ἀποστρέψαντες εἷλκον ὀπίσω. κἀγὼ

ἀγαθός, -ή, -όν: good
αἰχμάλωτος, -ον: captive, taken prisoner
ἀναστρέφω: to turn back, return
ἀποδίδωμι: to give back, restore, return
ἀποστρέφω: to turn back
ἀωρία, ἡ: the wrong time, dead of night
βαδίζω: to go, walk
γελάω: to laugh
γιγνώσκω: to know, perceive
δαιμόνιον, τό: a spirit
δείδω: to fear
δεῦρο: hither
δυστυχής, -ές: unlucky, unfortunate
ἕλκω: to draw, drag
ἥκω: to have come, be present

κάμνω: to work
καταλαμβάνω: to seize upon, lay hold of
λέγω: to say
ὁδός, ἡ: a way, path, road
οἰκεῖος, -α, -ον: domestic, related
ὀπίσω: backwards
παρθένος, ἡ: a maiden, girl
πολέμιος, -α, -ον: of war, hostile, enemy
πόρρωθεν: from afar
προστρέχω: to run forward
σαρδάνιος, -α, -ον: bitter, scornful
σελήνη, ἡ: the moon
σχίζω: to split, cleave
ταλαίπωρος, -ον: suffering, miserable
τριπλόος, -η, -ον: triple, threefold

πόρρωθεν: "from far off"
ἔγνωσαν: ao. of γιγνώσκω, "they recognized"
προσδραμόντες: ao. part. of προς-τρέχω, "having rushed up"
καλὴ κἀγαθὴ: "noble"
ἀωρίᾳ: dat. of time when, "at this bad time"
δέδοικας: perf. of δείδω, " have you no fear"
ἀποδώσομεν: fut. of ἀπο-δίδωμι, "we will ransom you"
ἀποστρέψαντες: ao. part. of ἀπο-στρέφω, "having turned around"
εἷλκον: impf. of ἕλκω, "they dragged"

περὶ τοῦ ποδὸς καὶ τοῦ τραύματος ἀναμνησθεὶς ἐχώλευον· οἱ
δέ, «Νῦν,» ἔφασαν, «χωλὸς ὅτε ἀποδιδράσκων ἑάλωκας; ἀλλ᾽
ὅτε φεύγειν ἐδόκει σοι, ὑγιαίνων ἵππου ὠκύτερος καὶ πετεινὸς
ἦσθα.» τοῖς δὲ λόγοις τούτοις τὸ ξύλον εἵπετο, καὶ ἤδη ἕλκος
τῷ μηρῷ εἶχον νουθετούμενος. ἐπεὶ δὲ εἴσω πάλιν
ἀνεστρέψαμεν, τὴν μὲν γραῦν εὕρομεν ἐκ τῆς πέτρας
κρεμαμένην ἐν καλῳδίῳ· δείσασα γάρ, οἷον εἰκός, τοὺς
δεσπότας ἐπὶ τῇ τῆς παρθένου φυγῇ κρημνᾷ ἑαυτὴν σφίγξασα

άλίσκομαι: to be taken, be captured
άναμιμνήσκω: to remind
άναστρέφω: to return
άποδιδράσκω: to run away, escape
γραῦς, γραός, ἡ: an old woman
δείδω: to fear
δεσπότης, -ου, ὁ: a master, lord
εἴσω: to within, into
ἕλκος, -εος, τό: a wound
ἕπω: to come after, (mid.) follow
εὑρίσκω: to find
ἵππος, ὁ: a horse
καλῴδιον, τό: a rope, cord
κρεμάννυμι: to hang, hang up
μηρός, ὁ: a thigh

νουθετέω: to admonish, warn
ξύλον, τό: a piece of wood, stick
πάλιν: back, backwards
παρθένος, ἡ: a maiden, girl
πετεινός, -ή, -όν: able to fly
πέτρα, ἡ: a rock
πούς, ποδός, ὁ: a foot
σφίγγω: to bind tight, bind fast
τραῦμα, -ατος, τό: a wound, injury
ὑγιαίνω: to be healthy
φεύγω: to flee, run away
φυγή, ἡ: flight
χωλεύω: to be lame, limp
χωλός, -ή, -όν: lame
ὠκύς, -εῖα, -ύ: quick, swift, fleet

ἀναμνησθεὶς: ao. pas. part. of ἀνα-μιμνήσκω, "having remembered" + gen.
ἐχώλευον: impf., "I started limping"
ἑάλωκας: perf. of ἁλίσκομαι, "now when you have been captured"
ἐδόκει σοι: "it seemed a good idea to you to" + inf.
ἵππου: gen. of comparison, "swifter than a horse"
ἦσθα: "you were winged"
εἵπετο: impf. of ἕπω, "the stick followed" + dat.
εἶχον: impf. of ἔχω, "I was getting a wound"
νουθετούμενος: pr. part., "from being admonished"
ἀνεστρέψαμεν: ao. of ἀνα-στρέφω, "we returned"
εὕρομεν: ao. of εὑρίσκω, "we found"
δείσασα: ao. part. of δείδω, "fearing"
οἷον εἰκός: "so it would seem"
κρημνᾷ : vivid pr. of κρήμνημι, "she hangs herself"
σφίγξασα: ao. part. of σφίγγω, "having bound tight"

ἐκ τοῦ τραχήλου. οἱ δὲ τὴν γραῦν θαυμάσαντες τῆς
εὐγνωμοσύνης, τὴν μὲν ἀπολύσαντες ἐς τὸν κρημνὸν κάτω
ἀφῆκαν ὡς ἦν ἐν τῷ δεσμῷ, τὴν δὲ παρθένον ἔνδον κατέδησαν,
εἶτα ἐδείπνουν, καὶ πότος ἦν μακρός.

The robbers resolve to kill the captive girl.

[25.] κἂν τούτῳ ἤδη περὶ τῆς κόρης διελέγοντο πρὸς
ἀλλήλους: «Τί ποιοῦμεν,» ἔφη τις αὐτῶν, «τὴν δραπέτιν;» «Τί
δὲ ἄλλο,» εἶπεν ἕτερος, «ἢ τῇ γραῒ ταύτῃ κάτω ἐπιρρίψωμεν
αὐτήν, ἀφελομένην μὲν ἡμᾶς χρήματα πολλὰ ὅσον ἐπ᾽ αὐτῇ,
καὶ προδοῦσαν ἡμῖν ὅλον τὸ ἐργαστήριον; εὖ ἴστε γάρ, ὦ

ἀπολύω: to loose from
ἀφαιρέω: to take from, take away from
ἀφίημι: to send forth
γραῦς, γραός, ἡ: an old woman
δειπνέω: to take a meal, have dinner
δεσμός, ὁ: a bond, noose
διαλέγω: to converse
δραπέτις, -ιδος, ἡ: a runaway
ἐπιρριπτέω: to throw, hurl
ἐργαστήριον, τό: a workshop, gang
εὐγνωμοσύνη, ἡ: considerateness, prudence
θαυμάζω: to wonder, marvel, admire
καταδέω: to bind down, tie up

κάτω: down, downwards
κόρη, ἡ: a maiden, girl
κρημνός, ὁ: an overhang, cliff
μακρός, -ά, -όν: long
οἶδα: to know
ὅλος, -η, -ον: whole, entire, complete
παρθένος, ἡ: a maiden, girl
ποιέω: to make, do
πότος, ὁ: a drink, drinking
προδίδωμι: to give over, betray
τράχηλος, ὁ: a neck, throat
χρῆμα, -ατος, τό: a thing that one uses, money

θαυμάσαντες: ao. part. of θαυμάζω, "being amazed"
τῆς εὐγνωμοσύνης: gen. of cause, "for her good sense"
ἀφῆκαν: ao. of ἀπο-ἵημι, "they sent her off"
ὡς ἦν: "as she was"
κατέδησαν: ao. of κατα-δέω, "they bound up"
κἂν (= καὶ ἐν) τούτῳ (sc. χρόνῳ): "meanwhile"
τὴν δραπέτιν: acc. of resp., "about this runaway"
Τί ἄλλο ... ἤ: "what else than...?"
ἐπιρρίψωμεν: ao. subj. of ἀπο-ρίπτω in delib. quest., "should we throw her down on" + dat.
ἀφελομένην: ao. part. of ἀπο-αἱρέω, "having taken from us"
ὅσον ἐπ᾽ αὐτῇ: "as much as is on her"
προδοῦσαν: ao. part. of προ-δίδωμι, "betraying"
ἡμῖν ὅλον: "our whole gang"

φίλοι, ὅτι αὕτη εἰ τῶν οἴκοι ἐδράξατο, οὐδὲ εἷς ἂν ἡμῶν ζῶν
ὑπελείπετο: πάντες γάρ ἂν ἑάλωμεν, τῶν ἐχθρῶν ἐκ
παρασκευῆς ἡμῖν ἐπιπεσόντων. ὥστε ἀμυνώμεθα μὲν τὴν
πολεμίαν: ἀλλὰ μὴ οὕτω ῥᾳδίως ἀποθνησκέτω πεσοῦσα ἐπὶ
τοῦ λίθου, θάνατον δὲ αὐτῇ τὸν ἀλγεινότατον καὶ μακρότατον
ἐξεύρωμεν καὶ ὅστις αὐτὴν χρόνῳ καὶ βασάνῳ φυλάξας
ὕστερον ἀπολεῖ.»

ἀλγεινός, -ή, -όν: painful, grievous
ἁλίσκομαι: to be taken, conquered
ἀμύνω: to ward off, defend oneself
ἀποθνήσκω: to die
ἀπόλλυμι: to destroy, kill
βάσανος, ἡ: agony, torture
δράττομαι: to grasp, reach
εἷς, μία, ἕν: one
ἐξευρίσκω: to find out, discover
ἐπιπίπτω: to fall upon, attack
ἐχθρός, -ά, -όν: hated, enemy
ζάω: to live
θάνατος, ὁ: death

λίθος, -ου, ὁ: a stone, rock
μακρός, -ά, -όν: long
οἴκοι: at home, in the house
παρασκευή, ἡ: a preparation
πίπτω: to fall
πολέμιος, -α, -ον: hostile, enemy
ῥᾴδιος, -α, -ον: easy, ready
ὑπολείπω: to leave remaining
ὕστερος, -α, -ον: later, afterward
φίλος, -η, -ον: beloved, dear
φυλάττω: to keep watch, guard
χρόνος, ὁ: time

εἰ τῶν οἴκοι ἐδράξατο ... οὐδὲ εἷς ἂν ὑπελείπετο: contrafactual condition, "if
  she had reached those at home ... not one of us would be spared"
ἐδράξατο: ao. of δράττομαι
ὑπελείπετο: impf. pas. of ὑπο-λείπω
ἂν ἑάλωμεν: ao. of ἁλίσκομαι an additional contrafactual apodosis, "we would
  have been captured"
τῶν ἐχθρῶν ... ἐπιπεσόντων: ao. part. of ἐπι-πίπτω in gen. abs., "our enemies
  having fallen upon us"
ὥστε ἀμυνώμεθα: result clause with jussive subj., "so that we should avenge
  ourselves"
μὴ ἀποθνησκέτω: pr. imper. 3 s., "let her not die"
πεσοῦσα: ao. part. of πίπτω, "falling"
ἐξεύρωμεν: ao. subj. jussive of ἐξ-ευρίσκω, "let us find"
ὅστις ... ἀπολεῖ: "(a death) which will destroy"
ἀπολεῖ: fut. of ἀπόλλυμι
φυλάξας: ao. part. of φυλάττω, "having kept her"

They decide on a devious plan to kill both the girl and the ass. (cf. Ap. Met. VI.31-2, p. 158)

εἶτα ἐζήτουν θάνατον, καί τις εἶπεν, «Οἶδα ὅτι ἐπαινέσεσθε τὸ ἀρχιτεκτόνημα. τὸν ὄνον δεῖ ἀπολέσαι ὀκνηρὸν ὄντα, νῦν δὲ καὶ χωλὸν εἶναι ψευδόμενον, καὶ μὴν καὶ τῆς φυγῆς τῆς παρθένου γενόμενον ὑπηρέτην καὶ διάκονον· τοῦτον οὖν ἔωθεν ἀποσφάξαντες ἀνατέμωμεν ἐκ τῆς γαστρὸς καὶ τὰ μὲν ἔγκατα πάντα ἔξω βάλωμεν, τὴν δὲ ἀγαθὴν ταύτην παρθένον τῷ ὄνῳ ἐγκατοικίσωμεν, τὴν μὲν κεφαλὴν ἔξω τοῦ

ἀγαθός, -ή, -όν: good
ἀνατέμνω: to cut open
ἀπόλλυμι: to destroy, kill, slay
ἀποσφάζω: to slaughter
ἀρχιτεκτόνημα, -ατος, τό: stroke of art
βάλλω: to throw
γαστήρ, γαστρός, ἡ: the belly
διάκονος, ὁ: a servant
ἔγκατα, τά: the innards, entrails
ἐγκατοικίζω: to place in
ἔξω: out
ἐπαινέω: to approve, applaud, commend
ἔωθεν: from morning

ζητέω: to seek, search for
θάνατος, ὁ: death
κεφαλή, ἡ: the head
οἶδα: to know
ὀκνηρός, -ά, -όν: shrinking, hesitating, timid
ὄνος, ὁ: an ass
παρθένος, ἡ: a maiden, girl
ὑπηρέτης, -ου, ὁ: an underling, attendant
φυγή, ἡ: flight
χωλός, -ή, -όν: lame
ψεύδομαι: to lie, pretend

ὅτι ἐπαινέσεσθε: fut. after οἶδα, "that you will praise"
ἀπολέσαι: ao. inf. of ἀπόλλυμι after δεῖ, "it is necessary to kill"
ὀκνηρὸν ὄντα: causal, "since he is troublesome"
νῦν δὲ καί: "now even"
χωλὸν εἶναι: implied ind. st. after ψευδόμενον, "lying *that he is lame*"
καὶ μὴν καί: indicating a climax, "furthermore"
γενόμενον: ao. part. of γίγνομαι, "having become the accomplice"
ἀποσφάξαντες: ao. part. of ἀπο-σφάττω, "having slaughtered this one"
ἀνατέμωμεν: ao. subj. of ἀνα-τέμνω, jussive, "let us cut up"
βάλωμεν: ao. subj. of βάλλω, jussive, "let us throw out"
ἀγαθήν: ironic, "this goodly"
ἐγκατοικίσωμεν: ao. subj. of ἐν-κατα-οἰκίζω, jussive, "let us house inside"

ὄνου πρόχειρον, ὡς ἂν μὴ εὐθὺς ἀποπνιγείη, τὸ δὲ ἄλλο σῶμα
πᾶν ἔνδον κρυπτόμενον, ὡς ἂν αὐτὴν κατακειμένην εὖ μάλα
συρράψαντες ῥίψωμεν ἔξω ἄμφω ταῦτα τοῖς γυψί, καινῶς
τοῦτο ἐσκευασμένον ἄριστον. σκοπεῖτε δέ, ὦ φίλοι, τῆς

ἄμφω: both
ἀποπνίγω: to choke, suffocate
ἄριστον, τό: a meal, breakfast
γύψ, ἡ: a vulture
ἔξω: out
καινός, -ή, -όν: new, fresh
κατάκειμαι: to lie down, lie outstretched
κρύπτω: to hide, cover

πρόχειρος, -ον: at hand, ready, accessible
ῥίπτω: to throw, cast, hurl
σκευάζω: to prepare, make ready
σκοπέω: to look after, consider
συρράπτω: to sew up, stitch together
σῶμα, -ατος, τό: a body
φίλος, -η, -ον: beloved, dear

ὡς ἂν μὴ εὐθὺς ἀποπνιγείη: neg. purpose clause, "so that she might not be
immediately choked." The ἂν is potential.
ἀποπνιγείη: ao. opt. pas. of ἀπο-πνίγω
ὡς ἂν ... ῥίψωμεν: ao. subj. of ῥίπτω in purpose clause, "so that we can hurl her"
συρράψαντες: ao. part. of συν-ράπτω, "having stitched her up"
ἐσκευασμένον: perf. part. of σκεύω, "this meal having been prepared"

Potential ἂν

The particle **ἂν** is used with the optative in main clauses to state a
future possibility as an opinion of the speaker. Its range of meaning includes
polite requests, to future less vivid conditions, to statements of what will prove to
be true. In dependent clauses that express purpose, fear, indefinite time, etc. it is
usual for the subjunctive to be used with **ἂν** in primary sequence, the optative
without **ἂν** in secondary sequence. However, potential **ἂν** can be used with the
optative in such clauses, where it will maintain its potential force. Here are some
examples from *The Ass*:

τὴν δὲ ἀγαθὴν ταύτην παρθένον τῷ ὄνῳ ἐγκατοικίσωμεν, τὴν μὲν
κεφαλὴν ἔξω τοῦ ὄνου πρόχειρον, <u>ὡς ἂν μὴ εὐθὺς ἀποπνιγείη</u>: "Let
us house this nice girl in the ass, with her head sticking out of the ass, *so
that she might not immediately be suffocated*"

Νέμεσις ἤγαγεν κἀμοὶ τὸν δεσπότην, <u>οἷον οὐκ ἂν εὐξαίμην</u>: "Nemesis
provided me with a master, *such as I might never have prayed for*"

ἱκέτευον αὐτὸν λαβόντα ἔχειν με ἐν φρουρᾷ <u>ἔστ' ἂν αὐτὸν πείσαιμι</u>: "I
begged him to take me and keep me in custody *until such time as I might
persuade him*"

<u>ἂν ποτε καὶ δέοι</u>, ὁ δὲ οὔτε κατῆλθεν οὔτε χεῖρά μοι ἐπέδωκεν: "*If ever it
might be necessary*, he never descended nor lent me a hand"

βασάνου τὸ δεινόν, πρῶτον μὲν τὸ νεκρῷ ὄνῳ συνοικεῖν, εἶτα
θέρους ὥρᾳ θερμοτάτῳ ἡλίῳ ἐν κτήνει καθεψεῖσθαι καὶ λιμῷ
ἀεὶ κτείνοντι ἀποθνήσκειν καὶ μηδὲ ἑαυτὴν ἀποπνῖξαι ἔχειν·
τὰ μὲν γὰρ ἄλλ' ὅσα πείσεται σηπομένου τοῦ ὄνου τῇ τε ὀδμῇ
καὶ τοῖς σκώληξι πεφυρμένη ἐῶ λέγειν. τέλος δὲ οἱ γῦπες διὰ
τοῦ ὄνου παρεισιόντες εἴσω καὶ ταύτην ὡς ἐκεῖνον ἴσως καὶ
ζῶσαν ἔτι διασπάσονται.»

ἀεί: always, for ever
ἀποθνήσκω: to die
ἀποπνίγω: to choke, suffocate
βάσανος, ἡ: agony, torture
γύψ, ἡ: a vulture
δεινός, -ή, -όν: fearful, terrible
διασπάω: to tear apart
εἴσω: to within, into
ζάω: to live
ἥλιος, ὁ: the sun
θερμός, -ή, -όν: hot, warm
θέρος, -εος, τό: summer
καθέψω: to boil, roast
κτείνω: to kill, slay

κτῆνος, -εος, τό: an animal, beast
λέγω: to speak, say
λιμός, -οῦ, ἡ: hunger
νεκρός, ὁ: a corpse
ὀσμή, ἡ: a smell
παρεισέρχομαι: to come through
πάσχω: to feel, suffer
σήπω: to rot
σκώληξ, -ηκος, ὁ: a worm
συνοικέω: to dwell with
τέλος, -εος, τό: fulfillment, end
φύρω: to mix
ὥρα, -ας, ἡ: period, season, time

τὸ νεκρῷ ὄνῳ συνοικεῖν: art. inf. in apposition to τὸ δεινόν, "first, living in an ass corpse"
(τὸ) καθεψεῖσθαι: art. inf. of κατα-ἔψω, "then, to be cooked"
λιμῷ ἀεὶ κτείνοντι: dat. of means, "by hunger which always kills"
(τὸ) ἀποθνήσκειν: art. inf., "dying"
(τὸ) μηδὲ ἔχειν: art. inf., "and not being able" + inf.
ἀποπνῖξαι: ao. inf. of ἀπο-πνίγω, "to choke"
ὅσα πείσεται: fut. of πάσχω, "which she will suffer," the obj. of ἔχειν
πεφυρμένη: perf. part. pas. of φύρω, "having been defiled by" + dat.
ἐῶ λέγειν: "I refrain to say"
παρεισιόντες: pr. part. of παρα-εἰς-ἔρχομαι, "penetrating"
ταύτην: i.e. the girl
ὡς ἐκεῖνον: "the same as that one" i.e. the ass.
ζῶσαν ἔτι: "her still living"
διασπάσονται: fut. of δια-σπάω, "will tear apart"

[26.] πάντες ἀνεβόησαν ὡς ἐπὶ ἀγαθῷ μεγάλῳ τῷ τερατώδει τούτῳ εὑρήματι. ἐγὼ δὲ ἀνέστενον ἐαυτὸν ὡς ἂν ἀποσφαγησόμενος καὶ μηδὲ νεκρὸς εὐτυχὴς κεισόμενος, ἀλλὰ παρθένον ἀθλίαν ἐπιδεξόμενος καὶ θήκη οὐδὲν ἀδικούσης κόρης ἐσόμενος.

Soldiers arrive and capture the band, freeing Lucius and the captive girl.

ὄρθρος δὲ ἦν ἔτι καὶ ἐξαίφνης ἐφίσταται πλῆθος στρατιωτῶν ἐπὶ τοὺς μιαροὺς τούτους ἀφιγμένον, καὶ εὐθέως πάντας ἐδέσμουν καὶ ἐπὶ τὸν τῆς χώρας ἡγεμόνα ἀπῆγον. ἔτυχε δὲ καὶ ὁ τὴν κόρην μεμνηστευμένος σὺν αὐτοῖς ἐλθών·

ἀγαθός, -ή, -όν: good
ἀδικέω: to do wrong
ἄθλιος, -α, -ον: struggling, unhappy, wretched
ἀναβοάω: to shout, utter a loud cry
ἀναστένω: to groan, moan
ἀπάγω: to lead away, carry off
ἀποσφάζω: to slaughter
ἀφικνέομαι: to arrive
δεσμεύω: to fetter, put in chains
ἐξαίφνης: suddenly
ἐπιδέχομαι: to admit
εὐθέως: immediately
εὕρημα, -ατος, τό: an invention, discovery
εὐτυχής, -ές: lucky, fortunate

ἐφίστημι: to set or place upon
ἡγεμών, -όνος, ἡ: a governor, ruler
θήκη, ἡ: a grave, tomb
κεῖμαι: to be laid
κόρη, ἡ: a maiden, girl
μιαρός, -ά, -όν: abominable, foul
μνηστεύω: to woo, court
νεκρός, ὁ: a dead body, corpse
ὄρθρος, ὁ: day-break, dawn
παρθένος, ἡ: a maiden, girl
πλῆθος, -εος, τό: a great number, crowd
στρατιώτης, -ου, ὁ: a soldier, recruit
τερατώδης, -ες: monstrous
τυγχάνω: to hit, happen upon
χώρα, ἡ: a place, space, land

ἀνεβόησαν: ao. of ἀνα-βοάω, "they shouted approval of" + dat.

ὡς ἐπὶ ἀγαθῷ μεγάλῳ (sc. ὄντι): implied ind. st. after ἀνεβόησαν, "as though it was good and great invention"

ὡς ἂν ἀποσφαγησόμενος: fut. part. pas. giving the reason for his groaning, "I was groaning *because I would be slaughtered*." The ἂν is potential.

(ὡς) μηδὲ κεισόμενος: "because I would *not even lie happily*"

(ὡς ἂν) ἐπιδεξόμενος: "because I would receive"

(ὡς ἂν) ἐσόμενος: "because I would be"

ἐφίσταται: pr. mid. of ἐπι-ἵστημι, "suddenly appeared"

ἀφιγμένον: perf. part. of ἀφικνέομαι modifying πλῆθος, "having arrived"

ἀπῆγον: impf. of ἀπο-ἄγω, "they led away to"

ἔτυχε: ao. of τυγχάνω, "happened to be" + part.

ὁ μεμνηστευμένος: perf. part. of μνηστεύω, "the one betrothed to" + acc.

ἐλθών: ao. part. of ἔρχομαι after ἔτυχεν, "happened to come"

αὐτὸς γὰρ ἦν ὁ καὶ τὸ καταγώγιον τῶν λῃστῶν μηνύσας. παραλαβὼν οὖν τὴν παρθένον καὶ καθίσας ἐπ' ἐμὲ οὕτως ἦγεν οἴκαδε. οἱ δὲ κωμῆται ὡς εἶδον ἡμᾶς ἔτι πόρρωθεν,

ἔγνωσαν εὐτυχοῦντας, εὐαγγέλιον αὐτοῖς ἐμοῦ προογκησαμένου, καὶ προσδραμόντες ἠσπάζοντο καὶ ἦγον ἔσω.

Lucius is treated kindly by the captive girl and her family. (cf. Ap. Met. VII.14, p. 161)

[27.] ἡ δὲ παρθένος πολὺν λόγον εἶχεν ἐμοῦ δίκαιον ποιοῦσα τοῦ συναιχμαλώτου συναποδράσαντος καὶ τὸν κοινὸν

ἄγω: to lead, bring
ἀσπάζομαι: to welcome, greet
γιγνώσκω: to know, to perceive
δίκαιος, -α, -ον: just, fair
ἔσω: to the interior, inside
εὐαγγέλιον, τό: good news
εὐτυχέω: to be well off
καθίζω: to make to sit down, seat
καταγώγιον, τό: a place of lodging
κοινός, -ή, -όν: common, shared
κωμήτης, -ου, ὁ: a villager, countryman
λῃστής, -οῦ, ὁ: a robber

λόγος, ὁ: a word
μηνύω: to disclose, reveal
οἴκαδε: to one's home, homewards
παραλαμβάνω: to receive, take up
παρθένος, ἡ: a maiden, girl
ποιέω: to make, do
πόρρωθεν: from afar
προογκάομαι: to bray before
προστρέχω: to run to
συναιχμάλωτος, ὁ: a fellow-prisoner
συναποδράω: to run away with, escape together

ὁ ... μηνύσας: ao. part. of μηνύω, "the one who disclosed"
παραλαβὼν: ao. part. of παρα-λαμβάνω, "having recovered"
καθίσας: ao. part. of καθίζω, "having sat her down"
ἔγνωσαν: ao. of γιγνώσκω, "they realized"
εὐτυχοῦντας: pr. part. after ἔγνωσαν, "that we were successful"
ἐμοῦ προογκησαμένου: ao. part. of προ-ογκέω in gen. abs., "me having brayed out in advance"
προσδραμόντες: ao. part. of προσ-τρέχω, "having run toward us"
δίκαιον ποιοῦσα: "making a just account"
συναποδράσαντος: ao. part. gen. s. of συν-ἀπο-δράω agreeing with ἐμοῦ causal, "since I had run off with"

αὐτῇ ἐκεῖνον θάνατον συγκινδυνεύσαντος. καί μοι παρὰ τῆς
κεκτημένης ἄριστον παρέκειτο μέδιμνος κριθῶν καὶ χόρτος
ὅσος καὶ καμήλῳ ἱκανός. ἐγὼ δὲ τότε μάλιστα κατηρώμην τὴν
Παλαίστραν ὡς ὄνον με καὶ οὐ κύνα τῇ τέχνῃ μεταθεῖσαν·
ἑώρων γὰρ τοὺς κύνας εἰς τοὐπτανεῖον παρεισιόντας καὶ
λαφύσσοντας πολλὰ καὶ ὅσα ἐν γάμοις πλουσίων νυμφίων.
ἡμέραις δὲ ὕστερον μετὰ τὸν γάμον οὐ πολλαῖς ἐπειδὴ χάριν
μοι ἡ δέσποινα ἔφη ἔχειν παρὰ τῷ πατρὶ καὶ ἀμείψασθαί με

ἄριστον, τό: a meal, breakfast
γάμος, ὁ: a wedding, marriage
δέσποινα, ἡ: a mistress, lady of the house
ἡμέρα, ἡ: a day
θάνατος, ὁ: death
ἱκανός, -ή, -όν: befitting (+ dat.)
κάμηλος, ὁ: a camel
καταράομαι: to curse
κριθή, ἡ: barley
κτάομαι: to get, gain, acquire
κύων, ὁ: a dog
λαφύσσω: to gulp down, devour
μέδιμνος, ὁ: a bushel
μετατίθημι: to change, alter

νυμφίος, ὁ: a newlywed
ὀπτάνιον, τό: a kitchen
Παλαίστρα, ἡ: Palaestra
παράκειμαι: to place before
παρέρχομαι: to go beside, go secretly
πατήρ, ὁ: a father
πλούσιος, -α, -ον: rich, wealthy, opulent
συγκινδυνεύω: to incur danger along
    with, share danger
τέχνη, ἡ: art, skill, craft
ὕστερος, -α, -ον: later, afterward
χάρις, -ιτος, ἡ: favor, grace
χόρτος, ὁ: feed, hay

συγκινδυνεύσαντος: ao. part. gen. s. also agreeing with ἐμοῦ causal, "since I had
    risked death with" + dat.
κεκτημένης: perf. part. gen. s. of κτάομαι, "from her who had taken possession of
    me"
κατηρώμην: impf. of κατα-ἀράομαι, "I cursed"
ὡς ... μεταθεῖσαν: ao. part. acc. s. f. of μετα-τίθημι causal after κατηρώμην,
    "because she (Palaestra) had changed me into"
ἑώρων: impf. of ὁράω, "for I saw"
παρεισιόντας: pr. part. of παρα-εἰς-ἔρχομαι in ind. st. after ἑώρων, "that the
    dogs were making their way into"
ἡμέραις οὐ πολλαῖς: dat. of degree of diff., "by not many days"
χάριν ... ἔχειν: ind. st. after ἔφη, "said that she was grateful"
ἀμείψασθαι: ao. inf. of ἀμείβω after θέλων, "wishing to reciprocate"

ἀμοιβῇ τῇ δικαίᾳ θέλειν ὁ πατὴρ ἐκέλευσεν ἐλεύθερον ἀφιέναι
ὑπαίθριον καὶ σὺν ταῖς ἀγελαίαις ἵπποις νέμεσθαι: «Καὶ γὰρ
ὡς ἐλεύθερος,» ἔφη, «ζήσεται ἐν ἡδονῇ καὶ ταῖς ἵπποις
ἐπιβήσεται.» καὶ αὕτη δικαιοτάτη ἀμοιβὴ ἐδόκει τότε, εἰ ἦν τὰ
πράγματα ἐν ὄνῳ δικαστῇ. καλέσας οὖν τῶν ἱπποφορβῶν τινα
τούτῳ με παραδίδωσιν, ἐγὼ δὲ ἔχαιρον ὡς οὐκέτι
ἀχθοφορήσων. ἐπεὶ δὲ ἥκομεν εἰς τὸν ἀγρόν, ταῖς ἵπποις με ὁ
νομεὺς συνέμιξεν καὶ ἦγεν ἡμᾶς τὴν ἀγέλην εἰς νομόν.

ἀγελαῖος, -α, -ον: of or in a herd
ἀγέλη, ἡ: a herd
ἀγρός, -οῦ, ὁ: a field, land
ἄγω: to lead, bring
ἀμοιβή, ἡ: a compensation, return, payment
ἀφίημι: to send forth, discharge
ἀχθοφορέω: to bear burdens
δίκαιος, -α, -ον: just, fair
δικαστής, -οῦ, ὁ: a judge
ἐθέλω: to will, wish
ἐλεύθερος, -α, -ον: free
ἐπιβαίνω: to go upon, mount
ζάω: to live
ἡδονή, ἡ: delight, enjoyment, pleasure

ἥκω: to have come, be present
ἵππος, ὁ/ἡ: a horse, mare
ἱπποφορβός, ὁ: a horse-keeper
καλέω: to call, summon
κελεύω: to bid, command, order
νέμω: to pasture, graze
νομεύς, -έως, ὁ: a shepherd, herdsman
νομός, ὁ: a pasture
οὐκέτι: no more, no longer
παραδίδωμι: to hand over
πρᾶγμα, -ατος, τό: that which has been done, a deed, matter
ὑπαίθριος, -α, -ον: in the open
χαίρω: to rejoice, be glad

ἀφιέναι: pr. inf. of ἀπο-ἵημι after ἐκέλευσεν, "he ordered to release"
νέμεσθαι: pr. inf. after ἐκέλευσεν, "to graze"
ζήσεται: fut. of ζέω, "he will live"
ἐπιβήσεται: fut. of ἐπι-βαίνω, "he will mount" + dat.
ἐδόκει ... εἰ ἦν: simple condition, "that seemed very just ... if the matter were"
ἐν ὄνῳ δικαστῇ: "before an ass judge"
ὡς οὐκέτι ἀχθοφορήσων: fut. part. expressing cause after ἔχαιρον, "because I would no longer carry burdens"
συνέμιξεν: ao. of συν-μίγνυμι, "mixed me with"
ἦγεν: impf. of ἄγω

Lucian

A cruel woman is put in charge of Lucius, who compels him to grind barley.

[28.] ἐχρῆν δὲ ἄρα κἀνταῦθα ὥσπερ Κανδαύλῃ κἀμοὶ γενέσθαι· ὁ γὰρ ἐπιστάτης τῶν ἵππων τῇ αὐτοῦ γυναικὶ Μεγαπόλῃ ἔνδον με κατέλιπεν· ἡ δὲ τῇ μύλῃ με ὑπεζεύγνυεν, ὥστε ἀλεῖν αὐτῇ καὶ πυροὺς καὶ κριθὰς ὅλας. καὶ τοῦτο μὲν ἦν μέτριον κακὸν εὐχαρίστῳ ὄνῳ ἀλεῖν τοῖς ἑαυτοῦ ἐπιστάταις· ἡ δὲ βελτίστη καὶ παρὰ τῶν ἄλλων τῶν ἐν ἐκείνοις τοῖς ἀγροῖς — πολλοὶ δὲ πάνυ ἦσαν — ἄλευρα τὸν μισθὸν αἰτοῦσα ἐξεμίσθου τὸν ἐμὸν ἄθλιον τράχηλον, καὶ τὰς μὲν κριθὰς τοὐμὸν ἄριστον φρύγουσα κἀμοὶ ὥστε ἀλεῖν ἐπιβάλλουσα,

---

ἀγρός, -οῦ, ὁ: field, country
ἄθλιος, -α, -ον: struggling, unhappy, wretched
αἰτέω: to ask, beg
ἄλευρον, τό: meal
ἀλέω: to grind
ἄριστον, τό: a meal, breakfast
βέλτιστος, -η, -ον: best
γυνή, γυναικός, ἡ: a woman, wife
ἐκμισθόω: to let out for hire, loan
ἐπιβάλλω: to throw or cast upon
ἐπιστάτης, -ου, ὁ: an overseer
εὐχάριστος, -ον: grateful, thankful
ἵππος, ὁ: a horse, mare

κακός, -ή, -όν: bad
Κανδαύλης, ὁ: Candaules
καταλείπω: to leave behind
κριθή, ἡ: barley
μετρέω: to measure
μισθός, ὁ: wages, pay
μύλη, ἡ: a millstone
ὅλος, -η, -ον: whole, entire, complete
πυρός, ὁ: wheat
τράχηλος, ὁ: a neck
ὑποζεύγνυμι: to put under the yoke
φρύγω: to roast
χρή: it is fated, necessary

ἐχρῆν: impf. 3 s. of χρή, "it was necessary" + inf.
ὥσπερ Κανδαύλῃ: "just as to Candaules" the Lydian king whose doom is related in Herodotus 1.8.
κἀμοὶ γενέσθαι: ao. inf. of γίγνομαι after ἐχρῆν, "to happen badly also to me"
ἔνδον: i.e. at home
κατέλιπεν: ao. of κατα-λείπω, "left me behind with" + dat.
ὑπεζεύγνυεν: impf. of ὑπο-ζεύγνυμι, "she would yoke me to" + dat.
ὥστε ἀλεῖν: result clause, "so that I might grind"
ἀλεῖν: in apposition to τοῦτο, "this... namely to grind"
τοῖς ἑαυτοῦ ἐπιστάταις: dat. of advantage, "for his own masters"
ἡ δὲ βελτίστη: "this best of women" with sarcasm
ἄλευρα τὸν μισθὸν: "seeking meal as payment"
ἐξεμίσθου: impf. of ἐκ-μισθόω, "she would hire out"
τοὐμὸν ἄριστον: acc. of resp., "meant *for my breakfast*"
κἀμοὶ (= καὶ ἐμοὶ) ἐπιβάλλουσα: "also inflicting on me to grind"

μάζας ὅλας ποιοῦσα κατέπινεν: ἐμοὶ δὲ πίτυρα τὸ ἄριστον ἦν.
εἰ δέ ποτε καὶ συνελάσειέ με ταῖς ἵπποις ὁ νομεύς, παιόμενός
τε καὶ δακνόμενος ὑπὸ τῶν ἀρσένων ἀπωλλύμην: ἀεὶ γάρ με
μοιχὸν ὑποπτεύοντες εἶναι τῶν ἵππων τῶν αὐτῶν γυναικῶν
ἐδίωκον ἀμφοτέροις εἰς ἐμὲ ὑπολακτίζοντες, ὥστε φέρειν οὐκ
ἠδυνάμην ζηλοτυπίαν ἱππικήν. λεπτὸς οὖν καὶ ἄμορφος ἐν οὐ
πολλῷ χρόνῳ ἐγενόμην, οὔτε ἔνδον εὐφραινόμενος πρὸς τῇ
μύλῃ οὔτε ὑπαίθριος νεμόμενος, ὑπὸ τῶν συννόμων
πολεμούμενος.

ἀεί: always, for ever	μοιχός, ὁ: an adulterer, paramour
ἄμορφος, -ον: misshapen, unsightly	μύλη, ἡ: a millstone
ἀμφότερος, -α, -ον: each, both	νέμω: to pasture, graze
ἀπόλλυμι: to destroy, kill, slay	νομεύς, -έως, ὁ: a shepherd, herdsman
ἄριστον, τό: a meal, breakfast	ὅλος, -η, -ον: whole, entire, complete
ἄρσην, ἄρσενος, ὁ: a male, stallion	παίω: to strike, beat
δάκνω: to bite	πίτυρον, τό: a husk
διώκω: to pursue	ποιέω: to make
δύναμαι: to be able, be capable	πολεμέω: to be at war, make war
εὐφραίνω: to cheer, delight, gladden	συνελαύνω: to drive together
ζηλοτυπία, ἡ: jealousy, rivalry	σύννομος, -ον: grazing together
ἱππικός, -ή, -όν: of a horse, equine	ὑπαίθριος, -α, -ον: in the open air, outside
ἵππος, ὁ/ἡ: a horse, mare	ὑπολακτίζω: to kick out
καταπίνω: to gulp down	ὑποπτεύω: to suspect, be suspicious
λεπτός, -ή, -όν: slight, thin	φέρω: to bear, carry, endure
μᾶζα, ἡ: a barley-cake	χρόνος, ὁ: time

κατέπινεν: impf., "she would gulp down"
εἰ συνελάσειε ... ἀπωλλύμην: past gen. cond., "if ever he would drive me out with
    ... I would be killed"
συνελάσειε: ao. opt. of συν-ελαύνω
με εἶναι: ind. st. after ὑποπτεύοντες, "suspecting me to be"
ἀμφοτέροις: "with both (sc. hooves)"
ὥστε φέρειν οὐκ ἠδυνάμην: indicative with ὥστε showing actual result, "so that
    I was no longer able to bear"
ἐγενόμην: ao. of γίγνομαι, "I became"

Lucian

Lucius is compelled to carry wood from the mountains, overseen by a sadistic boy. (cf. Ap. Met. VII.17-24, p. 162)

[29.] καὶ μὴν καὶ τὰ πολλὰ εἰς τὸ ὄρος ἄνω ἐπεμπόμην καὶ ξύλα τοῖς ὤμοις ἐκόμιζον. τοῦτο δὲ ἦν τὸ κεφάλαιον τῶν ἐμῶν κακῶν· πρῶτον μὲν ὑψηλὸν ὄρος ἀναβαίνειν ἔδει, ὀρθὴν δεινῶς ὁδόν, εἶτα καὶ ἀνυπόδητος ὄρει ἐν λιθίνῳ. καί μοι συνεξέπεμπον ὀνηλάτην, παιδάριον ἀκάθαρτον. τοῦτό με καινῶς ἑκάστοτε ἀπώλλυε· πρῶτον μὲν ἔπαιέ με καὶ τρέχοντα λίαν οὐ ξύλῳ ἁπλῷ, ἀλλὰ τῷ ὄζους πυκνοὺς ἔχοντι καὶ ὀξεῖς, καὶ ἀεὶ ἔπαιεν ἐς τὸ αὐτὸ τοῦ μηροῦ, ὥστε ἀνέῳκτό μοι κατ᾽

ἀεί: always, for ever
ἀκάθαρτος, -ον: unclean, foul
ἀναβαίνω: to go up, mount, ascend
ἀνοίγνυμι: to open
ἀνυπόδητος, -ον: unshod, barefoot
ἄνω: upwards
ἁπλοῦς, -ῆ, -οῦν: simple, plain
ἀπόλλυμι: to destroy, kill
δεινός, -ή, -όν: fearful, terrible, dreadful
ἑκάστοτε: each time, on each occasion
καινός, -ή, -όν: new, fresh
κακός, -ή, -όν: bad
κεφάλαιος, -α, -ον: chief, main, principle
κομίζω: to take care of, carry
λίαν: very much, exceedingly
λίθινος, -η, -ον: of stone, stony, craggy
μηρός, ὁ: a thigh

ξύλον, τό: a piece of wood, stick
ὁδός, ἡ: a way, path, road
ὄζος, ὁ: a stub, offshoot, twig
ὀνηλάτης, -ου, ὁ: a donkey-driver
ὀξύς, -εῖα, -ύ: sharp, keen
ὀρθός, -ή, -όν: straight, sharp, steep
ὄρος, -εος, τό: a mountain, hill
παιδάριον, τό: a young, little boy
παίω: to strike, hit
πέμπω: to send, dispatch
πυκνός, ή, όν: thick-set, crowded
συνεκπέμπω: to send out together, send with
τρέχω: to run
ὑψηλός, -ή, -όν: high, lofty
ὦμος, ὁ: a shoulder

καὶ μὴν καὶ: "furthermore"
ἄνω ἐπεμπόμην: impf. pas. of πέμπω, "I was (repeatedly) sent up"
τοῖς ὤμοις: dat., "on my shoulders"
ἔδει: impf., "it was necessary" + inf.
ὀρθὴν δεινῶς: "terribly steep"
συνεξέπεμπον: impf. of συν-ἐκ-πέμπω, "they sent out with"
ἀπώλλυε: impf. of ἀπόλλυμι, "kept killing me"
τῷ ἔχοντι: dat. agreeing with ξύλῳ, "but also with one having…"
τὸ αὐτὸ τοῦ μηροῦ: "the same (part) of the thigh"
ὥστε ἀνέῳκτό: plpf. of ἀνα-οἴγνυμι in result clause emphasizing actual result, "so that my thigh had been opened"
κατ᾽ ἐκεῖνο: "on that (spot of the thigh)"

ἐκεῖνο ὁ μηρὸς τῇ ῥάβδῳ· ὁ δὲ ἀεὶ τὸ τραῦμα ἔπαιεν. εἶτά μοι
ἐπετίθει φορτίον ὅσον χαλεπὸν εἶναι καὶ ἐλέφαντι ἐνεγκεῖν·
καὶ ἄνωθεν ἡ κατάβασις ὀξεῖα ἦν· ὁ δὲ καὶ ἐνταῦθα ἔπαιεν. εἰ
δέ μοι περιπῖπτον ἴδοι τὸ φορτίον καὶ εἰς τὸ ἕτερον ἐπικλῖνον,
δέον τῶν ξύλων ἀφαιρεῖν καὶ τῷ κουφοτέρῳ προσβάλλειν καὶ
τὸ ἴσον ποιεῖν, τοῦτο μὲν οὐδέποτε εἰργάσατο, λίθους δὲ
μεγάλους ἐκ τοῦ ὄρους ἀναιρούμενος εἰς τὸ κουφότερον καὶ
ἄνω νεῦον τοῦ φορτίου προσετίθει· καὶ κατῄειν ἄθλιος τοῖς

ἀεί: always, for ever
ἄθλιος, -α, -ον: struggling, unhappy, wretched
ἀναιρέω: to take up, raise
ἄνω: upwards
ἄνωθεν: from above
ἀφαιρέω: to take from, take away from
ἐλέφας, -αντος, ὁ: an elephant
ἐπικλίνω: to incline, tilt
ἐπιτίθημι: to place upon
ἐργάζομαι: to work, labor
ἴσος, -η, -ον: equal, the same
κατάβασις, -εως, ἡ: a way down, descent
κατέρχομαι: to go down
κοῦφος, -η, -ον: light, nimble
λίθος, -ου, ὁ: a stone

μηρός, ὁ: the thigh
νεύω: to decline, sink
ξύλον, τό: a piece of wood, stick
ὀξύς, -εῖα, -ύ: sharp, steep
ὄρος, -εος, τό: a mountain, hill
οὐδέποτε: not ever, never
παίω: to strike, hit
περιπίπτω: to fall around
προσβάλλω: to throw to
προστίθημι: to put to, place upon
ῥάβδος, ἡ: a rod, stick, switch
τραῦμα, -ατος, τό: a wound, injury
φέρω: to bear
φορτίον, τό: a load, burden
χαλεπός, -ή, -όν: hard to bear, painful, heavy

ἐπετίθει: impf. of ἐπι-τίθημι, "he kept piling on"
ὅσον χαλεπὸν εἶναι: "as much as would be difficult" + inf.
καὶ ἐλέφαντι: "even for an elephant"
ἐνεγκεῖν: ao. inf. of φέρω, "to bear"
εἰ ἴδοι … οὐδέποτε εἰργάσατο: past gen. cond., "if ever he saw … he never did"
ἴδοι: ao. opt. of εἶδον
εἰργάσατο: ao. of ἐργάζομαι
περιπῖπτον: pr. part. in ind. st. after ἴδοι, "saw that the load *was falling over*"
ἐπικλῖνον: pr. part. in ind. st., "that it was leaning"
δέον: pr. part. of δέω used absolutely, "it being necessary" + inf.
ἀφαιρεῖν: ao. inf. of ἀπο-αιρέω, "to remove" + gen.
καὶ τὸ ἴσον ποιεῖν: "and to make the load equal"
εἰργάσατο: ao. of ἐργάζομαι, "this he never did"
ἄνω νεῦον: pr. part., "(the side of the load) tilting upward"
προσετίθει: impf. of προσ-τίθημι, "he would add to"
κατῄειν: impf. of κατα-ἔρχομαι, "I would descend"

ξύλοις ὁμοῦ καὶ λίθους ἀχρείους περιφέρων. καὶ ποταμὸς ἦν
ἀέναος ἐν τῇ ὁδῷ· ὁ δὲ τῶν ὑποδημάτων φειδόμενος ὀπίσω
τῶν ξύλων ἐπ' ἐμοὶ καθίζων ἐπέρα τὸν ποταμόν.

The boy devises cruel punishments for Lucius.

[30.] εἰ δέ ποτε οἷα κάμνων καὶ ἀχθοφορῶν
καταπέσοιμι, τότε δὴ τὸ δεινὸν ἀφόρητον ἦν· οὐ γὰρ ἦν
καταβάντος τὴν χεῖρά μοι ἐπιδοῦναι κἀμὲ χαμόθεν ἐπεγείρειν
καὶ τοῦ φορτίου ἀφελεῖν, ἄν ποτε καὶ δέοι, ὁ δὲ οὔτε κατῆλθεν

ἀέναος, -ον: ever-flowing
ἀφαιρέω: to take from, take away from
ἀφόρητος, -ον: intolerable, insufferable
ἀχθοφορέω: to bear burdens
ἀχρεῖος, -α, -ον: useless, good for nothing
δεινός, -ή, -όν: fearful, terrible
ἐπεγείρω: to rouse up, raise
ἐπιδίδωμι: to give besides, lend
καθίζω: to make to sit down, seat
καιρός, ὁ: the proper time
κάμνω: to work
καταπίπτω: to fall down, drop
κατέρχομαι: to go down
λίθος, -ου, ὁ: a stone

ξύλον, τό: a piece of wood, stick
ὁδός, ἡ: a way, path, road
οἷος, -α, -ον: such as
ὁμοῦ: in the same place, together with (+ dat.)
ὀπίσω: backwards, behind
περάω: to cross, traverse
περιφέρω: to carry around
ποταμός, ὁ: a river, stream
ὑπόδημα, -ατος, τό: a shoe, sandal
φείδομαι: to spare
φορτίον, τό: a load, burden
χαμόθεν: from the ground
χείρ, χειρός, ἡ: a hand

ὁμοῦ καὶ περιφέρων: "at the same time also carrying around"
φειδόμενος: pr. part. showing purpose, "in order to spare" + gen.
ἐπέρα: impf. of περάω, "he would cross"
εἰ καταπέσοιμι: ao. opt. of κατα-πίπτω in past. gen cond., "if ever I fell...that would be..."
οὐ γὰρ ἦν: "for when it was possible" + inf.
οὗ: gen. of rel. pron. showing time when
καταβάντος: ao. part. of κατα-βαίνω in gen. abs., "(me) having gone down"
ἐπιδοῦναι: ao. inf. of ἐπι-δίδομαι after ἦν, "to give a helping hand"
χαμόθεν: "to raise me up from the ground"
ἀφελεῖν: ao. inf. of ἀπο-αἱρέω after ἦν, "to remove" + gen.
ἄν ποτε καὶ δέοι: pr. opt. in gen. temporal clause where ἄν is potential, "whenever it might be necessary"
κατῆλθεν: ao. of κατα-ἔρχομαι, "he never got down off"

οὔτε χεῖρά μοι ἐπέδωκεν, ἀλλ' ἄνωθεν ἀπὸ τῆς κεφαλῆς καὶ
τῶν ὤτων ἀρξάμενος συνέκοπτέ με τῷ ξύλῳ, ἕως ἐπεγείρωσί
με αἱ πληγαί. καὶ μὴν καὶ ἄλλο κακὸν εἰς ἐμὲ ἀφόρητον
ἔπαιζεν: συνενεγκὼν ἀκανθῶν ὀξυτάτων φορτίον καὶ τοῦτο
δεσμῷ περισφίγξας ἀπεκρέμα ὄπισθεν ἐκ τῆς οὐρᾶς, αἱ δὲ οἷον
εἰκὸς ἀπιόντος τὴν ὁδὸν ἀποκρεμάμεναι προσέπιπτόν μοι καὶ
πάντα μοι τὰ ὄπισθεν νύττουσαι ἐτίτρωσκον: καὶ ἦν μοι τὸ

ἄκανθα, -ης, ἡ: a thorn
ἄνωθεν: from above
ἀπέρχομαι: to go away, depart
ἀποκρεμάω: to let hang down
ἄρχω: to begin
ἀφόρητος, -ον: intolerable, insufferable
δεσμός, ὁ: a band, tie
ἐπεγείρω: to rouse up, raise
ἐπιδίδωμι: to give besides
ἕως: until, till
κακός, -ή, -όν: bad
κεφαλή, ἡ: a head
κρεμάννυμι: to hang
νύττω: to prick, spur, pierce
ξύλον, τό: a piece of wood, stick

ὁδός, ἡ: a way, path, road
ὀξύς, -εῖα, -ύ: sharp, keen
ὄπισθεν: behind, at the back
οὐρά, ἡ: the tail
οὖς, ὠτός, τό: an ear
παίζω: to play like a child, play a trick
περισφίγγω: to bind tight around
πληγή, ἡ: a blow, stroke
προσπίπτω: to fall upon
συγκόπτω: to beat up, thrash
συμφέρω: to bring together, gather, collect
τιτρώσκω: to wound
φορτίον, τό: a load, burden
χείρ, χειρός, ἡ: a hand

ἐπέδωκεν: ao. of ἐπι-δίδωμι, "he never lent a helping hand"
ἀρξάμενος: ao. part., "starting from" + gen.
συνέκοπτε: impf. of συν-κόπτω, "he would keep beating me"
ἕως ἐπεγείρωσι: pr. subj. in indef. temp. clause, "until such time as they caused me to rise"
καὶ μὴν καί: indicating a climax, "moreover"
συνενεγκών: ao. part. of συν-φέρω, "having collected"
περισφίγξας: ao. part. of περι-σφίγγω, "having bound this tightly around"
ἀπεκρέμα: impf. of ἀπο-κρεμάω, "he would suspend"
αἱ δέ: i.e. "the thistles"
οἷον εἰκός: "as would be expected"
ἀπιόντος: pr. part. of ἀπο-ἔρχομαι in gen. abs., "(me) going along"
προσέπιπτον: impf., "they kept falling forward upon" + dat.
πάντα μοι τὰ ὄπισθεν: "my entire behind"
ἐτίτρωσκον: impf., "they kept wounding"

ἀμύνειν ἀδύνατον, τῶν τιτρωσκόντων ἀεί μοι ἑπομένων κἀμοῦ ἠρτημένων. εἰ μὲν γὰρ ἀτρέμα προΐοιμι φυλαττόμενος τῶν ἀκανθῶν τὴν προσβολήν, ὑπὸ τῶν ξύλων ἀπωλλύμην, εἰ δὲ φεύγοιμι τὸ ξύλον, τότ᾽ ἤδη τὸ δεινὸν ὄπισθεν ὀξὺ προσέπιπτεν. καὶ ὅλως ἔργον ἦν τῷ ὀνηλάτῃ τῷ ἐμῷ ἀποκτενεῖν με.

Lucius kicks the boy, which only makes things worse.

[31.] ἐπεὶ δέ ποτε ἅπαξ κακὰ πάσχων πολλὰ οὐκέτι φέρων πρὸς αὐτὸν λὰξ ἐκίνησα, εἶχεν ἀεὶ τοῦτο τὸ λὰξ ἐν

ἀδύνατος, -ον: unable, impossible
ἀεί: always, for ever
ἄκανθα, -ης, ἡ: a thorn
ἀμύνω: to ward off, defend
ἅπαξ: once
ἀποκτείνω: to kill, slay
ἀπόλλυμι: to destroy, kill
ἀρτάω: to fasten to or hang
ἀτρέμα: gently, softly
δεινός, -ή, -όν: fearful, terrible, dire
ἕπω: to come after, follow
ἔργον, τό: a deed, work
κακός, -ή, -όν: bad
κινέω: to set in motion, move
λάξ: with the foot

ξύλον, τό: a piece of wood, stick
ὅλος, -η, -ον: whole, entire, complete
ὀνηλάτης, -ου, ὁ: a donkey-driver
ὀξύς, -εῖα, -ύ: sharp, keen
ὄπισθεν: behind, at the back
οὐκέτι: no more, no longer
πάσχω: to feel, suffer
προέρχομαι: to go forth, advance
προσβολή, ἡ: an attack, strike, impact
προσπίτνω: to fall upon
τιτρώσκω: to wound
φέρω: to bear, carry, endure
φεύγω: to flee, run away
φυλάττω: to keep watch, guard

τὸ ἀμύνειν: art. inf. nom. subj. of ἦν, "*to defend* myself was impossible"
τῶν τιτρωσκόντων: pr. part. in gen. abs., "the wounding (spikes) were always following"
ἠρτημένων: pf. part. of ἀρτάω, "having been suspended"
εἰ προΐοιμι … ἀπωλλύμην: past gen. cond., "if ever I went forward … I would be killed"
προΐοιμι: pr. opt. of προ-έρχομαι
ἀπωλλύμην: impf. of ἀπόλλυμι
εἰ δὲ φεύγοιμι … προσέπιπτεν: past gen. cond., "If ever I fled … the club would fall upon me"
φεύγοιμι: pr. opt.
ὅλως: "in general"
τῷ ὀνηλάτῃ: dat. of poss. with ἦν, "it was the task *of the driver*"
ἀποκτενεῖν: fut. inf. explaining ἔργον, "to kill me"
ποτε ἅπαξ: "on one occasion"
ἐκίνησα: ao. of κινέω, "I set in motion," "I directed toward him"
τὸ λάξ: the art. makes a noun of the adverb λάξ, "the kick"
εἶχεν: impf. of ἔχω, "he always kept"

μνήμη. καὶ ποτε κελεύεται στυππεῖον ἐξ ἑτέρου χωρίου εἰς ἕτερον χωρίον μετενεγκεῖν· κομίσας οὖν με καὶ τὸ στυππεῖον τὸ πολὺ συνενεγκὼν κατέδησεν ἐπ᾽ ἐμὲ καὶ δεσμῷ ἀργαλέῳ εὖ μάλα προσέδησέ με τῷ φορτίῳ κακὸν ἐμοὶ μέγα τυρεύων. ἐπεὶ δὲ προϊέναι λοιπὸν ἔδει, ἐκ τῆς ἑστίας κλέψας δαλὸν ἔτι θερμόν, ἐπειδὴ πόρρω τῆς αὐλῆς ἐγενόμεθα, τὸν δαλὸν ἐνέκρυψεν εἰς τὸ στυππεῖον. τὸ δὲ — τί γὰρ ἄλλο ἐδύνατο; — εὐθὺς ἀνάπτεται, καὶ λοιπὸν οὐδὲν ἔφερον ἄλλο ἢ πῦρ

ἀνάπτω: to light, kindle
ἀργαλέος, -α, -ον: painful, grievous
αὐλή, ἡ: a courtyard, house
δαλός, ὁ: a fire-brand, piece of burning wood
δεσμός, ὁ: a band, bond, tie
δύναμαι: to be able, capable, possible
ἐγκρύπτω: to hide in
ἑστία, ἡ: a hearth, fireside
θερμός, -ή, -όν: hot, warm
κακός, -ή, -όν: bad
καταδέω: to tie down
κελεύω: to bid, command, order
κλέπτω: to steal
κομίζω: to carry, bring

λοιπός, -ή, -όν: remaining, the rest
μάλα: very, exceedingly
μεταφέρω: to carry over, transfer
μνήμη, ἡ: a remembrance, memory
πόρρω: forwards, onwards, further (+ *gen.*)
προέρχομαι: to go forth, advance
προσδέω: to bind to, tie to, attach
πῦρ, πυρός, τό: fire
στυππεῖον, τό: flax
συμφέρω: to bring together, gather, collect
τυρεύω: to create mischief, cause trouble
φέρω: to bear
φορτίον, τό: a load, burden
χωρίον, τό: a place, spot

κελεύεται: vivid pr. for past tense
μετενεγκεῖν: ao. inf. of μετα-φέρω after κελεύεται, "he is ordered *to transfer*"
συνενεγκὼν: ao. part. of συν-φέρω, "having collected"
κατέδησεν: ao. of κατα-δέω, "he tied down"
προσέδησε: ao. of προσ-δέω, "he attached"
εὖ μάλα: "very well" i.e. "very tightly"
τυρεύων: pr. part. of τυρεύω, lit. "making cheese," fig. "concocting mischief"
προϊέναι: pr. inf. of προ-έρχομαι after ἔδει, "it was necessary to advance"
κλέψας: ao. part. of κλέπτω, "having stolen"
ἔτι θερμόν: "still hot"
ἐγενόμεθα: ao. of γίγνομαι, "when we were"
ἐνέκρυψεν: ao. of ἐν-κρύπτω, "he concealed in"
λοιπὸν: adv., "from then on"
οὐδὲν ἔφερον ἄλλο ἢ: "I was bearing nothing other than..."

ἄπλετον. μαθὼν οὖν ὡς αὐτίκα ὀπτήσομαι, ἐν τῇ ὁδῷ τέλματι
βαθεῖ ἐντυχὼν ῥίπτω ἐμαυτὸν τοῦ τέλματος ἐς τὸ ὑγρότατον·
εἶτα ἐκύλιον ἐνταῦθα τὸ στυππεῖον καὶ δινῶν καὶ στρέφων
ἐμαυτὸν τῷ πηλῷ κατέσβεσα τὸ θερμὸν ἐκεῖνο καὶ πικρὸν ἐμοὶ
φορτίον, καὶ οὕτω λοιπὸν ἀκινδυνότερον ἐβάδιζον τῆς ὁδοῦ τὸ
ἐπίλοιπον. οὐδὲ γὰρ ἔτι με ἀνάψαι τῷ παιδὶ δυνατὸν ἦν τοῦ
στυππείου πηλῷ ὑγρῷ πεφυρμένου. καὶ τοῦτό γε ὁ τολμηρὸς

ἀκίνδυνος, -ον: without danger, free from danger
ἀνάπτω: to light, kindle
ἄπλετος, -ον: boundless, immense, huge
αὐτίκα: straight away, at once
βαδίζω: to go, walk
βαθύς, -εῖα, -ύ: high, deep
δινόω: turn
δυνατός, -ή, -όν: strong, able
ἐντυγχάνω: to fall upon, meet with
ἐπίλοιπος, -ον: still left, remaining
θερμός, -ή, -όν: hot, warm
θέρμω: to heat, make hot
κατασβέννυμι: to put out, quench
κυλίω: to roll along

λοιπός, -ή, -όν: remaining, the rest
μανθάνω: to learn
ὁδός, ἡ: a way, path, road
ὀπτάω: to roast
παῖς, παιδός, ὁ: a slave, boy, boy
πηλός, ὁ: clay, mud
πικρός, -ά, -όν: pointed, sharp, painful
ῥίπτω: to throw, cast, hurl
στρέφω: to turn
στυππεῖον, τό: flax
τέλμα, -ατος, τό: a pond, marsh, swamp
τολμηρός, -ά, -όν: hardihood
ὑγρός, -ά, -όν: wet, moist, fluid
φορτίον, τό: a load, burden
φύρω: to mix

μαθὼν: ao. part. of μανθάνω, "having realized"
ὡς αὐτίκα ὀπτήσομαι: fut. in ind. st. after μαθὼν, "that I was to be roasted"
ἐντυχὼν: ao. part. of ἐν-τυγχάνω, "having come upon" + dat.
ἐκύλιον: impf., "I kept rolling"
δινῶν καὶ στρέφων: pr. part. with instrumental force, "by twisting and turning"
κατέσβεσα: ao. of κατα-σβέννυμι, "I extinguished"
ἀνάψαι: ao. inf. of after δυνατὸν, "nor was it possible to light up"
πεφυρμένου: perf. part. of φύρω agreeing with στυππείου, "since it was soaked"
τοῦτό γε: "even with respect to this"

παῖς ἐλθὼν ἐμοῦ κατεψεύσατο, εἰπὼν ὡς παριὼν ἑκὼν ἑαυτὸν ἐνσείσαιμι τῇ ἑστίᾳ. καὶ τότε μὲν ἐκ τοῦ στυππείου μηδὲ ἐλπίζων ὑπεξῆλθον.

ἑκών, ἑκοῦσα, ἑκόν: willing, voluntarily
ἐλπίζω: to hope for, expect
ἐνσείω: to plunge in, dive into
ἑστία, ἡ: a hearth
καταψεύδομαι: to tell lies against, speak falsely of

παῖς, παιδός, ὁ: a slave, boy, boy
παρέρχομαι: to go by, pass by
στυππεῖον, τό: flax
ὑπεξέρχομαι: to go out from under, escape

ἐλθών: ao. part. of ἔρχομαι used with κατεψεύσατο, "he went and lied"
κατεψεύσατο: ao. of κατα-ψεύδομαι
εἰπών: ao. part. of λέγω instrumental, "by saying"
παριών: pr. part. of παρα-ἔρχομαι, "going aside"
ὡς ... ἐνσείσαιμι: ao. opt. in sec. seq. of ind. st., "that I had bumped into" + dat.
ἐνσείσαιμι: ao. opt. of ἐν-σείω
ὑπεξῆλθον: ao. of ὑπο-ἐξ-ἔρχομαι, "I escaped from"

Indirect Statement in Secondary Sequence

One of the three main forms of indirect statement in Greek is ὅτι or ὡς + the indicative after verbs of saying, like φημι and λέγω. The mood of the direct speech can always be retained. But if the verb of saying is a past tense, the mood of the original statement can be changed to the corresponding tense of the optative. The difference between the two forms cannot be rendered in English, but the optative version is considered "less vivid" because it is not as close to the original words of the direct statement.

> κατεψεύσατο, εἰπὼν ὡς ἐνσείσαιμι τῇ ἑστίᾳ.
> κατεψεύσατο, εἰπὼν ὡς ἐνέσεισα τῇ ἑστίᾳ.
> He lied by saying *that I had bumped into the hearth.*

The original statement was ἐνέσεισε τῇ ἑστίᾳ: "he bumped into the hearth"

The same rule applies to indirect question and to the protasis of conditions.

> ἐγὼ μὲν ἠρόμην εἰ ἔνδον εἴη Ἵππαρχος:
> I asked *whether Hipparchus was inside.*

The original question was ἔνδον ἐστι Ἵππαρχος. In the *Onos* it is common to find the "more vivid" retention of the indicative.

> ἠπείλει, εἰ ἀνασταίη, ἀποκτενεῖν τῇ μαχαίρᾳ:
> He kept threatening *that if he got up,* he would kill him.

The original statement was a future more vivid condition: ἐὰν ἀναστῶ, ἀποκτενῶ τῇ μαχαίρᾳ: "If I get up, I will kill you"

The boy tells lies about Lucius to get him in trouble.

[32.] ἀλλ' ἕτερον ὁ ἀκάθαρτος παῖς ἐξεῦρεν ἐπ' ἐμὲ μακρῷ κάκιον: κομίσας γάρ με ἐς τὸ ὄρος καί μοι φορτίον ἁδρὸν ἐπιθεὶς ἐκ τῶν ξύλων, τοῦτο μὲν πιπράσκει γεωργῷ πλησίον οἰκοῦντι, ἐμὲ δὲ γυμνὸν καὶ ἄξυλον κομίσας οἴκαδε καταψεύδεταί μου πρὸς τὸν αὑτοῦ δεσπότην ἔργον ἀνόσιον: «Τοῦτον, δέσποτα, τὸν ὄνον οὐκ οἶδ' ὅ τι βόσκομεν δεινῶς ἀργὸν ὄντα καὶ βραδύν. ἀλλὰ μὴν νῦν ἐπιτηδεύει καὶ ἄλλο ἔργον: ἐπὰν γυναῖκα ἢ παρθένον καλὴν καὶ ὡραίαν ἴδῃ ἢ

ἁδρός, -ά, -όν: thick, bulky, heavy	**καταψεύδομαι**: to tell lies against, speak falsely of
ἀκάθαρτος, -ον: unclean, foul, vile	**κομίζω**: to carry, lead
ἀνόσιος, -α, -ον: unholy, profane	**μακρός, -ά, -όν**: long
ἄξυλος, -ον: with no wood, timberless	**ξύλον, τό**: a piece of wood, stick
ἀργός, -ή, -όν: lazy	**οἶδα**: to know
βόσκω: to keep, tend	**οἴκαδε**: to one's home, homewards
βραδύς, -εῖα, -ύ: slow	**οἰκέω**: to inhabit, live
γεωργός, ὁ: a farmer	**ὄνος, ὁ**: an ass
γυμνός, -ή, -όν: naked, unclad	**ὄρος, -εος, τό**: a mountain, hill
δεινός, -ή, -όν: fearful, terrible	**παῖς, παιδός, ὁ**: a slave, boy, boy
δεσπότης, -ου, ὁ: a master, lord	**παρθένος, ἡ**: a maiden, girl
ἐξευρίσκω: to find out, discover	**πιπράσκω**: to sell
ἐπιτηδεύω: to pursue, practice	**πλήσιος, -α, -ον**: close, near
ἐπιτίθημι: to lay on, place upon	**φορτίον, τό**: a load, burden
ἔργον, τό: a deed, work, act	**ὡραῖος, -α, -ον**: in season, ripe, young
κακός, -ή, -όν: bad, evil	

ἐξεῦρεν: ao. of ἐξ-ευρίσκω, "he discovered"
μακρῷ: dat. of degree of diff., "worse by much"
ἐπιθεὶς: ao. part. of ἐπι-τίθημι, "having placed upon me"
πλησίον οἰκοῦντι: dat. agreeing with γεωργῷ, "who lived nearby"
καταψεύδεταί μου: "he fabricates against me" + acc.
ὅ τι βόσκομεν: ind. quest., "why we feed him"
ὄντα: pr. part. causal, "since he is"
ἐπὰν (= ἐπεὶ ἄν) ... **ἴδῃ**: pres. gen. clause, "whenever he sees"
ἴδῃ: ao. subj. of εἶδον

παῖδα, ἀπολακτίσας ἵεται δρόμῳ ἐπ᾽ αὐτούς, ὡς εἴ τις ἐρᾷ
ἄνθρωπος ἄρρην ἐπὶ ἐρωμένῃ γυναικὶ κινούμενος, καὶ δάκνει
ἐν φιλήματος σχήματι καὶ πλησιάζειν βιάζεται, ἐκ δὲ τούτου
σοι δίκας καὶ πράγματα παρέξει, πάντων ὑβριζομένων,
πάντων ἀνατρεπομένων. καὶ γὰρ νῦν ξύλα κομίζων, γυναῖκα
εἰς ἀγρὸν ἀπιοῦσαν ἰδών, τὰ μὲν ξύλα πάντα χαμαὶ
ἐσκόρπισεν ἀποσεισάμενος, τὴν δὲ γυναῖκα ἐς τὴν ὁδὸν
ἀνατρέψας γαμεῖν ἐβούλετο, ἕως ἄλλος ἄλλοθεν ἐκδραμόντες

ἀγρός, -οῦ, ὁ: field, land	**ἐράω**: to love
ἄλλοθεν: from another place	**ἕως**: until, till
ἀνατρέπω: to overturn, upset	**ἵημι**: to send forth, (*mid.*) to hasten
ἄνθρωπος, ὁ: a man	**κινέω**: to set in motion, move
ἀπέρχομαι: to go away, depart	**κομίζω**: to carry, lead
ἀπολακτίζω: to kick away, shake off	**ξύλον, τό**: a piece of wood, stick
ἀποσείω: to shake off	**ὁδός, ἡ**: a way, path, road
ἄρρην, -εν: male, masculine	**παῖς, παιδός, ὁ**: a slave, boy
βιάζω: to force	**παρέχω**: to furnish, provide, supply
βούλομαι: to will, wish	**πλησιάζω**: to bring near
γαμέω: to marry, take as a lover	**πρᾶγμα, -ατος, τό**: a deed, action, matter
γυνή, γυναικός, ἡ: a woman, wife	**σκορπίζω**: to scatter, disperse
δάκνω: to bite	**σχῆμα, -ατος, τό**: form, appearance
δίκη, ἡ: justice, lawsuit	**ὑβρίζω**: to run riot, insult
δρόμος, ὁ: a course, running	**φίλημα, -ατος, τό**: a kiss
ἐκτρέχω: to run out	**χαμαί**: on the ground

ἀπολακτίσας: ao. part. of **ἀπο-λακτίζω**, "having kicked (me) away"
ἄνθρωπος ἄρρην: "male person"
ἐν φιλήματος σχήματι: "in the manner of a kiss"
πλησιάζειν βιάζεται: "he uses force to mount them"
παρέξει: fut. of **παρα-ἔχω**, "he will provide you with" + acc.
πάντων ὑβριζομένων, πάντων ἀνατρεπομένων: gen. abs., "all being violated,
    being terrified"
ἀπιοῦσαν: pr. part. of **ἀπο-ἔρχομαι** agreeing with **γυναῖκα**, "a woman going"
ἰδών: ao. part. of **εἶδον**, "having seen"
ἐσκόρπισεν: ao. of **σκορπίζω**, "he scattered"
ἀποσεισάμενος: ao. part. of **ἀποσείω**, "having shaken off"
ἀνατρέψας: ao. of **ἀνα-τρέπω**, "having overturned the woman"
ἕως ... ἠμύναμεν: ao. of **ἀμύνω**, "until we defended" + dat.
ἄλλος ἄλλοθεν: "some from here, some from there"
ἐκδραμόντες: ao. part. of **ἐκ-τρέχω**: having run up"

ἠμύναμεν τῇ γυναικὶ ἐς τὸ μὴ διασπασθῆναι ὑπὸ τοῦ καλοῦ
τούτου ἐραστοῦ.»

The boy's master decides to have Lucius killed.

[33.] ὁ δὲ ταῦτα πυθόμενος, «Ἀλλ' εἰ μήτε βαδίζειν,»
ἔφη, «ἐθέλει μήτε φορτηγεῖν καὶ ἔρωτας ἀνθρωπίνους ἐρᾷ ἐπὶ
γυναῖκας καὶ παῖδας οἰστρούμενος, ἀποσφάξατε αὐτόν, καὶ τὰ
μὲν ἔγκατα τοῖς κυσὶ δότε, τὰ δὲ κρέα τοῖς ἐργάταις
φυλάξατε· καὶ ἢν ἔρηται, πῶς οὗτος ἀπέθανε, λύκου τοῦτο

ἀμύνω: to keep off, defend
ἀνθρώπινος, -η, -ον: of man, human
ἀποθνήσκω: to die
ἀποσφάζω: to slaughter
βαδίζω: to go, walk
γυνή, γυναικός, ἡ: a woman, wife
διασπάω: to tear apart
δίδωμι: to give
ἔγκατα, τά: the entrails, bowels
ἐθέλω: to will, wish
ἐραστής, -οῦ, ὁ: a lover
ἐράω: to love

ἐργάτης, -ου, ὁ: a workman
ἔρως, -ωτος, ὁ: love, passion
ἐρωτάω: to ask, enquire
κρέας, τό: flesh, meat
κύων, ὁ: a dog
λύκος, ὁ: a wolf
οἰστράω: to drive mad
παῖς, παιδός, ὁ: a slave, boy
πυνθάνομαι: to learn
πῶς: how? in what way?
φορτηγέω: to carry loads
φυλάζω: to divide up

ἐς τὸ μὴ διασπασθῆναι: articular inf., "toward not being torn apart," i.e. "from
  being torn apart"
διασπασθῆναι: ao. pas. inf. of δια-σπάω
καλοῦ ἐραστοῦ: sarcastic, "from this handsome lover"
πυθόμενος: ao. part., "having learned"
μήτε βαδίζειν: pr. inf. after ἐθέλει, "if he wishes *neither to walk*"
ἔρωτας ἀνθρωπίνους: internal accusative with ἐρᾷ, "if he has human loves"
ἀποσφάξατε: ao. imper. of ἀποσφάττειν, "slaughter him"
δότε: ao. imper. of δίδωμι, "give"
φυλάξατε: ao. imper. of φυλάττω, "divide up the meat for" + dat.
ἢν ἔρηται ... καταψεύσασθε: fut. more. vivid cond., "if someone asks ... then
  falsely accuse" + gen.
ἔρηται: ao. subj. of ἐρωτάω
πῶς ἀπέθανε: ao. of ἀπο-θνήσκω in ind. quest., "how this one died"

καταψεύσασθε.» ὁ μὲν οὖν ἀκάθαρτος παῖς ὁ ἐμὸς ὀνηλάτης ἔχαιρε καί με αὐτίκα ἤθελεν ἀποσφάττειν.

A neighbor suggests castration instead of death for Lucius.

ἀλλ' ἔτυχε γάρ τις παρὼν τότε τῶν γειτόνων γεωργῶν· οὗτος ἐρρύσατό με ἐκ τοῦ θανάτου δεινὰ ἐπ' ἐμοὶ βουλευσάμενος.

«Μηδαμῶς,» ἔφη, «ἀποσφάξῃς ὄνον καὶ ἀλεῖν καὶ ἀχθοφορεῖν δυνάμενον· καὶ οὐ μέγα. ἐπειδὴ γὰρ εἰς ἀνθρώπους ἔρῳ καὶ οἴστρῳ φέρεται, λαβὼν αὐτὸν ἔκτεμε· τῆς γὰρ ἐπαφροδίτου ταύτης ὁρμῆς ἀφαιρεθεὶς, ἥμερός τε εὐθὺς καὶ

ἀκάθαρτος, -ον: unclean, foul, vile
ἀλέω: to grind, pound
ἄνθρωπος, ὁ: a man
ἀποσφάζω: to slaughter
αὐτίκα: forthwith, straightway, at once
ἀφαιρέω: to take from, take away from
ἀχθοφορέω: to bear burdens
βουλεύω: to take counsel, plan
γείτων, -ον: neighboring
γεωργός, ὁ: a farmer
δεινός, -ή, -όν: fearful, terrible
δύναμαι: to be able
ἐθέλω: to will, wish
ἐκτέμνω: to castrate
ἐπαφρόδιτος, -ον: charming, romantic

ἔρως, -ωτος, ὁ: love, desire
ἥμερος, -α, -ον: tame, tamed, reclaimed
θάνατος, ὁ: death
καταψεύδομαι: to tell lies about
μηδαμῶς: in no way, not at all
οἶστρος, ὁ: madness, frenzy
ὀνηλάτης, -ου, ὁ: a donkey-driver
ὄνος, ὁ: an ass
ὁρμή, ἡ: an attack, urge
παῖς, παιδός, ὁ: a slave, boy
πάρειμι: to be present
ῥύομαι: to rescue, save
τυγχάνω: to hit, happen
φέρω: to bear, carry
χαίρω: to rejoice, be delighted

καταψεύσασθε: ao. imper. of κατα-ψεύδομαι, "tell a lie about" + gen.
ἔτυχε: ao. of τυγχάνω, "someone happened to be" + part.
παρὼν: pr. part. of παρα-ειμι, "be present"
ἐρρύσατο: ao. of ἐρύω, "he defended"
βουλευσάμενος: ao. part., "by plotting terrible things"
μηδαμῶς ἀποσφάξῃς: ao. subj. of ἀπο-σφάττω in prohibition, "don't slaughter!"
δυνάμενον: "capable of" + inf.
οὐ μέγα: "it is not a big deal (to solve)"
φέρεται: pr. pas., "is carried away by" + dat.
λαβὼν: ao. part. of λαμβάνω, "having taken"
ἔκτεμε: ao. imper., "castrate him!"
ἀφαιρεθεὶς: ao. part. pas. of ἀπο-αἱρέω, "having been deprived of" + gen.

πίων ἔσται καὶ οἴσει φορτίον μέγα οὐδὲν ἀχθόμενος. εἰ δὲ αὐτὸς ἀπείρως ἔχεις ταύτης τῆς ἰατρείας, ἀφίξομαι δεῦρο μεταξὺ τριῶν ἢ τεττάρων ἡμερῶν καί σοι τοῦτον σωφρονέστερον προβατίου παρέξω τῇ τομῇ.»

οἱ μὲν οὖν ἔνδον ἅπαντες ἐπῄνουν τὸν σύμβουλον, ὡς εὖ λέγοι, ἐγὼ δὲ ἤδη ἐδάκρυον ὡς ἀπολέσων αὐτίκα τὸν ἐν τῷ ὄνῳ ἄνδρα καὶ ζῆν οὐκέτι ἐθέλειν ἔφην, εἰ γενοίμην εὐνοῦχος· ὥστε καὶ ὅλως ἀποσιτῆσαι τοῦ λοιποῦ ἐγνώκειν ἢ ῥῖψαι

ἀνήρ, ἀνδρός, ὁ: a man
ἄπειρος, -ον: inexperienced in (+ gen.)
ἀπόλλυμι: to kill, slay
ἀποσιτέω: to cease to eat, starve
αὐτίκα: immediately, at once
ἀφικνέομαι: to come to, arrive
ἄχθομαι: to be loaded
γιγνώσκω: to know
δακρύω: to weep
δεῦρο: hither, to this place
ἐθέλω: to will, wish
ἐπαινέω: to approve, applaud, commend
εὐνοῦχος, ὁ: a eunuch
ζάω: to live
ἡμέρα, ἡ: a day
ἰατρεία, ἡ: a medical procedure

λέγω: to speak
λοιπός, -ή, -όν: remaining, the rest
μεταξύ: between
ὅλος, -η, -ον: whole, entire, complete
οὐκέτι: no more, no longer
παρέχω: to furnish, provide, supply
πίων, -ον: fat, plump
προβάτιον, τό: a little sheep, lamb
ῥίπτω: to throw, cast, hurl
σύμβουλος, ὁ: an adviser, counselor
σώφρων, ὁ: temperate, moderate
τέσσαρες: four
τόμη, ἡ: a cutting, knife
τρεῖς: three
φέρω: to bear
φορτίον, τό: a load, burden

ἔσται: "he will be"
οἴσει: fut. of φέρω, "he will carry"
ἀπείρως ἔχεις: "if you are inexperienced"
ἀφίξομαι: fut. of ἀφικνέομαι, "I will return"
προβατίου: gen. of comparison after σωφρονέστερον, "more mild *than a lamb*"
παρέξω: fut. of παρα-ἔχω, "I will provide"
ἐπῄνουν: impf. of ἐπι-αινέω, "they were praising"
ὡς εὖ λέγοι: opt. in ind. st. in secondary sequence after ἐπῄνουν, "that he spoke well"
ὡς ἀπολέσων: fut. part. indicating cause, "because I would lose"
οὐκέτι ἐθέλειν: pr. inf. in ind. st. after ἔφην, "that I no longer wished" + inf.
εἰ γενοίμην: opt. in fut. less vivid protasis, "if I were to become"
γενοίμην: ao. opt. of γίγνομαι
ὥστε ... ἐγνώκειν: plpf. of γιγνώσκω in result clause, "so that I had decided to" + inf.
ἀποσιτῆσαι: ao. inf. of ἀπο-σιτέω, "to starve"
τοῦ λοιποῦ: "from that moment on"
ῥῖψαι: ao. inf. of ῥίπτω, "or to throw myself"

ἑαυτὸν ἐκ τοῦ ὄρους, ἔνθα ἐκπεσὼν θανάτῳ οἰκτίστῳ
ὁλόκληρος ἔτι καὶ ἀκέραιος νεκρὸς τεθνήξομαι.

News arrives that the newlywed masters died in an accident. The servants all
flee, taking Lucius with them.

[34.] ἐπεὶ δὲ ἦν νὺξ βαθεῖα, ἄγγελός τις ἀπὸ τῆς κώμης
ἧκεν εἰς τὸν ἀγρὸν καὶ τὴν ἔπαυλιν, ταύτην λέγων τὴν
νεόνυμφον κόρην τὴν ὑπὸ τοῖς λῃσταῖς γενομένην καὶ τὸν
ταύτης νυμφίον, περὶ δείλην ὀψίαν ἀμφοτέρους αὐτοὺς ἐν τῷ
αἰγιαλῷ περιπατοῦντας, ἐπιπολάσασαν ἄφνω τὴν θάλασσαν

ἄγγελος, ὁ: a messenger
ἀγρός, -οῦ, ὁ: field, land
αἰγιαλός, ὁ: the sea-shore, beach
ἀκέραιος, -ον: unharmed, inviolate
ἀμφότερος, -α, -ον: each, both
ἄφνω: suddenly
βαθύς, -εῖα, -ύ: high, deep
δείλη, ἡ: afternoon
ἐκπίπτω: to fall
ἔνθα: there
ἔπαυλις, -εως, ἡ: a farmhouse
ἐπιπολάζω: to come to the surface, rise up
ἥκω: to come
θάλασσα, ἡ: the sea
θάνατος, ὁ: death

κόρη, ἡ: a maiden, girl
κώμη, ἡ: a village
λέγω: to say
λῃστής, -οῦ, ὁ: a robber, plunderer
νεκρός, ὁ: a dead body, corpse
νεόνυμφος, -ον: newly married
νυμφίος, ὁ: a groom
νύξ, νυκτός, ἡ: night
οἴκτιστος, -η, -ον: most pitiable, lamentable
ὁλόκληρος, -ον: complete in all parts, whole
ὄρος, -εος, τό: a mountain, hill
ὄψιος, -α, -ον: late
περιπατέω: to walk around

ἐκπεσὼν: ao. part. of ἐκ-πίπτω used concessively, "although falling"
ὁλόκληρος ἔτι: "still whole"
τεθνήξομαι: fut. perf. of θνήσκω, "I will have died"
ἧκεν: impf. of ἥκω
λέγων: this pr. part. governs the inf. ἁρπάξαι and ποιῆσαι with acc. subject
    θάλασσαν in ind. st., "saying that the sea snatched them and made them"
τὴν ... γενομένην: ao. part. of γίγνομαι agreeing with κόρην, "the one who had
    been"
περιπατοῦντας: pr. part. agreeing with αὐτοὺς, the obj. of ἁρπάξαι, "snatched
    them while they were walking around"
ἐπιπολάσασαν: ao. part. agreeing with θάλασσαν, "having risen up"

ἁρπάξαι αὐτοὺς καὶ ἀφανεῖς ποιῆσαι, καὶ τέλος αὐτοῖς τοῦτο
τῆς συμφορᾶς καὶ θανάτου γενέσθαι. οἱ δὲ οἷα δὴ κεκενωμένης
τῆς οἰκίας νέων δεσποτῶν ἔγνωσαν μηκέτι μένειν ἐν τῇ
δουλείᾳ, ἀλλὰ πάντα διαρπάσαντες τὰ ἔνδον φυγῇ ἐσῴζοντο. ὁ
δὲ νομεὺς τῶν ἵππων κἀμὲ παραλαβὼν καὶ πάνθ' ὅσα δυνατὸς
συλλαβὼν ἐπικατέδησέ μοι καὶ ταῖς ἵπποις [καὶ κτήνεσιν
ἄλλοις]. ἐγὼ δὲ ἠχθόμην μὲν φέρων φορτίον ὄνου ἀληθινοῦ,
ἀλλ' οὖν ἄσμενος τὸ ἐμπόδιον τοῦτο τῆς ἐμῆς ἐδεξάμην

ἀληθινός, -ή, -όν: true, genuine
ἁρπάζω: to snatch away, carry off
ἄσμενος, -η, -ον: well-pleased, glad
ἀφανής, -ές: unseen, invisible, viewless
γιγνώσκω: to know
δείκνυμι: to bring to light, display, exhibit
δεσπότης, -ου, ὁ: a master, lord
διαρπάζω: to tear in pieces
δουλεία, ἡ: servitude, slavery, bondage
δυνατός, -ή, -όν: able, capable
ἐμπόδιος, τό: an impediment
ἔχθω: to hate
θάνατος, ὁ: death
ἵππος, ὁ/ἡ: a horse, mare
κενόω: to empty out, loot
κτῆνος, -εος, τό: a beast, animal

μένω: to stay, remain
μηκέτι: no more, no longer
νέος, νέα, νέον: young, youthful
νομεύς, -έως, ὁ: a shepherd, herdsman
οἰκία, ἡ: a house
οἷος, -α, -ον: such as
παραλαμβάνω: to take besides
ποιέω: to make
συλλαμβάνω: to collect, gather together
συμφορά, ἡ: an event, circumstance, chance
σῴζω: to save
τέλος, -εος, τό: an end
φέρω: to bear
φορτίον, τό: a load, burden
φυγή, ἡ: flight

γενέσθαι: ao. inf. also in ind. st. after λέγων, "and that this was"
οἷα δὲ: "seeing that" + part.
κεκενωμένης οἰκίας: pf. part. of κενόω in gen. abs., "the house having been
  emptied of" + gen.
ἔγνωσαν: ao. of γιγνώσκω, "they decided" + inf.
διαρπάσαντες: ao. of δια-αρπάζω, "having plundered"
παραλαβὼν: ao. part. of παρα-λαμβάνω, "having taken besides"
ὅσα δυνατὸς: "whatever he was able"
συλλαβὼν: ao. part. of συν-λαμβάνω, "having collected"
ἐπικατέδησε: ao. of ἐπι-κατα-δέω, "he tied it down upon" + dat.
ἠχθόμην: impf. of ἄχθομαι, "I was being burdened"
ἐμπόδιον: "impediment to" + gen
ἐδεξάμην: ao. of δέχομαι, "I welcomed"

ἐκτομῆς. καὶ τὴν νύκτα ὅλην ἐλθόντες ὁδὸν ἀργαλέαν καὶ
τριῶν ἄλλων ἡμερῶν τὴν ὁδὸν ἀνύσαντες ἐρχόμεθα ἐς πόλιν
τῆς Μακεδονίας Βέροιαν μεγάλην καὶ πολυάνθρωπον.

They travel to Macedonia where Lucius is sold to a priest of the Syrian goddess.

[35.] ἐνταῦθα ἔγνωσαν οἱ ἄγοντες ἡμᾶς ἱδρῦσαι καὶ
ἑαυτούς. καὶ τότε δὴ πρᾶσις ἦν ἡμῶν τῶν κτηνῶν καὶ κῆρυξ
εὔφημος ἐν ἀγορᾷ μέσῃ ἑστὼς ἐκήρυττεν. οἱ δὲ προσιόντες
ἰδεῖν ἤθελον τὰ στόματα ἡμῶν ἀνοίγοντες καὶ τὴν ἡλικίαν ἐν
τοῖς ὀδοῦσιν ἑκάστου ἔβλεπον, καὶ τοὺς μὲν ὠνήσαντο ἄλλος
ἄλλον, ἐμὲ δὲ ὕστατον ἀπολελειμμένον ὁ κῆρυξ ἐκέλευεν αὖθις

ἀγορά, -ᾶς, ἡ: a marketplace
ἄγω: to lead
ἀνοίγνυμι: to open
ἀνύω: to achieve, accomplish, complete
ἀπολείπω: to leave behind
ἀργαλέος, -α, -ον: painful, difficult
αὖθις: back, back again
Βέροια, ἡ: Beroea
βλέπω: to see
γιγνώσκω: to know
ἐθέλω: to will, wish
ἕκαστος, -η, -ον: every, each
ἐκτομή, ἡ: castration
εὔφημος, -ον: well-spoken
ἡλικία, ἡ: time of life, age
ἡμέρα, ἡ: a day
ἱδρύω: to make to sit down, to seat
ἵστημι: to make to stand
κελεύω: to bid, command, order

κῆρυξ, -υκος, ὁ: a herald, auctioneer
κηρύττω: to proclaim, shout
κτῆνος, -εος, τό: a beast, animal
Μακεδονία, ἡ: Macedonia
μέσος, -η, -ον: middle, in the middle
νύξ, νυκτός, ἡ: night
ὁδός, ἡ: a way, path, road, journey
ὀδούς, -όντος, ὁ: a tooth
ὅλος, -η, -ον: whole, entire, complete
πόλις, -εως, ἡ: a city
πολυάνθρωπος, -ον: full of people, populous
πρᾶσις, -εως, ἡ: a selling, sale
πρόσειμι: to approach
στόμα, τό: the mouth
τρεῖς: three
ὕστατος, -η, -ον: latest, last
ὠνέομαι: to buy, purchase

τὴν νύκτα ὅλην: acc. of duration, "for the whole night"
ἐλθόντες: ao. part. of ἔρχομαι, "having gone"
τριῶν ἄλλων ἡμερῶν: gen. of time within which, "within three days"
ἀνύσαντες: ao. part., "having finished"
ἔγνωσαν: ao. of γιγνώσκω, "they decided" + inf.
ἑστὼς: perf. part. of ἵστημι, "standing"
οἱ προσιόντες: pr. part. of προς-έρχομαι, "those approaching"
ὠνήσαντο: ao. of ὠνέομαι, "they bought"
ἀπολελειμμένον: pf. part. of ἀπο-λείπω, "having been left behind"

ἐπανάγειν ἐς οἶκον. «Ὁρᾷς,» ἔφη, «οὗτος μόνος οὐχ εὕρηκε κύριον.» ἡ δὲ πολλὰ πολλάκις δινουμένη καὶ μεταπίπτουσα Νέμεσις ἤγαγεν κἀμοὶ τὸν δεσπότην, οἷον οὐκ ἂν εὐξαίμην. κίναιδος γὰρ καὶ γέρων ἦν τούτων εἷς τῶν τὴν θεὸν τὴν Συρίαν εἰς τὰς κώμας καὶ τοὺς ἀγροὺς περιφερόντων καὶ τὴν θεὸν ἐπαιτεῖν ἀναγκαζόντων. τούτῳ πιπράσκομαι πολλῆς πάνυ τιμῆς, τριάκοντα δραχμῶν· καὶ στένων ἤδη τῷ δεσπότῃ εἱπόμην ἄγοντι.

ἀγρός, -οῦ, ὁ: field, land
ἄγω: to lead, carry, bring
ἀναγκάζω: to force, compel
γέρων, -οντος, ὁ: an old man
δεσπότης, -ου, ὁ: a master, lord
δινόω: to turn
δραχμή, ἡ: drachma
εἷς, μία, ἕν: one
ἐπαιτέω: to ask besides, beg
ἐπανάγω: to lead back
ἕπομαι: to follow
εὑρίσκω: to find
εὔχομαι: to pray
θεός, ἡ: a goddess
κίναιδος, ὁ: catamite
κύριος, ὁ: a lord, master

κώμη, ἡ: a village
μεταπίπτω: to fall differently, change
μόνος, -η, -ον: alone, only
Νέμεσις, -εως, ἡ: Nemesis, "Retribution"
οἶκος, ὁ: a house
πάνυ: altogether, entirely
περιφέρω: to carry around
πιπράσκω: to sell
πολλάκις: many times, often
πολύς, πολλή, πολύ: great, mighty, high
στένω: to moan, sigh, groan
Σύριος, -α, -ον: of or from Syria
τιμή, ἡ: a price
τριάκοντα: thirty

εὕρηκε: pf. of **εὑρίσκω,** "this one has found"
πολλὰ πολλάκις: "many times in many ways"
ἤγαγεν: ao. of **ἄγω,** "Nemesis led"
οὐκ ἂν εὐξαίμην: ao. indic. of **εὔχομαι** with potential **ἂν,** "such as I might never have prayed for"
τούτων εἷς … περιφερόντων … ἀναγκαζόντων: "one of those who carry around … and compel" + inf.
εἱπόμην: impf. of **ἕπομαι,** "I followed" + dat.

The Ass

Lucius is taken to home of the priests.

[36.] ἐπεὶ δὲ ἤκομεν ἔνθα ᾤκει Φίληβος – τοῦτο γὰρ
εἶχεν ὄνομα ὁ ὠνησάμενός με – μέγα εὐθὺς πρὸ τῆς θύρας
ἀνέκραγεν, «Ὦ κοράσια, δοῦλον ὑμῖν ἐώνημαι καλὸν καὶ ἁδρὸν
καὶ Καππαδόκην τὸ γένος.» ἦσαν δὲ τὰ κοράσια ταῦτα ὄχλος
κιναίδων συνεργῶν τοῦ Φιλήβου, καὶ πάντες πρὸς τὴν βοὴν
ἀνεκρότησαν· ᾤοντο γὰρ ἀληθῶς ἄνθρωπον εἶναι τὸν
ἐωνημένον. ὡς δὲ εἶδον ὄνον ὄντα τὸν δοῦλον, ἤδη ταῦτα ἐς
τὸν Φίληβον ἔσκωπτον, «Τοῦτον οὐ δοῦλον, ἀλλὰ νυμφίον

ἁδρός, -ά, -όν: thick, strong
ἀληθῶς: truly, in truth
ἀνακράζω: to cry out
ἀνακροτέω: to applaud
ἄνθρωπος, ὁ: a man
βοή, ἡ: a cry, shout
γένος, -εος, τό: race, stock, family
δοῦλος, ὁ: a slave
ἔνθα: there
ἤκω: to come
θύρα, ἡ: a door
Καππαδόκης: Cappadocian

κίναιδος, ὁ: catamite
κοράσιον, τό: a girl, maiden
νυμφίος, ὁ: a groom
οἰκέω: to inhabit, occupy
οἴομαι: to suppose, think, imagine
ὄνομα, -ατος, τό: a name
ὄχλος, ὁ: a crowd, a throng, mob
σκώπτω: to mock, jeer, scoff at
συνεργός, -όν: working together, sharing
   in a trade
Φίληβος, ὁ: Philebus
ὠνέομαι: to buy, purchase

ἔνθα ᾤκει: impf. of οἰκέω, "where he was living"
ὁ ὠνησάμενος: ao. part. of ὠνέομαι, "the one who bought"
ἐώνημαι: pf. of ὠνέομαι, "I have bought"
τὸ γένος: acc. of resp., "by race"
ἀνεκρότησαν: ao. of ἀνα-κρτοτέω, "they applauded"
εἶναι τὸν ἐωνημένον: ind. st. after ᾤοντο, "they supposed that the purchased one
   was"
ἐωνημένον: pf. part. of ὠνέομαι
ὄντα τὸν δοῦλον: ind. st. after εἶδον, "when they saw that the slave was"
ταῦτα: "in the following words"
ἔσκωπτον: impf., "they started jeering"

95

σαυτῇ πόθεν ἄγεις λαβοῦσα; ὄναιο δὲ τούτων τῶν καλῶν
γάμων καὶ τέκοις ταχέως ἡμῖν πώλους τοιούτους.»

Lucius carries the image of the goddess while the priests perform their rituals for alms.

[37.] καὶ οἱ μὲν ἐγέλων. τῇ δὲ ὑστεραίᾳ συνετάττοντο
ἐπ’ ἔργον, ὥσπερ αὐτοὶ ἔλεγον, καὶ τὴν θεὸν ἐνσκευασάμενοι
ἐμοὶ ἐπέθηκαν. εἶτα ἐκ τῆς πόλεως ἐξηλαύνομεν καὶ τὴν
χώραν περιῄειμεν. ἐπὰν δ’ εἰς κώμην τινὰ εἰσέλθοιμεν, ἐγὼ
μὲν ὁ θεοφόρητος ἱστάμην, ὁ δὲ αὐλητὴς ἐφύσα ὅμιλος ἔνθεον,

ἄγω: to lead, bring
αὐλητής, -οῦ, ὁ: a flute-player
γάμος, ὁ: a wedding, marriage
γελάω: to laugh
εἰσέρχομαι: to go into, enter
ἔνθεος, -ον: inspired, possessed
ἐνσκευάζω: to get ready, prepare
ἐξελαύνω: to ride out from
ἐπιτίθημι: to place upon
ἔργον, τό: a deed, work, act
θεοφόρητος, -ον: carrying a god
ἵστημι: to make to stand
κώμη, ἡ: a village
λέγω: to say

ὅμιλος, ὁ: a crowd, throng
ὀνίνημι: to profit, benefit
περιέρχομαι: to go around
πόθεν: whence? from where?
πόλις, -εως, ἡ: a city
πῶλος, ὁ: a foal, young horse
συντάττω: to arrange, make ready
ταχέως: quickly
τίκτω: to give birth to, bear
τοιοῦτος, -αύτη, -οῦτο: such as this
ὑστεραῖος, -α, -ον: on the day after, the next day
φυσάω: to blow
χώρα, ἡ: a place, country

σαυτῇ: dat. s. f. Philebus is addressed as a woman.
λαβοῦσα: ao. part. f. of **λαμβάνω**, "*having taken* for yourself"
ὄναιο ... τέκοις: opt. in wish for the future, "may you benefit ... and may you father"
ὄναιο: ao. opt. 2 s. of **ὀνίνημι**
τέκοις: ao. opt. 2 s. of **τέκνω**
ἡμῖν: dat. of advantage, "for us"
συνετάττοντο: impf. mid., "they organized themselves"
ἐνσκευασάμενοι: ao. part., "having prepared"
ἐπέθηκαν: ao. of **ἐπι-τίθημι**, "they placed upon" + dat.
περιῄειμεν: impf. of **περι-ἔρχομαι**, "we went around" + acc.
ἐπὰν (= **ἐπεὶ ἄν**) ... **εἰσέλθοιμεν**: past gen. temp. clause with potential **ἄν**, "whenever we might enter"
εἰσέλθοιμεν: ao. opt. of **εἰς-ἔρχομαι**
ἱστάμην: impf. intr. of **ἵστημι**, "I would stand"
ἐφύσα: impf. of **φυσάω**, "the flute-player would blow"
ὅμιλος: agreeing with **αὐλητής**, "altogether"

οἱ δὲ τὰς μίτρας ἀπορρί-
ψαντες τὴν κεφαλὴν
κάτωθεν ἐκ τοῦ αὐχένος
εἱλίσσοντες τοῖς ξίφεσιν
ἐτέμνοντο τοὺς πήχεις
καὶ τὴν γλῶτταν τῶν
ὀδόντων ὑπερβάλλων
ἕκαστος ἔτεμνε καὶ

ταύτην, ὥστε ἐν ἀκαρεῖ πάντα πεπλῆσθαι μαλακοῦ αἵματος.
ἐγὼ δὲ ταῦτα ὁρῶν τὰ πρῶτα ἔτρεμον ἑστώς, μή ποτε χρεία
τῇ θεῷ καὶ ὀνείου αἵματος γένοιτο. ἐπειδὰν δὲ κατακόψειαν

αἷμα, -ατος, τό: blood
ἀκαρής, -ές: very short
ἀπορρίπτω: to throw off
αὐχήν, -ένος, ὁ: the neck, throat
γλῶσσα, -ης, ἡ: the tongue
ἕκαστος, -η, -ον: every, each
ἑλίσσω: to turn around, twist around
ἐπειδάν: whenever
ἵστημι: to make to stand
κατακόπτω: to cut up
κάτωθεν: from below
κεφαλή, ἡ: the head
μαλακός, -ή, -όν: soft, weak, effeminate

μίτρα, ἡ: a head-dress
ξίφος, -εος, τό: a sword
ὀδούς, -όντος, ὁ: tooth
ὄνειος, -ον: of an ass
πῆχυς, ὁ: the forearm
πίμπλημι: to fill
πρῶτος, -η, -ον: first
τέμνω: to cut
τρέμω: to tremble in fear
ὑπερβάλλω: to throw beyond, stick out
    beyond
χρεία, ἡ: use, advantage, need (+ gen.)

οἱ δὲ: "others (of the group)"
ἀπορρίψαντες: ao. part. of ἀπο-ρίπτω, "having removed"
εἱλίσσοντες: pr. part., "were rolling"
καὶ ταύτην: "they would cut this too" (i.e. their tongue)
ἐν ἀκαρεῖ: "in a short while"
ὥστε ... πεπλῆσθαι: pf. inf. in result clause, "so that everything was filled with" +
    gen.
ἑστώς: pf. part. of ἵστημι, "standing"
μή ... γένοιτο: clause of fearing after ἔτρεμον, "that there might be a need" + gen.
γένοιτο: ao. opt. of γίγνομαι in sec. seq.
ἐπειδὰν (= ἐπειδή ἄν) κατακόψειαν: ao. opt. of κατα-κόπτω in past gen. temp.
    clause with potential ἄν, "whenever they would cut themselves"

οὕτως ἑαυτούς, ἐκ τῶν περιεστηκότων θεατῶν συνέλεγον ὀβολοὺς καὶ δραχμάς: ἄλλος ἰσχάδας καὶ τυροὺς καὶ οἴνου κάδον ἐπέδωκε καὶ πυροῦ μέδιμνον καὶ κριθῶν τῷ ὄνῳ. οἱ δὲ ἐκ τούτων ἐτρέφοντο καὶ τὴν ἐπ' ἐμοὶ κομιζομένην θεὸν ἐθεράπευον.

The priests bring home a young boy to abuse; Lucius accidentally betrays them to the townspeople.

[38.] καί ποτε εἰς κώμην τινὰ αὐτῶν εἰσβαλόντων ἡμῶν νεανίσκον τῶν κωμητῶν μέγαν ἀγρεύσαντες εἰσάγουσιν εἴσω ἔνθα καταλύοντες ἔτυχον. ἔπειτα ἔπασχον ἐκ τοῦ κωμήτου ὅσα συνήθη καὶ φίλια τοιούτοις ἀνοσίοις κιναίδοις ἦν. ἐγὼ δὲ

ἀγρεύω: to hunt
ἀνόσιος, -α, -ον: unholy, profane
δραχμή, ἡ: a drachma
εἰσάγω: to lead into
εἰσβάλλω: to throw into, fall upon
εἴσω: to within, into
ἔνθα: there
ἔπειτα: thereupon
ἐπιδίδωμι: to give besides, pay
θεατής, -οῦ, ὁ: one who sees, a spectator
θεραπεύω: to be an attendant, do service
ἰσχάς, -άδος, ἡ: a dried fig
κάδος, ὁ: a jar, vessel
καταλύω: to lodge
κίναιδος, ὁ: catamite
κομίζω: to carry, lead
κριθή, ἡ: barley

κώμη, ἡ: a village
κωμήτης, -ου, ὁ: a villager, countryman
μέδιμνος, ὁ: a corn-measure, bushel
νεανίσκος, ὁ: a youth, young man
ὀβολός, ὁ: an obol
οἶνος, ὁ: wine
πάσχω: to experience
περιΐστημι: to place round
πυρός, ὁ: wheat
συλλέγω: to collect, gather
συνήθης, -ες: accustomed, customary
τοιοῦτος, -αύτη, -οῦτο: such as this
τρέφω: to raise, support
τυγχάνω: to hit, happen upon
τυρός, ὁ: cheese
φίλιος, -η, -ον: beloved, dear

περιεστηκότων: pf. part. gen. pl. of περι-ἴστημι, "from those standing around"
συνέλεγον: impf., "they would collect"
ἐπέδωκε: ao. of ἐπι-δίδωμι, "others paid" + acc.
τῷ ὄνῳ: dat. of advant., "for the ass"
εἰσβαλόντων ἡμῶν: gen. abs., "when we invaded"
εἰσβαλόντων: ao. part. of εἰσ-βάλλω
ἀγρεύσαντες: ao. part., "having hunted down a youth"
ἔτυχον: ao. of τυγχάνω, "where they happened to" + part.
ἔπασχον: impf., "they experienced"
ὅσα συνήθη ... ἦν: "such things as were customary to" + dat.

ὑπεραλγήσας ἐπὶ τῇ ἐμαυτοῦ μεταβολῇ, «Καὶ μέχρι νῦν ἀνέχομαι κακῶν,» ἀναβοῆσαι, «ὦ Ζεῦ σχέτλιε,» ἠθέλησα, ἀλλ' ἡ μὲν φωνὴ οὐκ ἀνέβη μοι ἡ ἐμή, ἀλλ' ἡ τοῦ ὄνου ἐκ τοῦ φάρυγγος, καὶ μέγα ὠγκησάμην. τῶν δὲ κωμητῶν τινες ἔτυχον τότε ὄνον ἀπολωλεκότες, καὶ τὸν ἀπολωλότα ζητοῦντες ἀκούσαντές μου μέγα ἀναβοήσαντος παρέρχονται εἴσω οὐδενὶ οὐδὲν εἰπόντες ὡς ἐμοῦ τοῦ ἐκείνων ὄντος, καὶ καταλαμβάνουσι τοὺς κιναίδους ἄρρητα ἔνδον ἐργαζομένους· καὶ γέλως ἐκ τῶν ἐπεισελθόντων πολὺς γίνεται. ἔξω

ἀκούω: to hear
ἀναβαίνω: to go up, rise
ἀναβοάω: to shout aloud, cry out
ἀνέχω: to hold up
ἀπόλλυμι: to destroy utterly, kill, slay
ἄρρητος, -η, -ον: unspoken, unsaid
γέλως, ὁ: laughter
ἐθέλω: to will, wish
εἴσω: to within, into
ἔξω: out
ἐπεισέρχομαι: to come in after
ἐργάζομαι: to work, labor
ζητέω: to seek, search for
κακός, -ή, -όν: bad, evil

καταλαμβάνω: to seize upon, catch
κίναιδος, ὁ: catamite
κωμήτης, -ου, ὁ: a villager, countryman
μεταβολή, ἡ: a change, transformation
μέχρι: to a point, even so far
ὀγκάομαι: to bray
οὐδείς: and not one
παρέρχομαι: to pass by, go unnoticed
σχέτλιος, -α, -ον: unwearying, cruel
τυγχάνω: to hit, happen
ὑπεραλγέω: to feel pain
φάρυγξ, φάρυγγος, ἡ: a throat
φωνή, ἡ: a sound, tone

ὑπεραλγήσας: ao. part. of ὑπερ-αλγέω, "deeply pained"
μέχρι νῦν: "up until now"
ἀναβοῆσαι: ao. inf. after ἠθέλησα, "I wished to cry out"
ἀνέβη: ao. of ἀνα-βαίνω, "the voice did not rise up"
ὠγκησάμην: ao. of ὀγκάομαι, "I brayed"
ἔτυχον: ao. of τυγχάνω, "they happened to" + part.
ἀπολωλεκότες: pf. part. of ἀπόλλυμι after ἔτυχον, "to have lost"
ἀπολωλότα: pf. part. acc. s. of ἀπόλλυμι, "seeking *the lost one*"
ἀκούσαντες: ao. part., "having heard" + gen.
ἀναβοήσαντος: ao. part. agreeing with μου, "raising a shout"
ὡς ἐμοῦ ... ὄντος: gen. abs., "as though me being theirs (or so they thought)"
ἄρρητα: n. pl., "unspeakable acts"
τῶν ἐπεισελθόντων: ao. part. of ἐπι-εἰσ-έρχομαι, "from those coming upon them inside"

ἐκδραμόντες ὅλῃ τῇ κώμῃ τῷ λόγῳ διέδωκαν τῶν ἱερέων τὴν
ἀσέλγειαν.

Ashamed at having been exposed, they depart and punish Lucius.

οἱ δὲ αἰδούμενοι δεινῶς ταῦτα ἐληλεγμένα τῆς ἐπιούσης
νυκτὸς εὐθὺς ἔνθεν ἐξήλασαν, καὶ ἐπειδὴ ἐγένοντο ἐν τῇ ἐρήμῳ
τῆς ὁδοῦ ἐχαλέπαινον καὶ ὠργίζοντο ἐμοὶ τῷ μηνύσαντι τὰ
ἐκείνων μυστήρια. καὶ τοῦτο μὲν ἀνεκτὸν τὸ δεινὸν ἦν, κακῶς
τῷ λόγῳ ἀκούειν, ἀλλὰ τὰ μετὰ τοῦτο οὐκέτ᾽ ἀνεκτά· τὴν γὰρ
θεὸν ἀφελόντες μου καὶ χαμαὶ καταθέμενοι καὶ τὰ στρώματά

αἰδέομαι: to be ashamed	κακῶς: badly
ἀκούω: to hear	κατατίθημι: to place, put down
ἀνεκτός, -ή, -όν: bearable, sufferable, tolerable	κώμη, ἡ: a village
ἀσέλγεια, ἡ: licentiousness	λόγος, ὁ: a word, speech, story
ἀφαιρέω: to take from, take away	μηνύω: to disclose, reveal, betray
δεινός, -ή, -όν: fearful, terrible	μυστήριον, τό: a mystery, secret rite
δεινῶς: terribly, dreadfully	νύξ, νυκτός, ἡ: night
διαδίδωμι: to pass on	ὁδός, ἡ: a way, path, road
ἐκτρέχω: to run out	ὅλος, -η, -ον: whole, entire, complete
ἐλέγχω: to disgrace	ὀργίζομαι: to be angry, rage
ἐξελαύνω: to drive out	οὐκέτι: no more, no longer
ἐπέρχομαι: to come upon, approach	στρῶμα, -ατος, τό: trappings
ἔρημος, -ον: desolate, lonely, solitary	χαλεπαίνω: to be sore, be grievous
ἱερεύς, -έως, ὁ: a priest	χαμαί: on the ground

ἐκδραμόντες: ao. part. of ἐκ-τρέχω, "having run out"

διέδωκαν: ao. of δια-δίδωμι, "they spread abroad" + acc.

ταῦτα ἐληλεγμένα: pf. part. of ἐλέγχω, "these disgraces"

τῆς ἐπιούσης νυκτὸς: gen. of time within which, "in the course of the following night"

ἐξήλασαν: ao. of ἐξ-ἐλαύνω, "they drove out from there"

ἐγένοντο: ao. of γίγνομαι, "once they were"

ἐμοὶ τῷ μηνύσαντι: ao. part., "at me who had disclosed"

κακῶς ἀκούειν: serving as the pas. of λέγω, "to be spoken of badly," "to be abused" + dat. of instr.

τὰ μετὰ τοῦτο: "the things after this"

ἀφελόντες: ao. part. of ἀπο-αιρέω, "having removed"

καταθέμενοι: ao. part. of κατα-τίθημι, "having set down"

μου πάντα περισπάσαντες γυμνὸν ἤδη προσδέουσί με δένδρῳ
μεγάλῳ, εἶτα ἐκείνῃ τῇ ἐκ τῶν ἀστραγάλων μάστιγι παίοντες
ὀλίγον ἐδέησαν ἀποκτεῖναι, κελεύοντές με τοῦ λοιποῦ ἄφωνον
εἶναι θεοφόρητον. καὶ μὴν καὶ ἀποσφάξαι μετὰ τὰς μάστιγας
ἐβουλεύσαντο ὡς ἐς ὕβριν αὐτοὺς βαλόντα πολλὴν καὶ τῆς
κώμης οὐκ ἐργασαμένους ἐκβαλόντα· ἀλλ' ὥστε με μὴ
ἀποκτεῖναι, δεινῶς αὐτοὺς ἡ θεὸς ἐδυσώπησε χαμαὶ καθημένη
καὶ οὐκ ἔχουσα ὅπως ὁδεύοι.

ἀποκτείνω: to kill, slay
ἀποσφάζω: to slaughter
ἀστράγαλος, ὁ: knuckle bone
ἄφωνος, -ον: speechless, silent
βάλλω: to throw
βουλεύω: to take counsel, plan
γυμνός, -ή, -όν: naked, unclad
δεινῶς: terribly, dreadfully
δένδρον, τό: a tree
δυσωπέω: to put to shame
ἐκβάλλω: to throw out, cast out of
ἐργάζομαι: to work, labor
θεοφόρητος, -ον: carrying a god

κάθημαι: to be seated
κελεύω: to bid, command, order
κώμη, ἡ: a village
λοιπός, -ή, -όν: remaining, the rest
μάστιξ, -ιγος, ἡ: a whip, scourge
ὁδεύω: to go, travel
ὀλίγος, -η, -ον: few, little, small
παίω: to strike, hit
περισπάω: to strip off
προσδέω: to bind, tie to
ὕβρις, -εως, ἡ: wantonness, insolence,
  hubris
χαμαί: on the ground

περισπάσαντες: ao. part. of **περι-σπάω**, "having stripped off"
προσδέουσι: vivid pres., "they tie me to" + dat.
ἐκείνῃ τῇ μάστιγι: dat. instr., "with that whip" (although no whip has been
  mentioned yet; cf. the parallel passage in Apuleius *Met.* 8.30)
ὀλίγον ἐδέησαν: ao. of **δέω**, "they lacked by a little" i.e., "they almost" +inf.
ἀποκτεῖναι: ao. inf. after **ἐδέησαν**, "they almost killed me"
τοῦ λοιποῦ: gen. of indef. duration, "from then on"
καὶ μὴν καὶ: indicating a climax, "moreover"
ἀποσφάξαι: ao. inf. of **ἀπο-σφάττω** after **ἐβουλεύσαντο**, "they planned to
  slaughter"
ὡς ... βαλόντα ... ἐκβαλόντα: **ὡς** + part. giving an imputed motive, "because I cast
  them ... and caused them to be cast out (so I suppose)"
(ἐκ)βαλόντα: ao. part. acc. s. of **(ἐκ)βάλλω**
οὐκ ἐργασαμένους: ao. part., "not having completed"
ὥστε με μὴ ἀποκτεῖναι: result clause after **ἐδυσώπησεν**, "she shamed them so
  that they did not kill me"
καθημένη: pr. part. of **κατα-ἧμαι**, "being placed down"
οὐκ ἔχουσα: "not having a way"
ὅπως ὁδεύοι: opt. in ind. quest. in sec. seq. after **ἔχουσα**, "how she would make
  her way"

Lucian

At a rich man's estate, a cook plots to kill Lucius and substitute his meat for a ham he has lost.

[39.] ἐντεῦθεν οὖν μετὰ τὰς μάστιγας λαβὼν τὴν δέσποιναν ἐβάδιζον καὶ πρὸς ἑσπέραν ἤδη καταλύομεν εἰς ἀγρὸν πλουτοῦντος ἀνθρώπου. καὶ ἦν οὗτος ἔνδον καὶ τὴν θεὸν μάλα ἄσμενος τῇ οἰκίᾳ ὑπεδέξατο καὶ θυσίας αὐτῇ προσήγαγεν. ἐνθάδε οἶδα μέγαν κίνδυνον αὐτὸς ὑποστάς· τῶν φίλων γάρ τις τῷ δεσπότῃ τῶν ἀγρῶν ἔπεμψε δῶρον ὄνου ἀγρίου μηρόν· τοῦτον ὁ μάγειρος σκευάσαι λαβὼν ῥᾳθυμίᾳ ἀπώλεσε, κυνῶν πολλῶν λαθραίως εἴσω παρελθόντων·

ἄγριος, -α, -ον: savage, wild
ἀγρός, -οῦ, ὁ: field, land
ἄνθρωπος, ὁ: a man
ἀπόλλυμι: to destroy, kill, loose
ἄσμενος, -η, -ον: well-pleased, glad
βαδίζω: to go, walk
δέσποινα, ἡ: the mistress, lady
δεσπότης, -ου, ὁ: a master, lord
δῶρον, τό: a gift, present
εἴσω: to within, into
ἐνθάδε: thither, hither
ἐντεῦθεν: hence, thence
ἑσπέρα, ἡ: evening
θυσία, ἡ: an offering, sacrifice
καταλύω: to lodge
κίνδυνος, ὁ: a danger, risk, hazard
κύων, ὁ: a dog

λαθραίως: secretly
μάγειρος, ὁ: a cook
μάλα: very much
μάστιξ, -ιγος, ἡ: a whip, scourge
μηρός, ὁ: a thigh, ham
οἶδα: to know
οἰκία, ἡ: a house
παρέρχομαι: to go beside
πέμπω: to send
πλουτέω: to be rich, have wealth
προσάγω: to bring to
ῥᾳθυμία, ἡ: laziness, carelessness
σκευάζω: to prepare, make ready
ὑποδέχομαι: to receive (in one's home), host
ὑφίστημι: to place under
φίλος, ὁ: a friend

λαβὼν: ao. part. of λαμβάνω, "having taken"
πλουτοῦντος: pr. part. agreeing with ἀνθρώπου, "a man who is rich"
ὑπεδέξατο: ao. of ὑπο-δέχομαι, "he received the goddess"
προσήγαγεν: ao. of προσ-άγω, "he brought before" + dat.
αὐτὸς ὑποστάς: ao. part. intrans. of ὑπο-ἴστημι in ind. st. after οἶδα, "I knew that I was placed under" + acc.
ἔπεμψε δῶρον: ao. of πέμπω, "one of his friends sent as a gift"
σκευάσαι: ao. inf. of purpose, "in order to prepare"
λαβὼν: ao. part of λαμβάνω, "having taken"
ἀπώλεσεν: ao. of ἀπόλλυμι, "he lost it"
κυνῶν ... παρελθόντων: gen. abs., "the dogs having passed by"
παρελθόντων: ao. part. of παρα-ἔρχομαι

ὃς δεδιὼς πληγὰς πολλὰς καὶ βάσανον ἐκ τῆς ἀπωλείας τοῦ
μηροῦ ἔγνω κρεμάσαι ἑαυτὸν ἐκ τοῦ τραχήλου. ἡ δὲ γυνὴ ἡ
τούτου, κακὸν ἐξαίσιον ἐμόν, «Ἀλλὰ μήτε ἀπόθνησκε,» εἶπεν,
«ὦ φίλτατε, μήτε ἀθυμίᾳ τοιαύτῃ δῷς σεαυτόν· πειθόμενος
γάρ μοι πράξεις εὖ πάντα. τῶν κιναίδων τὸν ὄνον λαβὼν ἔξω
εἰς ἔρημον χωρίον κἄπειτα σφάξας αὐτὸν τὸ μέρος μὲν ἐκεῖνο
τὸν μηρὸν ἀποτεμὼν κόμιζε δεῦρο καὶ κατασκευάσας τῷ
δεσπότῃ ἀπόδος καὶ τὸ ἄλλο τοῦ ὄνου κάτω που ἐς κρημνὸν

ἀθυμία, ἡ: faintheartedness, despair
ἀποδίδωμι: to give over
ἀποθνήσκω: to die
ἀποτέμνω: to cut off, sever
ἀπώλεια, ἡ: destruction, loss
βάσανος, ἡ: torture
γιγνώσκω: to know
γυνή, γυναικός, ἡ: a woman, wife
δείδω: to fear
δεσπότης, -ου, ὁ: a master, lord
δεῦρο: hither
δίδωμι: to give
ἐξαίσιος, -α, -ον: portentous
ἔξω: out
ἔπειτα: thereupon
ἐρῆμος, -ον: desolate, lonely, solitary
κακός, -ή, -όν: bad, ill

κατασκευάζω: to prepare fully
κάτω: down, downwards
κίναιδος, ὁ: catamite
κομίζω: to carry, lead
κρεμάννυμι: to hang
κρημνός, ὁ: an overhang, cliff
μέρος, -εος, τό: a part, share
μηρός, ὁ: a thigh, ham
πείθω: to prevail upon, persuade
πληγή, ἡ: a blow, stroke
πράττω: to do, act
σφάζω: to slay, slaughter
τοιοῦτος, -αύτη, -οῦτο: such as this
τράχηλος, ὁ: the neck, throat
φίλτατος, -η, -ον: dearest
χωρίον, τό: a place, spot

ὅς: "that one" i.e. the chef
δεδιὼς: pf. part. of δείδω, "fearing"
ἔγνω: ao. of γιγνώσκω, "he decided" + inf.
κρεμάσαι: ao. inf. of κρεμάννυμι, "to hang himself"
κακὸν ἐξαίσιον: in apposition to γυνή, "my evil beyond fate"
μήτε ... δῷς: subj. of δίδωμι in prohibition, "don't give yourself"
πράξεις: fut. of πράττω, "you will do"
λαβὼν: ao. part of λαμβάνω, "having taken"
κἄπειτα: (= καὶ ἔπειτα)
σφάξας: ao. part of σφάττω, "having slaughtered"
ἀποτεμὼν: ao. part. of ἀπο-τέμνω, "having cut off"
κατασκευάσας: ao. part., "having prepared"
ἀπόδος: ao. imper. of ἀπο-δίδωμι, "give it" + dat.
που: "somewhere"

ἄφες: δόξει γὰρ ἀποδρὰς οἴχεσθαί ποι καὶ εἶναι ἀφανής. ὁρᾷς δὲ ὡς ἔστιν εὔσαρκος καὶ τοῦ ἀγρίου ἐκείνου πάντα ἀμείνων;»

ὁ δὲ μάγειρος τῆς γυναικὸς ἐπαινέσας τὸ βούλευμα, «Ἄριστα,» ἔφη, «σοι, ὦ γύναι, ταῦτα, καὶ τούτῳ μόνῳ τῷ ἔργῳ τὰς μάστιγας φυγεῖν ἔχω, καὶ τοῦτό μοι ἤδη πεπράξεται.»

ὁ μὲν οὖν ἀνόσιος οὗτος οὑμὸς μάγειρος ἐμοῦ πλησίον ἐστὼς τῇ γυναικὶ ταῦτα συνεβουλεύετο.

ἄγριος, -α, -ον: savage, wild
ἀμείνων, -ον: better (+ gen.)
ἀνόσιος, -α, -ον: unholy, profane
ἀποδιδράσκω: to run away, escape
ἄριστος, -η, -ον: best
ἀφανής, -ές: unseen, viewless
ἀφίημι: to send forth, throw away
βούλευμα, -ατος, τό: a design, plan
γυνή, γυναικός, ἡ: a woman, wife
δοκέω: to seem
ἐπαινέω: to approve, applaud, commend

εὔσαρκος, -ον: fleshy, plump
ἵστημι: to make to stand
μάγειρος, ὁ: a cook
μάστιξ, -ιγος, ἡ: a whip, scourge
μόνος, -η, -ον: alone, only
οἴχομαι: to be gone
πλήσιος, α, ον: near, close
πράττω: to do
συμβουλεύω: to advise, counsel
φεύγω: to flee, escape

ἄφες: ao. imper. of ἀπο-ἵημι, "dispatch the rest"
δόξει: fut., "he will seem" + inf.
ἀποδρὰς: ao. part. of ἀπο-διδράσκω, "having run off"
ποι: "to somewhere"
ὡς ἔστιν: ind. st. after ὁρᾷς, "that he is"
πάντα: acc. of resp., "in all ways"
ἐκείνου ἀμείνων: "better than that one" i.e. the wild ass
ἐπαινέσας: ao. part. of ἐπαινέω, "having praised the plan"
φυγεῖν ἔχω: "I am able to flee"
πεπράξεται: fut. pf. mid. of πράττω with passive force, "this will be done"
οὑμὸς: (= ὁ ἐμὸς)
ἐστὼς: pf. part. of ἵστημι, "standing"

Lucius manages to escape the plot of the cook.

[40.] ἐγὼ δὲ τὸ μέλλον ἤδη προορώμενος κράτιστον ἔγνων τὸ σῴζειν ἐμαυτὸν ἐκ τῆς κοπίδος καὶ ῥήξας τὸν ἱμάντα ᾧ διηγόμην καὶ ἀνασκιρτήσας ἵεμαι δρόμῳ εἴσω ἔνθα ἐδείπνουν οἱ κίναιδοι σὺν τῷ δεσπότῃ τῶν ἀγρῶν. ἐνταῦθα εἰσδραμὼν ἀνατρέπω πάντα τῷ σκιρτήματι καὶ λυχνίαν καὶ τραπέζας· κἀγὼ μὲν ᾤμην κομψόν τι τοῦτο πρὸς σωτηρίαν ἐμὴν εὑρηκέναι, καὶ τὸν δεσπότην τῶν ἀγρῶν κελεύειν εὐθέως ὡς ἀγέρωχον ὄνον ἐμὲ κατακλεισθέντα ποι φυλάττεσθαι

ἀγέρωχος, -ον: high-spirited
ἀγρός, -οῦ, ὁ: field, land
ἀνασκιρτάω: to leap, kick
ἀνατρέπω: to overturn, upset
γιγνώσκω: to know
δειπνέω: to take a meal, dine
δεσπότης, -ου, ὁ: a master, lord
διάγω: to lead across
δρόμος, ὁ: a course, running
εἰστρέχω: to run in
εἴσω: to within, into
ἔνθα: there
εὐθέως: immediately, straightaway
εὑρίσκω: to find
ἵεμαι: to speed, rush
ἱμάς, ὁ: a leather strap
κατακλείω: to shut in, enclose

κελεύω: to bid, command, order
κίναιδος, ὁ: catamite
κομψός, -ή, -όν: smart, clever, ingenious
κοπίς, -ίδος, ἡ: a cleaver
κράτιστος, -η, -ον: strongest, mightiest
λυχνία, ἡ: lampstand
μέλλω: to be going to, be about to
οἴομαι: to suppose, think, imagine
ὄνος, ὁ: an ass
προοράω: to foresee
ῥήγνυμι: to break
σκίρτημα, -ατος, τό: a leap, kick
σῴζω: to save
σωτηρία, ἡ: deliverance, safety
τράπεζα, -ης, ἡ: a table
φυλάττω: to keep watch, guard

τὸ μέλλον: pr. part. of μέλλω, "the future"
ἔγνων: ao. of γιγνώσκω, "I decided to"
τὸ σῴζειν: art. inf., subj. of ind. st. after ἔγνων, "that saving myself was best"
ῥήξας: ao. part. of ῥήγνυμι, "having broken"
ᾧ διηγόμην: impf. of δια-άγω, "by which I was being led"
ἀνασκιρτήσας: ao. part. of ἀνα-σκιρτάω, "having leapt"
ἵεμαι: pr. mid. of ἵημι, "I hurl myself"
εἰσδραμὼν: ao. part. of εἰσ-τρέχω, "having run in"
εὑρηκέναι: ao. inf. of εὑρίσκω in ind. st. after ᾤμην, "I supposed *that I had found*"
κελεύειν: ind. st. after ᾤμην, "and that the master would order"
ὡς ἀγέρωχον ὄνον (sc. ὄντα): ὡς + part. giving an imputed motive, "since I was a high-spirited ass"
κατακλεισθέντα: ao. pas. part. of κατα-κλείω agreeing with ἐμὲ, "me having been be locked up"
φυλάττεσθαι: pr. pas. inf. in ind. com. after κελεύειν, "order me to be guarded"

ἀσφαλῶς· ἀλλά με τοῦτο τὸ κομψὸν εἰς ἔσχατον ἤνεγκεν
κινδύνου. λυττᾶν δόξαντές με ξίφη πολλὰ ἤδη καὶ λόγχας ἐπ᾽
ἐμὲ ἐσπάσαντο καὶ ξύλα μακρά, καὶ εἶχον οὕτως ὥστε
ἀποκτενεῖν με. ἐγὼ δὲ ὁρῶν τοῦ δεινοῦ τὸ μέγεθος δρόμῳ εἴσω
παρέρχομαι ἔνθα οἱ ἐμοὶ δεσπόται κοιμηθήσεσθαι ἔμελλον. οἱ
δὲ θεασάμενοι τοῦτο συγκλείουσι τὰς θύρας εὖ μάλα ἔξωθεν.

Moving on to another village, the priests are accused of theft.

[41]. ἐπειδὴ δὲ ἤδη ὄρθρος ἦν, ἀράμενος τὴν θεὸν αὖθις
ἀπῄειν ἅμα τοῖς ἀγύρταις καὶ ἀφικόμεθα εἰς κώμην ἄλλην

ἀγύρτης, -ου, ὁ: a collector, beggar
αἴρω: to raise, take up
ἀπέρχομαι: to go away, depart
ἀποκτείνω: to kill, slay
ἀσφαλῶς: firmly, securely
αὖθις: back, again
ἀφικνέομαι: to come to, arrive
δεινός, -ή, -όν: fearful, terrible
δεσπότης, -ου, ὁ: a master, lord
δρόμος, ὁ: a course, running
εἴσω: to within, into
ἔνθα: there
ἔξωθεν: from without
ἔσχατος, -η, -ον: utmost, extreme
θεάομαι: to look on, see
θύρα, ἡ: a door
κίνδυνος, ὁ: a danger, risk, hazard

κοιμάω: to put to sleep
κομψός, -ή, -όν: smart, clever, ingenious
κώμη, ἡ: a village
λόγχη, ἡ: a spear
λυττάω: to be raging, be mad
μακρός, -ά, -όν: long
μάλα: very, very much
μέγεθος, -εος, τό: greatness, magnitude, size
μέλλω: to be going to, be about to
ξίφος, -εος, τό: a sword
ξύλον, τό: a piece of wood, stick
ὄρθρος, ὁ: daybreak, dawn
παρέρχομαι: to go
σπάω: to draw
συγκλείω: to shut up
φέρω: to bear, bring

τὸ κομψὸν: "the ruse"
ἤνεγκεν: ao. of **φέρω**, "brought (me) to"
λυττᾶν: pr. inf. after **δόξαντές**, "thinking me to be mad"
ἐσπάσαντο: ao. of **σπάω**, "they drew their swords"
εἶχον οὕτως: impf., "they began to be in such a manner," i.e. "they prepared themselves thus" + result clause
ὥστε ἀποκτενεῖν: fut. inf. in result clause, "so that they would kill me"
τοῦ δεινοῦ (sc. **κινδύνου**): "the magnitude of the terrible danger"
κοιμηθήσεσθαι: fut. pas. inf. of **κοιμέω** after **ἔμελλον**, "where they were about to go to bed"
εὖ μάλα ἔξωθεν: "completely from the outside"
ἀράμενος: ao. part. of **αἴρω**, "having lifted"
ἀπῄειν: impf. of **ἀπο-έρχομαι**, "I was going out"
ἀφικόμεθα: ao. of **ἀπο-ἱκνέομαι**, "we arrived"

μεγάλην καὶ πολυάνθρωπον, ἐν ᾗ καὶ καινότερόν τι
ἐτερατεύσαντο, τὴν θεὸν μὴ μεῖναι ἐν ἀνθρώπου οἰκίᾳ, τῆς δὲ
παρ' ἐκείνοις μάλιστα τιμωμένης ἐπιχωρίου δαίμονος τὸν ναὸν
οἰκῆσαι. οἱ δὲ καὶ μάλα ἄσμενοι τὴν ξένην θεὸν ὑπεδέξαντο τῇ
σφῶν αὐτῶν θεῷ συνοικίσαντες, ἡμῖν δὲ οἰκίαν ἀπέδειξαν
ἀνθρώπων πενήτων. ἐνταῦθα συχνὰς ἡμέρας οἱ δεσπόται
διατρίψαντες ἀπιέναι ἤθελον εἰς τὴν πλησίον πόλιν καὶ τὴν
θεὸν ἀπῄτουν τοὺς ἐπιχωρίους, καὶ αὐτοὶ ἐς τὸ τέμενος

ἄνθρωπος, ὁ: a man
ἀπαιτέω: to ask back, demand
ἀπέρχομαι: to go away, depart
ἀποδείκνυμι: to appoint, assign
ἄσμενος, -η, -ον: well-pleased, glad
δαίμων, -ονος, ὁ: divine spirit, god
δεσπότης, -ου, ὁ: a master, lord
διατρίβω: to spend time
ἐθέλω: to will, wish
ἐπιχώριος, -α, -ον: of or from a place, native
ἡμέρα, ἡ: a day
καινός, -ή, -όν: new, fresh, novel
μάλα: very, very much
μένω: to stay, remain
ναός, ὁ: a temple

ξένος, -α, -ον: foreign
οἰκέω: to inhabit, occupy
οἰκία, ἡ: a house
πένης, -ητος: poor
πλήσιος, α, ον: near, close
πόλις, -εως, ἡ: a city
πολυάνθρωπος, -ον: full of people, populous
συνοικίζω: to make to live with, house with
συχνός, -ή, -όν: long, many
σφός, σφή, σφόν: their, their own
τέμενος, -εος, τό: a sacred space
τερατεύομαι: to say monstrous things
ὑποδέχομαι: to receive (in one's home), host

ἐν ᾗ: "in which" (village)
μὴ μεῖναι: ao. inf. of μένω in apposition to the object of ἐτερατεύσαντο, "a more novel thing, namely *that the goddess not remain*." μὴ is used instead of οὐ.
τῆς ... δαίμονος: "the temple of the local goddess"
οἰκῆσαι: ao. inf. also after ἐτερατεύσαντο, "but that she inhabit"
ὑπεδέξαντο: ao. of ὑπο-δέχομαι, "they received"
συνοικίσαντες: ao. of συν-οικέω, "having housed her with" + dat.
ἀπέδειξαν: ao. of ἀπο-δείκνυμι, "they showed"
διατρίψαντες: ao. of δια-τρίβω, "having spent time"
ἀπιέναι: pr. inf. of ἀπο-ἔρχομαι after ἤθελον, "they desired to go away"
ἀπῄτουν: impf. of ἀπο-αἰτέω, "they were seeking"

παρελθόντες ἐκόμιζον αὐτὴν καὶ θέντες ἐπ᾽ ἐμοὶ ἤλαυνον ἔξω.
ἔτυχον δὲ οἱ δυσσεβεῖς εἰς τὸ τέμενος ἐκεῖνο παρελθόντες
ἀνάθημα φιάλην χρυσῆν κλέψαντες, ἣν ὑπὸ τῇ θεῷ ἔφερον· οἱ
δὲ κωμῆται αἰσθόμενοι τοῦτο εὐθὺς ἐδίωκον, εἶτα ὡς πλησίον
ἐγένοντο, καταπηδήσαντες ἀπὸ τῶν ἵππων εἴχοντο αὐτῶν ἐν
τῇ ὁδῷ καὶ δυσσεβεῖς καὶ ἱεροσύλους ἐκάλουν καὶ ἀπήτουν τὸ
κλαπὲν ἀνάθημα, καὶ ἐρευνῶντες πάντα εὗρον αὐτὸ ἐν τῷ
κόλπῳ τῆς θεοῦ. δήσαντες οὖν τοὺς γυνίας ἦγον ὀπίσω καὶ
τοὺς μὲν εἰς τὴν εἰρκτὴν ἐμβάλλουσι, τὴν δὲ θεὸν τὴν ἐπ᾽ ἐμοὶ

ἄγω: to lead, carry
αἰσθάνομαι: to perceive, notice
ἀνάθημα, -ατος, τό: a votive offering
ἀπαιτέω: to demand back
γύννις, -ίδος, ὁ: an effeminate man
διώκω: to pursue
δυσσεβής, -ές: ungodly, impious, profane
εἰρκτή, ἡ: a prison
ἐλαύνω: to drive, set in motion
ἐμβάλλω: to throw in, put in
ἔξω: out
ἐρευνάω: to seek, search
εὑρίσκω: to find
ἱερόσυλος, -α, -ον: sacrilegious, impious
ἵππος, ὁ: a horse, mare

καταπηδάω: to leap down
κλέπτω: to steal
κόλπος, ὁ: the bosom
κομίζω: to carry, lead
κωμήτης, -ου, ὁ: a villager
ὁδός, ἡ: a way, path, road
ὀπίσω: back
παρέρχομαι: to go beside, come to
πλήσιος, -α, -ον: near, close
τέμενος, -εος, τό: a sacred space
τίθημι: to set, put, place
τυγχάνω: to hit, happen
φέρω: to bear, carry
φιάλη, ἡ: a bowl
χρύσεος, -η, -ον: golden, of gold

παρελθόντες: ao. part. of παρα-ἔρχομαι, "having come to"
θέντες: ao. part. of τίθημι, "having placed"
ἔτυχον: ao. of τυγχάνω, "they happened to" + part.
παρελθόντες: ao. part. of παρα-ἔρχομαι, "having arrived
κλέψαντες: ao. part. of κλέπτω with ἔτυχον, "they happened to have stolen"
αἰσθόμενοι: ao. part. of αἰσθάνομαι, "having realized this"
ἐγένοντο: ao. of γίγνομαι, "as they became near"
καταπηδήσαντες: ao. part. of κατα-πηδάω, "having leapt down"
εἴχοντο: impf. mid. of ἔχω, "they detained" + gen.
ἐκάλουν: impf. of καλέω, "they called them impious"
τὸ κλαπέν: ao. part. pas. of κλέπτω, "the stolen object"
εὗρον: ao. of εὑρίσκω, "they found it"
δήσαντες: ao. part. of δέω, "having bound"

κομιζομένην ἀράμενοι ναῷ ἄλλῳ ἔδωκαν, τὸ δὲ χρυσίον τῇ πολίτιδι θεῷ πάλιν ἀπέδωκαν.

Lucius is sold to a miller, who puts him to work.

[42.] τῇ δὲ ὑστεραίᾳ τά τε σκεύη κἀμὲ πιπράσκειν ἔγνωσαν, καὶ ἀπέδοντό με ξένῳ ἀνθρώπῳ τὴν πλησίον κώμην οἰκοῦντι, τέχνην ἔχοντι ἄρτους πέττειν· οὗτός με παραλαβὼν καὶ πυρῶν μεδίμνους δέκα ὠνησάμενος, ἐπιθείς μοι τὸν πυρὸν οἴκαδε ἤλαυνεν ὡς ἑαυτὸν ὁδὸν ἀργαλέαν· ὡς δὲ ἥκομεν, εἰσάγει με εἰς τὸν μυλῶνα, καὶ ὁρῶ πολὺ πλῆθος ἔνδον

αἴρω: to take, lift up
ἄνθρωπος, ὁ: a man
ἀποδίδωμι: to give back, return
ἀργαλέος, -α, -ον: painful, grievous, difficult
ἄρτος, ὁ: a loaf of bread
γιγνώσκω: to know
δέκα: ten
δίδωμι: to give
εἰσάγω: to lead into
ἐλαύνω: to drive, set in motion
ἐπιτίθημι: to lay, put or place upon
ἔτος, -εος, τό: a year
ἥκω: to come
κομίζω: to carry, lead
κώμη, ἡ: a village
μέδιμνος, ὁ: a corn-measure, bushel
μυλών, -ῶνος, ὁ: a millhouse
ναός, ὁ: a temple

ξένος, -η, -ον: foreign, strange
ὁδός, ἡ: a way, path, road
οἴκαδε: home, homewards
οἰκέω: to inhabit, live
πάλιν: back, backwards
παραλαμβάνω: to receive from
πέττω: to bake
πιπράσκω: to sell
πλῆθος, -εος, τό: a great number
πλήσιος, -α, -ον: near, close
πόλιτις, -ιδος: belonging to one's city
πυρός, ὁ: wheat
σκεύη, τά: possessions, belongings
τέχνη, ἡ: art, skill, craft
ὑστεραῖος, -α, -ον: on the day after, the next day
χρυσίον, τό: a piece of gold
ὠνέομαι: to buy, purchase

ἀράμενοι: ao. part. of αἴρω, "having lifted"
ἔδωκαν: ao. part. of δίδωμι, "they gave her"
ἀπέδωκαν: ao. part. of ἀπο-δίδωμι, "they returned"
ἔγνωσαν: ao. part. of γιγνώσκω, "they decided to" + inf.
ἀπέδοντό: ao. mid. of ἀπο-δίδωμι, "they sold me"
πέττειν: pr. inf. after ἔχοντι, "having the skill *to bake*"
παραλαβὼν: ao. part. of παρα-λαμβάνω, "having received me"
ὠνησάμενος: ao. part. of ὠνέομαι, "having bought"
ἐπιθείς: ao. part. of ἐπι-τίθημι, "having placed upon" + dat.
ὡς ἑαυτὸν: "to his own (house)"

ὁμοδούλων κτηνῶν, καὶ μύλαι πολλαὶ ἦσαν, καὶ πᾶσαι τούτοις
ἐστρέφοντο, καὶ πάντα ἐκεῖνα μεστὰ ἦν ἀλεύρων. καὶ τότε μέν
με οἷα ξένον δοῦλον καὶ φορτίον βαρύτατον ἀράμενον καὶ ὁδὸν
ἀργαλέαν ἀφιγμένον ἀναπαύεσθαι ἔνδον ἀφῆκαν, τῇ δὲ
ὑστεραίᾳ ὀθόνῃ τὰ ὄμματά μου σκεπάσαντες ὑποζευγνύουσί με
τῇ κώπῃ τῆς μύλης, εἶτα ἤλαυνον. ἐγὼ δὲ ἠπιστάμην ὅπως
χρὴ ἀλεῖν πολλάκις παθών, προσεποιούμην δὲ ἀγνοεῖν· ἀλλὰ
μάτην ἤλπισα. λαβόντες γὰρ πολλοὶ τῶν ἔνδον βακτηρίας

ἀγνοέω: not to know
αἴρω: to take up, raise
ἄλευρον, τό: flour
ἀλέω: to grind
ἀναπαύομαι: to rest
ἀργαλέος, -α, -ον: painful, grievous,
    difficult
ἀφίημι: to send forth
ἀφικνέομαι: to come to, arrive
βακτηρία, ἡ: a staff, cane
βαρύς, -εῖα, -ύ: heavy
δοῦλος, ὁ: a slave
ἐλαύνω: to drive, set in motion
ἐλπίζω: to hope
ἐπίσταμαι: to know
κτῆνος, -εος, τό: a beast, animal
κώπη, ἡ: a handle, spoke

μάτην: in vain, idly, fruitlessly
μεστός, -ή, -όν: full of (+ gen.)
μύλη, ἡ: a millstone
ξένος, -η, -ον: foreign, strange
ὁδός, ἡ: a way, path, road
ὀθόνη, ἡ: a cloth
ὄμμα, -ατος, τό: an eye
ὁμόδουλος, ὁ: a fellow-slave
πάσχω: to suffer
πολλάκις: many times, often
προσποιέω: to pretend, affect
σκεπάζω: to cover
στρέφω: to turn
ὑποζεύγνυμι: to yoke under
ὑστεραῖος, -α, -ον: on the day after, the
    next day
φορτίον, τό: a load, burden

τούτοις: dat. of means, "by these beasts"
ἐστρέφοντο: pr. pas., "were being turned"
οἷα ... (sc. ὄντα) ... ἀράμενον ... ἀφιγμένον: The part. agree with με giving the
    ground of the action, "since I was ... since I had just carried ... since I had arrived"
ἀράμενον: ao. part. of αἴρω
ἀφιγμένον: pf. part. of ἀφικνέομαι
ἀφῆκαν: ao. of ἀπο-ίημι, "they allowed me to" + inf.
σκεπάσαντες: ao. part., "having covered my eyes"
ὅπως χρὴ ἀλεῖν: ind. quest. after ἠπιστάμην, "how it was necessary to grind"
παθών: ao. part. of πάσχω, "having experienced many times"
προσεποιούμην: impf. mid. of προσ-ποιέω, "I pretended to" + inf
ἤλπισα: ao. part. of ἐλπίζω, "I hoped"
λαβόντες: ao. part. of λαμβάνω, "having taken"
τῶν ἔνδον: "of those inside"

περιίστανταί με καὶ μὴ προσδοκήσαντα, ὡς οὐχ ὁρῶντα,
παίουσιν ἀθρόᾳ τῇ χειρί, ὥστε με ὑπὸ τῆς πληγῆς ὥσπερ
στρόμβον ἐξαπίνης στρέφεσθαι· καὶ πείρᾳ ἔμαθον ὅτι χρὴ τὸν
δοῦλον ἐς τὸ τὰ δέοντα ποιεῖν μὴ περιμένειν τὴν χεῖρα τοῦ
δεσπότου.

Lucius is sold to a nurseryman. (cf. Ap. Met. IX.32, p.178)

[43.] λεπτὸς οὖν πάνυ γίνομαι καὶ ἀσθενὴς τῷ σώματι,
ὥστε ἔγνω με ὁ δεσπότης πωλῆσαι, καὶ ἀποδίδοταί με
ἀνθρώπῳ κηπουρῷ τὴν τέχνην· οὗτος γὰρ εἶχε κῆπον λαβὼν

ἀθρόος, -α, -ον: crowded together, all at once
ἄνθρωπος, ὁ: a man
ἀποδίδωμι: to give over
ἀσθενής, -ές: without strength, feeble
γιγνώσκω: to know
δέον, τό: a duty
δεσπότης, -ου, ὁ: a master, lord
δοῦλος, ὁ: a slave
ἐξαπίνης: suddenly
κῆπος, ὁ: a garden
κηπουρός, ὁ: a gardener
λεπτός, -ή, -όν: thin, slight
μανθάνω: to learn

παίω: to strike, hit
πάνυ: altogether, entirely
πεῖρα, -ας, ἡ: a trial, attempt
περιίστημι: to place round
περιμένω: to wait for, await
πληγή, ἡ: a blow, stroke
προσδοκάω: to expect
πωλέω: to exchange, barter, sell
στρέφω: to turn around
στρόμβος, ὁ: a top
τέχνη, ἡ: art, skill, craft
χείρ, χειρός, ἡ: a hand
χρή: it is necessary

περιίστανται: pr., "they stand around" + acc.
μὴ προσδοκήσαντα: μὴ instead of οὐ indicating general force, "whenever I was not expecting it"
ὡς οὐχ ὁρῶντα: "since I couldn't see"
ἀθρόᾳ τῇ χειρί: dat. of means, "with multiple hands at once"
ὥστε ... στρέφεσθαι: pr. pas. inf. in result clause, "so that I was spun"
ὅτι χρὴ: obj. clause after ἔμαθον, "I learned *that it is necessary*" + acc. inf.
ἔμαθον: ao. of μανθάνω, "I learned"
τὸν δοῦλον ποιεῖν: after χρὴ, "that a slave does"
τὰ δέοντα: pr. part., "the things that must be done"
μὴ περιμένειν: "not to be waiting"
ἔγνω: ao. of γιγνώσκω, "he decided" + inf.
πωλῆσαι: ao. inf. πολέω, "to sell"
τὴν τέχνην: acc. of resp., "by trade"
εἶχε ... γεωργεῖν: "he was able to farm"
λαβὼν: ao. part. of λαμβάνω, "by taking (me)"

γεωργεῖν. καὶ τοῦτο εἴχομεν ἔργον· ὁ δεσπότης ἕωθεν ἐπιθείς
μοι τὰ λάχανα ἐκόμιζεν εἰς τὴν ἀγοράν, καὶ παραδοὺς τοῖς
ταῦτα πιπράσκουσιν ἦγέ με πάλιν εἰς τὸν κῆπον. εἶτα ἐκεῖνος
μὲν καὶ ἔσκαπτε καὶ ἐφύτευε καὶ τὸ ὕδωρ τῷ φυτῷ ἐπῆγεν,
ἐγὼ δὲ ἐν τούτῳ εἱστήκειν ἀργός. ἦν δέ μοι δεινῶς ἀλγεινὸς ὁ
τότε βίος, πρῶτον μὲν ἐπεὶ χειμὼν ἤδη ἦν κἀκεῖνος οὐδὲ αὐτῷ
στρῶμα εἶχεν ἀγοράσαι οὐχ ὅπως ἐμοί, καὶ ἀνυπόδητος πηλὸν

ἀγορά, -ᾶς, ἡ: a marketplace
ἀγοράζω: to conduct business, buy
ἄγω: to lead, bring
ἀλγεινός, -ή, -όν: giving pain, grievous, difficult
ἀνυπόδητος, -ον: unshod, barefoot
ἀργός, -ή, -όν: lazy, without work
βίος, ὁ: life
γεωργέω: to farm
δεινός, -ή, -όν: fearful, terrible
δεσπότης, -ου, ὁ: a master, lord
ἐπάγω: to bring on
ἐπιτίθημι: to put on, place upon
ἔργον, τό: a deed, work, act
ἕωθεν: from morning, at dawn

ἵστημι: to make to stand
κῆπος, ὁ: a garden
κομίζω: to carry, lead
λάχανον, -ου, τό: vegetables, greens
πάλιν: back, backwards
παραδίδωμι: to hand over
πηλός, ὁ: clay, earth
πιπράσκω: to sell
σκάπτω: to dig
στρῶμα, -ατος, τό: a bed
ὕδωρ, ὕδατος, τό: water
φυτεύω: to plant
φυτόν, τό: a plant
χειμών, -ῶνος, ὁ: winter

εἴχομεν: "we were able (to do) this" i.e. what follows
ἐπιθείς: ao. part of ἐπι-τίθημι, "having placed upon" + dat.
παραδοὺς: ao. part. of παρα-δίδωμι: having handed over to" + dat.
τοῖς πιπράσκουσιν: pr. part. dat., "to those who sell"
ἦγε: impf., "he would lead"
ἐπῆγεν: impf. of ἐπι-ἄγω, "he would direct to" + dat.
ἐν τούτῳ (sc. χρόνῳ): "meanwhile"
εἱστήκειν: plpf. of ἵστημι, "I would stand"
οὐδὲ αὐτῷ: "neither for himself"
ἀγοράσαι: ao. inf. of ἀγοράω after εἶχεν, "he was unable to buy"
οὐχ ὅπως: "let alone for me"

ὑγρὸν καὶ πάγον σκληρὸν καὶ ὀξὺν ἐπάτουν, καὶ τὸ φαγεῖν τοῦτο μόνον ἀμφοτέροις ἦν θρίδακας πικρὰς καὶ σκληράς.

Lucius' master encounters a soldier with whom he has a fight. (cf. Ap. Met. IX.40, p. 181)

[44.] καὶ ποτε ἐξιόντων ἡμῶν εἰς τὴν πόλιν ἐντυγχάνει ἀνὴρ γενναῖος *στρατιώτου στολὴν ἠμφιεσμένος*, καὶ τὰ μὲν πρῶτα λαλεῖ πρὸς ἡμᾶς τῇ Ἰταλῶν φωνῇ καὶ ἤρετο τὸν κηπουρὸν ὅποι ἀπάγει τὸν ὄνον ἐμέ· ὁ δέ, οἶμαι, τῆς φωνῆς ἀνόητος ὢν οὐδὲν ἀπεκρίνατο· ὁ δὲ ὀργιζόμενος, ὡς ὑπερορώμενος, παίει τῇ μάστιγι τὸν κηπουρόν, κἀκεῖνος

ἀμφότερος, -α, -ον: each, both
ἀνόητος, -ον: not understanding (+ *gen.*)
ἀπάγω: to lead away
ἀποκρίνομαι: to answer
γενναῖος, -α, -ον: noble
ἐντυγχάνω: to fall in with, meet with
ἐξέρχομαι: to go out
ἐρωτάω: to ask, enquire
ἐσθίω: to eat
θρίδαξ, -ακος, ἡ: lettuce
Ἰταλός, ὁ: an Italian
κῆπος, ὁ: a garden
κηπουρός, ὁ: a gardener
λαλέω: to talk
μάστιξ, -ιγος, ἡ: a whip, scourge
μόνος, -η, -ον: alone, only

οἴομαι: to suppose, think, imagine
ὀξύς, -εῖα, -ύ: sharp, keen
ὅποι: to which place, whither
ὀργίζομαι: to be angry, rage
πάγος, ὁ: a rock
παίω: to strike, hit
πατέω: to tread, walk
πικρός, -ά, -όν: sharp, bitter
πρῶτος, -η, -ον: first
σκληρός, -ά, -όν: hard
στολή, ἡ: an equipment, armament
στρατιώτης, -ου, ὁ: a soldier, recruit
ὑγρός, -ά, -όν: wet, damp, moist
ὑπεροράω: to look upon, disdain
φωνή, ἡ: a voice, speech

ἐπάτουν: impf. of πατέω, "I walked on" + acc.
τὸ φαγεῖν: ao. inf. of ἐσθίω, the art. inf. is subj. of ἦν, "*eating* lettuce was"
ἐξιόντων ἡμῶν: gen. abs., "as we were going out"
ἐξιόντων: pr. part. of ἐξ-έρχομαι
ἠμφιεσμένος: pf. part. of ἀμφι-έννυμι, "having put on," "wearing" + acc.
τῇ Ἰταλῶν φωνῇ: "in the Italian tongue" i.e. Latin
ἤρετο: ao. of ἐρωτάω, "he asked"
ὅποι ἀπάγει: ind. quest. after ἤρετο, "whither he was leading"
ἀνόητος ὢν: "since he was ignorant" + gen.
ἀπεκρίνατο: ao. of ἀπο-κρίνομαι, "he answered"
παίει: note the switch to the vivid present tense, "he strikes him"
ὡς ὑπερορώμενος: pr. part. of ὑπερ-οράω, "being despised (so he thought)"
ὑποσπάσας: ao. part. of ὑπο-σπάω, "having tripped him off his feet"

συμπλέκεται αὐτῷ καὶ ἐκ τῶν ποδῶν εἰς τὴν ὁδὸν ὑποσπάσας
ἐκτείνει, καὶ κείμενον ἔπαιεν οὕτω καὶ χειρὶ καὶ ποδὶ καὶ λίθῳ
τῷ ἐκ τῆς ὁδοῦ· ὁ δὲ τὰ πρῶτα καὶ ἀντεμάχετο καὶ ἠπείλει, εἰ
ἀνασταίη, ἀποκτενεῖν τῇ μαχαίρᾳ· ὁ δὲ ὥσπερ ὑπ' αὐτοῦ
ἐκείνου διδαχθείς, τὸ ἀκινδυνότατον, σπᾷ τὴν μάχαιραν αὐτοῦ
καὶ ῥιπτεῖ πόρρω, εἶτα αὖθις ἔπαιε κείμενον. ὁ δὲ τὸ κακὸν
ὁρῶν ἤδη ἀφόρητον ψεύδεται ὡς τεθνηκὼς ἐν ταῖς πληγαῖς· ὁ

ἀκίνδυνος, -ον: free from danger, safe
ἀνίστημι: to make to stand up, raise up
ἀντιμάχομαι: to fight back
ἀπειλέω: to threaten
ἀποκτείνω: to kill, slay
αὖθις: back, again
ἀφόρητος, -ον: intolerable, insufferable
διδάσκω: to teach
ἐκτείνω: to stretch out, lay out
θνήσκω: to die
κακός, -ή, -όν: bad, ill
κεῖμαι: to be laid
λίθος, -ου, ὁ: a stone

μάχαιρα, -ης, ἡ: a sword
ὁδός, ἡ a way, path, road
παίω: to strike, hit
πληγή, ἡ: a blow, stroke
πόρρω: forwards, onwards, further
πούς, ποδός, ὁ: a foot
πρῶτος, -η, -ον: first
ῥίπτω: to throw, cast, hurl
σπάω: to draw
συμπλέκω: to entangle, grapple
ὑποσπάω: to draw off
χείρ, χειρός, ἡ: a hand
ψεύδομαι: to lie, pretend

ἔπαιεν: impf., "he kept striking him"
τὰ πρῶτα: "at first"
εἰ ἀνασταίη, ἀποκτενεῖν: fut. more vivid cond. in ind. st. after ἠπείλει, "he kept
  threatening that if he got up, he would kill"
ἀνασταίη: ao. opt. of ἀνα-ίστημι representing the ao. subj. in sec. seq.
ἀποκτενεῖν: fut. inf. of ἀποκτείνω representing the fut. ind. The original
  statement would have been ἐάν ἀναστῶ, ἀποκτενῶ
ὁ δὲ: "but he" i.e. the gardener
ὥσπερ … διδαχθείς: ao. pas. part. of διδάσκω, "as though having been taught"
σπᾷ: switching back to the vivid present, "he draws and throws"
ἔπαιε: impf., "he started striking him"
ὡς τεθνηκὼς: ind. st. after ψεύδεται, "he pretended *that he was dead*"
τεθνηκὼς: pf. part. of θνήσκω

δὲ δείσας ἐπὶ τούτῳ τὸν μὲν αὐτοῦ ὡς εἶχε κείμενον ἀπολείπει, τὴν δὲ μάχαιραν βαστάσας ἐπ' ἐμοὶ ἤλαυνεν ἐς τὴν πόλιν.

The nurseryman and Lucius are hidden by friends to elude the angry soldier.(cf. Ap. Met. IX.42, p. 184)

[45.] ὡς δὲ ἤλθομεν, τὸν μὲν κῆπον αὐτοῦ συνεργῷ τινι ἐπέδωκεν γεωργεῖν, αὐτὸς δὲ τὸν κίνδυνον τὸν ἐκ τῆς ὁδοῦ δεδιὼς κρύπτεται ἅμα ἐμοὶ πρός τινος τῶν ἐν ἄστει συνήθων. τῇ δὲ ὑστεραίᾳ, δόξαν αὐτοῖς, οὕτω ποιοῦσιν· τὸν μὲν ἐμὸν δεσπότην κιβωτῷ ἐνέκρυψαν, ἐμὲ δὲ ἀράμενοι ἐκ τῶν ποδῶν κομίζουσιν ἄνω τῇ κλίμακι ἐς ὑπερῷον κἀκεῖ με ἄνω

αἴρω: to take up, raise, lift up
ἄνω: upwards
ἀπολείπω: to leave behind, abandon
ἄστυ, -εος, τό: a city, town
βαστάζω: to lift up, raise
γεωργέω: to farm
δείδω: to fear
δεσπότης, -ου, ὁ: a master, lord
δόξα, ἡ: a notion
ἐγκρύπτω: to hide, conceal in
ἐλαύνω: to drive, set in motion
ἐπιδίδωμι: to give besides
κεῖμαι: to be laid
κῆπος, ὁ: a garden

κιβωτός, ἡ: a wooden box, chest
κίνδυνος, ὁ: a danger, risk, hazard
κλῖμαξ, -ακος, ἡ: a ladder
κομίζω: to carry, lead
κρύπτω: to hide
μάχαιρα, -ης, ἡ: a sword
ὁδός, ἡ: a way, path, road
ποιέω: to make
πόλις, -εως, ἡ: a city
πούς, ποδός, ὁ: a foot
συνεργός, -όν: working together
ὑπερῷος, -α, -ον: above, upper
ὑστεραῖος, -α, -ον: on the day after, the next day

δείσας: ao. part. of δείδω, "fearing"
αὐτοῦ: "in the very spot"
ὡς εἶχε: "just as he was"
βαστάσας: ao. of βαστάζω, "having raised it up upon me"
ἤλθομεν: ao. of ἔρχομαι, "we came"
ἐπέδωκεν: ao. of ἐπι-δίδωμι, "he handed over to" + dat
δεδιὼς: pf. part. of δείδω, "being afraid of" + acc.
τὸν ἐκ τῆς ὁδοῦ: "the risk of the road"
πρός τινος: "under the protection of one"
δόξαν: ao. part. acc. s. n. of δοκέω used absolutely, "it having seemed a good idea" + dat.
ἐνέκρυψαν: ao. of ἐν-κρύπτω, "they hid"
ἀράμενοι: ao. part. of εἴλω, "having lifted"

συγκλείουσιν. ὁ δὲ στρατιώτης ἐκ τῆς ὁδοῦ τότε μόλις ἐξαναστάς, ὡς ἔφασαν, καρηβαρῶν ταῖς πληγαῖς ἧκεν εἰς τὴν πόλιν καὶ τοῖς στρατιώταις τοῖς σὺν αὐτῷ ἐντυχὼν λέγει τὴν ἀπόνοιαν τοῦ κηπουροῦ· οἱ δὲ σὺν αὐτῷ ἐλθόντες μανθάνουσιν ἔνθα ἦμεν κεκρυμμένοι, καὶ παραλαμβάνουσι τοὺς τῆς πόλεως ἄρχοντας. οἱ δὲ εἴσω τινὰ πέμπουσι τῶν ὑπηρετῶν καὶ τοὺς ἔνδον ἅπαντας προελθεῖν ἔξω κελεύουσιν· ὡς δὲ προῆλθον, ὁ κηπουρὸς οὐδαμοῦ ἐφαίνετο. οἱ μὲν οὖν στρατιῶται ἔνδον

ἅπας, ἅπασα, ἅπαν: all, every
ἀπόνοια, ἡ: senselessness
ἄρχων, -οντος, ὁ: a ruler
εἴσω: to within, into
ἔνθα: there
ἐντυγχάνω: to fall in with, meet with
ἐξανίστημι: to raise up
ἔξω: out
ἥκω: to come
καρηβαρέω: to be dizzy
κελεύω: to bid, command, order
κηπουρός, ὁ: a gardener
κρύπτω: to hide
λέγω: to say

μανθάνω: to learn
μόλις: scarcely
ὁδός, ἡ: a way, path, road
οὐδαμοῦ: nowhere
παραλαμβάνω: to take
πέμπω: to send, dispatch
πληγή, ἡ: a blow, stroke
πόλις, -εως, ἡ: a city
προέρχομαι: to go forth
στρατιώτης, -ου, ὁ: a soldier, recruit
συγκλείω: to shut up, enclose
ὑπηρέτης, -ου, ὁ: a public slave, assistant
φαίνομαι: to appear, seem

ἐξαναστάς: ao. part. of ἐξ-ανα-ἵστημι, "having raised himself up"

ὡς ἔφασαν: ao. of φημί, "as they told us"

ἐντυχών: ao. part. of τυγχάνω, "having come upon" + dat.

ἐλθόντες: ao. part. of ἔρχομαι, "having come"

ἔνθα ἦμεν κεκρυμμένοι: pf. periphrastic of κρύπτω in ind. quest. after μανθάνουσιν, "where we were hidden"

οἱ δὲ εἴσω: "but these inside"

ἅπαντας προελθεῖν: ao. inf. of προ-ἔρχομαι in ind. com., "they order all to come forward"

προῆλθον: ao. of προ-ἔρχομαι, "they came forward"

ἔφασαν εἶναι τὸν κηπουρὸν κἀμὲ τὸν ἐκείνου ὄνον· οἱ δὲ οὐδὲν ἄλλο ὑπολελεῖφθαι ἔλεγον οὔτε ἄνθρωπον οὔτε ὄνον.

Lucius peeps out to see what is happening and betrays the nurseryman.

θορύβου δὲ ἐν τῷ στενωπῷ καὶ πολλῆς βοῆς ἐκ τούτων γινομένης ὁ ἀγέρωχος καὶ πάντα περίεργος ἐγὼ βουλόμενος μαθεῖν τίνες εἶεν οἱ βοῶντες, διακύπτω ἄνωθεν κάτω διὰ τῆς θυρίδος. οἱ δέ με ἰδόντες εὐθὺς ἀνέκραγον· οἱ δὲ ἑαλώκεσαν ψευδῆ λέγοντες· καὶ οἱ ἄρχοντες εἴσω παρελθόντες καὶ πάντα ἀνερευνῶντες εὑρίσκουσιν τὸν ἐμὸν δεσπότην τῇ κιβωτῷ

ἀγέρωχος, -ον: high-minded	**εὑρίσκω**: to find
ἁλίσκομαι: to be taken, be caught	**θόρυβος, ὁ**: a noise, uproar, clamor
ἀνακράζω: to cry out	**θυρίς, -ίδος, ἡ**: a window
ἀνερευνάω: to examine closely, investigate	**κάτω**: down, downwards
ἄνθρωπος, ὁ: a man	**κηπουρός, ὁ**: a gardener
ἄνωθεν: from above	**κιβωτός, ἡ**: a wooden box, chest
ἄρχων, -οντος, ὁ: a ruler	**λέγω**: to say
βοάω: to shout	**μανθάνω**: to learn
βοή, ἡ: a loud cry, shout	**παρέρχομαι**: to go beside
βούλομαι: to will, wish	**περίεργος, -ον**: inquisitive, curious
δεσπότης, -ου, ὁ: a master, lord	**στενωπός, ὁ**: a narrow lane, ally
διακύπτω: to peep through, look out	**ὑπολείπω**: to leave remaining
εἴσω: to within, into	**ψευδής, -ές**: lying, false

εἶναι τὸν κηπουρὸν: ind. st. after **ἔφασαν**, "they claimed that the gardener was inside"

ὑπολελεῖφθαι: pf. inf. pas. of **ὑπο-λείπω** after **ἔλεγον**, "but they kept saying none to have been left behind"

θορύβου ... βοῆς γινομένης: gen abs., "a din and shout occurring"

μαθεῖν: ao. inf. of **μανθάνω**, "wishing *to know*"

τίνες εἶεν: opt. in ind. quest. in sec. seq., "who were the shouting ones"

ἰδόντες: ao. part. of **εἶδον**, "having seen"

ἀνέκραγον: ao. of **ἀνα-κράζω**, "they immediately began crying out"

ἑαλώκεσαν: plpf. of **ἁλίσκομαι**, "they were caught" + part.

παρελθόντες: ao. part. of **παρα-ἔρχομαι**, "having come along"

ἐγκείμενον καὶ λαβόντες τὸν μὲν εἰς τὸ δεσμωτήριον ἔπεμψαν
λόγον τῶν τετολμημένων ὑφέξοντα, ἐμὲ δὲ κάτω βαστάσαντες
τοῖς στρατιώταις παρέδοσαν. πάντες δὲ ἄσβεστον ἐγέλων ἐπὶ

τῷ μηνύσαντι ἐκ τῶν
ὑπερῴων καὶ προδόντι τὸν
ἑαυτοῦ δεσπότην· κἀκ τότε
ἐξ ἐμοῦ πρώτου ἦλθεν εἰς
ἀνθρώπους ὁ λόγος οὗτος,
«Ἐξ ὄνου παρακύψεως.»

ἄνθρωπος, ὁ: a man
ἄσβεστος, -η, -ον: ceaseless
βαστάζω: to lift, lift up, raise
γελάω: to laugh
δεσμωτήριον, τό: a prison
δεσπότης, -ου, ὁ: a master, lord
ἔγκειμαι: to lie in
κάτω: down, downwards
λόγος, ὁ: a word, phrase
μηνύω: to disclose, reveal, betray

παραδίδωμι: to hand over
παράκυψις, -εως, ἡ: peeping
πέμπω: to send, dispatch
προδίδωμι: to give away, betray
πρῶτος, -η, -ον: first
στρατιώτης, -ου, ὁ: a soldier, recruit
τολμάω: to dare
ὑπερῷον, τό: an upper room
ὑπέχω: to undergo

λαβόντες: ao. part. of λαμβάνω, "having arrested"
ἔπεμψαν: ao. of πέμπω, "they sent"
τῶν τετολμημένων: pf. part. of τολμάω, "on account *of the things dared*"
ὑφέξοντα: fut. part. acc. s. of ὑπο-ἔχω indicating purpose, "they sent him *in order to await an account*"
παρέδοσαν: ao. of παρα-δίδωι, "they handed me over to" + dat.
ἐγέλων: impf., "they started laughing"
τῷ μηνύσαντι: ao. part., "at the one disclosing"
προδόντι: ao. part., "and the one betraying"
ἦλθεν: ao. of ἔρχομαι, "came"
ὁ λόγος οὗτος: "this saying"
ἐξ ὄνου παρακύψεως: "from the peeping of an ass," a phrase from Menander referring to a frivolous lawsuit

118

The soldier sells Lucius to a cook.

[46.] τῇ δὲ ὑστεραίᾳ τί μὲν ἔπαθεν ὁ κηπουρὸς ὁ ἐμὸς δεσπότης, οὐκ οἶδα, ὁ δὲ στρατιώτης πωλήσειν με ἔγνω, καὶ πιπράσκει με πέντε καὶ εἴκοσιν Ἀττικῶν· ὁ δὲ ὠνησάμενος θεράπων ἦν ἀνδρὸς σφόδρα πλουσίου πόλεως τῶν ἐν Μακεδονίᾳ τῆς μεγίστης Θεσσαλονίκης. οὗτος τέχνην εἶχε ταύτην, τὰ ὄψα τῷ δεσπότῃ ἐσκεύαζεν, καὶ εἶχεν ἀδελφὸν σύνδουλον ἄρτους πέττειν καὶ μελίπηκτα κιρνᾶν ἐπιστάμενον. οὗτοι οἱ ἀδελφοὶ σύσκηνοί τε ἀεὶ ἦσαν ἀλλήλοις καὶ κατέλυον ἐν ταὐτῷ καὶ τὰ σκεύη τῶν τεχνῶν εἶχον ἀναμεμιγμένα, καὶ μετὰ ταῦτα κἀμὲ ἵστασαν ἔνθα κατέλυον.

ἀδελφός, ὁ: a brother
ἀεί: always, for ever
ἀναμείγνυμι: to mix together
ἄρτος, ὁ: a loaf of bread
Ἀττικός, -ή, -όν: Attic, Athenian
γιγνώσκω: to know
δεσπότης, -ου, ὁ: a master, lord
εἴκοσι: twenty
ἐπίσταμαι: to know
θεράπων, -οντος, ὁ: an attendant, servant
ἵστημι: to make to stand
καταλύω: to lodge
κηπουρός, ὁ: a gardener
κιρνάω: to mix
Μακεδονία, ἡ: Macedonia
μελίπηκτον, τό: a honey-cake
οἶδα: to know
ὄψον, τό: cooking, cooked food

πάσχω: to experience, suffer
πέντε: five
πέττω: to bake
πιπράσκω: to sell
πλούσιος, -α, -ον: rich, wealthy, opulent
πόλις, -εως, ἡ: a city
πωλέω: to sell
σκευάζω: to prepare, make ready
σκεύη, τά: possessions, belongings
στρατιώτης, -ου, ὁ: a soldier, recruit
σύνδουλος, ὁ: a fellow-slave
σύσκηνος, ὁ: a messmate
σφόδρα: very, very much
τέχνη, ἡ: art, skill, craft
ὑστεραῖος, -α, -ον: on the day after, the next day
ὠνέομαι: to buy, purchase

τί μὲν ἔπαθεν: ao. of πάσχω in ind. quest. after οἶδα, "what he suffered"
ἔγνω: ao. part. of γιγνώσκω, "he decided" + inf.
Ἀττικῶν: gen. of price, "for 25 Attic drachmas"
ὁ δὲ ὠνησάμενος: ao. part. of ὠνέομαι, "the one who bought"
τῶν ἐν Μακεδονίᾳ: "the largest of those (cities) in Macedonia"
πέττειν καὶ κιρνᾶν: pr. inf. after ἐπιστάμενον, "knowing how to bake and mix"
ἐν ταὐτῷ: "in the same (place)"
ἀναμεμιγμένα: pf. part. of ἀνα-μίγνυμι, "their tools mixed together"
μετὰ ταῦτα: "and among these (tools)"
ἵστασαν: impf. of ἵστημι, "they stood me"

Lucian

Unobserved, Lucius helps himself to the human food in the kitchen.

καὶ οὗτοι μετὰ τὸ δεῖπνον τοῦ δεσπότου πολλὰ λείψανα
ἄμφω εἴσω ἐκόμιζον ὁ μὲν κρεῶν καὶ ἰχθύων, ὁ δὲ ἄρτων καὶ
πλακούντων. οἱ δὲ κατακλείσαντες ἔνδον ἐμὲ μετὰ τούτων καὶ
φυλακὴν ἐμοὶ γλυκυτάτην περιστήσαντες ἀπῄεσαν ὥστε
ἀπολούσασθαι: κἀγὼ τοῖς παρακειμένοις κριθιδίοις μακρὰ
χαίρειν λέγων ταῖς τέχναις καὶ τοῖς κέρδεσι τῶν δεσποτῶν
ἐδίδουν ἐμαυτόν, καὶ διὰ μακροῦ πάνυ ἐγεμιζόμην ἀνθρωπείου
τροφῆς. οἱ δὲ ἀναστρέψαντες εἴσω τὰ μὲν πρῶτα οὐδὲν
ᾐσθάνοντο τῆς ὀψοφαγίας τῆς ἐμῆς ἐκ τοῦ πλήθους τῶν

αἰσθάνομαι: to perceive, notice
ἄμφω: both
ἀναστρέφω: to turn back, return
ἀνθρώπειος, -α, -ον: human
ἀπέρχομαι: to go away, depart
ἄρτος, ὁ: a loaf of bread
γεμίζω: to fill full
γλυκύς, -εῖα, -ύ: sweet
δεῖπνον, τό: a dinner
δεσπότης, -ου, ὁ: a master, lord
δίδωμι: to give
εἴσω: to within, into
ἰχθῦς, -ύος, ὁ: fish
κατακλείω: to shut in, enclose
κέρδος, -εος, τό: gain, profit, advantage
κομίζω: to carry, lead

κρέας, τό: meat
κριθίδιον, τό: barley
λέγω: to say
λείψανον, τό: a remnant, leftover
μακρός, -ά, -όν: long
ὀψοφαγία, ἡ: luxurious eating
παράκειμαι: to lay before
περιΐστημι: to place round
πλακοῦς, -οῦντος, ὁ: a cake
πλῆθος, -εος, τό: a great number,
   multitude
πρῶτος, -η, -ον: first
τέχνη, ἡ: art, skill, craft
τροφή, ἡ: nourishment, food
χαίρω: to bid farewell

ὁ μὲν, ὁ δὲ: "the one brought leftovers of meat, the other of breads"
περιστήσαντες: ao. part. trans. of περι-ἵστημι, "placing around me"
ἀπῄεσαν: impf. of ἀπο-ἔρχομαι, "they departed"
ὥστε ἀπολούσασθαι: ao. inf. mid., "so that they could wash themselves"
χαίρειν λέγων: "bidding farewell to" + dat.
ἐδίδουν ἐμαυτόν: impf. of δίδωμι, "I would give myself over to" + dat.
ἀναστρέψαντες: ao. part. of ἀνα-στρέφω, "having returned"
ᾐσθάνοντο: impf., "they would perceive not at all"

παρακειμένων, κᾀμοῦ ἔτι ἐν φόβῳ καὶ φειδοῖ κλέπτοντος τὸ
ἄριστον. ἐπεὶ δὲ καὶ τέλεον ἤμην αὐτῶν καταγνοὺς ἄγνοιαν,
τὰς καλλίστας τῶν μερίδων καὶ ἄλλα πολλὰ κατέτρωγον, καὶ
ἐπειδὴ ᾔσθοντο ἤδη τῆς ζημίας, τὰ μὲν πρῶτα ἄμφω ὕποπτον
ἐς ἀλλήλους ἔβλεπον καὶ κλέπτην ὁ ἕτερος τὸν ἕτερον καὶ
ἅρπαγα τῶν κοινῶν καὶ ἀναίσχυντον ἔλεγον, καὶ ἦσαν
ἀκριβεῖς λοιπὸν ἄμφω καὶ τῶν μερίδων ἀριθμὸς ἐγίνετο.

ἄγνοια, ἡ: ignorance
αἰσθάνομαι: to perceive, notice
ἀκριβής, -ές: exact, accurate, precise
ἄμφω: both
ἀναίσχυντος, -ον: shameless, impudent
ἀριθμός, ὁ: number
ἄριστον, τό: a meal
ἅρπαξ, -αγος, ὁ: a robber
βλέπω: to see, look at
ζημία, ἡ: loss, damage
καταγιγνώσκω: to remark, discover
κατατρώγω: to eat up

κλέπτης, -ου, ὁ: a thief
κλέπτω: to steal
κοινός, -ή, -όν: common, shared
λέγω: to say
λοιπός, -ή, -όν: remaining, the rest
μερίς, -ίδος, ἡ: a part, portion, share
παράκειμαι: to lie beside
πρῶτος, -η, -ον: first
τέλεος, -α, -ον: finished, at the end
ὕποπτος, -ον: viewed with suspicion
φειδώ, -οῦς, ἡ: a sparing, thrift
φόβος, ὁ: fear

κᾀμοῦ ... κλέπτοντος: gen. abs., "and me stealing"
ἐν φόβῳ καὶ φειδοῖ: dat. of manner, "in a timid and sparing manner"
τέλεον: acc. s. f. agreeing with ἄγνοιαν, "their complete ignorance"
ἤμην καταγνοὺς: ao. part. of κατα-γιγνώσκω in plpf. periphrastic, "after *I had realized*"
κατέτρωγον: impf. of κατα-τρώγω, "I began gulping down"
ᾔσθοντο: ao. of αἰσθάνομαι, "they perceived" + gen.
ἔβλεπον: impf., "they started looking suspiciously"
ὁ ἕτερος τὸν ἕτερον: "each called the other"
λοιπὸν: acc. of duration, "for the rest of the time"
ἀριθμὸς ἐγίνετο: "there was an accounting"

121

Lucian

The cooks suspect Lucius and catch him eating human food.

[47.] ἐγὼ δὲ τὸν βίον εἶχον ἐν ἡδονῇ καὶ τρυφῇ, καὶ τὸ σῶμά μου ἐκ τῆς συνήθους τροφῆς πάλιν καλὸν ἐγεγόνει καὶ τὸ δέρμα ἐπανθούσῃ τῇ τριχὶ ἀπέστιλβεν. οἱ δὲ γενναιότατοι μέγαν τέ με καὶ πίονα ὁρῶντες καὶ τὰ κριθίδια μὴ δαπανώμενα, ἀλλ᾽ ἐν ταὐτῷ μέτρῳ ὄντα, εἰς ὑπόνοιαν ἔρχονται τῶν τολμημάτων τῶν ἐμῶν, καὶ προελθόντες ὡς εἰς τὸ βαλανεῖον ἀπιόντες, ἔπειτα τὰς θύρας συγκλείσαντες, προσβαλόντες ὀπῇ τινι τὰ ὄμματα τῆς θύρας ἐσκοποῦντο τἄνδον. κἀγὼ τότε μηδὲν τοῦ δόλου εἰδὼς ἠρίστων

ἀπέρχομαι: to go away, depart
ἀποστίλβω: to shine
ἀριστάω: to eat a meal
βαλανεῖον, τό: a bath
βίος, ὁ: life
γενναῖος, -α, -ον: noble
δαπανάω: to spend, consume
δέρμα, -ατος, τό: skin, hide, coat
δόλος, ὁ: a trick
ἐπανθέω: to bloom, be bright
ἔπειτα: thereupon
ἡδονή, ἡ: delight, enjoyment, pleasure
θρίξ, τριχός, ἡ: hair
θύρα, ἡ: a door
κριθίδιον, τό: barley
μέτρον, τό: a measure

οἶδα: to know
ὄμμα, -ατος, τό: an eye
ὀπή, ἡ: an opening, hole
πάλιν: back, again
πίων, -ον: fat, plump
προέρχομαι: to go forth
προσβάλλω: to throw against, put to
σκοπέω: to look
συγκλείω: to shut, close up
συνήθης, -ες: accustomed, customary
σῶμα, -ατος, τό: a body
τόλμημα, -ατος, τό: an enterprise, daring deed
τροφή, ἡ: nourishment, food
τρυφή, ἡ: softness, delicacy, luxury
ὑπόνοια, ἡ: a suspicion

ἐγεγόνει: plpf. of γίγνομαι, "had become"
ἐπανθούσῃ: pr. part. dat. s. f. of ἐπι-ανθέω, "with blooming hair"
μέγαν τέ με (sc. ὄντα): in ind.st. after ὁρῶντες, "seeing that I was big"
μὴ δαπανώμενα: "and that the barley was not being eaten"
ἀλλ᾽ ... ὄντα: "but that it was"
προελθόντες: ao. part. of προ-έρχομαι, "having gone forth"
ὡς ... ἀπιόντες: "as though they were departing"
προσβαλόντες: ao. part. of προσ-βάλλω, "having cast their eyes upon" + dat.
τἄνδον: (= τά ἔνδον) "the things inside"
εἰδὼς: ao. part. of οἶδα, "knowing nothing"

προσελθών. οἱ δὲ τὰ μὲν πρῶτα ἐγέλων ὁρῶντες ἄριστον
ἄπιστον· εἶτα δὲ τοὺς ὁμοδούλους ἐκάλουν ἐπὶ τὴν ἐμὴν θέαν,
καὶ γέλως πολὺς ἦν, ὥστε καὶ ὁ δεσπότης αὐτῶν ἤκουσεν τοῦ
γέλωτος, θορύβου ὄντος ἔξωθεν, καὶ ἤρετο τινα ἐφ᾽ ᾧ
τοσοῦτον οἱ ἔξω
γελῶσιν. ἐπεὶ δὲ
ἤκουσεν, ἐξανίσταται
τοῦ συμποσίου καὶ
διακύψας εἴσω ὁρᾷ με
συὸς ἀγρίου μερίδα
καταπίνοντα, καὶ μέγα
ἐν γέλωτι ἀναβοήσας
εἰστρέχει εἴσω.

ἄγριος, -α, -ον: savage, wild
ἀκούω: to hear
ἀναβοάω: to shout aloud, cry
ἄπιστος, ον: incredible, unbelievable
ἄριστον, τό: a meal
γελάω: to laugh
γέλως, ὁ: laughter
δεσπότης, -ου, ὁ: a master, lord
διακύπτω: to peep through
εἰστρέχω: to run in
εἴσω: to within, into
ἐξανίστημι: to raise up
ἔξω: out
ἔξωθεν: from without

ἐρωτάω: to ask, enquire
θέα, ἡ: a sight, view
θόρυβος, ὁ: a noise, uproar, clamor
καλέω: to call, summon
καταπίνω: to gulp down
μερίς, -ίδος, ἡ: a part, portion, share
ὁμόδουλος, ὁ: a fellow-slave
προσέρχομαι: to go to
πρῶτος, -η, -ον: first
συμπόσιον, τό: a drinking-party,
    symposium
σῦς, συός, ὁ: a pig, boar
τοσοῦτος, -αύτη, -οῦτο: so great, so
    much

προσελθών: ao. part. of προσ-έρχομαι, "having approached"
ὥστε … ἤκουσεν: result clause, "so that he heard" + gen.
θορύβου ὄντος: gen. abs., "since there was a din"
ἤρετο: ao. of ἐρωτάω, "he asked"
ἐφ᾽ ᾧ … γελῶσιν: ind. quest. after ἤρετο, "about what were they laughing"
ἐξανίσταται: vivid pr., "he arises"
διακύψας: ao. part., "having peeped through"
με … καταπίνοντα: ind. st. after ὁρᾷ, "that I am wolfing down"

123

Lucian

Lucius' unusual eating habits become a form of entertainment.

κἀγὼ σφόδρα ἠχθόμην ἐπὶ τοῦ δεσπότου κλέπτης ἅμα
καὶ λίχνος ἑαλωκώς. ὁ δὲ πολὺν εἶχεν ἐπ' ἐμοὶ γέλωτα, καὶ τὰ
μὲν πρῶτα κελεύει με εἴσω ἄγεσθαι εἰς τὸ ἐκείνου συμπόσιον,
ἔπειτα τράπεζάν μοι παραθεῖναι εἶπε καὶ εἶναι ἐπ' αὐτῇ πολλὰ
τῶν ὅσα μὴ δυνατὸν ἄλλῳ ὄνῳ καταφαγεῖν, κρέα λοπάδας
ζωμοὺς ἰχθῦς, τοῦτο μὲν ἐν γάρῳ καὶ ἐλαίῳ κατακειμένους,
τοῦτο δὲ νάπυϊ ἐπικεχυμένους. κἀγὼ τὴν τύχην ὁρῶν ἤδη
ἀπαλόν μοι προσμειδιῶσαν καὶ μαθὼν ὅτι με τοῦτο μόνον τὸ

ἄγω: to lead, bring
ἁλίσκομαι: to be taken, be caught
ἀπαλός, -ή, -όν: soft, tender, kind
γάρος, ὁ: fish sauce
γέλως, -ωτος, ὁ: laughter
δεσπότης, -ου, ὁ: a master, lord
δυνατός, -ή, -όν: able, possible
εἴσω: to within, into
ἔλαιον, τό: olive oil
ἔπειτα: thereupon
ἐπιχέω: to pour over
ἔχθω: to hate
ζωμός, ὁ: a broth, soup
ἰχθῦς, -ύος, ὁ: fish
κατάκειμαι: to lie down
κατεσθίω: to eat up, devour

κελεύω: to bid, command, order
κλέπτης, -ου, ὁ: a thief
κρέας, τό: meat
λίχνος, -η, -ον: greedy, gluttonous
λοπάς, -άδος, ἡ: shellfish
μανθάνω: to learn
μόνος, -η, -ον: alone, only
νᾶπυ, τό: mustard
παρατίθημι: to place before
προσμειδιάω: to smile upon
πρῶτος, -η, -ον: first
συμπόσιον, τό: a drinking-party,
 symposium
σφόδρα: very, very much
τράπεζα, -ης, ἡ: a table
τύχη, ἡ: chance, fortune

ἠχθόμην: impf., "I was vexed at" + part.
ἑαλωκώς: pf. part. of ἁλίσκομαι, "having been caught as a thief"
με ἄγεσθαι: pr. pas. inf. in ind. com., "he ordered me to be led"
παραθεῖναι: ao. inf. pas. of παρα-τίθημι in ind. com. after εἶπε, "to be set
 alongside me"
ἐπ' αὐτῇ: "upon it" (i.e. the table)
καταφαγεῖν: ao. inf. of κατα-ἐσθίω after μὴ δυνατὸν, "what was not possible to
 eat"
τοῦτο μὲν ... τοῦτο δὲ: "some of it soused in ... some drenched with..."
ἐπικεχυμένους: pf. part. of ἐπι-χέω, "having been drenched with" + dat.
τὴν τύχην ... προσμειδιῶσαν: pr. part. in ind. st. after ὁρῶν, "that my fate was
 smiling"
μαθὼν: ao. part. of μανθάνω, "having realized"

124

παίγνιον ἀνασώσει, καίτοι ἤδη ἐμπεπλησμένος ὅμως ἠρίστων
τῇ τραπέζῃ παραστάς. τὸ δὲ συμπόσιον ἐκλονεῖτο τῷ γέλωτι.
καί τις εἶπεν, «Καὶ πίεται οἶνον οὗτος ὁ ὄνος, ἤν τις αὐτῷ
ἐγκερασάμενος ἐπιδῷ:» καὶ ὁ δεσπότης ἐκέλευσεν κἀγὼ τὸ
προσενεχθὲν ἔπιον.

Lucius is turned over to a freedman for training in human behavior.

[48.] ὁ δὲ οἷον εἰκὸς ὁρῶν ἐμὲ κτῆμα παράδοξον τὴν
μὲν τιμὴν τὴν ἐμὴν κελεύει τῶν διοικητῶν τινι καταβαλεῖν τῷ
ἐμὲ ὠνησαμένῳ καὶ ἄλλο τοσοῦτον, ἐμὲ δὲ παρέδωκεν

ἀνασώζω: to recover, rescue
ἀριστάω: to take a meal
γέλως, -ωτος, ὁ: laughter
δεσπότης, -ου, ὁ: a master, lord
διοικητής, -οῦ, ὁ: an administrator
ἐγκεράννυμι: to mix
ἐπιδίδωμι: to give besides
καταβάλλω: to throw down
κελεύω: to bid, command, order
κλονέω: to drive in confusion
κτῆμα, -ατος, τό: a possession
οἶνος, ὁ: wine
παίγνιον, τό: a game, comic performance

παραδίδωμι: to hand over
παράδοξος, -ον: incredible, paradoxical
παρίστημι: to make to stand beside
πίνω: to drink
προσφέρω: to bring to
συμπόσιον, τό: a drinking-party,
   symposium
τιμή, ἡ: value, price, compensation
τοσοῦτος, -αύτη, -οῦτο: so great, so
   much
τράπεζα, -ης, ἡ: a table
ὠνέομαι: to buy, purchase

ὅτι ἀνασώσει: fut. of ἀνα-σώζω, "that this will save me"
ἐμπεπλησμένος: pf. part. of ἐν-πίμπλημμι, "although already full"
παραστάς: ao. part. intrans. of παρα-ἵστημι, "standing by"
πίεται: fut. of πίνω, "he will also drink"
ἤν τις ... ἐπιδῷ: ao. subj. of ἐπι-δίδωμι in fut. more vivid cond., "if someone will
   give him"
ἐγκερασάμενος: ao. part. of ἐν-κεράννυμι, "having mixed (with water)"
τὸ προσενεχθὲν: ao. pas. part. of προσ-φέρω, "the thing brought forth"
ἔπιον: ao. of πίνω, "I drank"
οἷον εἰκὸς: "as you would expect"
ἐμὲ κτῆμα (sc. ὄντα): ind. st. after ὁρῶν, "seeing *that I was a possession*"
καταβαλεῖν: ao. inf. of κατα-βάλλω, "he ordered *to pay to*" + dat.
τῷ ... ὠνησαμένῳ: ao. part., "to the one who sold me"
καὶ ἄλλο τοσοῦτον: "the same amount again"
παρέδωκεν: ao. of παρα-δίδωμι, "he handed me over to" + dat.

ἀπελευθέρῳ τῶν αὐτοῦ τινι νεανίσκῳ καὶ εἶπε κατηχεῖν ὅσα
ποιῶν μάλιστα ψυχαγωγεῖν αὐτὸν δυναίμην. τῷ δέ γε ῥᾴδια ἦν
πάντα· ὑπήκουον γὰρ εὐθὺ εἰς ἅπαντα διδασκόμενος. καὶ
πρῶτον μὲν κατακλίνεσθαί με ἐπὶ κλίνης ὥσπερ ἄνθρωπον ἐπ'
ἀγκῶνος ἐποίησεν, εἶτα καὶ προσπαλαίειν αὐτῷ καὶ μὴν καὶ
ὀρχεῖσθαι ἐπὶ τοὺς δύο ἐπανιστάμενον ὀρθὸν καὶ κατανεύειν
καὶ ἀνανεύειν πρὸς τὰς φωνὰς καὶ πάνθ' ὅσα ἐδυνάμην μὲν καὶ
δίχα τοῦ μανθάνειν, ποιεῖν·

ἀγκών, -ῶνος, ὁ: an elbow
ἀνανεύω: to nod "no"
ἄνθρωπος, ὁ: a man
ἀπελεύθερος, ὁ: a freedman
διδάσκω: to teach
δίχα: apart from, without (+ gen.)
δύναμαι: to be able
δύο: two
ἐπανίστημι: to set up again
εὐθύς, -εῖα, -ύ: straight
κατακλίνω: to lay down
κατανεύω: to nod "yes"

κατηχέω: to instruct
κλίνη, ἡ: a couch, bed
μανθάνω: to learn
νεάνισκος, ὁ: youth, young man
ὀρθός, -ή, -όν: straight
ὀρχέομαι: to dance
ποιέω: to make, do
προσπαλαίω: to wrestle
ῥᾴδιος, -α, -ον: easy, ready
ὑπακούω: to listen, obey
φωνή, ἡ: a voice, speech
ψυχαγωγέω: to beguile, entertain

εἶπε κατηχεῖν: "he told him to instruct me"
ὅσα ... δυναίμην: pr. opt. in gen rel. clause, "whatever I might be able to" + inf.
ποιῶν: "by doing (whatever)..."
τῷ δέ γε: "for him (the youth) to be sure"
ὑπήκουον: impf., "I would obey"
κατακλίνεσθαί με: acc. + inf. after ἐποίησεν, "he caused me to lie down"
(με) προσπαλαίειν: "then to wrestle with" + dat.
καὶ μὴν καί: indicating a climax, "moreover"
ὀρχεῖσθαι (με) ἐπανιστάμενον: "to dance standing upright"
ἐπανιστάμενον: pr. part. of ἐπι-ἀνα-ἵστημι
ὅσα ἐδυνάμην: "all which I was able do"
δίχα τοῦ μανθάνειν: art. inf., "apart from learning"

Lucius' tricks become the talk of the town.

καὶ τὸ πρᾶγμα περιβόητον ἦν, ὄνος ὁ τοῦ δεσπότου,
οἰνοπότης, παλαίων, ὄνος ὀρχούμενος. τὸ δὲ μέγιστον, ὅτι
πρὸς τὰς φωνὰς ἀνένευον ἐν καιρῷ καὶ κατένευον· καὶ πιεῖν δὲ
ὁπότε θελήσαιμι, ᾔτουν τοῖς ὀφθαλμοῖς τὸν οἰνοχόον κινήσας.
καὶ οἱ μὲν ἐθαύμαζον τὸ πρᾶγμα ὡς παράδοξον ἀγνοῦντες
ἄνθρωπον ἐν τῷ ὄνῳ κείμενον· ἐγὼ δὲ τρυφὴν ἐποιούμην τὴν
ἐκείνων ἄγνοιαν. καὶ μὴν καὶ βαδίζειν ἐμάνθανον καὶ κομίζειν
τὸν δεσπότην ἐπὶ νώτου καὶ τρέχειν δρόμον ἀλυπότατον καὶ
τῷ ἀναβάτῃ ἀναίσθητον. καὶ σκεύη μοι ἦν πολυτελῆ, καὶ

ἄγνοια, ἡ: ignorance
αἰτέω: to ask, beg
ἄλυπος, -ον: without pain
ἀναβάτης, -ου, ὁ: a rider
ἀναίσθητος, -ον: unfeeling, not noticing
ἀνανεύω: to nod "no"
βαδίζω: to go, walk
δεσπότης, -ου, ὁ: a master, lord
δρόμος, ὁ: a course, running
ἐθέλω: to will, wish
θαυμάζω: to wonder, marvel, be amazed
καιρός, ὁ: the proper time
κατανεύω: to nod "yes"
κεῖμαι: to be laid, lie
κινέω: to set in motion, move
κομίζω: to carry, lead
μανθάνω: to learn
νῶτον, τό: a back
οἰνοπότης, -ου, ὁ: wine-drinking

οἰνόχοος, ὁ: a cupbearer
ὄνος, ὁ: an ass
ὁπότε: when
ὀρχέομαι: to dance
ὀφθαλμός, ὁ: the eye
παλαίω: to wrestle
παράδοξος, -ον: incredible, paradoxical
περιβόητος, -ον: much talked of, famous
πίνω: to drink
ποιέω: to make
πολυτελής, -ές: very expensive, very
    costly
πρᾶγμα, -ατος, τό: a deed, act, matter
σκεύη, τά: equipment, possessions,
    baggage
τρέχω: to run
τρυφή, ἡ: softness, delicacy, luxury
φωνή, ἡ: a voice, speech

τὸ δὲ μέγιστον ὅτι: the biggest thing (was) that..."
ὁπότε θελήσαιμι: past gen clause, "whenever I wished"
θελήσαιμι: ao. opt. of ἐθέλω
πιεῖν: ao. inf. of πίνω, "to drink"
κινήσας: ao. part. of κινέω, "nudging the wine pourer"
ὡς παράδοξον: "as though strange"
ἄνθρωπον κείμενον: ind. st. after ἀγνοῦντες, "not knowing *that a man was
    abiding*"
ἐποιούμην: impf. mid., "I made for my purposes"
καὶ μὴν καί: indicating a climax
τῷ ἀναβάτῃ: dat. after ἀναίσθητον, "imperceptible to the rider"

στρώματα πορφυρᾶ ἐπιβάλλομαι, καὶ χαλινοὺς εἰσεδεχόμην
ἀργύρῳ καὶ χρυσῷ πεποικιλμένους, καὶ κώδωνες ἐξήπτοντό
μου μέλος μουσικώτατον ἐκφωνοῦντες.

Lucius' antics become part of a gladiatorial show.

[49.] ὁ δὲ Μενεκλῆς ὁ δεσπότης ἡμῶν, ὥσπερ ἔφην, ἐκ
τῆς Θεσσαλονίκης δεῦρο ἐληλύθει ἐπ' αἰτίᾳ τοιαύτῃ· ὑπέσχετο
τῇ πατρίδι θέαν παρέξειν ἀνδρῶν ὅπλοις πρὸς ἀλλήλους
μονομαχεῖν εἰδότων· καὶ οἱ μὲν ἄνδρες τῆς μάχης ἤδη ἦσαν ἐν
παρασκευῇ, καὶ ἀφῖκτο ἡ πορεία. ἐξελαύνομεν ἔωθεν, κἀγὼ
τὸν δεσπότην ἔφερον εἴ ποτε χωρίον εἴη τῆς ὁδοῦ τραχὺ καὶ

αἰτία, ἡ: a cause	ὁδός, ἡ: a way, path, road
ἀνήρ, ἀνδρός ὁ: a man	οἶδα: to know
ἄργυρος, ὁ: silver	ὅπλον, τό: a tool, weapon
ἀφικνέομαι: to come to, arrive	παρασκευή, ἡ: preparation, training
δεσπότης, -ου, ὁ: a master, lord	παρέχω: to furnish, provide, supply
δεῦρο: hither	πατρίς, -ίδος, ἡ: native land
εἰσδέχομαι: to take into, admit, receive	ποικίλλω: to work in embroidery,
ἐκφωνέω: to pronounce	decorate
ἐξάπτω: to fasten from	πορεία, ἡ: a march, journey
ἐξελαύνω: to ride out	πορφύρεος, -η, -ον: purple
ἐπιβάλλω: to throw or cast upon	στρῶμα, -ατος, τό: trappings
ἔωθεν: from morning, at dawn	τοιοῦτος, -αύτη, -οῦτο: such as this
θέα, ἡ: a sight, view, spectacle	τραχύς, -εῖα, -ύ: rugged, rough
κώδων, -ωνος, ἡ: a bell	ὑπισχνέομαι: to promise
μάχη, ἡ: battle, fight, combat	φέρω: to bear, carry
μέλος, -εος, τό: a tune, melody	χαλινός, ὁ: a bridle
Μενεκλῆς, ὁ: Menecles	χρυσός, ὁ: gold
μονομαχέω: to fight in single combat	χωρίον, τό: a place, spot
μουσικός, -ή, -όν: musical	

εἰσεδεχόμην: impf. of εἰσ-δέχομαι, "I received on my body"
πεποικιλμένους: pf. part. of ποικίλλω agreeing with χαλινούς, "bridles having
    been dappled"
ἐξήπτοντο: impf. pas., "were fitted"
ὥσπερ ἔφην: "as I said"
ἐληλύθει: plpf. of ἔρχομαι, "he had come"
ὑπέσχετο: ao. of ὑπο-ισχνέομαι, "he promised" + fut. inf.
παρέξειν: fut. inf. of παρέχω, "to provide"
ἀνδρῶν ... εἰδότων: pf. part. of οἶδα, "of men who know how to" + inf.
ἀφῖκτο: plpf. of ἀφ-ικνέομαι, "the journey (time) had arrived"
εἴ ποτε χωρίον εἴη: past. gen. cond., "if ever the place was rough"
εἴη: pr. opt. of εἰμι

τοῖς ὀχήμασιν ἐπιβαίνειν χαλεπόν. ὡς δὲ κατέβημεν ἐπὶ
Θεσσαλονίκην, οὐκ ἦν ὅστις ἐπὶ θέαν οὐκ ἠπείγετο καὶ τὴν
ὄψιν τὴν ἐμήν· ἡ γὰρ ἐμὴ δόξα προεληλύθει ἐκ μακροῦ καὶ τὸ
πολυπρόσωπον καὶ τὸ ἀνθρώπινον τῶν ἐμῶν ὀρχημάτων καὶ
παλαισμάτων. ἀλλ᾽ ὁ μὲν δεσπότης τοῖς ἐνδοξοτάτοις τῶν
αὐτοῦ πολιτῶν παρὰ τὸν πότον ἐδείκνυέ με καὶ τὰ παράδοξα
ἐκεῖνα τὰ ἐν ἐμοὶ παίγνια ἐν τῷ δείπνῳ παρετίθει.

ἀνθρώπινος, -η, -ον: of man, human
δείκνυμι: to display, exhibit
δεῖπνον, τό: a meal
δεσπότης, -ου, ὁ: a master, lord
δόξα, ἡ: a belief, reputation
ἔνδοξος, -ον: esteemed, honored
ἐπείγω: to press down, weigh down
ἐπιβαίνω: to go upon
θέα, ἡ: a seeing, view, spectacle
καταβαίνω: to go down
μακρός, -ά, -όν: long, far
ὄρχημα, -ατος, τό: dancing

ὄχημα, -ατος, τό: a carriage
ὄψις, -εως, ἡ: a look, view
παίγνιον, τό: a game, comic performance
πάλαισμα, -ατος, τό: wrestling
παράδοξος, -ον: incredible, paradoxical
παρατίθημι: to place beside
πολίτης, -ου, ὁ: a citizen
πολυπρόσωπος, -ον: many-faced, with
    many acting roles
πότος, ὁ: a drinking
προέρχομαι: to go forward, advance
χαλεπός, -ή, -όν: hard, difficult

ἐπιβαίνειν: epexegetic inf., "difficult *to traverse*"
κατέβημεν: ao. of κατα-βαίνω, "as we reached"
ἠπείγετο; impf. mid. of ἐπείγω, "who was not pressing forward"
προεληλύθει: plpf. of προ-ἔρχομαι, "had already gone before"
ἐκ μακροῦ: "from a great distance"
καὶ τὸ: "and so had the..."
ἐδείκνυε: impf., "he would show me" + dat.
παρετίθει: impf., "he would set forth"

Lucian

Lucius' keeper charges admission to see Lucius.

[50.] ὁ δὲ ἐμὸς ἐπιστάτης πρόσοδον εὖρεν ἐξ ἐμοῦ
πολλῶν πάνυ δραχμῶν· κατακλείσας γάρ με ἔνδον εἶχεν
ἑστῶτα, καὶ τοῖς βουλομένοις ἰδεῖν ἐμὲ καὶ τἀμὰ παράδοξα
ἔργα μισθοῦ τὴν θύραν ἤνοιγεν. οἱ δ᾽ εἰσεκόμιζον ἄλλος ἄλλο
τι τῶν ἐδωδίμων, μάλιστα τὸ ἐχθρὸν εἶναι ὄνου γαστρὶ
δοκοῦν· ἐγὼ δὲ ἤσθιον. ὥστε ὀλίγων ἡμερῶν τῷ δεσπότῃ καὶ
τοῖς ἐν τῇ πόλει συναριστῶν μέγας τε καὶ πίων δεινῶς ἤδη
ἐγεγόνειν.

ἀνοίγνυμι: to open
βούλομαι: to will, wish
γαστήρ, γαστρός, ἡ: the belly, stomach
δεινός, -ή, -όν: fearful, terrible
δεσπότης, -ου, ὁ: a master, lord
δραχμή, ἡ: a drachma
ἐδώδιμος, -η, -ον: eatable
εἰσκομίζω: to carry into
ἐπιστάτης, -ου, ὁ: an overseer, caretaker
ἔργον, τό: a deed, work, act
ἐσθίω: to eat
εὑρίσκω: to find

ἐχθρός, -ά, -όν: hated, hostile
ἡμέρα, ἡ: a day
θύρα, ἡ: a door
ἵστημι: to make to stand
κατακλείω: to shut in, enclose
μισθός, ὁ: a fee
ὀλίγος, -η, -ον: few, little, scanty, small
παράδοξος, -ον: incredible, paradoxical
πίων, -ον: fat, plump
πόλις, -εως, ἡ: a city
πρόσοδος, ἡ: a income, profit
συναριστάω: to share a meal

εὖρεν: ao. of εὑρίσκω, "he discovered"
πρόσοδον: "a means of" + gen.
ἑστῶτα: pf. part. of ἵστημι, "he kept me standing there"
τοῖς βουλομένοις: "for those wishing" + inf.
μισθοῦ: gen. of price, "for a fee"
ἤνοιγεν: impf. of ἀνοίγνυμι, "he would open the door"
τὸ ... δοκοῦν: pr. part. of δοκέω, "the (food) seeming" + inf.
ὥστε ἐγεγόνειν: plpf. of γίγνομαι in result clause, "so that I had become"
ὀλίγων ἡμερῶν: gen. of time within which, "in the course of a few days"
συναριστῶν: pr. part., "by eating with" + dat.

A foreign lady pays to be able to sleep with Lucius. (cf. Ap. Met. X.19-23, p. 186)

καί ποτε γυνὴ ξένη οὐ μέτρια κεκτημένη, τὴν ὄψιν
ἱκανή, παρελθοῦσα ἔσω ἰδεῖν ἐμὲ ἀριστῶντα εἰς ἔρωτά μου
θερμὸν ἐμπίπτει, τοῦτο μὲν τὸ κάλλος ἰδοῦσα τοῦ ὄνου, τοῦτο
δὲ τῷ παραδόξῳ τῶν ἐμῶν ἐπιτηδευμάτων εἰς ἐπιθυμίαν
συνουσίας προελθοῦσα· καὶ διαλέγεται πρὸς τὸν ἐπιστάτην
τὸν ἐμὸν καὶ μισθὸν αὐτῷ ἁδρὸν ὑπέσχετο, εἰ συγχωρήσειεν
αὐτῇ σὺν ἐμοὶ τὴν νύκτα ἀναπαύσεσθαι· κἀκεῖνος οὐδὲν

ἁδρύς, -ά, -όν: thick, fine, fat
ἀναπαύω: to make to cease, to stop or hinder from
ἀριστάω: to have a meal
γυνή, γυναικός, ἡ: a woman, wife
διαλέγω: to speak to
ἐμπίτνω: fall upon
ἐπιθυμία, ἡ: desire, yearning, longing
ἐπιστάτης, -ου, ὁ: an overseer
ἐπιτήδευμα, -ατος, τό: a pursuit, practice
ἔρως, -ωτος, ὁ: love, desire
ἔσω: inside
θερμός, -ή, -όν: hot, warm
ἱκανός, -ή, -όν: becoming, befitting

κάλλος, -εος, τό: beauty
κτάομαι: to get, gain, acquire
μέτριος, -α, -ον: within measure
μισθός, ὁ: pay, reward, a bribe
νύξ, νυκτός, ἡ: night
ξένος, -η, -ον: foreign, strange
ὄψις, -εως, ἡ: look, appearance, aspect
παράδοξος, -ον: incredible, paradoxical
προέρχομαι: to go forward, go on, advance
συγχωρέω: to come together, meet
συνουσία, ἡ: a being with, intercourse
ὑπισχνέομαι: to promise

οὐ μέτρια κεκτημένη: pf. part. of κτάομαι, "having acquired (possessions) not normal," i.e. "very rich"
ὄψιν: acc. of resp., "becoming *in looks*"
παρελθοῦσα: ao. part. of παρα-έρχομαι, "having come inside"
ἰδεῖν: ao. inf. of εἶδον expressing purpose, "in order to see me"
τοῦτο μὲν ... τοῦτο δὲ: "partly for this, partly for that" explaining the passion of the woman
ἰδοῦσα: ao. part. of εἶδον, "because she had seen"
προελθοῦσα: ao. part. of προ-έρχομαι, "because *she had progressed* into desire"
ὑπέσχετο: ao. of ὑπο-ισχνέομαι, "she promised (to pay) money"
εἰ συγχωρήσειεν: the protasis of a fut. more vivid cond. changed from subj. to opt. in ind. st. after ὑπέσχετο, "she promised that if he would allow her to" + inf.
ἀναπαύσεσθαι: fut. inf. mid. after συγχωρήσειεν, "to spend the night"

φροντίσας, εἴτε ἀνύσει τι ἐκείνη ἐξ ἐμοῦ εἴτε καὶ μή, λαμβάνει
τὸν μισθόν.

She comes at night and has a tryst with Lucius.

[51.] κἀπειδὴ ἑσπέρα τε ἦν ἤδη κἀκ τοῦ συμποσίου
ἀφῆκεν ἡμᾶς ὁ δεσπότης, ἀναστρέφομεν ἔνθα ἐκαθεύδομεν, καὶ
τὴν γυναῖκα εὕρομεν πάλαι ἀφιγμένην ἐπὶ τὴν ἐμὴν εὐνήν.
κεκόμιστο δὲ αὐτῇ προσκεφάλαια μαλακὰ καὶ στρώματα εἴσω
κατέθεντο καὶ χαμεύνιον ἡμῖν εὐτρεπὲς ἦν. εἶτα οἱ μὲν τῆς
γυναικὸς θεράποντες αὐτοῦ που πλησίον πρὸ τοῦ δωματίου
ἐκάθευδον, ἡ δὲ λύχνον ἔνδον ἔκαιε μέγαν τῷ πυρὶ

ἀναστρέφω: to turn back, return
ἀνύω: to effect, achieve, accomplish
ἀφίημι: to send away, discharge
ἀφικνέομαι: to come to
γυνή, γυναικός, ἡ: a woman, wife
δεσπότης, -ου, ὁ: a master, lord
δωμάτιον, τό: a bed-chamber
εἴσω: to within, into
εἴτε... εἴτε: either...or
ἔνθα: there
ἑσπέρα, ἡ: evening
εὐνή, ἡ: a bed
εὑρίσκω: to find
εὐτρεπής, -ές: prepared, ready
θεράπων, -οντος, ὁ: an attendant, servant
καθεύδω: to sleep

καίω: to light, kindle
κατατίθημι: to place, put
κομίζω: to carry, lead
λύχνος, ὁ: a lamp
μαλακός, -ή, -όν: soft
μισθός, ὁ: pay, reward, a bribe
πάλαι: for a long time
πλήσιος, -α, -ον: near, close
προσκεφάλαιον, τό: a cushion, pillow
πῦρ, πυρός, τό: fire
στρῶμα, -ατος, τό: bedding
συμπόσιον, τό: a drinking-party,
    symposium
φροντίζω: to think, consider, have a care
χαμεύνιον, τό: a small pallet bed

οὐδὲν φροντίσας: ao. part. of φροντίζω, "since he didn't care"
εἴτε ... εἴτε καὶ μή: ind. quest. after φροντίσας, "whether she would accomplish ...
    or not"
κἀκ: (= καὶ ἐκ)
ἀφῆκεν: ao. of ἀπο-ΐημι, "he sent us away"
εὕρομεν: ao. of εὑρίσκω, "we found the woman"
ἀφιγμένην: pf. part. of ἀφικνέομαι, "long ago arrived"
κεκόμιστο: plpf. of κομίζω, "she had placed on it (i.e. the bed)"
κατέθεντο: ao. of κατα-τίθημι, "she had deposited"
ἡ δὲ: "but she"

λαμπόμενον· ἔπειτα ἀποδυσαμένη παρέστη τῷ λύχνῳ γυμνὴ ὅλη καὶ μύρον ἔκ τινος ἀλαβάστρου προχεαμένη τούτῳ ἀλείφεται, κἀμὲ δὲ μυρίζει ἔνθεν, μάλιστα τὴν ῥῖνά μου μύρων ἐνέπλησεν, εἶτά με

καὶ ἐφίλησε καὶ οἷα πρὸς αὐτῆς ἐρώμενον καὶ ἄνθρωπον διελέγετο καί με ἐκ τῆς φορβειᾶς ἐπιλαβομένη ἐπὶ τὸ χαμεύνιον εἷλκε· κἀγὼ

οὐδέν τι τοῦ παρακαλέσαντος εἰς τοῦτο δεόμενος καὶ οἴνῳ δὲ παλαιῷ πολλῷ ὑποβεβρεγμένος καὶ τῷ χρίσματι τοῦ μύρου

ἀλάβαστρος, ὁ: an alabaster vase	**μύρον, τό**: an unguent, sweet oil
ἀλείφω: to anoint (with oil)	**οἶνος, ὁ**: wine
ἄνθρωπος, ὁ: a man	**οἷος, -α, -ον**: such as
ἀποδύνω: to strip off	**ὅλος, -η, -ον**: whole, entire, complete
γυμνός, -ή, -όν: naked, unclad	**παλαιός, -ά, -όν**: old, ancient
διαλέγω: to speak to	**παρακαλέω**: to call to
ἕλκω: to draw, drag	**παρίστημι**: to make to stand, place beside
ἐμπίπλημι: to fill up	**προχέω**: to pour forth
ἔνθεν: thereafter	**ῥίς, ῥινός, ἡ**: a nose
ἔπειτα: thereupon	**ὑποβεβρεγμένος, -η, -ον**: somewhat drunk
ἐπιλαμβάνω: to take hold of	
ἐρώμενος, ὁ: beloved	**φιλέω**: to love, kiss
λάμπω: to shine, beam, be bright	**φορβειά, ἡ**: a halter
λύχνος, ὁ: a lamp	**χαμεύνιον, τό**: a small pallet bed
μυρίζω: to rub with unguent	**χρίσμα, -ατος, τό**: an anointing

---

ἀποδυσαμένη: ao. part., "she having undressed"
παρέστη: ao. of **παρα-ἵστημι**, "she stood completely naked"
προχεαμένη: ao. part. mid. of **προ-χέω**, "she having poured out"
ἀλείφεται: pr. mid., "she anoints herself"
ἐνέπλησεν: ao. of **ἐν-πίμπλημι**, "she filled up my nose"
οἷα πρὸς αὐτῆς ἐρώμενον: "just as toward her beloved"
ἐπιλαβομένη: "having taken hold of my halter"
εἷλκε: impf. of **ἕλκω**, "she drew me toward the bed"
οὐδέν τι: acc. of resp., "in no respect whatsoever"
τοῦ παρακαλέσαντος: ao. part. gen. s. after **δεόμενος**, "lacking *something summoning me*"
ὑποβεβρεγμένος: pf. part. of **ὑποβρέχω**, "having been soaked"

οἰστρημένος καὶ τὴν παιδίσκην δὲ ὁρῶν πάντα καλὴν
κλίνομαι, καὶ σφόδρα ἠπόρουν ὅπως ἀναβήσομαι τὴν
ἄνθρωπον· καὶ γὰρ ἐξ ὅτου ἐγεγόνειν ὄνος, συνουσίας ἀλλ᾽
οὐδὲ τῆς ὄνοις συνήθους ἔτυχον ἀψάμενος οὐδὲ γυναικὶ
ἐχρησάμην ὄνῳ·

Lucius fears he will destroy the woman, but his fears are groundless.

καὶ μὴν καὶ τοῦτό μ᾽ εἰς δέος οὐχὶ μέτριον ἦγε, μὴ οὐ
χωρήσασα ἡ γυνὴ διασπασθῇ, κἀγὼ ὥσπερ ἀνδροφόνος καλὴν

ἄγω: to lead, carry
ἀναβαίνω: to go up, mount
ἀνδροφόνος, ον: murderous, homicidal
ἄνθρωπος, ἡ: a woman
ἀπορέω: to be at a loss
ἅπτω: to touch
γυνή, γυναικός, ἡ: a woman, wife
δέος, δέους, τό: fear, alarm, affright
διασπάω: to tear apart
κλίνω: to lay down
μέτριος, -α, -ον: within measure

οἰστράω: to drive mad, arouse
ὄνος, ἡ: a female ass
παιδίσκη, ἡ: a young girl, maiden
συνήθης, -ες: accustomed, customary, usual
συνουσία, ἡ: a being with, intercourse
σφόδρα: very, very much
τυγχάνω: to hit, happen upon
χράομαι: to use (+ dat.)
χωρέω: to make room, give way

οἰστρημένος; pr. part. of οἰστράω, "having been aroused"
πάντα: acc. of resp., "in every way"
ὅπως ἀναβήσομαι: ind quest. after ἠπόρουν, "I was very worried *how I would mount*"
ἀναβήσομαι: fut. of ἀνα-βαίνω
ἐξ ὅτου: gen. of rel. pron. ὅστις, "from whatever time"
ἐγεγόνειν: plpf. of γίγνομαι, "I had become"
τῆς ὄνοις συνήθους: "the intercourse *customary for asses*"
ἔτυχον: ao. of τυγχάνω, "I happened to" + part.
ἀψάμενος: ao. part. mid. of ἅπτω after ἔτυχον, "to have engaged in" + gen.
ἐχρησάμην: ao. mid. of χράω, "nor had I used (sexually)" + dat.
εἰς δέος: "this led me *into a fear*"
μὴ ... διασπασθῇ: ao. subj. pas. of διασπάω in clause of fearing, "lest she be torn apart." The use of the subjunctive instead of the optative after ἦγε is the more vivid construction.
οὐ χωρήσασα: ao. part. of χωρέω, "not making room for me"

134

δώσω δίκην. ἠγνόουν δὲ οὐκ εἰς δέον δεδιώς. ἡ γὰρ γυνὴ
πολλοῖς τοῖς φιλήμασι, καὶ τούτοις ἐρωτικοῖς, προσκαλουμένη
ὡς εἶδεν οὐ κατέχοντα, ὥσπερ ἀνδρὶ παρακειμένη
περιβάλλεταί με καὶ ἄρασα εἴσω ὅλον παρεδέξατο. κἀγὼ μὲν ὁ
δειλὸς ἐδεδοίκειν ἔτι καὶ ὀπίσω ἀπῆγον ἐμαυτὸν ἀτρέμα, ἡ δὲ
τῆς τε ὀσφύος τῆς ἐμῆς εἴχετο, ὥστε μὴ ὑποχωρεῖν, καὶ αὐτὴ
εἵπετο τὸ φεῦγον. ἐπεὶ δὲ ἀκριβῶς ἐπείσθην ἔτι μοι καὶ
προσδεῖν πρὸς τὴν τῆς γυναικὸς ἡδονήν τε καὶ τέρψιν, ἀδεῶς

ἀγνοέω: not to perceive, not to know
ἀδεής, -ές: without fear, fearless
αἴρω: to raise, lift up
ἀκριβῶς: certainly
ἀνήρ, ἀνδρός ὁ: a man
ἀπάγω: to lead away, carry off
ἀτρέμα: (adv.) without motion
γυνή, γυναικός, ἡ: a woman, wife
δείδω: to fear
δειλός, -ή, -όν: cowardly, miserable
δίδωμι: to give
δίκη, ἡ: justice, lawsuit
εἴσω: to within, into
ἕπομαι: to follow
ἐρωτικός, -ή, -όν: amatory, passionate

ἡδονή, ἡ: delight, enjoyment, pleasure
κατέχω: to hold fast, hold back
ὅλος, -η, -ον: whole, entire, complete
ὀπίσω: backwards
ὀσφῦς, ὀσφύος, ἡ: loins
παραδέχομαι: to receive
παράκειμαι: to lie beside
πείθω: to prevail upon, persuade
περιβάλλω: to throw around, embrace
προσδέω: to need besides
προσκαλέω: to call to, summon
τέρψις, -εως, ἡ: enjoyment, delight
ὑποχωρέω: to go back, withdraw
φεύγω: to flee, run away
φίλημα, -ατος, τό: a kiss

δώσω: fut. of **δίδωμι**, "and I will pay a penalty" logically still part of the fear he has, but expressed vividly with the indicative.
ἠγνόουν: impf. of **ἀγνοέω**, "I didn't realize"
δεδιώς: pf. part. of **δείδω** in ind. st. after **ἠγνόουν**, "I failed to recognize that I was fearing"
οὐκ εἰς δέον: pr. part. of **δέω**, "not to anything binding"
οὐ κατέχοντα: pr. part. in ind. st. after **εἶδεν**, "as she saw that I was not holding back"
ἄρασα: ao. part. of **αἴρω**, "having taken it in"
παρεδέξατο: ao. of **παρα-δέχομαι**, "she received it whole"
ἐδεδοίκειν: plpf. of **δείδω**, "I was afraid still"
ἀπῆγον: impf., "I kept withdrawing"
εἴχετο: impf. mid., "she took hold of" + gen.
ὥστε μὴ ὑποχωρεῖν: result clause, "so that I would not draw back"
εἵπετο: impf. of **ἕπομαι**, "she kept pursuing"
τὸ φεῦγον: "the fleeing (member)"
ἐπείσθην: ao. pas. of **πείθω**, "after I was persuaded"
προσδεῖν: pr. inf. in ind st. after **ἐπείσθην**, "that more was needed from me"

λοιπὸν ὑπηρέτουν ἐννοούμενος ὡς οὐδὲν εἴην κακίων τοῦ τῆς
Πασιφάης μοιχοῦ. ἡ δὲ γυνὴ οὕτως ἦν ἄρα ἐς τὰ ἀφροδίσια
ἑτοίμη καὶ τῆς ἀπὸ τῆς συνουσίας ἡδονῆς ἀκόρεστος, ὥστε
ὅλην τὴν νύκτα ἐν ἐμοὶ ἐδαπάνησεν.

*The master finds out about the woman and resolves to have Lucius perform with
a condemned woman in public.*

[52.] ἅμα δὲ τῇ ἡμέρᾳ ἡ μὲν ἀναστᾶσα ἀπῄει συνθεμένη
πρὸς τὸν ἐπιστάτην τὸν ἐμὸν οἴσειν ἐπὶ τοῖς αὐτοῖς τὸν
μισθὸν τὸν αὐτὸν τῆς νυκτός. ὁ δὲ ἅμα μὲν πλουσιώτερος ἐκ
τῶν ἐμῶν γενόμενος καὶ τῷ δεσπότῃ καινότερον ἐν ἐμοὶ

ἀκόρεστος, -ον: insatiate
ἀνίστημι: to make to stand up, raise up
ἀπέρχομαι: to go away, depart
ἀφροδίσιος, -α, -ον: belonging to Aphrodite, (*subst.*) lust, sex
γυνή, γυναικός, ἡ: a woman, wife
δαπανάω: to spend
δεσπότης, -ου, ὁ: a master, lord
ἐννοέω: to think, consider, reflect
ἐπιστάτης, -ου, ὁ: an overseer, caretaker
ἑτοῖμος, -ον: at hand, ready, prepared
ἡδονή, ἡ: delight, enjoyment, pleasure
ἡμέρα, ἡ: a day

καινός, -ή, -όν: new, fresh
κακός, -ή, -όν: bad
λοιπός, -ή, -όν: remaining, the rest
μισθός, ὁ: pay, reward, bribe
μοιχός, ὁ: an adulterer, paramour
νύξ, νυκτός, ἡ: night
ὅλος, -η, -ον: whole, entire, complete
Πασιφάη, ἡ: Pasiphae
πλούσιος, -α, -ον: rich, wealthy
συνουσία, ἡ: a being with, intercourse
συντίθημι: to put together, arrange
ὑπηρετέω: to service
φέρω: to bear, carry

λοιπὸν: acc. of duration, "for the rest of the time"
ὑπηρέτουν: impf. of ὑπηρετέω, "I kept serving"
ὡς οὐδὲν εἴην: opt. in ind. st. after ἐννοούμενος, "thinking that I was no worse"
τοῦ τῆς Πασιφάης μοιχοῦ: gen. of comp. after κακίων. Pasiphae was loved by
    the bull of Poseidon.
ἄρα: "as it appeared"
οὕτως ἦν ... ὥστε: "was so ready and insatiable... that she..."
ὅλην τὴν νύκτα: acc. of duration, "the whole night long"
ἐδαπάνησεν: ao. of δαπανάω, "she spent"
ἀναστᾶσα: ao. part. of ἀνα-ἵστημι, "having arisen"
ἀπῄει: impf. of ἀπο-ἔρχομαι, "she left"
συνθεμένη: ao. part. of συν-τίθημι, "having arranged" + inf.
οἴσειν: fut. inf. of φέρω after συνθεμένη, "arranged *to bring*"
ἐπὶ τοῖς αὐτοῖς: "on the same terms"
τῆς νυκτός: gen. of time within which, "during the night"
γενόμενος: ao. part. of γίγνομαι, "having become"

ἐπιδειξόμενος συγκατακλείει με τῇ γυναικί· ἡ δὲ κατεχρήσατό
μοι δεινῶς. καί ποτε ἐλθὼν ὁ ἐπιστάτης ἀπαγγέλλει τῷ
δεσπότῃ τὸ ἔργον, ὡς ἂν αὐτὸς διδάξας, καὶ ἐμοῦ μὴ εἰδότος
ἄγει αὐτὸν ἑσπέρας ἤδη ἔνθα ἐκαθεύδομεν, καὶ διά τινος ὀπῆς
τῆς θύρας δείκνυσί με ἔνδον τῇ μείρακι συνευναζόμενον. ὁ δὲ
ἡσθεὶς τῇ θέᾳ καὶ δημοσίᾳ με ταῦτα ποιοῦντα δεῖξαι
ἐπεθύμησε, καὶ κελεύει πρὸς μηδένα ἔξω τοῦτο εἰπεῖν, «Ἵνα,»
ἔφη, «ἐν τῇ ἡμέρᾳ τῆς θέας παραγάγωμεν τοῦτον ἐς τὸ
θέατρον σύν τινι τῶν καταδεδικασμένων γυναικῶν, κἂν

ἄγω: to lead, bring
ἀπαγγέλλω: to report, announce
γυνή, γυναικός, ἡ: a woman, wife
δείκνυμι: to show, display
δεινῶς: terribly, dreadfully
δεσπότης, -ου, ὁ: a master, lord
δημόσιος, -α, -ον: of the people, public
διδάσκω: to teach
ἐπιδείκνυμι: to show off, display
ἐπιθυμέω: to desire
ἐπιστάτης, -ου, ὁ: an overseer, caretaker
ἔργον, τό: a deed, work, act
ἑσπέρα, ἡ: evening
ἥδομαι: to enjoy oneself, take delight, take
    one's pleasure
ἡμέρα, ἡ: a day

θέα, ἡ: a seeing, sight, spectacle
θέατρον, τό: a theater
θύρα, ἡ: a door
καθεύδω: to lie down, sleep
καταδικάζω: to pass judgment against,
    condemn
καταχράομαι: to make full use of (+ dat.)
κελεύω: to bid, command, order
μεῖραξ, -ακος, ἡ: a young girl, lass
οἶδα: to know
ὀπή, ἡ: an opening, hole
παράγω: to lead by
ποιέω: to make, do
συγκατακλείω: to shut in together
συνευνάζω: to lay down with

ἐπιδειξόμενος: fut. part. of ἐπι-δείκνυμι, "in order to show"
κατεχρῆσατο: impf. of κατα-κράομαι, "she made full use of me"
ἐλθὼν: ao. part. of ἔρχομαι
ὡς ἂν αὐτὸς διδάξας: ao. part. of διδάσκω, "as though he himself had taught."
    The use of ἂν + indic. indicates it is contrary-to-fact.
ἐμοῦ μὴ εἰδότος: gen. abs., "with me not knowing"
ἑσπέρας: gen. of time within which, "in the course of the evening"
με ... συνευναζόμενον: "he shows me sleeping with"
ἡσθεὶς: ao. part. of ἥδομαι, "having enjoyed" + dat.
με ταῦτα ποιοῦντα: "to show me doing these things"
δεῖξαι: fut. inf. of δείκνυμι, "to show"
ἐπεθύμησεν: ao. of ἐπι-θυμέω, "he desired" + fut. inf.
πρὸς μηδένα ἔξω: "to no one else"
ἵνα ... παραγάγωμεν: ao. subj. of παρα-άγω in purpose clause, "in order to lead
    along"
τῶν καταδεδικασμένων: pf. part. of κατα-δικάζω, "with someone of those
    condemned"

πάντων ὀφθαλμοῖς ἐπὶ τὴν γυναῖκα ἀναβήσεται.» καί τινα τῶν γυναικῶν, ἥτις κατεκέκριτο θηρίοις ἀποθανεῖν, ἄγουσιν ἔνδον παρ᾽ ἐμὲ καὶ προσιέναι τε ἐκέλευον καὶ ψαύειν ἐμοῦ.

Lucius and the condemned woman are brought to the amphitheater.

[53.] εἶτα τὸ τελευταῖον τῆς ἡμέρας ἐκείνης ἐνστάσης, ἐν ᾗ τὰς φιλοτιμίας ἦγεν ὁ ἐμὸς δεσπότης, εἰσάγειν ἔγνωσάν με εἰς τὸ θέατρον. καὶ εἰσῄειν οὕτω· κλίνη ἦν μεγάλη, ἀπὸ χελώνης Ἰνδικῆς πεποιημένη, χρυσῷ ἐσφηκωμένη, ἐπὶ ταύτης με ἀνακλίνουσιν κἀκεῖ μοι τὴν γυναῖκα παρακατέκλιναν. εἶτα οὕτως ἡμᾶς ἐπέθηκαν ἐπί τινος μηχανήματος καὶ εἴσω εἰς τὸ

ἄγω: to lead, bring
ἀναβαίνω: to go up, mount
ἀνακλίνω: to lean, lay down
ἀποθνήσκω: to die
γιγνώσκω: to know
δεσπότης, -ου, ὁ: a master, lord
εἰσάγω: to lead in
εἰσέρχομαι: to go into, enter
εἴσω: to within, into
ἐνίστημι: to be upon, present
ἐπιτίθημι: to place upon
ἡμέρα, ἡ: a day
θέατρον, τό: a theater
θηρίον, τό: a wild animal, beast
Ἰνδικός, -ή, -όν: Indian

κατακρίνω: to give a sentence, condemn
κελεύω: to bid, command, order
κλίνη, ἡ: a couch, bed
μηχάνημα, -ατος, τό: a machine, a mechanical stage device for lifting things and people
ὀφθαλμός, ὁ: an eye
παρακατακλίνω: to lay down beside
προσίημι: to admit, submit
σφηκόω: to bind tightly
τελευταῖος, -α, -ον: last, final
φιλοτιμία, ἡ: munificence
χελώνη, ἡ: a tortoise
χρυσός, ὁ: gold
ψαύω: to touch

κἀν (= καὶ ἐν) πάντων ὀφθαλμοῖς: "in front of all"
ἀναβήσεται: fut. part. of ἀνα-βαίνω, "he will mount"
κατεκέκριτο: plpf. of κατα-κρίνω, "who had been condemned"
ἀποθανεῖν: ao. inf. of ἀπο-θνήσκω after κατεκέκριτο, "condemned to die"
προσιέναι τε καὶ ψαύειν: ind. com. after ἐκέλευον, "they ordered her to approach and touch me"
ἡμέρας ἐνστάσης: gen. abs., "that day being at hand"
ἐνστάσης: ao. part. intrans. of ἐν -ἵστημι
ἐν ᾗ: "the day on which"
ἔγνωσάν: ao. part. of γιγνώσκω, "they decided to" + inf.
εἰσῄειν: impf. of εἰσ-έρχομαι, "I went"
πεποιημένη: pf. part. of ποιέω, "constructed"
ἐσφηκωμένη: pf. part. of σφηκόω, *"bound together by gold"*
παρακατέκλιναν: ao. part. of παρα-κατα-κλίνω, "they caused her to lie down beside"
ἐπέθηκαν: ao. of παρα-τίθημι, "they disposed us"

138

θέατρον παρενέγκαντες κατέθηκαν ἐν τῷ μέσῳ, καὶ οἱ
ἄνθρωποι μέγα ἀνεβόησαν καὶ κρότος πάσης χειρὸς ἐξήλατο
ἐπ᾽ ἐμοί, καὶ τράπεζα ἡμῖν παρέκειτο καὶ πολλὰ ἐσκευασμένα
ἐπ᾽ αὐτῇ ἔκειτο ὅσα τρυφῶντες ἄνθρωποι ἐν δείπνῳ ἔχουσιν.
καὶ παῖδες ἡμῖν παρειστήκεισαν οἰνοχόοι καλοὶ τὸν οἶνον ἡμῖν
χρυσίῳ διακονούμενοι. ὁ μὲν οὖν ἐμὸς ἐπιστάτης ἑστὼς
ὄπισθεν ἐκέλευέν με ἀριστᾶν· ἐγὼ δὲ ἅμα μὲν ἠδούμην ἐν τῷ
θεάτρῳ κατακείμενος, ἅμα δὲ ἐδεδίειν μή που ἄρκτος ἢ λέων
ἀναπηδήσεται.

αἰδέομαι: to be ashamed
ἀναβοάω: to shout aloud, cry out
ἀναπηδάω: to leap up
ἄνθρωπος, ὁ: a man
ἀριστάω: to eat a meal
ἄρκτος, ἡ: a bear
δείδω: to fear
δεῖπνον, τό: a meal, dinner
διακονέω: to serve
ἐξάλλομαι: to leap up, swell
ἐπιστάτης, -ου, ὁ: an overseer, caretaker
θέατρον, τό: a theater
ἵστημι: to make to stand
κατάκειμαι: to lie down
κατατίθημι: to put down
κελεύω: to bid, command, order

κρότος, ὁ: a striking, clapping
λέων, -οντος, ὁ: a lion
μέσος, -η, -ον: middle, in the middle
οἶνος, ὁ: wine
οἰνόχοος, ὁ: a cupbearer
ὄπισθεν: behind, at the back
παῖς, παιδός, ὁ: a slave, boy
παράκειμαι: to lie beside
παραφέρω: to bring to
παρίστημι: to make to stand beside
σκευάζω: to prepare, make ready
τράπεζα, -ης, ἡ: a table
τρυφάω: to live luxuriously
χείρ, χειρός, ἡ: a hand
χρυσίον, τό: a golden object

παρενέγκαντες: ao. part. of παρα-φέρω, "having carried into"
κατέθηκαν: ao. part. of κατα-τίθημι, "they set us down"
ἀνεβόησαν: ao. part. of ἀνα-βοάω, "they shouted"
ἐξήλατο: ao. of ἐξάλλομαι, "applause *leapt up*"
ἐσκευασμένα: pf. part. of σκευάζω, "many prepared things lay on it"
παρειστήκεισαν: plpf. of παρα-ἵστημι, "were standing around"
χρυσίῳ: dat., "in a gold (cup)"
ἑστὼς: pf. part. of ἵστημι, "my keeper standing behind"
με ἀριστᾶν: ind. com. after ἐκέλευεν, "ordered me to sup"
ἅμα μέν ... ἅμα δέ: "partly ... partly"
ἠδούμην: impf. of αἰδέομαι, "I was ashamed to be" + part.
ἐδεδίειν: plpf. of δείδω, "I was afraid"
μή ... ἀναπηδήσεται: vivid fut. indic. in a clause of fearing (instead of opt.), "lest
  some bear shall leap out"

139

By chance Lucius eats some roses and is turned back into a man.

[54.] ἐν τούτῳ δέ τινος ἄνθη φέροντος παροδεύοντος ἐν τοῖς ἄλλοις ἄνθεσιν ὁρῶ καὶ ῥόδων χλωρῶν φύλλα, καὶ μηδὲν ἔτι ὀκνῶν ἀναπηδήσας τοῦ λέχους ἐκπίπτω· καὶ οἱ μὲν ᾤοντό με ἀνίστασθαι ὀρχησόμενον· ἐγὼ δὲ ἐν ἐξ ἑνὸς ἐπιτρέχων καὶ ἀπανθιζόμενος ἀπ᾽ αὐτῶν τῶν ἀνθῶν τὰ ῥόδα κατέπινον. τῶν δὲ ἔτι θαυμαζόντων ἐπ᾽ ἐμοὶ ἀποπίπτει ἐξ ἐμοῦ ἐκείνη ἡ τοῦ κτήνους ὄψις καὶ ἀπόλλυται, καὶ ἀφανὴς ἐκεῖνος ὁ πάλαι ὄνος, ὁ δὲ Λούκιος αὐτὸς ἔνθεν μοι γυμνὸς εἱστήκει. τῇ δὲ παραδόξῳ

ἀναπηδάω: to leap up
ἄνθος, ὁ: a blossom, flower
ἀνίστημι: to make to stand up, raise up
ἀπανθίζω: to pick out flowers
ἀπόλλυμι: to destroy, loose
ἀποπίπτω: to fall off
ἀφανής, -ές: unseen, invisible
γυμνός, -ή, -όν: naked, unclad
εἷς, μία, ἕν: one
ἐκπίπτω: to fall
ἐπιτρέχω: to run at, attack
θαυμάζω: to wonder, marvel, be amazed
ἵστημι: to make to stand
καταπίνω: to gulp down

κτῆνος, -εος, τό: a beast, animal
λέχος, -εος, τό: a couch, bed
Λούκιος, ὁ: Lucius
οἴομαι: to suppose, think, imagine
ὀκνέω: to shrink back, hesitate
ὀρχέομαι: to dance
ὄψις, -εως, ἡ: a look, appearance
πάλαι: long ago, for a long time
παράδοξος, -ον: incredible, paradoxical
παροδεύω: to pass by
ῥόδον, τό: a rose
φέρω: to bear
φύλλον, τό: a leaf, petal
χλωρός, -ά, -όν: green, fresh, blooming

ἐν τούτῳ (χρόνῳ): "meanwhile"
τινος φέροντος παροδεύοντος: gen. abs., "someone carrying and parading around flowers"
ἀναπηδήσας: ao. part. of ἀνα-πηδάω, "having leapt up"
ᾤοντο: impf., "they supposed"
με ἀνίστασθαι: ind. st. after ᾤοντο, "that I was getting up"
ὀρχησόμενον: fut. part. showing purpose, "in order to dance"
ἐν ἐξ ἑνὸς: "one by one"
κατέπινον: impf., "I started gulping down"
τῶν δὲ ἔτι θαυμαζόντων: gen. abs., "while these were still marveling"
ἔνθεν: "from within"
εἱστήκει: plpf. of ἵστημι, "was standing there naked"

ταύτῃ καὶ μηδέποτε ἐλπισθείσῃ θέᾳ πάντες ἐκπεπληγμένοι
δεινὸν ἐπεθορύβησαν καὶ τὸ θέατρον εἰς δύο γνώμας ἐσχίζετο·
οἱ μὲν γὰρ ὥσπερ φάρμακα δεινὰ ἐπιστάμενον καὶ κακόν τι
πολύμορφον ἠξίουν εὐθὺς ἔνδον πυρί με ἀποθανεῖν, οἱ δὲ
περιμεῖναι καὶ τοὺς ἀπ' ἐμοῦ λόγους ἔλεγον δεῖν καὶ πρότερον
διαγνῶναι, εἶθ' οὕτως δικάσαι περὶ τούτων. κἀγὼ δραμὼν
πρὸς τὸν ἄρχοντα τῆς ἐπαρχίας – ἔτυχεν δὲ τῇ θέᾳ ταύτῃ
παρών – ἔλεγον κάτωθεν ὅτι γυνή με Θετταλὴ γυναικὸς

ἀξιόω: to think worthy	**θέατρον, τό**: a theater
ἀποθνήσκω: to die	**κακός, -ή, -όν**: bad, evil
ἄρχων, -οντος, ὁ: a ruler	**κάτωθεν**: from below, up from below
γνώμη, ἡ: a thought, judgment, opinion	**λέγω**: to say
γυνή, γυναικός, ἡ: a woman, wife	**λόγος, ὁ**: a word
δεινός, -ή, -όν: fearful, terrible	**μηδέποτε**: never
διαγιγνώσκω: to distinguish, discern	**πάρειμι**: to be present
δικάζω: to judge, to give judgment on	**περιμένω**: to wait for, await
δύο: two	**πολύμορφος, -ον**: multiform
ἐκπλήσσω: to strike out of	**πρότερος, -α, -ον**: before, earlier
ἐλπίζω: to hope, look for, expect	**πῦρ, πυρός, τό**: fire
ἐπαρχία, ἡ: a district, province	**σχίζω**: to split, divide
ἐπιθορυβέω: to shout	**τρέχω**: to run
ἐπίσταμαι: to know	**τυγχάνω**: to hit, happen upon
θέα, ἡ: a seeing, sight, spectacle	**φάρμακον, τό**: a drug, medicine

ἐλπισθείσῃ: ao. part. of **ἐλπίζω** modifying **θέᾳ**, "by this never expected sight"
ἐκπεπληγμένοι: pf. part. of **ἐκ-πλήσσω**, "having been shocked"
ἐπεθορύβησαν: ao. of **ἐπι-θορυβέω**, "all raised a din"
ἐσχίζετο: impf. pas., "was divided"
ὥσπερ...ἐπιστάμενον: "on the grounds that I knew"
ἠξίουν: impf. of **ἀξιόω**, "some deemed it worthy"
με ἀποθανεῖν: acc. + inf. after **ἠξίουν**, "that I die"
οἱ δὲ περιμεῖναι: ao. inf. after **ἠξίουν**, "others (deemed it worthy) to wait"
λόγους ἔλεγον: obj. of **διαγνῶναι**, "to discern the words (which) I would say"
δεῖν: pr. inf. also after **ἠξίουν**, "that it was necessary" + inf.
διαγνῶναι: ao. inf. of **δια-γιγνώσκω** after **δεῖν**, "necessary *to discern*"
εἶτα ... δικάσαι: ao. inf. of **δικάζω** after **δεῖν**, "*then* it was necessary *to judge*"
δραμὼν: ao. part. of **τρέχω**, "having run"
ἔτυχεν: ao. of **τυγχάνω**, "he happened to be" + part.
παρών: pr. part. of **παρα-ειμι** after **ἔτυχεν**, "happened *to be present*"
ὅτι ... ποιήσειεν: ao. opt. of **ποιέω** in sec. seq. after **ἔλεγον**, "that a woman had made me an ass"

Θετταλῆς δούλη χρίσματι μεμαγευμένῳ ἐπαλείψασα ὄνον
ποιήσειεν, καὶ ἱκέτευον αὐτὸν λαβόντα ἔχειν με ἐν φρουρᾷ ἔστ᾽
ἂν αὐτὸν πείσαιμι, ὡς οὐ καταψεύδομαι οὕτω γεγονός.

Lucius reveals his identity to the magistrate, who knows his family.

[55.] καὶ ὁ ἄρχων, «Λέγε,» φησίν, «ἡμῖν ὄνομα τὸ σὸν
καὶ γονέων τῶν σῶν καὶ συγγενῶν, εἴ τινας φὴς ἔχειν τῷ γένει
προσήκοντας, καὶ πόλιν.»

κἀγώ, «Πατὴρ μέν,» ἔφην, «... ἔστι μοι Λούκιος, τῷ δὲ
ἀδελφῷ τῷ ἐμῷ Γάϊος: ἄμφω δὲ τὰ λοιπὰ δύο ὀνόματα κοινὰ
ἔχομεν. κἀγὼ μὲν ἱστοριῶν καὶ ἄλλων εἰμὶ συγγραφεύς, ὁ δὲ

ἀδελφός, ὁ: a brother	κοινός, -ή, -όν: common, shared
ἄμφω: both	λέγω: to say
ἄρχων, -οντος, ὁ: a ruler	λοιπός, -ή, -όν: remaining, the rest
Γάϊος, ὁ: Gaius	μαγεύω: to use magic, enchant
γένος, -εος, τό: race, stock, family	ὄνομα, -ατος, τό: a name
γονεύς, -έως, ὁ: a begetter, parent	πατήρ, ὁ: a father
δοῦλος, ὁ: a slave	πείθω: to win over, persuade
δύο: two	ποιέω: to make
ἐπαλείφω: to smear over, anoint	πόλις, -εως, ἡ: a city
ἔστε: until	προσήκω: to come to, be akin
Θετταλός, -ή, -όν: Thessalian	συγγενής, -ές: born with, related
ἱκετεύω: to beg	συγγραφεύς, -έως, ὁ: a writer
ἱστορία, ἡ: a history	φρουρά, ἡ: a watch, guard
καταψεύδομαι: to lie	χρῖσμα, -ατος, τό: an ointment

μεμαγευμένῳ: pf. part. dat. of μαγεύω, "by bewitched oil"
ἐπαλείψασα: ao. part. of ἐπι-αλείφω, "by anointing"
λαβόντα: ao. part. of λαμβάνω agreeing with αὐτὸν, "having taken"
αὐτὸν ἔχειν: ind. com., "I begged him to keep me"
ἔστ᾽ ἂν αὐτὸν πείσαιμι: ao. opt. of πείθω in gen. temp. clause, "until such time as
   I might persuade," ἂν is potential
οὕτω γεγονός: pf. part. of γίγνομαι in ind. st., "I am not lying *that it happened
   thus*"
εἴ τινας φὴς ἔχειν: "if you claim to have any persons"
προσήκοντας: pr. part., "related"
Πατὴρ: the father's name has dropped out
ὁ δὲ: "but he" (his brother)

ποιητὴς ἐλεγείων ἐστὶ καὶ μάντις ἀγαθός: πατρὶς δὲ ἡμῖν
Πάτραι τῆς Ἀχαΐας.»

ὁ δὲ δικαστὴς ἐπεὶ ταῦτα ἤκουσε, «Φιλτάτων ἐμοί,»
ἔφη, «λίαν ἀνδρῶν υἱὸς εἶ καὶ ξένων οἰκίᾳ τέ με ὑποδεξαμένων
καὶ δώροις τιμησάντων, καὶ ἐπίσταμαι ὅτι οὐδὲν ψεύδῃ παῖς
ἐκείνων ὤν:» καὶ τοῦ δίφρου ἀναπηδήσας περιβάλλει τε καὶ
πολλὰ ἐφίλει, καί με οἴκαδε ἦγεν ὡς ἑαυτόν. ἐν τούτῳ δὲ καὶ ὁ
ἐμὸς ἀδελφὸς ἀφίκετο ἀργύριον καὶ ἄλλα μοι πολλὰ κομίζων,
κἂν τούτῳ με ὁ ἄρχων δημοσίᾳ πάντων ἀκουόντων ἀπολύει.

ἀγαθός, -ή, -όν: good
ἄγω: to lead, bring
ἀδελφός, ὁ: brother
ἀκούω: to hear
ἀναπηδάω: to leap up
ἀνήρ, ἀνδρός ὁ: a man
ἀπολύω: to release
ἀργύριον, τό: silver, money
ἄρχων, -οντος, ὁ: a ruler
ἀφικνέομαι: to come to, arrive
Ἀχαία, ἡ: Achaia (a region)
δημοσίᾳ: (*adv.*) "at the public expense"
δικαστής, -οῦ, ὁ: a judge
δίφρος, ὁ: a seat, throne
δῶρον, τό: a gift, present
ἐλεγεῖον, τό: an elegy
ἐπίσταμαι: to know
κομίζω: to carry, lead

λίαν: very, exceedingly
μάντις, -εως, ὁ: a seer, prophet
ξένος, ὁ: a foreigner, guest
οἴκαδε: home, homewards
οἰκία, ἡ: a house
παῖς, παιδός, ὁ: a slave, boy
Πάτραι, -ῶν, αἱ: Patras (a city)
πατρίς, -ίδος, ἡ: native land
περιβάλλω: to throw around, embrace
ποιητής, -οῦ, ὁ: a poet
τιμάω: to honor
υἱός, ὁ: a son
ὑποδέχομαι: to receive (in one's home),
   host
φιλέω: to love, kiss
φίλτατος, -η, -ον: dearest
ψεύδομαι: to lie

ὑποδεξαμένων: ao. part. gen. pl. agreeing with **ξένων**, "of hosts who have received
   me"
τιμησάντων: ao. part. also agreeing with **ξένων**, "and who have honored me with
   gifts"
ὅτι οὐδὲν ψεύδῃ: pr. 2. s m. of **ψεύδομαι** in ind. st. after **ἐπίσταμαι**, "I know *that
   you are not lying*"
ὤν: causal, "since you are the son of these"
ἀναπηδήσας: ao. part., "having leapt up"
ὡς ἑαυτόν: "to his own house"
ἀφίκετο: ao. of **ἀφικνέομαι**, "arrived"
κἂν (= καὶ ἐν) τούτῳ (sc. χρόνῳ): "meanwhile"
πάντων ἀκουόντων: gen. abs., "with all hearing"

καὶ ἐλθόντες ἐπὶ θάλασσαν ναῦν ἐσκεψάμεθα καὶ τὴν
ἀποσκευὴν ἐνεθέμεθα.

Before departing for home, Lucius decides to visit the lady who loved him as an ass.

[56.] ἐγὼ δὲ κράτιστον εἶναι ἔγνων ἐλθεῖν παρὰ τὴν
γυναῖκα τὴν ἐρασθεῖσάν μου τοῦ ὄνου, καλλίων αὐτῇ
φανεῖσθαι λέγων νῦν ἐν ἀνθρώπῳ ὤν. ἡ δὲ ἀσμένη τέ μ'
εἰσεδέξατο τῷ παραδόξῳ, οἶμαι, τοῦ πράγματος ἐπιτερπομένη,
καὶ δειπνεῖν σὺν αὐτῇ καὶ καθεύδειν ἱκέτευε· κἀγὼ ἐπειθόμην
νεμέσεως ἄξιον εἶναι νομίζων τὸν ὄνον τὸν ἀγαπηθέντα νῦν

ἀγαπάω: to treat with affection, love
ἄνθρωπος, ὁ: a man
ἄξιος, -ία, -ον: worthy, deserving
ἀποσκευή, ἡ: baggage
ἄσμενος, -η, -ον: well-pleased, glad
γιγνώσκω: to know
δειπνέω: to have a meal, dine
εἰσδέχομαι: to take in, admit
ἐντίθημι: to put into
ἐπιτέρπομαι: to rejoice, delight
ἔραμαι: to love
θάλασσα, ἡ: the sea
ἱκετεύω: to beg

καθεύδω: to lie down, sleep
κάλλος, -εος, τό: beauty
κράτιστος, -η, -ον: best
λέγω: to say
ναῦς, ἡ: a ship
νέμεσις, -εως, ἡ: retribution
νομίζω: to believe, think
οἴομαι: to suppose, think, imagine
παράδοξος, -ον: incredible, paradoxical
πείθω: to win over, persuade
πρᾶγμα, -ατος, τό: a deed, act, matter
σκέπτομαι: to look about, look for

ἐλθόντες: ao. part. of ἔρχομαι, "having come"
ἐσκεψάμεθα: ao. of σκέπτομαι, "we looked about for"
ἐνεθέμεθα: ao. of ἐν-τίθημι, "we stored in it"
ἔγνων: ao. of γιγνώσκω, "I decided"
κράτιστον εἶναι: ind. st. after ἔγνων, "that it would be best"
ἐλθεῖν: epexegetic inf. after κράτιστον, "best to go"
ἐρασθεῖσάν: ao. pas. part. acc. s. f. of ἐράω, "the one who was smitten with me"
φανεῖσθαι: fut. inf. in ind. st after λέγων, "calculating that I would appear"
ὤν: causal, "since I am a man"
εἰσεδέξατο: ao. of εἰς-δέχομαι, "she received me"
δειπνεῖν καὶ καθεύδειν: inf. after ἱκέτευεν, "she begged me to sup and to sleep"
ἐπειθόμην: impf., "I obeyed"
ἄξιον εἶναι: ind. st. after νομίζων, "that it would be worthy of" + gen.
τὸν ὄνον .... ὑπερτρυφᾶν καὶ ὑπερορᾶν: epexegetic infinties explaining ἄξιον,
    "for the ass to be excessively haughty and to look down on"
τὸν ἀγαπηθέντα: ao. pas. part. acc. m. of ἀγαπάω, "the ass who had been loved"

γενόμενον ἄνθρωπον ὑπερτρυφᾶν καὶ τὴν ἐρασθεῖσαν
ὑπερορᾶν: καὶ δειπνῶ σὺν αὐτῇ καὶ πολὺ ἐκ τοῦ μύρου
ἀλείφομαι καὶ στεφανοῦμαι τῷ φιλτάτῳ ἐς ἀνθρώπους με
ἀνασώσαντι ῥόδῳ.

After dining with her, he strips naked, but the lady is not impressed.

ἐπεὶ δὲ ἦν νὺξ βαθεῖα ἤδη καὶ καθεύδειν ἔδει, κἀγὼ δ᾽
ἐπανίσταμαι καὶ ὡσπερεὶ μέγα τι ἀγαθὸν ποιῶν ἀποδύομαι
καὶ ἵσταμαι γυμνὸς ὡς δῆθεν ἔτι μᾶλλον ἀρέσων ἐκ τῆς πρὸς
τὸν ὄνον συγκρίσεως. ἡ δὲ ἐπειδὴ εἶδέ με πάντα ἀνθρώπινα
ἔχοντα, προσπτύσασά μοι, «Οὐ φθείρῃ ἀπ᾽ ἐμοῦ,» ἔφη, «καὶ
τῆς ἐμῆς οἰκίας καὶ μακράν ἀπελθὼν κοιμήσῃ;»

ἀγαθός, -ή, -όν: good	κοιμάω: to put to sleep
ἀλείφω: to anoint (with oil)	μακρός, -ά, -όν: long, far
ἀνασώζω: to recover, rescue	μύρον, τό: an unguent, sweet oil
ἀνθρώπινος, -η, -ον: of man, human	νύξ, νυκτός, ἡ: night
ἄνθρωπος, ὁ: a man	οἰκία, ἡ: a house
ἀπέρχομαι: to go away, depart from	ποιέω: to make
ἀποδύνω: to strip off	προσπτύω: to spit upon (+ *dat.*)
ἀρέσκω: to please, satisfy	ῥόδον, τό: a rose
βαθύς, -εῖα, -ύ: high, deep	στεφανόω: to wreathe, garland
γυμνός, -ή, -όν: naked, unclad	σύγκρισις, -εως, ἡ: a comparison
δειπνέω: to have a meal, dine	ὑπεροράω: to look down upon, disdain
ἐπανίστημι: to set up again	ὑπερτρυφάω: to be excessively haughty
ἔραμαι: to love	φθείρω: to ruin, destroy
ἵστημι: to make to stand	φίλτατος, -η, -ον: dearest
καθεύδω: to lie down, sleep	

γενόμενον: ao. part. of **γίγνομαι**, "the ass now become a man"
ὑπερτρυφᾶν: pr. inf. of **ὑπερ-τρυφάω**
ἐρασθεῖσαν: ao. pas. part. acc. f. of **ἔραμαι**, "her who had loved him"
ὑπερορᾶν: pr. inf. of **ὑπερ-οράω**
δειπνῶ: note the change to the vivid present tense, "and I dine with her…"
τῷ φιλτάτῳ … ῥόδῳ: dat. of means, "with the dearest rose"
με ἀνασώσαντι: ao. part. dat. of **ἀνα-σώζω** agreeing with **ῥόδῳ**, "the one that
    saved me"
ἐπανίσταμαι: pr. mid. of **ἐπι-ανα-ἵστημι**, "I get up"
ὡσπερεὶ (ὡς-περ-εἰ): "just as if"
ὡς δῆθεν ἀρέσων: fut. part. of **ἀρέσκω**, "(supposing) that I would be more
    pleasing"
οὐ φθείρῃ: 2 s. fut. pas., "will you not be damned"
ἀπελθὼν: ao. part of **ἔρχομαι**, "having departed"
κοιμήσῃ: fut., "will you take yourself"

ἐμοῦ δ' ἐρομένου, «Τί γὰρ καὶ ἡμάρτηταί μοι τοσοῦτο;» «Ἐγώ,» ἔφη, «μὰ Δί' οὐχὶ σοῦ, ἀλλὰ τοῦ ὄνου τοῦ σοῦ ἐρῶσα τότε ἐκείνῳ καὶ οὐχὶ σοὶ συνεκάθευδον, καὶ ᾤμην σε καὶ νῦν κἂν ἐκεῖνό γε μόνον τὸ μέγα τοῦ ὄνου σύμβολον διασώζειν καὶ σύρειν· σὺ δέ μοι ἐλήλυθας ἐξ ἐκείνου τοῦ καλοῦ καὶ χρησίμου ζῴου ἐς πίθηκον μεταμορφωθείς.»

καὶ καλεῖ εὐθὺς ἤδη τοὺς οἰκέτας καὶ κελεύει με τῶν νώτων μετέωρον κομισθῆναι ἔξω τῆς οἰκίας, καὶ ἐξωσθεὶς πρὸ τοῦ δωματίου ἔξω γυμνὸς καλῶς ἐστεφανωμένος καὶ μεμυρισμένος τὴν γῆν γυμνὴν περιλαβὼν ταύτῃ συνεκάθευδον.

ἀμαρτάνω: to do wrong
γῆ, ἡ: earth
γυμνός, -ή, -όν: naked, unclad
διασῴζω: to preserve, maintain
δωμάτιον, τό: a bed chamber
ἐξωθέω: to thrust out, force out
ἐράω: to love
ἐρωτάω: to ask, enquire
Ζεύς, Διός, ὁ: Zeus
ζῷον, τό: an animal
καλέω: to call, summon
κελεύω: to bid, command, order
κομίζω: to carry, lead
μεταμορφόω: to transform
μετέωρος, -ον: raised from the ground

μόνος, -η, -ον: alone, only
μυρίζω: to rub with unguent, anoint
νῶτον, τό: a back
οἰκέτης, -ου, ὁ: a house slave
οἰκία, ἡ: a house
οἴομαι: to suppose, think, imagine
περιλαμβάνω: to seize around, embrace
πίθηκος, ὁ: an ape, monkey
στεφανόω: to crown, wreath
συγκαθεύδω: to lie down with, sleep with
σύμβολον, τό: a sign, symbol
σύρω: to draw, drag
τοσοῦτος, -αύτη, -οῦτο: so large, so great
χρήσιμος, -η, -ον: useful, serviceable

ἐμοῦ δ' ἐρομένου: gen. abs., "when I asked"
ἡμάρτηται: pf. pas. of ἀμαρτάνω, "what has been neglected by me?"
ἐρῶσα: pr. part. of ἐράω, "(not) because I loved" + gen.
συνεκάθευδον: impf., "I used to sleep with" + dat.
κἂν (= καὶ ἐὰν) ἐκεῖνό γε μόνον: "even if that one thing only"
σε … διασῴζειν καὶ σύρειν: ind. st. after ᾤμην, "I supposed that you would be keeping and dragging along"
ἐλήλυθας: pf. of ἔρχομαι, "you have come"
μεταμορφωθείς: ao. pas. part., *"having been transformed* into a monkey"
κομισθῆναι: ao. inf. pas. of κομίζω in ind. com. after κελεύει, "she orders me to be escorted"
μετέωρον: "me high up on" + gen.
ἐξωσθεὶς: ao. part. pas. of ἐξωθέω, "having been forced out"
ἐστεφανωμένος: pf. part. of στεφανόω, "all garlanded handsomely"
μεμυρισμένος: pf. part., "all anointed"
περιλαβὼν: ao. part. of περι-λαμβάνω, "having embraced the ground"

146

The Ass

Lucius returns home and thanks the gods for his safety.

ἅμα δὲ τῷ ὄρθρῳ γυμνὸς ὢν ἔθεον ἐπὶ ναῦν καὶ λέγω
πρὸς τὸν ἀδελφὸν τὴν ἐμαυτοῦ ἐν γέλωτι συμφοράν. ἔπειτα ἐκ
τῆς πόλεως δεξιοῦ πνεύσαντος ἀνέμου πλέομεν ἔνθεν, καὶ
ὀλίγαις ἡμέραις ἔρχομαι εἰς τὴν ἐμὴν πατρίδα. ἐνταῦθα θεοῖς
σωτῆρσιν ἔθυον καὶ ἀναθήματα ἀνέθηκα, μὰ Δί' οὐκ ἐκ κυνὸς
πρωκτοῦ, τὸ δὴ τοῦ λόγου, ἀλλ' ἐξ ὄνου περιεργίας διὰ μακροῦ
πάνυ, καὶ οὕτω δὲ μόλις, οἴκαδε ἀνασωθείς.

ἀδελφός, ὁ: brother
ἀνάθημα, -ατος, τό: a votive offering
ἀνασῴζω: to recover, rescue
ἄνεμος, ὁ: wind
γέλως, -ωτος, ὁ: laughter
γυμνός, -ή, -όν: naked, unclad
δεξιός, -ά, -όν: on the right, fortunate
ἔνθεν: from there
ἔπειτα: thereupon
ἡμέρα, ἡ: a day
θεός, ὁ: a god
θέω: to run
θύω: to sacrifice
κύων, ὁ: a dog
λέγω: to say

λόγος, ὁ: a word
μακρός, -ά, -όν: long
μόλις: scarcely
ναῦς, ἡ: a ship
οἴκαδε: home, homewards
ὀλίγος, -η, -ον: few, little, small
ὄρθρος, ὁ: the dawn
πατρίς, -ίδος, ἡ: native land
περιεργία, ἡ: curiosity
πλέω: to sail
πνέω: to blow
πόλις, -εως, ἡ: a city
πρωκτός, ὁ: a bottom, rear
συμφορά, ἡ: a circumstance
σωτήρ, -ῆρος, ὁ: a savior, deliverer

γυμνὸς ὤν: "still being naked"
δεξιοῦ πνεύσαντος ἀνέμου: gen. abs., "a fair wind having risen"
πνεύσαντος: ao. part. of πνεύω
ὀλίγαις ἡμέραις: "within a few days"
θεοῖς σωτῆρσιν: dat. ind. obj., "to the gods, my saviors"
ἀναθήματα: n. pl. internal acc. with ἀνέθηκα, "I dedicated *dedications*"
ἀνέθηκα: ao. of ἀνα-τίθημι, "I set up"
ἐκ κυνὸς πρωκτοῦ: "from the dog's bottom," making an unclear reference to the
    fable when a dog is about to poop on a reed.
τὸ δὴ τοῦ λόγου: "as the saying goes"
ἐξ ὄνου περιεργίας: "but rather from the curiosity of an ass" cf. the phrase from
    Menander cited above p. 118: ἐξ ὄνου παρακύψεως
διὰ μακροῦ (sc. χρόνῳ): "throughout a very long time"
καὶ οὕτω δὲ μόλις οἴκαδε: "and thus just barely homeward having been saved"
ἀνασωθείς: ao. part. of ἀνα-σῴζω

147

Apuleius' *Metamorphoses*: Selected Passages

[Selection 1: Apuleius, *Met.* I.22]

Et cum dicto modico secus progressus ostium accedo et ianuam firmiter oppessulatam pulsare vocaliter incipio. Tandem adulescentula quaedam procedens: "Heus tu" inquit "qui tam fortiter fores verberasti, sub qua specie mutuari cupis? An tu solus ignoras praeter aurum argentumque nullum nos pignus admittere?"

"Meliora" inquam "ominare et potius responde an intra aedes erum tuum offenderim."

---

accedo (3): to approach
admitto (3): to admit, receive
adulescentula, -ae f: a young woman
aedes, -is f: a temple, shrine
an: could it be that...? (*introduces question expecting negative answer*)
argentum, -i n: silver
aurum, -i n: gold
cupio (3): to wish, desire
erus, -i m: a master, lord
firmiter: really, strongly, firmly
foris, -is n: a door, gate
fortiter: strongly
heus: hey!
ianua, -ae f: a door
ignoro (1): to not know, be ignorant
incipio (3): to begin
inquam: to say
inquit: he said
intra: within, inside
melior, –ius: better (*comp.* of bonus)

modicum, -i, n: a small amount
mutuo (1): to lend, exchange
nullus, -a, -um: no, none
offendo (3): to come upon, meet with, find
ominor (3): to forebode, give an omen
oppessulatus, -a, -um: bolted
ostium, -i n: a door, gate, mouth
pignus, -oris n: a wager, bet, security
potius: rather, more
praeter: besides, beyond, except (+ *acc.*)
procedo (3): to proceed, advance, appear
progredior (3): to go forth
pulso (1): to beat, knock
respondeo (2): to answer
secus: (*adv.*) near
solus, -a, -um: alone, only
species, -ei n: an appearance, form
tandem: finally
verbero (1): to beat, strike
vocaliter: out loud, noisily

---

cum dicto: "with this word," a common Apuleian expression
modico: abl. of spec. with *secus*, "nearer *by a little*"
progressus: perf. part. of dep. *progredior*, "having gone forth"
qui: relative pronoun with antecedent *tu* "you who have..."
verberasti: syncopated 2 s. perf. (= *verberavisti*)
sub qua specie: "under what form?" referring to the type of loan security mentioned below
mutuari: pas. inf., "do you wish *to be lent* (to)" i.e. *"to be granted a loan"*
nos admittere: acc. + inf. in ind. st. after *ignoras*, "are you unaware *that we accept?*"
pignus: the collateral offered as security for a loan"
meliora ominare: pres. imper. of deponent *ominor*, "Give better omens!"
an ... offenderim: perf. subj. in ind. question after *responde*, "*whether I might find* your master"

151

Apuleius

"Plane," inquit "sed quae causa quaestionis huius?"

"Litteras ei a Corinthio Demea scriptas ad eum reddo."

"Dum annuntio," inquit "hic ibidem me opperimino," et cum dicto rursum foribus oppessulatis intro capessit. Modico deinde regressa patefactis aedibus: "Rogat te" inquit.

Intuli me eumque accumbentem exiguo admodum grabattulo et commodum cenare incipientem invenio. Assidebat pedes uxor et

---

accumbo (3): to lie down
admodum: very, quite
aedes, -is f: a temple, shrine
annuntio (1): to announce, report, say
assideo (2): to sit by, sit down to
capesso (3): to take, seize
causa, -ae f: a cause, reason
ceno (1): to dine, eat a meal
commodum: just, even now
Corinthius, -a, -um: Corinthian
deinde: then, next
Demea, -ae m: Demeas
dictium, -i n: word
exiguus, -a, -um: small
foris, -is f: a door, gate
grabattulus, -i m: a small bed, couch
ibidem: in that very place
incipio (3): to begin, start

infero, inferre, intuli, illatus: to carry in
inquam: to say
intro: within, inside
invenio (4): to find, discover
littera, -ae f: a letter
modicum, -i, n: a small amount
opperior (4): to wait
oppessulatus, -a, -um: bolted
patefacio (3): to open
pes, pedis m: foot
plane: clearly, plainly
quaestio, -onis f: a question, inquiry
reddo (3): to return, deliver
regredior (3): to go back, return
rogo (1): to ask
rursum: back, backward, again
scribo (3): to write
uxor, -oris f: wife

---

a Corinthio Demea: abl. of agent, "letters written *by Demeas the Corinthian*"
opperimino: archaic 2 s. imper. of dep. *opperior*, "*await me*"
foribus oppessulatis: abl. abs. "with the doors bolted"
intro capessit (sc. *se*): "she took (herself) inside"
modico: abl. time within which, "in a short time"
regressa: perf. part. nom. f. s., "*having returned*"
patefactis aedibus: abl. abs., "with the doors opened"
Intuli me: "I carried myself in" i.e. "I entered"
exiguo admodum grabattulo: abl. place where, "lying *upon a very small couch*"
accumbentem, incipientem: pres. part. acc. m. s. modifying *eum*, "I found him *lying...* and *beginning*"
pedes: acc. place to which with *ad-sideo*, "his wife was sitting *at this feet*" in subservience

152

mensa vacua posita, cuius monstratu: "En" inquit "hospitium."

"Bene" ego, et ilico ei litteras Demeae trado. Quibus properiter lectis: "Amo" inquit "meum Demeam qui mihi tantum conciliavit hospitem."

---

amo (1): to like, love

concilio (1): to bring together, commend (+ *acc.*) to (+ *dat.*)

Demea, -ae m: Demeas

en: behold! see!

hospes, -itis n: a guest

hospitium, -i n: hospitality, guest entertainment

ilico: immediately, on the spot

inquam: to say

lego (3): to read

littera, -ae f: a letter

mensa, -ae f: a table

monstro (1): to show, point out

pono (3): to put, place, set

properiter: quickly, speedily

tantus, -a, -um: so much, so great

trado (3): to hand over, deliver

vacuus, -a, -um: empty, bare

---

mensa vacua posita: abl. abs. "an empty table having been set"

cuius monstratu: abl. supine in rel. clause, "with a pointing out of which (table)"

quibus lectis: abl. abs., "which (letters) having been read"

qui...hospitem: relative clause with causal force, modifying **Demeam**, "my Demeas, who has (i.e. because he has) commended so great a guest to me."

Apuleius

[Selection 2: Apuleius, *Met.* III.25]

Ac dum salutis inopia cuncta corporis mei considerans non avem me sed asinum video, querens de facto Photidis sed iam humano gestu simul et voce privatus, quod solum poteram, postrema deiecta labia umidis tamen oculis oblicum respiciens ad illam tacitus expostulabam. Quae ubi primum me talem aspexit, percussit faciem suam manibus infestis et: "Occisa sum misera:"

---

ac: and, besides
asinus, -i m: an ass, donkey
aspicio (3): to see, observe
avis, -is f: a bird
consider: to look over, examine
corpus, -oris n: a body
cunctus, -a, -um: all, entire
deicio (3): to cast down, hang
expostulo (1): to remonstrate, complain about
facies, faciei f: face
gestus, -us m: gesture
humanus, -a, -um: human, of man
infestus, -a, -um: hostile, disturbed
inopia, -ae f: a lack, need, want + gen.
labia, -ae f: lip
manus, -us f: a hand
miserus, -a, -um: wretched, miserable
oblicum: obliquely, askance

occido (3): to kill, destroy
oculus, -i m: eye
percutio (3): to beat, strike
Photis, Photidis f: Photis
possum, posse, potui, -: to be able
postremus, -a, -um: last, lowest
primum: at first
privo (1): to deprive, rob
queror (3): to complain, protest
respicio (3): to look back, gaze at
salus, salutis f: health, safety
simul: at the same time, also
solus, -a, -um: alone, only
tacitus, -a, -um: silent
talis, -is, -e: such
umidus, -a, -um: moist, wet
video (2): to see
vox, vocis f: voice

---

inopia: abl. of manner "with want of salvation"
cuncta corporis: obj. of *considerans* "examining all (parts) of my body"
non avem me sed asinum (sc. *esse*): ind. st. after *video*, "I saw *that I was not a bird but an ass*"
humano gestu, voce: abl. of separation after *privatus*, "deprived *of human gesture* and also *voice*"
postrema deiecta labia: ab. abs. "my bottom lip cast down""
umidis oculis: "with moist eyes" i.e. "crying"
quae: nom. f. s. referring to Fotis
me talem: "me in such a state"
manibus infestis: abl. of means, "she struck her face *with hostile hands*"
occisa sum: "I have died miserably!"

clamavit "me trepidatio simul et festinatio fefellit et pyxidum similitudo decepit. Sed bene, quod facilior reformationis huius medela suppeditat. Nam rosis tantum demorsicatis exibis asinum statimque in meum Lucium postliminio redibis. Atque utinam vesperi de more nobis parassem corollas aliquas, ne moram talem patereris vel noctis unius. Sed primo diluculo remedium festinabitur tibi."

---

asinus, -i m: an ass
clamo (1): to shout, cry out
corolla, -ae f: a garland
decipio (3): to decive, cheat
demorsico (1): to bit off, nibble at
diluculum, -i n: dawn, daybreak
exeo, exire, exivi, exitus: to leave, emerge
facilior, -or, -us: easier, rather easily
fallo (3): to decive, beguile
festinatio, -onis f: speed, haste
festino (1): to hasten, hurry
Lucius, -i m: Lucius
medela, -ae f: cure, treatment
mora, -ae f: a delay, hindrance
mos, moris m: custom, habit
nox, noctis f: a night
paro (1): to prepare, obtain

patior (3): to suffer
postliminio: back again, anew
pyxis, pyxidis f: a small box
redeo, redire, redivi, reditus: to return, go back, revert
reformatio, -onis f: transformation
remedium, -i n: a remedy, cure
rosa, -ae f: a rose
similitudo, -inis f: likeness, similarity
statim: immediately, at once
suppedito (1): to be available, be supplied
talis, -is, -e: such, so great
trepidation, -onis f: fear
unus, -a, -um: one, single
utinam: if only, would that
verperi: in the evening

---

me: d.o. of *fefellit* and *decepit*
pyxidum: gen. pl., "the similarity *of the boxes*"
bene, quod: "but it will be *fine because...*"
rosis demorsicatis: abl. abs., "with roses nibbled"
redibis: 2 s. fut., "*you will turn back* into my Lucius"
de more: "as usual"
utinam ... parassem: plupf. subj. (=*paravissem*) in contrafactual wish, "*would that I had prepared* some garlands*"
ne ... patereris: impf. subj. also contrafactual, "would that you would not suffer"
primo diluculo: abl. of time when, "at daybreak"
festinabitur: 3 s. fut. pas., "a cure *will be hastened* to you"

[Selection 3: Apuleius, Met. VI.30]

Tunc ingratis ad promptum recurrens exitium reminiscor doloris ungulae et occipio nutanti capite claudicare. Sed: "Ecce," inquit ille qui me retraxerat "rursum titubas et vacillas, et putres isti tui pedes fugere possunt, ambulare nesciunt? At paulo ante pinnatam Pegasi vincebas celeritatem." Dum sic mecum fustem quatiens benignus iocatur comes, iam domus eorum extremam

---

ambulo (1): to walk
ante: before
benignus, -a, -um: kind, favorable
caput, capitis n: head
celeritas, -tatis f: speed, swiftness
claudico (1): to limp
comis, -e: gracious, obliging, kind
dolor, doloris m: grief, pain
domus, -i f: house, home
ecce: see! behold!
exitium, -i n: destruction, ruin
extremus, -a, -um: last, farthest
fugio: to flee
fustis, -is m: a stick, club
ingratis: against one's wishes, unwilling
inquam: to say
ioco (1): to joke, jest
nescio (4): not to know, be ignorant
nuto (1): to waver

occipio (3): to begin
paulo: by a little
Pegasus, -i m: Pegasus, mythical winged horse of the Muses
pes, pedis m: a foot
pinnatus, -a, -um: winged
possum: to be able
promptus, -a, -um: ready, eager
putris, -e: rotten, stinking
quatio (3): to shake
recurro (3): to hurry back, return
reminiscor (3): to recall, remember + gen.
retraho (3): to drag back, bring back
rursum: back, again
titubo (1): to stagger, falter
ungula, -ae f: a hoof
vacillo (1): to totter
vinco (3): to conquer, defeat, surpass

---

ad promptum exitium: "returning *to my ready destruction*"
nutanti capite: abl. absolute, "with my head shaking"
retraxerat: 3 s. plupf. act. in relative clause with *qui*, "that one, who *had dragged* me back"
fugere: complementary inf. with *possunt*, "they are able *to flee*"
ambulare: complementary inf. after *nesciunt*, "they do not know how *to walk*"
paulo ante: "a little while earlier"
pinnatam Pegasi celeritatem: transferred epithet, "the winged speed of Pegasus" i.e. "the speed of winged Pegasus"

loricam perveneramus. Et ecce de quodam ramo procerae cupressus induta laqueum anus illa pendebat.

---

anus, -us f: an old woman
cupressus, -i f: crypress tree
ecce: see! behold!
induo (3): to put on, cover
laqueus, -i m: a noose

lorica, -ae f: a fortification
pendo (3): to hang
pervenio (4): to come to, reach, arrive
procerus, -a, -um: tall, high
ramus, -i m: a branch

---

perveneramus: 1 pl. plupf., "*we had arrived* at the outermost fortification"
procerae cupressus: gen. f. s., "from a branch *of a tall cypress tree*"
induta: perf. part. with middle sense, "having put on"

Apuleius

[Selection 4: Apuleius, Met. VI.31-32]

[31] Nec vos memoria deseruit utique quid iam dudum decreveritis de isto asino semper pigro quidem sed manducone summo nunc etiam mendaci fictae debilitatis et virginalis fugae sequestro ministroque. Hunc igitur iugulare crastino placeat totisque vacuefacto praecordiis per mediam alvum nudam virginem, quam praetulit nobis, insuere, ut sola facie praeminente ceterum

---

alvus, -i f: belly
asinus, -i m: an ass
ceterus, -a, -um: the rest, remaining
crastino: tomorrow
debilitas, -tatis f: infirmity, lameness
decerno (3): to decide, determine
desero (3): to leave behind, forsake, desert
dudum: a while ago, formerly
facies, faciei f: face
fictus, -a, -um: false, pretended
fuga, -ae f: flight, escape
igitur: therefore, so then
insuo (3): to sew up in
iugulo (1): to slit the throat, slaughter
manduco, -onis m: a glutton
medius, -a, -um: middle, in the middle
memoria, -ae f: memory
mendax, -acis m: a liar

minister, ministri m: an aide, accomplice
nudus, -a, -um: nude, naked, stripped
piger, pigra, pigrum: lazy, slow
placeo (2): to please, satisfy
praecordium, -i n: entrails, innards
praefero, -ferre, -tuli, -latis: to carry before, prefer
praemineo (2): to be prominent, stand out
semper: always
sequester, sequestri m: a go-between, intermediary
solus, -a, -um: alone, only
totus, -a, -um: all, whole
utique: certainly, by all means
vacuefacio (3): to empty out, make room
virginalis, -is, -e: virginal, of a maiden
virgo, virginis f: maiden, young woman

---

memoria deseruit: "memory has not left you" i.e. you haven't forgotten
quid ... decreveritis: perf. subj. in ind. quest. "what you decided"
semper pigro quidem sed manducone summo nunc etiam: "always slow, to be sure, but a glutton and now also"
virginalis fugae: "of the virginal flight," i.e. "of the maiden's escape"
manducone, mendaci, sequestro ministroque: abl. in apposition to *isto asino*
placeat: pr. subj. jussive "may it please you" + inf.
vacuefacto (sc. ei): "(to him) having been gutted"
totis ... praecordiis: abl. of sep. with *vacuefacto* "from all his innards"
quam praetulit nobis: "the maiden, *whom he* (Lucius) *preferred to us*"
insuere: complimentary inf. after *placeat*, "may it be pleasing *to sew up inside*"
ut ... coerceat: pr. subj. in result clause, "so that he encloses"
sola facie praeminente: ab. abs., "only her face sticking out"

158

corpus puellae nexu ferino coerceat, tunc super aliquod saxum
scruposum insiciatum et fartilem asinum exponere et solis ardentis
vaporibus tradere. [32] Sic enim cuncta quae recte statuistis ambo
sustinebunt, et mortem asinus quam pridem meruit, et illa morsus
ferarum, cum vermes membra laniabunt, et ignis flagrantiam, cum
sol nimiis caloribus inflammarit uterum, et patibuli cruciatum, cum

---

ambo: both, together
ardeo (2): to be hot, burn
asinus, -i m: an ass
calor, -oris m: heat
coerceo (2): to enclose
corpus, corporis n: body
cruciatus, -us m: torture, cruelty
cunctus, -a, -um: all
expono (3): to set out
fartilis, -is, -e: crammed, stuff
fera, -ae f: a wild beast
ferinus, -a, -um: wild, beastly
flagrantia, -ae f: burning, scorching
ignis, -is m: fire, flame
inflammo (1): to inflame, set fire to
insiciatus, -a, -um: stuffed (with meat)
lanio (1): to tear, rend, mangle
membrum, -i n: a limb
mereo (2): to earn, deserve

mors, mortis f: death
morsus, -us m: a bite, sting
nexus, -us, m: knot
nimius, -a, -um: excessive, too great
patibulum, -i n: a gibbet, gallows
pridem: previously
puella, -ae f: a girl
recte: rightly, correctly
saxum, -i n: a rock, stone
scruposus, -a, -um: rough, sharp
sol, solis m: the sun
sol, solis m: the sun
statuo (3): to set up, establish
super: upon (+ acc.)
sustineo (2): to support, endure
trado (3): to hand over, deliver
uterus, -i m: womb, belly
vapor, -oris m: heat, warmth
vermis, -is m: a worm, maggot

---

exponere, tradere: complimentary inf. after **placeat**, "may it please *to set out... and to hand over*"
ardentis vaporibus: dat. i.o., "hand (him) over *to the buring heat* of the sun"
quae recte statuistis: relative clause after **cuncta**, "all those (punishments) *which you have rightly determined*"
mortem (sc. **sustinebit**) **asinus**: "the ass (will endure) a death which..."
illa (sc. **sustinebit**) **morsus**: "*she (will endure) the bites* of wild beasts"
cum laniabunt: fut. indic. in temporal clause, "*while the worms will tear* her limbs"
ignis flagrantiam: "(and she will endure) the scorching of fire"
inflammarit: syncopated fut. perf. (=**inflammaverit**) "when the sun will have burned"
uterum: "the belly (of the ass)"
patibuli cruciatum: "(and she will endure) the torture of the gallows"

canes et vultures intima protrahent viscera. Sed et ceteras eius aerumnas et tormenta numerate: mortuae bestiae ipsa vivens ventrem habitabit, tum faetore nimio nares aestuabit, et inediae diutinae letali fame tabescet, nec suis saltem liberis manibus mortem sibi fabricare poterit."

---

aerumna, -ae f: trouble, affliction
aestuo (1): to burn, seeth, be agitated
bestia, -ae f: a beast, animal
canis, -is m: a dog
ceterus, -a, -um: the rest, remaining
diutinus, -a, -um: long lasting, enduring
fabrico (1): to create, contrive
faetor, -oris m: stench, stink
fames, -is f: hunger
habito (1): to inhabit, dwell in
inedia, -ae f: starvation
intimus, -a, -um: inmost, interior
letalis, -is, -e: lethal, deadly
liber, libera, liberum: free, unrestricted

manus, -us f: hand
mors, mortis f: death
mortuus, -a, -um: dead
naris, -is f: nostril, nose
nimio: far, greatly
numero (1): to count, reckon
possum, posse, potui, -: to be able
protraho (3): to drag forth
tabesco (3): to dry up, waste away
tormentum, -i n: torment, torture
venter, ventris m: stomach, belly
viscus, visceris n: entrails
vivo (3): to be alive, live
vultur, vulturis m: a vulture, bird of prey

---

numerate: pl. imper., "*Count up* the rest of the afflictions!"
faetore: abl. of cause, "on account of the stench"
nares: pl. acc. of respect, "she will burn greatly *with respect to her nose*"
letali fame: abl. of means, "from a fatal hunger"
nec ... saltem: "*not even* with her own"
suis manibus: abl. of means, "by her own hands"
sibi: dat. of reference, "to contrive a death *for herself*"

[Selection 5: Apuleius, Met. VII.14]

Exin me suum sospitatorem nuncupatum matrona prolixe curitabat ipsoque nuptiarum die praesepium meum ordeo passim repleri iubet faenumque camelo Bactrinae sufficiens apponi. Sed quas ego condignas Photidi diras devotiones imprecarer, quae me formavit non canem, sed asinum, quippe cum viderem largissimae cenae reliquiis rapinisque canes omnes inescatos atque distentos.

---

appono (3): to place by, set out
asinus, -i m: an ass
Bactrinus, -a, -um: Bactrian
camelus, -i m: a camel
canis, -is m: a dog
cena, -ae f: a dinner
condignus, -a, -um: worthy, deserved
curito (1): to attend to, take care of
devotio, -onis f: a prayer, curse
dies, diei m: a day
dirus, -a, -um: awful, terrible, dire
distendo (3): to stretch, spread out
exin: then, thereafter
faenum, i n: hay
formo (1): to shape, transform
imprecor (1): to invoke, pra for, call down
inesco (1): to fill (with food)

iubeo (2): to order
largus, -a, -um: lavish, bountiful
matron, -ae f: lady, mistress
nuncupo (1): to name, call
nuptial, -ae f: wedding, (pl.) marriage
ordeum, -i n: barley
passim: everywhere
Photis, Photidis f: Photis
praesepium, -i n: a manger
prolixe: amply, lavishly
quippe: of course, obviously
rapina, -ae f: robbery, booty
reliquia, -ae f: remnant, (pl.) remains
repleo (2): to fill up
sospitor, -oris m: savior
sufficio (3): to be sufficient, be adequate
video (2): to see

---

me ... nuncupatum: "me having been called"
ipsoque die: abl. of time when, "*on the very day* of the wedding"
repleri: pas. inf. after *iubet*, "she orders my manger *to be filled*" + abl.
apponi: pas. inf. after *iubet*, "she orders hay *to be set out*"
camelo Bactrinae: dat. of reference after *sufficiens*, "hay enough *for a Bactrian camel*"
quas ... imprecarer: impf. subj. in exclamation, " what curses I called down on Fotis"
cum viderem: impf. subj. in circumstantial clause, "I called down curses *when I saw...* "
reliquiis rapinisque: abl. of cause, "*from the leavings and snatchings* of that meal"

[Selection 6: Apuleius, Met. VII.17-24]

Delegor enim ligno monte devehundo, puerque mihi praefectus imponitur, omnibus ille quidem puer deterrimus. Nec me montis excelsi tantum arduum fatigabat iugum, nec saxeas tantum sudes incursando contribam ungulas, verum fustium quoque crebris ictibus prolixe dedolabar, ut usque plagarum mihi medullaris insideret dolor; coxaeque dexterae semper ictus incutiens et unum feriendo locum dissipato corio et ulceris latissimi facto foramine,

---

arduus, -a, -um: steep, tall
contreo, -ire, -ivi, -itus: to destroy, crush
corium, -i n: skin, hide
coxa, -ae f: hip
creber, crebra, cerebrum: frequent, repeated
dedolo (1): to beat
delego (1): to assign, appoint
deterrimus, -a, -um: lowest, meanest
deveho (3): to convey, carry down
dexter, dextera, dexterum: right
dissipo (1): to disperse, destroy
dolor, -oris m: grief, pain
excelsus, -a, -um: high, tall
facio (3): to make, create
fatigo (1): to weary, tire
ferio (4): to hit, strike
foramen, -minis n: a hole
fustis, -is m: a stick, club
ictus, -us m: a blow, stroke
impono (3): to impose, place in command
incurso (1): to strike, dash against

insido (3): to penetrate, sink in
iugum, -i n: a ridge, summit
latus, -a, -um: wide, broad
lignum, -i n: wood
locus, -i m: a place, location
medullaris, -is, -e: of the marrow, innermost
mons, montis m: a mountain, hill
omnis, -is, -e: all
plaga, -ae f: a stroke, blow
praefectus, -i m: commander, overseer
prolixe: generously, in quantity
puer, pueri m: a boy
saxeus, -a, -um: rocky, stony
semper: always
sudis, -is f: a crag, peak
tantus, -a, -um: so much, so great
ulcus, ulceris n: a sore
ungula, -ae f: a hoof
unus, -a, -um: one, single
verus, -a, -um: true

---

devehundo: abl. gerundive modifying **ligno**, "I was appointed *for the wood that had to be carried down*" i.e. "to carry down the wood"
mihi: dat. with compound verb *in-pono*, "A boy was imposed *on me*"
omnibus ... deterrimus: "the worst of all"
Nec ... nec ... verum: "not only ... but also"
incursando: abl. gerund of cause, "destroyed *by striking* such rocky crags"
ungulas: acc. of respect, "I was destroyed *with respect to my hooves*"
crebris ictibus: abl. of cause, "I was grieved *by the frequent blows*"
ut ... insideret: impf. subj. in result cl. "so that grief was penetrating" + dat.
ictus: internal acc. "striking *blows* against" + dat.
feriendo: abl. gerund "by hitting"
dissipato corio: ab. abs., "the skin having been destroyed"
facto foramine: abl. abs., "with a hole created"

immo fovea vel etiam fenestra nullus tamen desinebat identidem vulnus sanguine delibutum obtundere. Lignorum vero tanto me premebat pondere, ut fascium molem elephanto, non asino paratam putares. Ille vero etiam quotiens in alterum latus praeponderans declinarat sarcina, cum deberet potius gravantis ruinae fustes demere et levata paulisper pressura sanare me vel certe in alterum

---

alter, altera, alterum: one, another
asinus, -i m: an ass
certe: surely, certainly
debeo (2): to owe, ought, should
declino (1): to descend, sink down
delibutus, -a, -um: stained, smeared, dripping
demo (3): to take away
desino (3): to stop, desist
elephantus, -i m: an elephant
fascis, -is m: a bundle (of sticks)
fenestra, -ae f: a window
fovea, -ae f: a pit, trench
fustis, -is m: a club, stick
gravo (1): to load down, burden
identidem: repeatedly, again and again
immo: more correctly, indeed
latus, lateris n: a side

levo (1): to lift up, lighten
lignum, -i n: wood
moles, -is f: mass, heap, pile
nullus, -a, -um: no, none
obtundo (3): to beat, batter
paro (1): to prepare, furnish
paulisper: for a short time, briefly
pondus, ponderis n: a weight, burden
potius: rather, more
praepondero (1): to weigh more
premo (3): to press, oppress, overwhelm
quotiens: as often as
ruina, -ae f: a fall, collapse
sanguis, sanguinis m: blood
sano (1): to cure, heal, correct
sarcina, -ae f: a pack, bundle
tantus, -a, -um: so much, so great
vulnus, vulneris n: a wound

---

immo: "*or rather* a trench"
vel etiam: "*or even* a window"
sanguine: abl. of manner, "the wound dripping *with blood*"
obtundere: complementary inf. after **desinebat**, "he would not cease *beating* the wound"
tanto pondere: abl. of means, "he burdened me *with so great a weight*"
ut...putares: result clause after **tanto**, "so great *that you would think...*"
molem...paratam (sc. **esse**): ind. st. after **putares**, "you would think *that the heap was prepared...*"
elephanto, asino: dat. of reference, "prepared *for an elephant*, not *for an ass*"
in alterum latus: acc. place to which, "sinking down *onto one side*"
cum deberet: concessive clause, "*although he ought* to take away..."
demere, sanare, peraequare: complementary inf. after **deberet**

163

translatis peraequare, contra lapidibus additis insuper sic iniquitati ponderis medebatur.

[18] Nec tamen post tantas meas clades inmodico sarcinae pondere contentus, cum fluvium transcenderemus, qui forte praeter viam defluebat, peronibus suis ab aquae madore consulens ipse quoque insuper lumbos meos insiliens residebat, exiguum scilicet et illud tantae molis superpondium. Ac si quo casu limo caenoso ripae supercilia lubricante oneris inpatientia prolapsus deruissem, cum

---

addo (3): to add
aqua, -ae f: water
caenosus, -a, -um: filthy, foul
casus, -us m: a fall, chance
clades, cladis f: ruin, calamity
consulo (3): to look after, care for (+ dat.)
contentus, -a, -um: content, pleased, satisfied with (+ abl.)
contra: on the contrary
defluo (3): to flow down
deruo (3): to fall down
exiguus, -a, -um: small, meager
fluvius, -i m: river, stream
forte: by chance
iniquitas, -tatis f: an inequality, unevenness
inmodicus, -a, -um: excessive
inpatientia, -ae f: inability to bear
insilio (4): to leap upon
insuper: on top, in addition
insuper: on top, in addition to
lapis, lapidis m: a stone, rock
limus, -i m: mud, mire
lubrico (1): to make slippery

lumbus,-i m: loins
mador, -oris m: moisture, wetness
medeor (2): to cure, remedy, correct (+ dat.)
moles, molis f: a mass, heap, pile
onus, oneris n: load, burden
peraequo (1): to equalize, make even
pero, -onis m: a boot
pondus, ponderis n: a weight, burden
praeter: besides, before, in front of
prolabor (3): to collapse
resideo (2): to sit down , settle
ripa, -ae f: bank
sarcina, -ae f: pack, bundle
scilicet: certainly, of course
supercilium, -i, n: eyebrow, edge
superpondium, -i n: an overweight
tamen: yet, nevertheless
tantus, -a, -um: so much, so great
transcendo (3): to go across
transfero, -ferre, -tuli, -latus: to transfer, carry across
via, -ae f: way, road

---

translatis (sc. *lapidibus*): ab. abs., "with stones shifted over"
lapidibus additis: abl. abs., "instead, *with stones added*"
iniquitati: dat. obj. of *medebatur*, "he corrected *the unevenness* of the burden"
inmodico pondere: abl. after *contentus*, "satisfied *with the excessive weight* of the pack"
transcenderemus: impf. act. subj. in circumstantial clause with cum, "when *we would cross* a steam"
qui...defluebat: relative clause modifying *fluvium*, "a river, *which was flowing...*"
peronibus suis: dat., "caring *for his boots* away from the water's wetness"
exiguum scilicet: "*surely a small* addition," spoken ironically
quo casu: "by some chance"
limo ... lubricante: ab. abs., "*the mud making slippery* the top of the bank"
si ... deruissem: plupf. subj. in past gen. cond., "if ever I would fall down"

deberet egregius agaso manum porrigere, capistro suspendere, cauda sublevare, certe partem tanti oneris, quoad resurgerem saltem, detrahere, nullum quidem defesso mihi ferebat auxilium, sed occipiens a capite, immo vero et ipsis auribus totum me compilabat fusti grandissimo, donec fomenti vice ipsae me plagae suscitarent. Idem mihi talem etiam excogitavit perniciem. Spinas

---

agaso, -onis *m*: a driver
auris, -is *f*: ear
auxilium, -i *n*: help, assistance
capistrum, -i *n*: a halter, harness
caput, capitis *n*: a head
cauda, -ae *f*: a tail
certe: surely, certainly
compilo (1): to cudgel
debeo (2): owe, ought, should
defessus, -a, -um: worn out, tired
detraho (3): to draw off, remove
donec: while, until
egregious, -a, -um: distinguished
excogito (1): to think out, devise
fero, ferre, tuli, latus: to bring, bear
fomentum, -i *n*: a poultice, remedy
fustis, -is *m*: a club, stick
grandis, -is, -e: large, great

immo: more correctly, indeed
manus, -us *f*: a hand
nullus, -a, -um: no, none, not any
occipio (3): to begin
onus, oneris *n*: load, burden
pars, partis *f*: part, portion
pernicies, perniciei *f*: ruin; disaster
plaga, -ae *f*: a stroke, blow
porrigo (3): to stretch out, extend
quoad: as long as, until
resurgo (3): to rise again, lift oneself
saltem: at least
sublevo (1): to raise, lift up
suscito (1): to awaken, rouse
suspendo (3): to lift up, support
talis, -is, -e: such, the following
vero: truly
vicis, -is *f*: a turn, exchange

---

deberet: impf. subj. in a concessive *cum* clause, "when a good diligent diver *ought* to extend a hand"
porrigere ... suspendere ... sublevare ... detrahere: all complimentary inf. after **deberet**
quoad resurgerem: impf. subj. in indef. temporal clause, "until such time as I rise again"
defesso mihi: dat. i.o., "he would bring no help *to tired me*"
occipiens a capite: "starting at the head"
immo vero et: "*or rather* with my ears"
compilabat: "he would beat me"
fomenti vice: "blows *in the place of medicine*"
donec ... suscitarent: impf. subj. in indef. clause, "until such time as these blows would rouse me"
mihi: dat. of reference, "such ruin *for me*"

acerrumas et punctu venenato viriosas in fascem tortili nodo constrictas caudae meae pensilem deligavit cruciatum, ut incessu meo commotae incitataeque funestis aculeis infeste me convulnerarent.

[19] Ergo igitur ancipiti malo laborabam. Nam cum me cursu proripueram fugiens acerbissimos incursus, vehementiore nisu spinarum feriebar: si dolori parcens paululum restitissem, plagis compellebar ad cursum. Nec quicquam videbatur aliud excogitare

acer, acris, acre: sharp, pointed
acerbus, -a, -um: harsh, bitter, painful
aculeus, aculei m: a sting, spike, prick
alius, alia, aliud: other, another
anceps, ancipitis: on both sides
cauda, -ae f: tail
commoveo (2): to agitate, shake up
compello (3): to force, compel
constringo (3): to tie together, bind fast
convulnero: to inflict severe wounds
cruciatus, -us m: a torture device
cursus, -us m: a course, running
deligo (1): to tie, fasten
dolor, -oris m: pain, grief
excogito (1): to think out, devise
fascis, -is m: a bundle (of sticks)
ferio (4): to hit, strike
fugio (3): to run away, flee
funestus, -a, -um: deadly, fatal
igitur: therefore
incessus, -us m: a walking, advancing

incito (1): to urge, arouse, incite
incursus, -us m: an assault, attack
infeste: dangerously, savagely
laboro (1): to be troubled
nisus, -us m: pressure, effort
nodus, -i m: a knot
parco (3): to forbear, spare
paululum: a little, for a little while
pensilis, -is, -e: hanging, pendant
plaga, -ae f: a stroke, blow
proripio (3): to rush forth
punctus, -us m: a prick, sting
quicquam: any, anything
resto (1): to stop, stand still
spina, -ae f: a thorn
tortilis, -is, -e: twisted, coiled
vehementiore: more vehemently
venenatus, -a, -um: poisoned, poisonous
video (2): to see
viriosus, -a, -um: strong, violent

punctu venenato: abl. of respect with **viriosas**, "thorns violent *in their poisonous sting*"
tortili nodo: abl. of means, "bound together *with a twisted knot*"
caudae meae: f. s. dat. with compound verb **de-ligo**, "he fastened the hanging torture *from my tail*"
incessu meo: abl. of means, "agitated and incited *by my advancing*"
ut ... convulnerarent: impf. subj. in result clause, "so that (the thorns) *would wound* me savagely"
cum ... proripueram: plupf. indic. in temporal clause, "whenever I rushed forth"
feriebar: 1 s. impf. pas., "*I was struck* by their force more violently"
restitissem: the protasis of a fut. cond. changed to the plupf. subj. because it is viewed from the past "if I were to stand still"
compellebar: impf. pas., "*I was compelled* to my course"
excogitare: complimentary inf. after **videbatur**, "that most wicked boy seemed *to devise*"

puer ille nequissimus quam ut me quoquo modo perditum iret, idque iurans etiam non numquam comminabatur. En plane fuit, quod eius detestabilem malitiam ad peiores conatus stimularet; nam quadam die nimia eius insolentia expugnata patientia mea calces in eum validas extuleram. Denique tale facinus in me comminiscitur. Stuppae sarcina me satis onustum probeque funiculis constrictum producit in viam deque proxima villula spirantem carbunculum

---

calx, calcis f: heel
carbunculus, -i m: an ember, coal
comminisco (3): to devise, think up
comminor (1): to threaten
conatus, -us m: attempt, endeavor
constringo (3): to bind fast, tie up
denique: finally, in the end
detestabilis, -is, -e: detestable
effero, -ferre, -tuli, -latus: to carry out
expugno (1): to conquer, overcome
facinus, facinoris n: deed, crime
funiculus, -i m: a rope, cord
insolentia, -ae f: insolence
iuro (1): to swear
malitia, -ae f: malice, wickedness
nequissimus, -a, -um: most wicked
nimius, -a, -um: too great, excessive
numquam: never

onustus, -a, -um: laden
patientia, -ae f: endurance, patience
peior, peius: worse, more evil
perditus, -us m: ruin, death
plane: clearly, plainly
probe: properly, rightly
produco (3): to lead forth, lead out
proximus, -a, -um: nearest, next
puer, pueri m: a boy
sarcina, -ae f: pack, bundle
satis: enough, adequately
spiro (1): to breath, be alive
stimulo (1): to incite, stir up
stuppa, -ae f: flax
talis, -is, -e: such, the following
validus, -a, -um: strong, powerful
via, -ae f: way, road
villula, -ae f: a small farmhouse

Nec quicquam aliud ... quam: "nothing other than"
ut...iret: impf. subj. in noun clause explaining **aliud**, "to devise nothing other *than to bring* ruin"
quoquo modo: "by any means"
non numquam: litotes, "not never" i.e. "sometimes"
quod ... stimularet: impf. subj. in noun clause, "it was clear *that an attempt would goad his maliciousness*"
expugnata patientia: abl. abs., "*when my patience was overcome* by his excessive insolence "
extuleram: plupf. of *effero*, "*I lashed out* my hooves"
in me: "a crime *against me*"
onustum, constrictum: perf. pas. part. modifying **me**, "he led me, *laden* with a bundle ... and *bound* with ropes"
spirantem carbunculum: "a burning coal"

furatus oneris in ipso meditullio reponit. Iamque fomento tenui calescens et enutritus ignis surgebat in flammas et totum me funestus ardor invaserat, nec ullum pestis extremae suffugium nec salutis aliquod apparet solacium, et ustrina talis moras non sustinet et meliora consilia praevertitur. [20] Sed in rebus scaevis adfulsit Fortunae nutus hilarior nescio an futuris periculis me reservans,

---

adfulgeo (2): to shine forth, smile upon
appareo (2): to appear, be evident
ardor, -oris m: fire, flame, heat
calesco (3): to grow hot, be inflamed
consilium, -i n: advice, council
enutrio (4): to nurture
extremus, -a, -um: extreme, dire, utter
flamma, -ae f: flame
fomentum, -i n: kindling
Fortuna, -ae f: the goddess Fortune
funestus, -a, -um: deadly, disastrous
furor (1): to steal
futurus, -a, -um: about to be, future
hilarior, -or, -us: more kindly
ignis, -is m: fire
invado (3): : to attack, assault
meditullium, -i n: middle, midpoint
melior, -or, -us: better
mora, -ae f: delay, pause
nescio (4): not to know, be ignorant

nutus, -us m: a nod
onus, oneris n: load, burden
periculum, -i n: danger, peril, trial
pestis, -is f: curse, destruction
praeverto (3): to forestall
repono (3): to put back, store
res, rei f: a thing, matter, circumstance
reservo (1): to reserve, spare
salus, salutis f: health, safety
scaevus, -a, -um: awkward, unfavorable
solacium, -i n: comfort, solace
suffugium, -i n: shelter, refuge
surgo (3): to rise, grow
sustineo (2): to support, endure
talis, -is, -e: such, so great
tenuis, -is, -e: light, fine, tender
totus, -a, -um: whole, entire
ullus, ulla, ullum: any
ustrina, -ae f: burning

---

furatus: perf. part. of dep. *furor*, " (the boy) *having stolen* a coal"
in ipso meditullio: "*in the very middle* of the load"
enutritus: "the fire having been nurtured (sc. by the flax)"
totum me: "me all over"
nec ullum suffugium … nec salutis aliquod solacium: "neither any refuge … nor any comfort"
apparet … sustinet …praevertitur: vivid present tenses
an: distributive particle after *nescio* governing both *reservans* and *liberans*. The position indicates doubt about the former. "I know not *whether* she was sparing… *but certainly* she was releasing…"
futuris periculis: dat. of reference, "sparing me *for future perils*"

certe praesente statutaque morte liberans. Nam forte pluviae pridianae recens conceptaculum aquae lutulentae proximum conspicatus ibi memet inprovido saltu totum abicio flammaque prorsus extincta tandem et pondere levatus et exitio liberatus evado. Sed ille deterrimus ac temerarius puer hoc quoque suum nequissimum factum in me retorsit gregariisque omnibus adfirmavit me sponte vicinorum foculos transeuntem titubanti gradu

abicio (3): to throw, hurl
adfirmo (1): to declare, affirm
aqua, -ae f: water
certe: surely, certainly
conceptaculum, -i n: a receptacle
conspicor (1): to catch sight of
deterrimus, -a, -um: most wicked
evado (3): to escape
exitium, -i n: destruction, ruin, death
extinguo (3): to quench, extinguish
factum, -i n: deed, act
flamma, -ae f: flame
foculus, -i m: a brazier
forte: by chance, as luck would have it
gradus, -us m: a step
improvidus, -a, -um: thoughtless, unwary
levo (1): to raise, lighten, relieve
libero (1): to free, release
libero (1): to free, release

lutulentus, -a, -um: muddy, murky
mors, mortis f: death
nequissimus, -a, -um: most wicked
pluvia, -ae f: rain
pondus, ponderis n: weight, burden
praesens, praesentis: present, current
pridianus, -a, -um: of the day before
prorsus: straightaway, entirely
proximus, -a, -um: nearest, next
puer, pueri m: boy
recens, recentis: recent, fresh
retorqueo (2): to twist back
saltus, saltus m: leap, jump
sponte: of one's own will, voluntarily
statuo (3): to set up, establish, decided
temerarius, -a, -um: rash, reckless
titubo (1): to totter, stagger
transeo, -ire, -ivi, -itus: to go over, cross
vicinus, -i m: a neighbor

praesente statutaque morte: abl. of separation, "freeing me *from a present and decided death*"
pluviae pridianae recens conceptaculum aquae lutulentae: i.e. "a mud puddle"
conspicatus ... abicio: having spotted it, I throw myself"
memet: *me* + intensive enclitic *–met*, "myself"
pondere, exitio: abl. of separation with **levatus** and **liberatus**, "relieved *of my burden* and freed *from ruin*"
retorsit: perf. of **retorqueo**, "turned back against me"
me ... accersisse mihi: perf. inf. in ind. st. after **adfirmavit**, "that I had brought upon myself"
me ... transeuntem: pr. part., "that I crossing"
titubanti gradu: abl. of manner, "with a faltering step"

prolapsum ignem ultroneum accersisse mihi, et arridens addidit: "Quo usque ergo frustra pascemus igninum istum?"

Nec multis interiectis diebus longe peioribus me dolis petivit. Ligno enim quod gerebam in proximam casulam vendito vacuum me ducens iam se nequitiae meae proclamans imparem miserrimumque istud magisterium renuens querelas huius modi concinnat: [21] Videtis istum pigrum tardissimumque et nimis

---

accerso (3): to invoke, fetch, bring on one-self
addo (3): to add, say in addition
arrideo (2): to laugh at
casula, -ae f: a small cottage
concinno (1): to make up, concoct
dies, diei m: a day
dolus, -i m: a trick, deceit, treachery
duco (3): to lead
frustra: in vain; for nothing
gero (3): to bear, carry
igninus, -i, m: fireman
ignis, -is m: fire
impar, imparis: unequal to (+ dat.)
interiacio (3): to throw between
lignum, -i n: wood
longe: far, by far
magisterium, -i n: an office, duty

miser, misera, miserum: wretched, pitiable
nequitia, -ae f: wickedness
nimis: very much, too much
pasco (3): to feed, keep
peior, peius: worse, more evil
peto (3): to seek, attack
piger, pigra, pigrum: lazy, slow
proclamo (1): to cry out, proclaim
prolabor (3): to fall forward
proximus, -a, -um: nearest, next
querela, -ae f: a complaint, grievance
renuo (3): to refuse
tardus, -a, -um: slow, limping
ultroneus, -a, -um: voluntary, deliberate
usque: up to
vacuus, -a, -um: empty, unladen
vendo (3): to sell
video (2): to see

---

me ... prolapsum: perf. part., "that I having fallen forward"
arridens: pr. part., "with a laugh"
quo usque: "up to what point," i.e. "for how long?"
nec multis interiectis diebus: abl. abs., "and with not many days thrown in" i.e. "a few days later"
longe peioribus dolis: abl. of means, "he attacked me *with far worse tricks*"
Ligno ... vendito: abl. abs., "with the wood sold"
quod gerebam: relative clause after *ligno*, "the wood, *which I was bearing*"
querelas huius modi: "complaints of the following kind"
se (sc. *esse*) *imparem*: ind. st. after *proclamans*, "proclaiming that he was unequal to" + dat.
nimis asinum: "too much an ass"

asinum? Me post cetera flagitia nunc novis periculis etiam angit. Ut quemque enim viatorem prospexerit, sive illa scitula mulier seu virgo nubilis seu tener puellus est, ilico disturbato gestamine, non numquam etiam ipsis stramentis abiectis, furens incurrit et homines amator talis appetit et humi prostratis illis inhians illicitas atque incognitas temptat libidines et ferinas voluptates, aversaque Venere invitat ad nuptias. Nam imaginem etiam savii mentiendo ore

---

abicio (3): to throw down, cast off
amator, -oris m: a lover
ango: to vex, trouble
appeto (3): to seek after, assail
asinus, -i m: an ass
aversus, -a, -um: averse, hostile
ceterus, -a, -um: other, the rest
disturbo (1): to disturb, upset
ferinus, -a, -um: of wild beasts
flagitium, -i n: shame, disgrace
furo (3): to rage, be wild
gestamen, gestaminis n: a burden, load
homo, hominis m: a man
humi: on the ground
ilico: on the spot; immediately
illicitus, -a, -um: forbidden, unlawful
imago, imaginis f: a likeness, image
incognitus, -a, -um: unknown, unheard of
incurro (3): to run at, attack (3)
inhio (1): to gape
invite: to invite, incite

libido, libidinis f: desire, lust
mentior (4): to pretend, imitate
mulier, mulieris f: a woman
novus, -a, -um: new
nubilis, nubile: marriageable
nuptia, -ae f: marriage
os, oris n: a mouth
periculum, -i n: danger, trial
prospicio (3): to foresee, see far off
prosterno (3): to knock down, lay low
puellus, -i m: boy
savium, -i n: a kiss
scitulus, -a, -um: handsome
sive: whether, or
stramentum, -i n: thatch, covering
tempto (q): to try
tener, tenera, tenerum: soft, tender
Venus, Veneris f: the goddess Venus
viator, -oris m: traveler
virgo, virginis f: maiden, young woman
voluptas, -tatis f: pleasure, delight

---

novis periculis: ab. of means, "with new dangers"
ut (= *utcumque*)... *prospexerit*: perf. subj. in temp. clause, "as soon as he has seen"
disturbato gestamine: abl. abs., "with this burden upset"
non numquam: litotes, "not never" i.e. "sometimes"
stramentis abiectis: ab. abs., "his coverings having been thrown off"
prostratis illis: ab. abs., "with those (the females) having been cast down"
aversa Venere: abl. abs., "with Venus opposed" i.e. contrary to normal love
mentiendo: gerund, "with his mouth *pretending* a likeness of a kiss"

improbo compulsat ac morsicat. Quae res nobis non mediocres lites atque iurgia, immo forsitan et crimina pariet. Nunc etiam visa quadam honesta iuvene, ligno quod devehebat abiecto dispersoque, in eam furiosos direxit impetus et festivus hic amasio humo sordida prostratam mulierem ibidem incoram omnium gestiebat inscendere. Quod nisi ploratu questuque femineo conclamatum viatorum praesidium accurrisset ac de mediis ungulis ipsius esset erepta

---

abicio (3): to throw down, cast away
accurro (3): to run to
amasio, -onis m: a lover
compulso (1): to pound, batter
conclamo (1): to cry out loud, summon
crimen, criminis n: a crime
deveho (3): to convey
dirigo (3): to turn, direct
dispergo (3): to scatter
eripio (3): to snatch away, rescue
femineus, -a, -um: womanly, feminine
festivus, -a, -um: festive, jovial
forsitan: perhaps
furiosus, -a, -um: mad, frantic, wild
gestio (4): to be eager, wish
honestus, -a, -um: honorable, upright
humus, -i f: ground
ibidem: in that very place, at that very moment
immo: on the contrary, indeed
impetus, -us m: attack, assault
improbus, -a, -um: wicked, rude

incoram: in front of (+ gen.)
inscendo (3): to mount
iurgium, -i n: dispute, strife
juvenis, -is f: a young woman
lignum, -i n: wood
lis, litis f: a suit, quarrel
mediocris, -is, -e: average, trivial
medius, -a, -um: middle, the middle of
morsico (1): to bite
mulier, mulieris f: woman
nisi: if not, except
pario: to produce, create
ploratus, -us m: a wailing, crying
praesidium, -i n: protection, help
prosterno (3): to know down, lay low
questus, -us m: complaint
res, rei f: a thing, matter
sordidus, -a, -um: dirty, filthy
ungula, -ae f: hoof
viator, -oris m: traveler
video (2): to see

---

quae res: "This thing," referring to Lucius' supposed amorous advances
non mediocres: "not trivial" i.e. "serious"
nobis: dat. of reference, "quarrels and disputes *for us*"
visa quadam honesta iuvene: abl. abs., "with a certain good woman seen"
ligno abiecto dispersoque: abl. abs., "with the wood thrown down and scattered"
humo sordida: abl. of place where, "*on the filthy ground*"
nisi accurrisset...esset erepta liberataque: plupf. subj. in past contrafactual protatis, "if help had not arrived ... if she had not been snatched and freed"

liberataque, misera illa compavita atque dirupta ipsa quidem cruciabilem cladem sustinuisset, nobis vero poenale reliquisset exitium."

[22] Talibus mendaciis admiscendo sermones alios, qui meum verecundum silentium vehementius premerent, animos pastorum in meam perniciem atrociter suscitavit. Denique unus ex illis: "Quin igitur publicum istum maritum" inquit "immo communem omnium adulterum illis suis monstruosis nuptiis condignam victimamus hostiam?" et "Heus tu, puer," ait

---

admisceo (2): to mix together
adulter, adulteri m: adulterer, illicit lover
alius, alia, aliud: other, another
animus, -i m: a mind, spirit
atrociter: cruelly, savagely
clades, cladis f: slaughter, death
communis, -is, -e: common
compavio (4): to trample on
condignus, -a, -um: appropriate, worthy
cruciabilis, -is, -e: agonizing, painful
denique: finally, then
dirumpo (3): to break apart, shatter
exitium, -i n: destruction, ruin, death
heus: hey!
hostia, -ae f: victim, sacrifice
igitur: therefore
immo: more correctly, indeed
inquam: to say
libero (1): to free, release
maritus, -i m: a lover

mendacium, -i n: a lie
miser, misera, miserum: wretched
monstruosus, -a, -um: monstrous
nuptia, -ae f: marriage
pastor, -oris m: shepherd
pernicies, perniciei f: ruin, destruction
poenalis, -is, -e: of punishment, penal
premo (3): to oppress
publicus, -a, -um: public, common
puer, pueri m: a boy
quin: why not (+ *indic.* = *imper.*)
relinquo (3): to leave behind
sermo, sermonis m: speech, talk
silentium, -i n: silence
suscito: (1) to stir up, rouse
sustineo (2): to sustain, endure
unus, -a, -um: one
vehementius: more vehemently
verecundus, -a, -um: shameful
victimo (1): to offer as a sacrifice

---

sustinuisset: plupf. subj. in past contrafactual apodosis, "that miserable woman *would have suffered* a torturous death"

reliquisset: 3 s. plupf. subj. in past contrafactual apodosis, "a penal ruin *would have remained* for us"

admiscendo: gerund abl. of means, "*by mixing up* other speeches with such lies"

qui ... premerent: impf. subj. in rel. clause of characteristic, "which would oppress"

quin igitur...victimamus: "So why don't we sacrifice...?"

illis suis monstruosis nuptiis: abl. with **condignam**, "a victim worthy *of his own monstrous nuptials*"

"obtruncato protinus eo intestina quidem canibus nostris iacta, ceteram vero carnem omnem operariorum cenae reserva. Nam corium adfirmatum cineris inspersu dominis referemus eiusque mortem de lupo facile mentiemur."

Sublata cunctatione accusator ille meus noxius, ipse etiam pastoralis exsecutor sententiae, laetus et meis insultans malis calcisque illius admonitus, quam inefficacem fuisse mehercules doleo, protinus gladium cotis adtritu parabat.

---

accusator, -oris m: accuser, prosecutor
adfirmo (1): to confirm, assert
admoneo (2): to warn, remind
adtritus, -us m: a grinding, sharpening
calx, calcis f: heel
canis, -is m: a dog
carnis, -is f: meat, flesh
cena, -ae f: dinner
ceterus, -a, -um: other, the rest
cinis, -eris m: ashes, dust
corium, -i n: skin, hide
cos, cotis f: a whetstone
cunctatio, -onis f: delay, hesitation
doleo (2): to grieve
dominus, -i m: a master
exsecutor, -oris m: executor, performer
facile: easily, readily
gladius, -i m: sword
iacio (3): to throw
inefficax, inefficacis: useless, ineffectual

inspergo: to sprinkle upon
insulto (1): to mock, jeer at
intestina, -ae f: intestines
laetus, -a, -um: happy, cheerful
lupus, lupi m: wolf
malus, -a, -um: bad, evil
mehercules: by Hercules!
mentior (4): to lie, pretend
mors, mortis f: death
noxius, -a, -um: harmful, criminal
obtrunco (1): to kill
operarius, -i m: laborer, worker
paro (1): to furnish, draw
pastoralis, -is, -e: of or for a shepherd
protinus: immediately, at once
protinus: immediately, at once
refero, -ferre, -tuli, -latus: to carry back
reservo (1): to reserve, hold on to
sententia, -ae f: sentence, judgment
tollo, -ere, sustulli, sublatum: to remove

---

obtruncato protinus eo: ab. abs., "once he has been slaughtered"
iacta: imper., "*cast out* his innards"
cenae: dat. of purpose, "keep the rest *for dinner*"
cineris inspersu: ab. of means, "confirmed *by a sprinking of ash*"
dominis: dat. i.o. of *referemus*, "we will bring back *to the masters*"
mentiemur: fut., "we will fake"
sublata cunctatione: ab. abs., "delay having been removed"
admonitus: "having been admonished by" + gen.
quam: anteced. *calcis*, "of the heel *which*"
inefficacem fuisse: ind. st. after *doleo*, "which I grieve *to have been ineffectual*"

[23] Sed quidam de coetu illo rusticorum: "Nefas" ait "tam bellum asinum sic enecare et propter luxuriem lasciviamque amatoriam criminatum opera servitioque tam necessario carere, cum alioquin exsectis genitalibus possit neque in venerem nullo modo surgere vosque omni metu periculi liberare, insuper etiam longe crassior atque corpulentior effici. Multos ego scio non modo asinos inertes, verum etiam ferocissimos equos nimio libidinis

---

alioquin: otherwise
amatorius, -a, -um: amorous
asinus, -i m: an ass
bellus, -a, -um: beautiful, fine
careo (2): to lack, lose , be without
coetus, -us m: a meeting, assembly
corpulentior, -or, -us: larger, fatter
crassior, -or, -us: heavier, thicker
crimino (1): to accuse, denounce
efficio (3): to cause, effect
eneco (1): to kill, slay
equus, equi m: a horse
exseco (1): to cut off, excise
ferox, ferocis: wild, fierce
genital, genitalis n: genitals
iners, inertis: sluggish, lazy
insuper: on top, in addition

lascivia, -ae f: wantonness
libero (1): to free, release
libido, libidinis f: desire, lust
longe: far, by far
luxuries, -ei f: luxury, extravagance
metus, -us m: fear
necessarius, -a, -um: necessary, essential
nefas: wrong, sin, violation
opera, -ae f: work, service
periculum, -i n: danger, peril
possum: to be able, be possible
propter: on account of (+ acc.)
rusticus, -i m: a peasant, farmer
scio (4): to know
servitium, -i n: slavery, servitude
surgo (3): to rise, grow
venus, veneris f: lust

---

enecare ... carere: pr. inf. after **nefas**, "it is a shame *to slay ... to be without*"
criminatum: agreeing with **asinum**, "him having been charged"
opera servitioque: abl. of separation after **carere**, "to be without (his) *work and necessary servitude*"
cum ... possit: pres. subj. in circumstantial clause, "*when it is possible*" + inf.
exsectis genitalibus: ab. abs., "his genitals having been cut out"
nullo modo: "in no way"
metu: abl. of separation, "to free you *from all fear* of danger"
effici: pres. pas. inf. of **efficio** also complementing **possit**, "possible that he be made"
non modo...verum etiam: "not only... but also"
asinos ... equos ... factos (esse): ind. st. after **scio**, "I know many asses and even horse to have been made tame"

laborantes atque ob id truces vesanosque adhibita tali detestatione
mansuetos ac mites exinde factos et oneri ferundo non inhabiles et
cetero ministerio patientes. Denique nisi vobis suadeo nolentibus,
possum spatio modico interiecto, quo mercatum obire statui, petitis
e domo ferramentis huic curare praeparatis ad vos actutum redire
trucemque amatorem istum atque insuavem dissitis femoribus
emasculare et quovis vervece mitiorem efficere."

---

actutum: immediately, without delay
adhibeo (2): to use, employ
amator, -oris *m*: lover
ceterus, -a, -um: other, the rest
curo (1): to take care of, provide
denique: finally, and then
detestatio, -onis *f*: castration, gelding
dissitus, -a, -um: lying apart
domus, domi *f*: house
emasculo (1): to castrate
exinde: thence, after that
facio (3): to make, do, create
femur, -oris, n: thigh
fero, ferre, tuli, latus: to bear, carry
ferramentum, -i *n*: an iron tool
inhabilis, -e: unmanageable, unfit
insuavis, -is, -e: unpleasant, disagreeable
intericio (3): to throw between, insert
laboro (1): to work, be troubled
mansuetus, -a, -um: tame, gentle
mercatus, -us *m*: a market

ministerium, -i *n*: a duty, task
mitior, -or, -us: milder, gentler
mitis, -e: mild, meek
modicus, -a, -um: moderate, reasonable
nisi: if not, except, unless
nolo: to be unwilling, refuse
ob: on account of (+ *acc.*)
oboe, -ire, -ivi, -itus: to go to, visit
onus, oneris *n*: load, burden
patior (3): to suffer, endure, permit
peto (3): to seek
possum: to be able
praeparo (1): to prepare
redeo, -ire, -ivi, -itus: to return
spatium, i *n*: space, span, interval
statuo (3): to establish, decide, think
suadeo (2): to urge, recommend to (+ *dat.*)
trux, trucis: wild, savage
trux, trucis: wild, savage, fierce
vervex, vervecis *m*: a wether, castrated goat
vesanus, -a, -um: mad, frenzied

---

adhibita tali detestatione: abl. abs., "such a castration having been employed"
oneri ferundo: gerundive in dat. of purpose after **inhabiles**, "not unfit *for a load to be carried*" i.e. "fit *for carrying a load*"
cetero ministerio: also dat. of purpose after **patientes**, "suffering other duties"
nisi vobis nolentibus: part. with conditional force, "I urge *you, unless you are unwilling*"
spatio modico interiecto: abl. abs., "with a moderate interval thrown in," i.e. "after some time has passed"
quo: abl. of time within which, "*in which (time)* I have decided..."
petitis ... ferramentis ... praeparatis: ab. abs. "implements having been sought and prepared"
redire .. emasculare ... efficere: inf. with possum "I am able to return ... and emasculate and to make him"
dissitis femoribus: ab. abs. "his thighs having been spread apart"
vervece: abl. of comparison after **mitiorem**, "gentler *than a wether*"

[24] Tali sententia mediis Orci manibus extractus, set extremae poenae reservatus maerebam et in novissima parte corporis totum me periturum deflebam. Inedia denique vel praecipiti ruina memet ipse quaerebam extinguere moriturus quidem nihilo minus sed moriturus integer.

---

corpus, corporis n: body
defleo (2): to weep, lament, bewail
extinguo (3): to extinguish, kill
extraho (3): to extract, rescue
inedia, -ae f: fasting, starvation
integer, integra, integrum: whole, entire
maereo (2): to grieve, mourn
manus, -us f: a hand
medius, -a, -um: middle, in the middle
morior (3): to die, perish
novissimus, -a, -um: newest, last, rear

Orcus, Orci m: god of the underworld
pars, partis f: part, region
pereo, -ire, -ivi, -itus: to die, be ruined
poena, -ae f: a penalty, punishment
praeceps, praecipitis: headlong, precipitous
quaero (3): to seek, strive for
reservo (1): to save, spare
ruina, -ae f: fall, destruction
sententia, -ae f: an opinion, judgment, sentence

---

set: (= *sed*)
mediis Orci manibus: abl. of sep., "having been saved *from the hands of Hell*"
extremae poenae: dat. of purp., "reserved for a severe punishment"
totum me periturum (sc. *esse*): fut. inf. in ind. st. after *deflebam*, "I was lamenting *that I was going to perish entirely*"
memet: "my own self"
praecipiti ruina: abl. of means, "to kill myself *by a precipitous fall*" i.e. from a cliff
moriturus: fut. act. part. "about to die"
nihilo minus: "nevertheless"

Apuleius

[Selection 7: Apuleius, Met. IX.32]

Matutino me multis holeribus onustum proxumam civitatem deducere consuerat dominus atque ibi venditoribus tradita merce, dorsum insidens meum, sic hortum redire. Ac dum fodiens, dum irrigans, ceteroque incurvus labore deservit, ego tantisper otiosus placita quiete recreabar. Sed ecce siderum ordinatis ambagibus per numeros dierum ac mensuum remeans annus post mustulentas

---

ambages, ambagis f: a circuit, orbit
annus, -i m: year
ceterus, -a, -um: other, remaining, rest
civitas, -tatis f: a city, town
consuesco (3): to be accustomed
deduco (3): to lead down
deservio (4): to devote oneself to (+ abl.)
dies, diei m: day
dorsum, -i n: back
ecce: see! behold!
fodio (3): to dig
holus, holeris n: vegetables
hortus, -i m: a garden
ibi: there, then
incurvus, -a, -um: bent, curved
insideo (2): to sit on
irrigo (1): to water
labor, -oris m: labor, work, toil

matutinus, -a, -um: early, of early morning
mensis, -is m: a month
merx, mercis f: merchandise, goods
mustulentus, -a, -um: wine-filled
numerus, -i m: a number, sum
onustus, -a, -um: laden
ordinatus, -a, -um: ordered, appointed
otiosus, -a, -um: idle, at leisure
placitus, -a, -um: pleasing, agreeable
proxumus, -a, -um: nearest, next
quies, quietis f: quiet, calm, rest
recreo (1): to renew, revive
redeo, -ire, -ivi, -itus: to go back, return
remeo (1): to go back, return
sidus, sideris n: a star, constellation
tantisper: for such time, meanwhile
trado (3): to hand over, deliver
venditor, -oris m: a seller, merchant

---

matutino: abl. of time when, "in the early morning"
multis holeribus: abl. of means, "me laden *with many vegetables*"
proxumam civitatem: acc. place to which, "to lead me *to the next town*"
deducere: complementary inf. after *consuerat*, "he was accustomed *to lead...*"
tradita merce: abl. abs., "*with the merchandise delivered* to the vendors"
hortum: acc. place to which, "to return *to the garden*"
dum ... deservit: "while he devoted himself to" + part.
cetero labore: bent over *by other labor*
ordinatis ambagibus: abl. of manner "according to their appointed orbits"
annus ... deflexerat: "the year had turned away"

autumni delicias ad hibernas Capricorni pruinas deflexerat, et adsiduis pluviis nocturnisque rorationibus sub dio et intecto conclusus stabulo continuo discruciabar frigore, quippe cum meus dominus prae nimia paupertate ne sibi quidem nedum mihi posset stramen aliquod vel exiguum tegimen parare, sed frondoso casulae contentus umbraculo degeret. Ad hoc matutino lutum nimis

---

adsiduus, -a, -um: constant, unremitting
autumnus, -i m: autumn
Capricornus, -i m: Capricorn (a sign of the zodiac)
casula, -ae f: a hut
concludo (3): to shut up, confine
contentus, -a, -um: content with (+ abl.)
continuus, -a, -um: continuous, constant
deflecto (3): to bend down, change course
dego (3): to spend time, live
delicia, -ae f: a delight, charm
discrucio (1): to torture
dium, dii n: the open sky
dominus, -i m: owner, master
exiguus, -a, -um: small, meager
frigor, frigoris m: cold
frondosus, -a, -um: leafy, thatched
hibernus, -a, -um: wintry, hoary

intectus, -a, -um: uncovered, without a roof
lutum, -i n: mud, dirt
matutinus, -a, -um: of early morning
nimis: very much, too much
nimius, -a, -um: excessive, too much
nocturnus, -a, -um: nocturnal, nightly
paro (1): to prepare, furnish, supply
paupertas, -tatis f: poverty
pluvia, -ae f: rain, shower
possum: to be able
prae: because of (+ abl.)
pruina, -ae f: frost
quippe: of course, as you see
roratio, -onis f: dew
stabulum, -i n: a stall, enclosure, pen
stramen, straminis n: straw for bedding
tegimen, tegiminis n: cover, protection
umbraculum, -i n: shelter, shade

Capricorni: "the frosts *of Capricorn*" i.e. December and January
sub dio: "in the open air"
intecto conclusus stabulo: "shut up in an uncovered stable"
cum posset... degeret: impf. subj. in concessive clause, "*although he was able* to provide"
ne sibi quidem: "not even for himself"
nedum mihi: "much less for me"
sed ... degeret: "*but he lived* content"
Ad hoc: "for this (purpose)"

frigidum gelusque praeacuta frusta nudis invadens pedibus enicabar ac ne suetis saltem cibariis ventrem meum replere poteram. Namque et mihi et ipso domino cena par ac similis oppido tamen tenuis aderat, lactucae veteres.

---

cena, -ae f: a dinner, meal
cibarium, -i n: ration, food
dominus, -i m: owner, master
enico (1): to kill
frigidus, -a, -um: cold, frigid
frustum, -i, n: piece
gelus, -us m: frost, ice
invado (3): to walk on
lactuca, -ae f: lettuce
nudus, -a, -um: naked, bare
oppido: exceedingly, altogether

par, paris: equal
pes, pedis m: foot
possum: to be able
praeacutus, -a, -um: sharp, pointed
repleo (2): to fill
saltem: at least, anyhow
suetus, -a, -um: accustomed, familiar
tenuis, -is, -e: slight
venter, ventris m: stomach, belly
vetus, veteris: old

---

nudis invadens pedibus: walking with bare feet on" + acc.
ne suetis saltem: "with not even the customary rations"

[Selection 8: Apuleius, Met. IX.40]

Sed ubi nullis precibus mitigari militem magisque in suam perniciem advertit efferari iamque inversa vite de vastiore nodulo cerebrum suum diffindere, currit ad extrema subsidia simulansque sese ad commovendam miserationem genua eius velle contigere, summissus atque incurvatus, arreptis eius utrisque pedibus sublimem terrae graviter adplodit et statim qua pugnis qua cubitis

---

adplodo (3): to strike, dash
adverto (3): to observe
arripio: to take hold of, seize
cerebrum, -i n: a brain, head
commoveo: to excite, arouse
contingo (3): to touch
cubitum, -i n: an elbow
curro (3): to run
diffindo (3): to split, divide
effero: to make wild, enrage
extremus, -a, -um: last, farthest
genu, genus n: a knee
graviter: violently
incurvo (1): to bend down
inversus, -a, -um: turned around
miles, -itis m: a soldier
miseratio, -onis f: pity, compassion

mitigo (1): to mitigate
nodulus, -i: a knot, knob
nullus, -a, -um: no, none
pernicies, -ei f: harm
pes, pedis m: foot
prex, -ecis, f: prayer
pugnus, -i m: a fist
simulo (1): to pretend, imitate
statim: at once, immediately
sublimis, -e: raised
subsidium, -i n: relief, succor
summitto (3): to lower, set down
terra, terrae f: earth, ground
uter, utra, utrum: both
vastus, -a, -um: immense, huge, thick
vitis, -is m: a staff
volo: to wish

---

mitigari militem: pr. pas. inf. in ind st. after **advertit**, "when he observed *that the soldier was being softened*"
efferari (**militem**): also in ind. st., "and that he was becoming more fierce"
inversa vite: abl. of means, "with his staff inverted"
diffindere: inf. of purpose, "in order to split"
ad extrema subsidia: "to his last resort"
ad commovendam miserationem: gerundive of purpose, "for the sake of seeking pity"
sese ... velle contigere: ind. st. after **simulans** "pretending *that he wished to touch* his knees" (a gesture of supplication)
arreptis utrisque pedibus: abl. abs., "with both his legs seized"
terrae adplodit: "he struck him to the ground"
qua...qua...qua: repeated in partitive sense, "*partly* with fists, *partly* with elbows, *partly* with bites"

qua morsibus, etiam de via lapide correpto, totam faciem manusque
eius et latera converberat. Nec ille, ut primum humi supinatus est,
vel repugnare vel omnino munire se potuit, sed plane identidem
comminabatur, si surrexisset, sese concisurum eum machaera sua
frustatim. Quo sermone eius commonefactus hortulanus eripit ei
spatham eaque longissime abiecta rursum saevioribus eum plagis

---

abicio (3): to throw away
comminor (1): to threaten
commonefacio: to warn
concido (3): to cut up, chop up
converbero (1): to beat, batter
corripio (3): to seize, snatch up
eripio (3): to snatch away
facies, faciei f: face
frustatim: into pieces
hortulanus, -i m: a gardener
humi: on the ground
identidem: repeatedly, again and again
lapis, lapidis m: stone
latus, lateris n: side, flank
longissime: very far off
machaera, -ae f: a sword

manus, -us f: hand
morsus, -us m: bite, teeth
munio (4): to defend, protect
omnino: entirely, at all
plaga, -ae f: a stroke, blow
plane: clearly, plainly
possum: to be able
primum: at first
repugno (1): to fight back
rursum: back, again
saevior, -or, -us: more savage, fiercer
sermo, -onis m: speech, talk
spatha, -ae f: a sword
supino (1): to lay on ones back, lay flat
surgo (3): to rise
via, -ae f: way, road

---

lapide correpto: abl. abs., "and even *with a stone snatched up* from the road"
Nec ille: i.e. the soldier
ut primum: "as soon as"
supinatus est: perf. pass. of **supino**, "as soon as *he was laid on his back*"
si surrexisset: protasis of fut. cond. changed to the plup. subj. because it is from the
  point of view of the past, "he was threatening that that *if he were to get up*"
sese concisurum (sc. **esse**): fut. act. inf. in ind. st. after comminabatur, representing
  the apodosis of the fut. condition "he was threatening *that he would cut* him into
  pieces"
Quo sermone: abl. of means, "having been warned *by his speech*"
eaque abiecta: abl. abs., "*with it (the sword) thrown* a long way off"
saevioribus plagis: abl. of means, "he assailed him *with fiercer blows*"

adgreditur. Nec ille prostratus et praeventus vulneribus reperire saluti quiens subsidium, quod solum restabat, simulat sese mortuum. Tunc spatham illam secum asportans hortulanus inscenso me concito gradu recta festinat ad civitatem nec hortulum suum saltem curans invisere ad quempiam sibi devertit familiarem.

---

adgredior (3): to attack, assail
asporto (1): to carry away, remove
civitas, -tatis f: a city, town
concitus, -a, -um: agitated, rapid
curo (1): to have a care for, worry about
deverto (3): to divert, put up, lodge
familiaris, -is m: an acquaintance, friend
festino (3): to hasten, hurry
gradus, -us m: a step, course
hortulanus, -i m: gardener
hortulus, -i m: a little garden
inscendo (3): to climb on, mount
inviso (3): to go to see, visit
morior (3): to die

praevenio (4): to prevent, hinder
prosterno (3): to strike down, lay low
queo: to be able
quispiam, quaepiam, quodpiam: some, one
recta: directly, straight
reperio (4): to discover, find
resto (1): to remain
salus, salutis f: health, safety
simulo (1): to pretend, feign
solus, -a, -um: alone, only
spatha, -ae f: a sword
subsidium, -i n: help, relief
vulnus, vulneris n: wound

---

nec ...reperire quiens: "and not being able to find"
saluti: dat. of purp., "for his welfare"
sese mortuum (sc. *esse*): ind. st. after *simulat,* "he pretended *that he was dead*"
inscenso me: ab. abs., "me having been mounted"
curans invisere: "not caring to visit"
ad quempiam familiarem: acc. place to which, "he lodged *with one of this friends*"
sibi: dat. of possession, "one of *his* friends"

Apuleius

[Selection 9: Apuleius, Met. IX.42]

Qua contentione et clamoso strepitu cognito, curiosus alioquin et inquieti procacitate praeditus asinus, dum obliquata cervice per quandam fenestrulam quidnam sibi vellet tumultus ille prospicere gestio, unus e commilitonibus casu fortuito conlimatis oculis ad umbram meam cunctos testatur incoram. Magnus denique continuo clamor exortus est et emensis protinus scalis iniecta manu

---

alioquin: otherwise, besides, in general
asinus, -i m: an ass
casus, -us m: a fall, chance
cervix, cervicis f: neck
clamor, clamoris m: a shout, outcry
clamosus, -a, -um: noisy, shouted
cognosco (3): to recognized, find out
commilito, -onis m: a fellow soldier
conlimo (1): to direct (the eyes) sideways, glance away
contentio, -onis f: stretching, controversy, struggle
continuo: immediately, at once
curiosus, -a, -um: curious, meddlesome
emetior: to pass over, measure out
exorior (4): to come out, arise
fenestrula, -ae f: a little window
fortuitus, -a, -um: casual, accidental
gestio (3): to be eager, wish

incoram: openly, publicly
inicio (3): to throw in, lay (hands) on
inquietus, -a, -um: restless
magnus, -a, -um: large, great
manus, -us f: a hand
obliquo (3): to turn aside, twist
oculus, -i m: eye
praeditus, -a, -um: gifted, provided with
procacitas, -tatis f: impudence
prospicio: to watch for, foresee
protinus: straight on, immediately
scalae, -arum f: (pl.) ladder
strepitus, -us m: noise, racket
testor (1): to give evidence, swear, call to witness (+ acc.)
tumultus, -us m: commotion, confusion
umbra, umbrae f: a shadow
unus, -a, -um: one, single
volo: to wish, will

Qua contentione...cognito: abl. abs., "with this controversy and noisy racket having been recognized" i.e. "When I heard the racket"
inquieti procacitate: abl. with **praeditus**, "an ass gifted *with a restless impudence*"
dum ... gestio: "as I wish" + inf.
obliquata cervice: abl. abs., "with my neck turned sideways"
quidnam sibi vellet: impf. subj. in ind. quest. after **prospicere**, "I am eager to see *what that tumult meant*," the impf. subj. is used after the vivid present *gestio*.
casu fortuito: abl. of cause, "by an accidental chance"
conlimatis oculis: abl. abs., "with his eyes cast sideways"
cunctos testatur: "called attention of all to"
exortus est: perf. of dep. *exorior*, "a great uproar *arose*"
emensis protinus scalis: abl. abs., "with a ladder brought over straightaway"
iniecta manu: "with a hand laid on (me)"

quidam me velut captivum detrahunt. Iamque omni sublata cunctatione scrupulosius contemplantes singula, cista etiam illa revelata, repertum productumque et oblatum magistratibus miserum hortulanum poenas scilicet capite pensurum in publicum deducunt carcerem summoque risu meum prospectum cavillari non desinunt. Unde etiam de prospectu et umbra asini natum est frequens proverbium.

---

asinus, -i m: an ass
captivus, -i m: a prisoner, captive
carcer, carceris m: a prison, jail
cavillor (1): to jest, mock
cista, -ae f: a chest, box
contemplo (1): to notice, look hard at
cunctatio, -onis f: delay
deduco (3): to lead away, lead off
desino (3): to stop, finish, cease
detraho (3): to drag down
frequens, frequentis: frequent, repeated
hortulanus, -i m: a gardener
magistratus, -us m: a magistrate, official
miser, misera, miserum: poor, wretched,
    pitiable
nascor (3): to be born, come into existence
offero, offerre, obtuli, oblatus: to being be-
    fore, present to

pendo (3): to weigh out, pay
poena, -ae f: a penalty, punishment
produco (3): to lead out, bring out
prospectus, -us m: a view, sight, looking out
proverbium, -i n: a proverb, saying
publicus, -a, -um: public, of the state
reperio (4): discover, learn of
revelo (1): show, reveal
risus, -us m: a laugh, laughter
scilicet: one may know, certainly
scrupulosus, -a, -um: careful, accurate
singulus, -a, -um: single, each
tollo, -ere, sustulli, sublatum: to remove
umbra, -ae f: a shadow
unde: whence
velut: just as, as if

---

velut captivum: "as if I were a prisoner"
sublata cunctatione: ab. abs., "all delay set aside"
cista revelata: ab. abs., "the chest having been revealed"
repertum productumque et oblatum: acc. part. agreeing with **hortulanum**,
    "discovered, led forward and handed over"
pensurum: fut. act. part. of **pendo** expressing purpose, "they led him off *in order to
    pay*"
scilicet capite: abl., "surely with his head"
summoque risu: abl. of manner, "with the greatest laughter"
meum prospectum: acc. dir. obj. of **cavillari**, "mocking *my looking out* (from the
    window)"
cavillari: pres. inf. of dep. **cavillor**, "they did not cease *mocking*"
natum est: perf. of dep. **nascor**, "Whence the repeated saying *has come into existence*"

Apuleius

[Selection 10: Apuleius, Met. X.19-23]

Fuit in illo conventiculo matrona quaedam pollens et opulens. Quae more ceterorum visum meum mercata ac dehinc multiformibus ludicris delectata per admirationem adsiduam paulatim in admirabilem mei cupidinem incidit; nec ullam vesanae libidini medelam capiens ad instar asinariae Pasiphaae complexus meos ardenter exspectabat. Grandi denique praemio cum altore meo depecta est noctis unius concubitum; at ille nequaquam anxius

---

admirabilis, -is, -e: astonishing
admiratio, -onis f: wonder, astonishment
adsiduus, -a, -um: constant, unremitting
altor, altoris m: nourisher, keeper
anxius, -a, -um: anxious, uneasy, concerned
ardenter: passionately, ardently
asinarius, -a, -um: asanine, of or to asses
capio (3): to take, seize
complexus, -us m: an embrace, (pl.) inter-
    course
concubitus, -us m: a lying together, inter-
    course
conventiculum, -i n: a small assembly, group
cupido, cupidinis m: desire, love
dehinc: hereafter, then
delecto (1): to delight, please
depeciscor (3): to bargain for, come to terms
exspecto (1): to look for, hope for, desire
grandis, -is, -e: great, large
incido (3): to happen, fall into

instar: equal to, in the form of (+ gen.)
libido, libidinis f: desire, lust
ludicrum, -i n: a play, show
matrona, -ae f: a wife, woman
medela, -ae f: a cure, treatment
mercor (1): to buy, pay
mos, moris m: custom, habit
multiformis, -e: with many shapes
nequaquam: by no means
nox, noctis f: night
opulens, opulentis: wealthy, rich
Pasiphae -aae f: Pasiphae
paulatim: little by little, gradually
pollens, pollentis: with power, important
praemium, -i n: a reward, gift, bribe
ullus, --a, -ullum: any
unus, -a, -um: one, single
vesanus, -a, -um: mad, frenzied, wild
video (2): to see

---

more ceterorum: "in the manner of others"
mercata ... delectata: perf. part. modifying *quae* (*matrona*), "she having purchased ... having delighted in"
visum meum: "my sight," i.e. "the sight of me"
in mei cupidinem incidit: "she fell into love of me"
vesanae libidini: dat. of ref., "any cure *for her mad passion*"
instar asinariae Pasiphaae: "like some ass-version of Pasiphae." Pasiphae was the wife of Minos of Krete who, after falling in love and mating with a bull, gave birth to the Minotaur.
complexus meos: acc. m. pl., "she was desiring *my embraces*"
grandi praemio: abl. of price, "with a great bribe"
depecta est: perf. dep., "she bargained for" + acc.
noctis unius: gen. f. s., "the intercourse *of a single night*"

186

quidnam posset de me suave provenire, lucro suo tantum contentus, adnuit.

[20] Iam denique cenati a triclinio domini decesseramus et iamdudum praestolantem cubiculo meo matronam offendimus. Dii boni, qualis ille quamque praeclarus apparatus! Quattuor eunuchi confestim pulvillis compluribus ventose tumentibus pluma delicata terrestrem nobis cubitum praestruunt, sed et stragula veste auro ac murice Tyrio depicta probe consternunt ac desuper brevibus

---

adnuo (3): to nod, agree
apparatus, -us m: a preparation
aurum, auri n: gold
bonus, -a, -um: good
brevis, -e: short, small
ceno (1): to dine
complures, -a: many, several
confestim: immediately, suddenly
consterno (3): to cover, lay
contentus, -a, -um: pleased, satisfied with (+ abl.)
cubiculum, -i n: bedroom, chamber
cubitus, -us m: a bed
decedo (3): to withdraw, depart, leave
delicatus, -a, -um: luxurious, sumptuous
depingo (3): to paint, color, dye
desuper: over, above
dominus, -i m: lord, master
eunuchus, -i m: a eunuch
iamdudum: immediately
lucrum, -i n: gain, profit
matrona, -ae f: a wife, woman

murex, muricis m: purple (dye)
offendo (3): to meet with, stumble upon
pluma, -ae f: feather, plume
possum: to be able
praeclarus, -a, -um: splendid, bright
praestolor (1): to stand ready, wait
praestruo (3): to arrange in advance
provenio (4): to proceed
pulvillus, -i m: little pillow
quails, -e: of what sort, how
quam: how
quattuor: four
quidnam: interrogative particle
stragulum, -i n: a bed cover
suavis, -e: agreeable, pleasant
tantus, -a, -um: so great, so much
terrester, terrestris, terrestre: on the ground
triclinium, -i n: a (dining) couch, dining room
tumeo (2): to swell
ventose: windy
vestis, -is f: clothing, a blanket

---

quidnam posset: impf. subj. in ind. quest., "worried not at all *that he would be able to*" + inf.
a triclinio domini: "from the dining couch of my master"
cubiculo meo: abl. of place where, "in my chamber"
quam praeclarus: "how splendid!"
pulvillis compluribus tumentibus : abl. abs., "with many pillows puffing up"
pluma delicata: abl. of means, "with delicate plume"
stragula...depicta: nom. pl., "bedcovers painted with" + *abl.*
auro ac murice Tyrio: abl. of means, "colored *with gold and Tyrian purple*"

admodum, sed satis copiosis pulvillis aliis nimis modicis, quis maxillas et cervices delicatae mulieres suffulcire consuerunt, superstruunt. Nec dominae voluptates diutina sua praesentia morati, clausis cubiculis foribus facessunt. At intus cerei praeclara micantes luce nocturnas nobis tenebras inalbabant.

[21] Tunc ipsa cuncto prorsus spoliata tegmine, taenia quoque, qua decoras devinxerat papillas, lumen propter adsistens, de stagneo vasculo multo sese perungit oleo balsamino meque indidem largissime perfricat, sed multo tanto impensius curans

---

admodum: very, exceedingly
adsisto (3): to stand (near)
balsaminus, -a, -um: of balsam, balsamic
cereus, -i m: a candle
cervix, cervicis f: neck
clavis, clavis f: a key
consuesco (3): to be accustomed
copiosus, -a, -um: abundant, plentiful
cunctus, -a, -um: whole, entire
decorus, -a, -um: beautiful, glorious
delicatus, -a, -um: delicate, elegant
devincio (4): to tie up, bind, hold fast
diutinus, -a, -um: long lasting
domina, -ae f: mistress
facesso (3): to go away
foris, foris f: door, gate
impensius: more lavishly
inalbo (1): to brighten, make light
indidem: from the same place
intus: within, inside
largissime: most liberally
lumen, luminis n: a light, lamp
lux, lucis f: light
maxilla, -ae f: a jaw, face

micans, micantis: gleaming, sparkling
mulier, mulieris f: woman
nimis: very much, too much
nocturnus, -a, -um: nocturnal, of night
oleum, olei n: oil
papilla, -ae f: breast, bosom
perfrico (1): to rub all over
perungo (3): to annoit thoroughly
praeclarus, -a, -um: splendid, bright
propter: near, on account of
prorsus: entirely, utterly
pulvillus, -i m: a little pillow
satis: enough, adequate
spolio (1): to strip
stagneus, -a, -um: made of stagnum, tin
suffulcio (4): to underprop, support
superstruo (3): to set over, set up on top
taenia, -ae f: a bandeau, brassiere
tegmen, tegminis n: covering, clothing
tenebra, -ae f: darkness, shadow
tunc: then, thereupon
vasculum, -i n: a small vessel
voluptas, -tatis f: pleasure, delight

---

quis: (= *quibus*), "by which"
consuerunt: pr. of *consuesco*, "women are accustomed to" + *inf.*
nec ... morati: "(the eunuchs) *not delaying* by their presence"
clausis cubiculis foribus: ab. abs., "the doors having been closed"
praeclara luce: abl. of means, "with splendid light"
nobis: dat. of reference, "brightened the nocturnal darkness *for us*"
qua: abl. of means, "even her bandeau, *with which* she had bound..."
multo tanto: abl. of degree of difference after *impensius*, "more lavishly *by so much more*"

etiam nares perfundit meas. Tunc exosculata pressule, non qualia in lupanari solent basiola iactari vel meretricum poscinummia vel adventorum negantinummia, sed pura atque sincera instruit et blandissimos adfatus: "Amo" et "Cupio" et "Te solum diligo" et "Sine te iam vivere nequeo" et cetera, quis mulieres et alios inducunt et suas testantur adfectationes, capistroque me prehensum more, quo didiceram, reclinat facile, quippe cum nil novi nihilque difficile facturus mihi viderer, praesertim post tantum

---

adfatus, -um m: speech, utterance
adfectatio, -onis f: a seeking, affection
adventor, -oris m: a visitor, customer
alius, alia, aliud: other, another
amo (1): to love
basiolum, -i n: little kiss
blandissimus, -a, -um: most flattering, very pleasant
capistrum, -i n: halter, harness
cupido: to desire
difficile: with difficulty
diligo (3): to hold dear, love
disco (3): to leave, become acquainted with
exosculor (1): to kiss
facile: easily, readily
facio: to make, do
iacto (1): to toss
induco (3): to bring in, introduce
instruo (3): to furnish
lupanar, -aris n: brothel
meretrix, meretricis f: courtesan, prostitute
mos, moris m: custom, habit

mulier, mulieris f: a woman
naris, -is f: nostril, (*pl.*) nose
negantinummius, -a, -um: refusing to pay, stingy
nequeo: to be unable
novus, -a, -um: new
perfundo (3): to pour over, wet, coat
poscinummius, -a, -um: money-seeking
praesertim: especially, particularly
prehendo (3): to take hold of, grasp
pressule: adv. while pressing against
purus, -a, um: pure, clean, chaste
qualis, -e: what kind, as
quippe: of course, as you see
recline: to cause to lie down
sincerus, -a, -um: genuine, sincere
sine: without (+ *abl.*)
soleo (2): to be accustomed to
solus, -a, -um: alone, only
testor: to testify, swear
video (2): to see
vivo (3): to live

---

non qualia ... solent basiola iactari: "not such as are customary to be tossed out"
vel poscinummia ... vel negantinummia: agreeing with *basiola*, "kisses either money-seeking or stingy"
pura atque sincera: also agreeing with *basiola*
quis: (= *quibus*), "with which"
capistro: abl. of means, "me, taken hold of *by my harness*"
quo didiceram: plup. indic. of *disco*, "in the manner, *which I had learned*" quo is attracted into the abl. case by its antecedent more
nil novi: "nothing of new"
facturus (esse): fut. inf. after *viderer*, "I seemed to be about to do"
cum ... viderer: impf. pas. subj. of *video*, "since I seemed" + inf.
post tantum temporis: "after so much of time"

temporis tam formosae mulieris cupientis amplexus obiturus; nam
et vino pulcherrimo atque copioso memet madefeceram et unguento
flagrantissimo prolubium libidinis suscitaram. [22] Sed angebar
plane non exili metu reputans, quem ad modum tantis tamque
magis cruribus possem delicatam matronam inscendere vel tam
lucida tamque tenera et lacte ac melle confecta membra duris
ungulis complecti labiasque modicas ambroseo rore purpurantes

---

ambrosius, -a, -um: lovely, sweet
amplexus, -us m: an embrace, intercourse
ango (3): to choke, distress
complector (3): to embrace
conficio (3): to make, prepare
copiosus, -a, -um: abundant, plentiful
crus, cruris n: leg
cupio (3): to wish, long for, desire
delicatus, -a, -um: delicate, dainty
durus, -a, -um: hard, rough
exilis, -e: small, thin
flagrans, flagrantis: scorching, fiery
formosus, -a, -um: beautiful, fine
inscendo (3): to mount
labia, -ae f: a lip
lac, lactis n: milk
libido, libidinis f: desire, lust, passion
lucidus, -a, -um: bright, shining, white
madefacio (3): to wet, drench, intoxicate
matrona, -ae f: a woman, matron

mel, mellis n: honey
membrum, -i n: a member, limb
metus, -us m: fear, anxiety
modicus, -a, -um: moderate, small
mulier, mulieris f: woman
oboe, -ire, -ivi, -itus: to go to meet, attend
plane: clearly, plainly
possum: to be able
prolubium, -i n: desire, inclination
pulcher, pulchra, pulchrum: beautiful
purpuro (1): to be purple, be adorned
reputo (1): to think over, reflect
ros, roris m: dew
suscito (1): to encourage, arouse, excite
tantus, -a, -um: of such size, so great
tempus, temporis n: time, condition
tener, tenera, tenerum: soft, delicate
unguentum, -i n: an unguent, oil
ungula, -ae f: a hoof
vinum, -i n: wine

---

obiturus: fut. act. part., "(I) *about to engage* the embraces"
memet madefeceram: plupf. of *madefacio*, "*I had intoxicated* myself with wine"
suscitaram: syncopated plupf. (= *suscitaveram*), "*I had aroused* a desire of lust"
non exili metu: litotes, "by no small fear," i.e. "a great fear"
quem ad modum ... possem: impf. subj. in ind. quest. after *angebar*, "I was worried in
    what manner I might be able to" + inf.
tantis ... cruribus: abl. of means
tam lucida tamque tenera: agreeing with *membra*, "limbs so white and delicate"
lacte ac melle: abl. of means after *confecta*, "limbs made *of milk and honey*"
complecti: pres. inf. of dep. of *complector* also after *possem*, "how I might be able *to
    embrace* her limbs..."
ambroseo rore: abl. of means, "reddened *with lovely dew*"

tam amplo ore tamque enormi et saxeis dentibus deformi saviari,
novissime quo pacto, quanquam ex unguiculis perpruriscens, mulier
tam vastum genitale susciperet: heu me, qui dirrupta nobili femina
bestiis obiectus munus instructurus sim mei domini! Molles
interdum voculas et adsidua savia et dulces gannitus
commorsicantibus oculis iterabat illa, et in summa: "Teneo te"

---

adsiduus, -a, -um: constant, repeated
amplus, -a, -um: large, great
bestia, -ae f: a beast, animal
commorsico (1): to devour
deformis, -is, -e: deformed, misshapen
dens, dentis m: a tooth
dirrumpo (3): to break apart, shatter
dominus, -i m: owner, master
dulcis, -is, -e: sweet, kind
enormis, -is, -e: immense, huge
femina, -ae f: a woman
gannitus, -us m: a whimper
genital, genitalis n: genitals, member
heu: oh! alas!
instruo (3): to furnish, equip
interdum: sometimes, meanwhile
itero (1): to repeat
mollis, -is, -e: soft, mild
mulier, mulieris f: woman

munus, muneris n: a service, public duty,
   here public entertainment
nobilis, -is, -e: noble, prominent
novissime: lastly
obicio (3): to cast out, throw to
oculus, -i m: eye
os, oris n: mouth
pactum, -i n: agreement, manner
perprurisco: to itch all over
quanquam: although, yet
savior (1): to kiss
savium, -i n: kiss
saxeus, -a, -um: stony, of stone
suscipio (3): to accept, receive
teneo (2): to hold
unguiculus, -i m: a fingernail, finger tip
vastus, -a, -um: huge, monstrous
vocula, -ae f: a low voice, small speech

---

tam amplo ore tamque enormi et ... deformi: abl. of means, "with so big and ugly a
   mouth"
saxeis dentibus: abl. of description, "with stony teeth"
saviari: pres. inf. of dep. of **savior** after **possem**, "how I might be able *to kiss* her lips..."
quo pacto ... susciperet: impf. subj. in ind. quest. after **angebar**, "in what matter the
   woman might receive..."
ex unguiculis: "from the fingertips" i.e. "all over"
perpruriscens: "although *itching* (with desire) all over"
qui ... sim: pres. subj. in rel. cl. of char. which is also the apodosis of a condition, "alas
   for me, *who would be*"
dirrupta nobili femina: abl. abs. taking the place of the protasis of a future less vivid
   condition "a noble woman having been shattered," i.e. if a noble woman were to
   be shattered
obiectus: perf. pass. part. with instrumental force, "*by being thrown* to the beasts"
instructurus: fut. pas. part. used periphrasitically with **sim**, "I would *serve* the
   gladiatorial show of my master"
commorsicantibus oculis: abl. of manner, "with her devouring eyes"

inquit "teneo, meum palumbulum, meum passerem" et cum dicto
vanas fuisse cogitationes meas ineptumque monstrat metum.
Artissime namque complexa totum me prorsus, sed totum recepit.
Illa vero quotiens ei parcens nates recellebam, accedens toties nisu
rabido et spinam prehendens meam adplicitiore nexu inhaerebat, ut
hercules etiam deesse mihi aliquid ad supplendam eius libidinem
crederem, nec Minotauri matrem frustra delectatam putarem

---

adplicitior, -oris: closer, more intimate
artissime: very closely, most tightly
cogitatio, -onis f: thinking, contemplation
complector (3): to embrace
credo (3): to belive, suppose
delector (1): to delight, take pleasure
desum: be wanting, lack
frustra: in vain, for nothing
Hercules, Herculis m: Hercules
ineptus, -a, -um: silly, foolish
inhaereo (2): to stick to, hang on
inquam: to say
libido, libidinis f: desire, lust
mater, matris f: mother
metus, -us m: a fear, anxiety
Minotaurus, -i m: Minotaur, the mythical
    half-man, half-bull
monstro (1): to show, reveal

natis, -is f: rump, (*pl.*) haunches
nexus, -us m: a tie, bond, joining
nisus, -us m: a pressing, pressure
palumbulus, -i m: a little pigeon
parco (3): to spare
passer, passeris m: sparrow
prehendo (3): to take hold of, grasp
prorsus: entirely, utterly
puto (1): to think
quotiens: how often, as often as
rabidus, -a, -um: mad, raging, wild
recello (3): to pull back
recipio (3): to accept, take in
spina, -ae f: a spine
suppleo (2): to supply, satisfy
vanus, -a, -um: empty, vain
vero: truly, indeed

---

cum dicto: "with this word," i.e. "in accordance with this word"
fuisse: perf. inf. of sum in ind. st. after *monstrat*, "she showed that my
    contemplations *were* in vain and my fear *was* silly."
quotiens... toties: "*as often as* I was pulling back...*so often* she kept hanging on"
ei parcens: "sparing her"
ut ... crederem: impf. subj. in result clause, "so that I believed"
deesse mihi aliquid: inf. in ind. st. after *crederem*, "that something was lacking from
    me"
ad supplendam eius libidinem: acc. gerundive expressing purpose, "to satisfy her
    lust"
nec ... putarem: impf. subj. in continuation of the result clause, "nor was I supposing"
matrem frustra delectatam (sc. *esse*): ind. st. after *putarem*, "that the mother had
    been loved in vain"
Minotauri matrem: "mother of the Minotaur," i.e. Pasiphae

adultero mugiente. Iamque operosa et pervigili nocte transacta, vitata lucis conscientia facessit mulier condicto pari noctis futurae pretio. [23] Nec gravate magister meus voluptates ex eius arbitrio largiebatur partim mercedes amplissimas acceptando, partim novum spectaculum domino praeparando. Incunctanter ei denique libidinis nostrae totam detegit scaenam. At ille liberto magnifice munerato destinat me spectaculo publico. Et quoniam neque egregia

---

accepto (3): to receive, take
adulter, adulteri m: adulterer, illicit lover
amplissimus, -a, -um: largest
arbitrium, -i n: choice, judgment, decision
condico (3): to agree on, appoint
conscientia, -ae f: knowledge, complicity
destino (1): to determine, arrange
detego (3): to reveal, expose
dominus, -i m: an owner, master
egregious, -a, -um: distinguished
facesso (3): to go away, depart
futurus, -a, -um: about to be, future
gravate: reluctantly, unwillingly
incunctanter: without hesitation
largior (4): to grant
libertus, liberti m: freedman
libido, libidinis f: desire, lust
lux, lucis f: light, daylight
magister, magistri m: a master, keeper

magnifice: splendidly, handsomely
merces, mercedis f: pay, bribe
mugio (4): to low, moo
mulier, mulieris f: a woman
munero (1): to give, present
novus, -a, -um: new
nox, noctis f: night
operosus, -a, -um: laborious, painstaking
partim: partly
pervigil, pervigilis: sleepless
praeparo (1): to prepare
pretium, -i n: price
publicus, -a, -um: public
quoniam: because, since
scaena, -ae f: a scene
spectaculum, -i n: a show, spectacle
transigo (3): to complete, accomplish
vito (1): to avoid
voluptas, -tatis f: pleasure, delight

---

adultero mugiente: "by her mooing lover," i.e. the bull
nocte transacta: ab. abs., "the night have been completed"
vitata lucis conscientia: ab. abs., "the complicity of night having been avoided"
condicto pretio: abl. abs., "*with the price* of a future night *agreed upon*"
partim acceptando ... partim praeparando: abl. gerunds of means, "partly by accepting ... partly by preparing"
domino: dat. of advantage, "for his master"
liberto magnifice munerato: abl. abs., "with his freedman handsomely rewarded"
spectaculo publico: dat. of purpose, "for the public spectacle"
neque...neque: "neither...nor"

illa uxor mea propter dignitatem neque prorsus ulla alia inveniri potuerat grandi praemio, quae mecum incoram publicans pudicitiam populi caveam frequentaret. Eius poenae talem cognoveram fabulam.

---

cavea, -ae f: a cage
cognosco (3): to learn, find out
dignitas, -tatis f: honor, excellence
fabula, -ae f: story, tale
frequento (1): to frequent, go repeatedly
grandis, -e: great, large, grand
incoram: openly, publicly
invenio (4): to find, discover

poena, -ae f: penalty, punishment
praemium, -i n: a reward, recompense
prorsus: entirely, utterly
publico: to show publicly
pudicitia, -ae f: chastity, modesty
ullus, -a, -um: any
uxor, uxoris f: wife

---

propter dignitatem: "for the sake of propriety"
inveniri: pres. pas. inf. after *potuerat*, "was able *to be found*"
grandi praemio: abl. of price, "for a great reward"
quae ... frequentaret: impf. subj. in rel. cl. of characteristic, "who would frequent"

List of Verbs

List of Verbs

 The following is a list of verbs that have some irregularity in their conjugation. The principal parts of the Greek verb in order are 1. Present 2. Future 3. Aorist 4. Perfect Active 5. Perfect Middle 6. Aorist Passive, 7. Future Passive. We have not included the future passive below, since it occurs very rarely. For many verbs not all forms are attested or are only poetic. Verbs are alphabetized under their main stem, followed by various compounds that occur in the *Ass* with a brief definition. A dash (-) before a form means that it occurs only or chiefly with a prefix. The list is based on the list of verbs in H. Smythe, *A Greek Grammar*.

ἄγω: to lead **ἄξω**, 2 aor. **ἤγαγον, ἦχα, ἦγμαι, ἤχθην**
    ἀπάγω: to lead away, divert
    διάγω: to lead across
    ἐπάγω: to bring on, charge
    ἐπανάγω: to lead back
    κατάγω: to lead down, bring down
    προσάγω: to bring forth, lead to

αἱρέω: to take **αἱρήσω**, 2 aor. **εἷλον, ᾕρηκα, ᾕρημαι, ᾑρέθην**
    ἀναιρέω: to take up, raise
    ἀφαιρέω: to take away, exclude, set aside, remove
    ἐξαιρέω: to take out

αἴρω: to lift **ἀρῶ, ἦρα, ἦρκα, ἦρμαι, ἤρθην**
    ἐπαίρω: to lift up and set on

αἰσθάνομαι: to perceive **αἰσθήσομαι**, 2 aor. **ᾐσθόμην, ᾔσθημαι**

ἀκούω: to hear **ἀκούσομαι, ἤκουσα**, 2 perf. **ἀκήκοα**, 2 plup. **ἠκηκόη** or **ἀκηκόη, ἠκούσθην**
    ὑπακούω: to listen, attend

ἀλείφω: to anoint **ἀλείψω, ἤλειψα, ἀπ-αλήλιφα, ἀλήλιμμαι, ἠλείφθην**

ἁλίσκομαι: to be taken **ἁλώσομαι**, 2 aor. **ἑάλων, ἑάλωκα**

ἁμαρτάνω: to fail, go wrong **ἁμαρτήσομαι**, 2 aor. **ἥμαρτον, ἡμάρτηκα, ἡμάρτημαι, ἡμαρτήθην**

ἀμείβω: to change **ἀμείψω, ἤμειψα**

ἀνύω: to effect **ἀνύσω, ἤνυσα, ἤνυκα**

ἅπτω: to fasten, (*mid.*) to touch **ἅψω, ἧψα, ἧμμαι, ἥφθην**

ἀμύνω: to ward off ἀμυνῶ, ἤμυνα; (*mid.*) ἀμύνομαι defend myself ἀμυνοῦμαι, ἠμυνάμην

ἀρύω: to draw (water) ἤρυσα, ηρύθην

ἄρχω: to be first, begin ἄρξω, ἦρξα, ἦργμαι, ἤρχθην

ἀφικνέομαι: to arrive at ἀφ-ίξομαι, 2 aor. ἀφ-ικόμην, ἀφ-ῖγμαι

ἄχθομαι: to be vexed, be loaded down ἀχθέσομαι, ἠχθέσθην

βαίνω: to step βήσομαι, 2 aor. ἔβην, βέβηκα
    ἐμβαίνω: to step in, walk into
    ἐπιβαίνω: to go upon, trample
    καταβαίνω: to go down

βάλλω: to throw βαλῶ, 2 aor. ἔβαλον, βέβληκα, βέβλημαι, ἐβλήθην
    ἐκβάλλω: to throw out
    εἰσβάλλω: to throw into, fall upon
    ἐμβάλλω: to throw in, charge
    καταβάλλω: to throw down, proscribe
    παραβάλλω: to throw beside
    περιβάλλω: to throw around, put on
    προσβάλλω: to throw against
    συμβάλλω: to throw together, infer
    ὑπερβάλλω: to throw beyond, stick out beyond
    ὑποβάλλω: to throw down, put under, suggest

βλέπω: to look at, see βλέψομαι, ἔβλεψα
    ὑποβλέπω: to look up

βοάω: to shout βοήσομαι, ἐβόησα βέβωμαι, ἐβώσθην
    ἀναβοάω: to shout aloud, utter a loud cry

βούλομαι: to wish βουλήσομαι, βεβούλημαι, ἐβουλήθην

γαμέω: to marry γαμῶ, ἔγημα, γεγάμηκα

γελάω: to laugh γελάσομαι, ἐγέλασα, ἐγελάσθην

γίγνομαι: to become γενήσομαι, 2 aor. ἐγενόμην, 2 perf. γέγονα, γεγένημαι, ἐγενήθην

γιγνώσκω: to know γνώσομαι, ἔγνων, ἔγνωκα, ἔγνωσμαι, ἐγνώσθην
    διαγινώσκω: to distinguish, discern, resolve
    καταγιγνώσκω: to remark, discover

δάκνω: to bite δήξομαι, 2 aor. ἔδακον, δέδηγμαι, ἐδήχθην, δαχθήσομαι

δείδω: to fear δείσομαι, ἔδεισα, δέδοικα

δείκνυμι: to show **δείξω, ἔδειξα, δέδειχα, δέδειγμαι, ἐδείχθην**
  ἀποδείκνυμι: to show, demonstrate
  ἐπιδείκνυμι: to show, exhibit

δέω (1): to bind **δήσω, ἔδησα, δέδεκα, δέδεμαι, ἐδέθην**
  καταδέω: to bind down, tie up
  προσδέω: to bind to, tie to, attach

δέω (2) : to need, lack (*mid*) ask: **δεήσω, ἐδέησα, δεδέηκα, δεδέημαι, ἐδεήθην**

δέομαι: want, ask: **δεήσομαι, δεδέημαι, ἐδεήθην**. (from **δέω** 2)

δέχομαι: to receive **δέξομαι, ἐδεξάμην, δέδεγμαι, -εδέχθην**
  εἰσδέχομαι: to take in, admit, receive
  ἐπιδέχομαι: to admit
  ὑποδέχομαι: to receive beneath

διδάσκω: to teach, (*mid.*) learn **διδάξω, ἐδίδαξα, δεδίδαχα, δεδίδαγμαι, ἐδιδάχθην**

δίδωμι: to give **δώσω**, 1 aor. **ἔδωκα** in s., 2 aor. **ἔδομεν** in pl. **δέδωκα, δέδομαι, ἐδόθην**
  ἀποδίδωμι: to give back, return, render
  ἐνδίδωμι: to give in, allow
  ἐπιδίδωμι: to give besides, lend, hand over
  παραδίδωμι: to hand over
  προδίδωμι: to give away, betray

διώκω: to pursue **διώξομαι, ἐδίωξα, δεδίωχα, ἐδιώχθην**

δοκέω: to think, seem **δόξω, ἔδοξα, δέδογμαι**

ἐθέλω: to wish **ἐθελήσω, ἠθέλησα, ἠθέληκα**

εἶδον: I saw (pr. system provided by **ὁράω**), perf. **οἶδα** "know," fut. **εἴσομαι** "shall know"

εἰμί: to be, fut. **ἔσομαι**
  πάρειμι: to be present, stand by
  πρόσειμι: to be present, be added

ἐγείρω: to wake up **ἐγερῶ, ἤγειρα**, 2 perf. **ἐγρήγορα, ἐγήγερμαι, ἠγέρθην**
  ἀνεγείρω: to wake up, rouse

ἐλαύνω: to drive **ἐλῶ, ἤλασα, -ελήλακα, ἐλήλαμαι, ἠλάθην**
  παρελαύνω: to drive past

ἕλκω: to draw up **ἕλξω, εἵλκυσα, εἵλκυκα**

ἐλέγχω: to shame **ἐλέγξω, ἤλεγξα, ἐλήλεγμαι, ἠλέγχθην**

ἕπομαι: to follow **ἕψομαι**, 2 aor. **ἑσπόμην**

ἐράω: to love, imp. *ἤρων* aor. *ἠράσθην*

ἐργάζομαι: to work *ἠργαζόμην, ἐργάσομαι, ἠργασάμην, εἴργασμαι, ἠργάσθην*

ἔρχομαι: to come or go to: fut. *εἶμι*, 2 aor. *ἦλθον*, 2 perf. *ἐλήλυθα*
    ἀπέρχομαι: to go away, depart from
    εἰσέρχομαι: to go in, enter
    ἐξέρχομαι: to come out, go out, leave
    ἐπεισέρχομαι: to come in (besides)
    ἐπέρχομαι: to go upon, attack
    κατέρχομαι: to go down from
    παρεισέρχομαι: to come in beside
    παρέρχομαι: to go by, to pass by
    περιέρχομαι: to go around, wander
    προέρχομαι: to come forward, advance, go forth
    προσέρχομαι: to go to
    ὑπεξέρχομαι: to go out from under, escape

ἐσθίω: to eat *ἔδομαι*, 2 aor. *ἔφαγον*

εὑρίσκω: to find *εὑρήσω*, 2 aor. *ηὗρον* or *εὗρον, ηὕρηκα* or *εὕρηκα, εὕρημαι, εὑρέθην*

εὐφραίνω: to cheer, delight, gladden *εὐφρανῶ, ηὔφρανα, ηὐφράνθην*

εὔχομαι: to pray *εὔξομαι, ηὐξάμην, ηὖγμαι*
    ἐξευρίσκω: to find out, discover

ἔχω: to have *ἕξω*, 2 aor. *ἔσχον, ἔσχηκα*, imperf. *εἶχον*.
    ἀνέχω: to hold back
    ἀντέχω: to hold against
    παρέχω: to furnish, provide, supply
    προσέχω: to hold to, offer
    συνέχω: to hold together
    ὑπέχω: to undergo

ζάω: to live *ζήσω, ἔζησα, ἔζηκα*

ζεύγνυμι: to yoke *ζεύξω, ἔζευξα, ἔζευγμαι, ἐζεύχθην*
    ὑποζεύγνυμι: to put under the yoke

ἥδομαι: to be happy *ἡσθήσομαι, ἥσθην*

θαυμάζω: to wonder, admire, fut. *θαυμάσομαι*

θέω: to run *θεύσομαι*

θνήσκω: to die *θανοῦμαι*, 2 aor. *-έθανον, τέθνηκα*
    ἀποθνήσκω: to die

θύω: to sacrifice *θύσω, ἔθυσα, τέθυκα, τέθυμαι, ἐτύθην*

ἵημι: to let go, relax, to send forth **ἥσω, ἧκα, εἷκα, εἷμαι, εἵθην**
    ἀφίημι: to send forth, send away
    συνίημι: to bring or set together

ἵστημι: to make to stand, set **στήσω** shall set, **ἔστησα** set, caused to stand, 2 aor.
    ἔστην stood, 1 perf. **ἕστηκα** stand, plupf. **εἱστήκη** stood, **ἐστάθην**
    ἀνίστημι: to make to stand up, raise up
    ἐνίστημι: to set against, resist
    ἐξανίστημι: to raise up
    ἐπανίστημι: to set up again
    ἐφίστημι: to set upon
    παρίστημι: to stand up beside
    περιίστημι: to place round
    ὑφίστημι: to place or set under

καίω: to burn **καύσω, ἔκαυσα, -κέκαυκα, κέκαυμαι, ἐκαύθην**

καλέω: to call **καλῶ, ἐκάλεσα, κέκληκα, κέκλημαι, ἐκλήθην**
    ἐγκαλέω: to call in, blame, accuse
    παρακαλέω: to call to, summon, invite

κελεύω: to urge **κελεύσω, ἐκέλευσα, κεκέλευκα, κεκέλευσμαι, ἐκελεύσθην**

κηρυττω: to proclaim **κηρύξω, ἐκήρυξα, -κεκήρυχα, κεκήρυγμαι, ἐκηρυχθην**

κλάω: to break **ἔκλασα, -κέκλασμαι, -εκλάσθην**

κλέπτω: to steal **κλέψω , ἔκλεψα, κέκλοφα, κέκλεμμαι**, 2 aor. pass. **ἐκλάπην**

κλείω: to shut **κλείσω, ἔκλεισα, κέκλειμαι, ἐκλείσθην**
    συγκλείω: to shut, close up, enclose

κλίνω: to bend **κλινῶ, ἔκλινα, κέκλικα, κέκλιμαι, -εκλίνην**
    ἀνακλίνω: to lean, lay down
    ἐπικλίνω: to incline, tilt
    παρακατακλίνω: to lay down beside

κομίζω: to take care of **κομιῶ, ἐκόμισα, κεκόμικα, κεκόμισμαι, ἐκομίσθην**

κόπτω: to strike **κόψω, ἔκοψα, -κέκοφα, κέκομμαι, -εκόπην**

κρίνω: to decide **κρινῶ, ἔκρινα, κέκρικα, κέκριμαι, ἐκρίθην**
    ἀποκρίνω: to separate, set apart; (*mid.*)answer

κρούω: to strike **κρούσω, ἔκρουσα, -κέκρουκα, -κέκρουμαι, -εκρούσθην**

κρύπτω: to hide from **κρύψω, ἔκρυψα, κέκρυμμαι, ἐκρύφθην**

κτάομαι: to acquire **κτήσομαι, ἐκτησάμην, κέκτημαι** possess

κτείνω: to kill **κτενῶ, ἔκτεινα**, 2 perf. **-έκτονα**
    ἀποκτείνω: to kill, slay

λαμβάνω: to take **λήψομαι, ἔλαβον, εἴληφα, εἴλημμαι, ἐλήφθην**
    ἐπιλαμβάνω: to lay hold of, seize, attack
    καταλαμβάνω: to seize, overtake
    παραλαμβάνω: to take beside
    περιλαμβάνω: to seize around, embrace
    συλλαμβάνω: to collect, seize

λαγχάνω: to obtain by lot **λήξομαι, ἔλαχον, εἴληχα, εἴλημμαι, ἐλήχθην**

λανθάνω: to escape notice **λήσω, ἔλαθον, λέληθα**

λάμπω: to shine **λάμψω, ἔλαμψα, λέλαμπα, -λέλησμαι**

λέγω: to speak **ἐρέω, εἶπον, εἴρηκα, λέλεγμαι, ἐλέχθην** and **ἐρρήθην**
    διαλέγω: to speak with, converse

λείπω: leave **λείψω, ἔλιπον, λέλοιπα, λέλειμμαι, ἐλείφθην**
    καταλείπω: to abandon

λύω: to loose **λύσω, ἔλυσα, λέλυκα, λέλυμαι, ἐλύθην**

μανθάνω: to learn **μαθήσομαι, ἔμαθον, μεμάθηκα**

μάχομαι: to fight **μαχοῦμαι, ἐμαχεσάμην, μεμάχημαι**
    ἀντιμάχομαι: to fight back

μέμφομαι: to blame **μέμψομαι, ἐμεμψάμην, ἐμέμφθην**

μένω: to stay **μενῶ, ἔμεινα, μεμένηκα**
    περιμένω: to wait for, await
    προσμένω: to bide one's time, await
    ὑπομένω: to endure, survive

μίγνυμι: to mix **μείξω, ἔμειξα, μέμειγμαι, ἐμείχθην**
    ἀναμείγνυμι: to mix together

νομίζω: to believe **νομιῶ, ἐνόμισα, νενόμικα, νενόμισμαι, ἐνομίσθην**

οἴομαι: to suppose **ᾠήθην** imperf. **ᾤμην**

ὁράω: to see **ὄψομαι**, 2 aor. **εἶδον, ἑόρακα** and **ἑώρακα, ὤφθην**, imperf. **ἑώρων**

ὀργίζω: to make angry **-οργιῶ, ὤργισα, ὤργισμαι, ὠργίσθην**

ὄλλυμι: to destroy **ολῶ, -ώλεσα, -ολώλεκα, -όλωλα**
    ἀπόλλυμι: to destroy, lose

παίω: to strike **παίσω, ἔπαισα, -πέπαικα, ἐπαίσθην**

παλαίω: to wrestle **ἐπάλαισα, ἐπαλαίσθην**

πάσχω: to experience **πείσομαι**, 2 aor. **ἔπαθον**, 2 perf. **Πέπονθα**

πείθω: to persuade **πείσω, ἔπεισα**, 2 perf. **πέποιθα, πέπεισμαι, ἐπείσθην**

πεινάω: to be hungry **πεινήσω, ἐπείνησα, πεπαίνηκα**

πέμπω: to send, convey **πέμψω, ἔπεμψα**, 2 perf. **πέπομφα, πέπεμμαι, ἐπέμφθην**

πέτομαι: to fly **πτήσομαι**, 2 aor. **-επτόμην**

πήγνυμι: to fix, make fast **πήξω, ἔπηξα**, 2 perf. **πέπηγα**, 2 aor. pass. **ἐπάγην**

πίνω: to drink **πίομαι**, 2 aor. **ἔπιον, πέπωκα, -πέπομαι, -επόθην**
    καταπίνω: to gulp down
    προπίνω: to drink before

πίπτω: to fall **πεσοῦμαι**, 2 aor. **ἔπεσον, πέπτωκα**
    ἀναπίπτω: to fall back
    ἐπιπίπτω: to fall upon, attack
    καταπίπτω: to fall down, drop down
    μεταπίπτω: to fall differently, change
    περιπίπτω: to fall around, encounter
    συμπίπτω: to fall together

πλέω: to sail **πλεύσομαι, ἔπλευσα, πέπλευκα, πέπλευσμαι, ἐπλεύσθην**

πνέω: to blow **πνεύσομαι, ἔπνευσα, -πέπνευκα**

ποθέω: to desire, miss **ποθήσω** or **ποθέσομαι, ἐπόθησα** or **ἐπόθεσα**

πράττω: to do **πράξω, ἔπραξα**, 2 perf. **πέπραχα, πέπραγμαι, ἐπράχθην**

πυνθάνομαι: to learn **πεύσομαι**, 2 aor. **ἐπυθόμην, πέπυσμαι**

ῥήγνυμι: to break **-ρήξω, ἔρρηξα, -έρρωγα, ἐρράγην**

ῥιπτω: throw **ῥίψω, ἔρριψα**, 2 perf. **ἔρριφα, ἔρριμμαι, ἐρρίφην**
    ἐπιρριπτέω: throw oneself

σκάπτω: to dig **σκάψω, -έσκαψα**, 2 perf. **-έσκαφα, ἔσκαμμαι**, 2 aor. pass. **εσκάφην**

σκέπτομαι: to view **σκέψομαι, ἐσκεψάμην, ἔσκεμμαι**

σκώπτω: to mock **σκώψομαι, ἔσκωψα, ἐσκώφθην**

σπάω: to draw **σπάσω, ἔσπασα, -έσπακα, ἔσπασμαι, -εσπάσθην**

στάζω: to drip **ἔσταξα, -έσταγμαι, -εστάχθην**

στρέφω: to turn **στρέψω, ἔστρεψα, ἔστραμμαι, ἐστρέφθην**
    ἀναστρέφω: to turn back, return
    ἀποστρέφω: to turn around, turn back

σῴζω: to save *σώσω, ἔσωσα, σέσωκα, ἐσώθην* **ὑπεροράω**: to look down upon, despise

τείνω: stretch *τενῶ, -έτεινα, -τέτακα, τέταμαι, -ετάθην*

τέμνω: to cut *τεμῶ*, 2 aor. *ἔτεμον, -τέτμηκα, τέτμημαι, ἐτμήθην*
    ἀνατέμνω: to cut open
    ἀποτέμνω: to cut off, sever

τίθημι: to place *θήσω, ἔθηκα, τέθηκα, τέθειμαι* (but usu. instead *κεῖμαι*), *ἐτέθην*
    ἐπιτίθημι: to put upon, add to
    ἐντίθημι: to put in
    μετατίθημι: to place differently, transpose
    προστίθημι: to put to, put forth, impose
    παρατίθημι: to place beside
    συντίθημι: to put together, arrange

τιτρώσκω: to wound *-τρώσω, ἔτρωσα, τέτρωμαι, ἐτρώθην*

τρέφω: to nourish *θρέψω, ἔθρεψα*, 2 perf. *τέτροφα, τέθραμμαι, ἐτράφην*

τρέχω: to run *δραμοῦμαι, ἔδραμον, -δεδράμηκα*

τρίβω: to rub *τρίψω, ἔτριψα*, 2 perf. *τέτριφα, τέτριμμαι, ἐτρίβην*
    διατρίβω: to spend time
    ἐκτρίβω: to rub out, wear out

τρέπω: to turn *τρέψω, ἔτρεψα, τέτροφα, ἐτράπην*
    ἐπιτρέπω: to turn towards, attack

τυγχάνω: to happen *τεύξομαι, ἔτυχον, τετύχηκα. τέτυγμαι, ἐτύχθην*
    ἐντυγχάνω: to fall in with, meet with

ὑπισχνέομαι: to promise *ὑπο-σχήσομαι*, 2 aor. *ὑπ-εσχόμην*

φαίνω: to show *φανῶ, ἔφηνα, πέφηνα, πέφασμαι, ἐφάνην*

φέρω: to bear *οἴσω*, 1 aor. *ἤνεγκα*, 2 aor. *ἤνεγκον*, 2 perf. *ἐνήνοχα, ἐνήνεγμαι, ἠνέχθην*
    μεταφέρω: to carry over, transfer
    παραφέρω: to bring to one's side
    περιφέρω: to carry around
    προσφέρω: to bring to, apply
    συμφέρω: to bring together, compare

φεύγω: to flee *φεύξομαι, ἔφυγον, πέφευγα*

φημί: to say *φήσω, ἔφησα*

φυλάττω: to guard **φυλάξω, ἐφύλαξα, πεφύλαχα, πεφύλαγμαι, ἐφυλάχθην**

φύω: to bring forth **φύσω, ἔφυσα**, 2 aor. **ἔφυν, πέφυκα**
     ἐκφύω: to grow out

χαίρω: to rejoice at **χαιρήσω, κεχάρηκα, κεχάρημαι, ἐχάρην**

χαλεπαίνω: to be offended **χαλεπανῶ, ἐχαλέπηνα, ἐχαλεπάνθην**

χέω: to pour fut. **χέω**, aor. **ἔχεα, κέχυκα, κέχυμαι, ἐχύθην**
     ἐπιχέω: to pour over

χράομαι: to use **χρήσομαι, ἐχρησάμην, κέχρημαι, ἐχρήσθην**

χρίω: to anoint **χρίσω, ἔχρισα, κέχριμαι, ἐχρίσθην**

ψεύδομαι: to lie **ψεύσω, ἔψευσα, ἔψευσμαι, ἐψεύσθην**

Glossary

Glossary

A α

ἀγαθός, -ή, -όν: good
ἀγαπάω: to treat with affection, love
ἀγγέλλω: to bear a message, report
ἄγγελος, ὁ: a messenger
ἄγε: come! come on! well!
ἀγελαῖος, -α, -ον: of or in a herd
ἀγέλη, ἡ: a herd
ἀγέρωχος, -ον: high-minded, high-spirited
ἀγκών, -ῶνος, ὁ: an elbow
ἀγνοέω: not to know, not perceive, be ignorant
ἄγνοια, ἡ: ignorance
ἀγορά, -ᾶς, ἡ: a marketplace
ἀγοράζω: to conduct business, buy
ἀγρεύω: to hunt
ἄγριος, -α, -ον: of the field, savage, wild
ἀγρός, -οῦ, ὁ: a field, land, country
ἀγύρτης, -ου, ὁ: a collector, beggar
ἄγω: to lead, carry, convey, bring
ἀγών, -ου, ὁ: a competition
ἀγωνίζομαι: to contend for a prize
ἀδαμάντινος, -η, -ον: adamant
ἀδεής, -ές: without fear, fearless, with impunity
ἀδελφός, ὁ: a brother
ἀδικέω: to do wrong
ἀδρός, -ά, -όν: thick, strong, heavy, fat
ἀδύνατος, -ον: unable, impossible
ἀεί: always, for ever
ἀέναος, -ον: ever-flowing
ἀθλέω: to contend, practice athletics
ἄθλιος, -α, -ον: struggling, unhappy, wretched
ἀθρόος, -α, -ον: crowded together, all at once
ἀθυμία, ἡ: faintheartedness, despair
αἰγιαλός, ὁ: the sea-shore, beach
αἰδέομαι: to be ashamed
αἷμα, -ατος, τό: blood
αἱρέω: to take up, grasp
αἴρω: to raise, lift up, take up
αἰσθάνομαι: to perceive, notice , see, hear

αἰσχρός, -ά, -όν: shameful, low, ugly
αἰτέω: to ask, beg
αἰτία, ἡ: a cause
αἰτιάομαι: to charge, accuse, blame
αἰχμαλωσία, ἡ: captivity
αἰχμάλωτος, -ον: taken prisoner, held captive
αἰωρέω: to lift up, raise
ἀκάθαρτος, -ον: unclean, foul, vile
ἄκαιρος, -ον: ill-timed, inopportune
ἄκανθα, -ης, ἡ: a thorn
ἀκαρής, -ές: very short
ἀκέραιος, -ον: unharmed, inviolate
ἀκίνδυνος, -ον: free from danger, safe
ἀκολουθέω: to follow
ἀκόρεστος, -ον: insatiate
ἀκούω: to hear
ἀκριβής, -ές: exact, accurate, precise
ἀκριβῶς: certainly
ἀλαβάστρος, ὁ: an alabaster vase
ἀλγεινός, -ή, -όν: painful, grievous, difficult
ἀλείφω: to anoint (with oil)
ἄλευρον, τό: flour, meal
ἀλέω: to grind, pound
ἀλή, ἡ: salt
ἀληθινός, -ή, -όν: genuine, real, true
ἀληθῶς: truly, in truth
ἁλίσκομαι: to be taken, be captured
ἀλλά: but
ἄλλοθεν: from another place
ἄλλος, -η, -ον: another, other
ἀλλότριος, -α, -ον: of or belonging to another
ἄλλως: in another way or manner
ἄλυπος, -ον: without pain
ἅμα: (adv.) at once, at the same time, (prep.) together with (+ dat.)
ἁμαρτάνω: to do wrong, miss, mistake
ἁμαρτία, ἡ: a failure, mistake
ἀμείβω: to exchange, respond
ἀμείνων, -ον: better (+ gen.)
ἀμελέω: to have no care for
ἅμμα, -ατος, τό: anything tied, a knot, clinch
ἀμοιβή, ἡ: a compensation, return, payment
ἄμορφος, -ον: misshapen, unsightly
ἀμύνω: to keep off, ward off, defend, (mid.) to take revenge

Glossary

ἀμφότερος, -α, -ον: each, both
ἄμφω: both
ἄν: (indefinite particle; generalizes
    dependent clauses with subjunctive;
    indicates contrary-to-fact with
    independent clauses)
ἀνά: up, upon (+ acc.)
ἀναβαίνω: to go up, mount, ascend,
    climb
ἀναβάτης, -ου, ὁ: a rider
ἀναβοάω: to shout, cry out
ἀναγελάω: to laugh loud
ἀναγκάζω: to force, compel
ἀνάθημα, -ατος, τό: a votive offering
ἀναιρέω: to take up, raise
ἀναίσθητος, -ον: unfeeling, not
    noticing, without sense of (+ gen.)
ἀναίσχυντος, -ον: shameless, impudent
ἀνακαγχάζω: to burst out laughing
ἀνακλάω: to bend back
ἀνακλίνω: to lean, lay down
ἀνακράζω: to cry out
ἀνακροτέω: to applaud
ἀναλίσκω: to use up, spend, waste
    (time)
ἀναμείγνυμι: to mix together
ἀναμιμνήσκω: to remind
ἀνανεύω: to nod "no"
ἀναπαύομαι: to rest
ἀναπαύω: to make to cease, to stop,
    hinder (from)
ἀναπηδάω: to leap up, jump on
ἀναπίπτω: to fall back
ἀνάπτω: to light, kindle
ἀνασκιρτάω: to leap, kick
ἀνασπάω: to pull back, withdraw
ἀναστένω: to groan, moan
ἀναστρέφω: to turn back, return
ἀνασώζω: to recover, rescue
ἀνατέμνω: to cut open
ἀνατρέπω: to overturn, upset
ἀνδρεῖος, -α, -ον: of or for a man
ἀνδροφόνος, ον: murderous, homicidal
ἀνεγείρω: to rouse
ἀνεκτός, -ή, -όν: bearable, sufferable,
    tolerable
ἄνεμος, ὁ: wind
ἀνεξίκακος, -ον: enduring, tolerant
ἀνερευνάω: to examine closely,
    investigate

ἀνέχω: to hold up, bear, endure
ἀνήρ, ἀνδρός, ὁ: a man
ἄνθινος, -η, -ον: of or like flowers,
    blooming, fresh
ἄνθος, ὁ: a blossom, flower
ἀνθρώπειος, -α, -ον: human
ἀνθρώπινος, -η, -ον: of man, human
ἄνθρωπος, ὁ/ἡ: a man, (fem.) a woman
ἀνίστημι: to make to stand up, raise up
ἀνόητος, -ον: not understanding (+
    gen.)
ἀνοίγνυμι: to open
ἀνόσιος, -α, -ον: unholy, profane
ἀνταγωνιστής, -οῦ, ὁ: an opponent,
    competitor, rival
ἀντέχω: to cling
ἀντί: instead of (+ gen.)
ἀντιμάχομαι: to fight back
ἀνυπόδητος, -ον: unshod, barefoot
ἀνύω: to effect, achieve, accomplish,
    complete
ἄνω: upwards
ἄνωθεν: from above
ἀνώτερος, -α, -ον: higher, above
ἄξιος, -ία, -ον: worthy, deserving
ἀξιόω: to think worthy
ἄξυλος, -ον: with no wood, timberless
ἀπαγγέλλω: to report, announce
ἀπαγορεύω: to give up, grow weary
ἀπάγω: to lead away, carry off
ἀπαιτέω: to ask back, demand
ἀπαλός, -ή, -όν: soft, tender, kind
ἀπανθίζω: to pick out flowers
ἅπαξ: once
ἅπας, ἅπασα, ἅπαν: all, every
ἀπειλέω: to threaten
ἄπειρος, -ον: inexperienced,
    unacquainted with (+ gen.)
ἀπελεύθερος, ὁ: a freedman
ἀπέρχομαι: to go away, depart
ἄπιστος, ον: incredible, unbelievable
ἄπλετος, -ον: boundless, immense,
    huge
ἁπλοῦς, -ῆ, -οῦν: simple, plain
ἀπό: from, away from (+ gen.)
ἀποδείκνυμι: to appoint, assign
ἀποδιδράσκω: to run away, escape
ἀποδίδωμι: to give back, restore, return
ἀποδύνω: to strip off, undress, shed
ἀποδύομαι: to strip down, strip naked

Glossary

ἀποθνήσκω: to die
ἀποκρεμάω: to let hang down
ἀποκρίνομαι: to answer
ἀποκτείνω: to kill, slay
ἀπολακτίζω: to kick away, shake off, kick back
ἀπολείπω: to leave behind, abandon
ἀπόλλυμι: to destroy, kill, loose
ἀπολύω: to loose, release, dismiss
ἀπονοέομαι: to have lost all sense
ἀπόνοια, ἡ: senselessness
ἀποπίπτω: to fall off
ἀποπνίγω: to choke, suffocate
ἀπορέω: to be without, lack, be at a loss
ἀπορρίπτω: to throw off
ἀποσείω: to shake off
ἀποσιτέω: to cease to eat, starve
ἀποσκευή, ἡ: baggage
ἀποστίλβω: to shine
ἀποστρέφω: to turn back
ἀποσφάζω: to cut the throat, slaughter
ἀποτέμνω: to cut off, sever
ἀποχωρέω: to go away from
ἅπτω: to touch, fasten upon
ἀπώλεια, ἡ: destruction, loss
ἀπωτέρω: further off
ἀράζω: snarl, growl
ἀργαλέος, -α, -ον: painful, difficult, grievous
ἀργός, -ή, -όν: lazy, without work
ἀργύρεος, -ᾶ, -οῦν: silver, of silver
ἀργύριον, τό: a piece of silver, money
ἄργυρος, ὁ: silver
ἄρδω: to water
ἀρέσκω: to please, satisfy
ἀριθμός, ὁ: number
ἀριστάω: to eat a meal, take breakfast
ἄριστον, τό: a meal, breakfast
ἄρκτος, ἡ: a bear
ἁρπάζω: to snatch away, carry off
ἅρπαξ, -αγος, ὁ: a robber
ἄρρην, -εν: male, masculine
ἄρρητος, -η, -ον: unspoken, unsaid
ἄρσην, ὁ: a male, stallion
ἀρτάω: to fasten to or hang
ἄρτος, ὁ: a loaf of bread
ἀρύω: to draw
ἀρχή, ἡ: a beginning, origin, first cause
ἀρχιτεκτόνημα, -ατος, τό: a stroke of art

ἄρχω: to begin, rule
ἄρχων, -οντος, ὁ: a ruler
ἄσβεστος, -η, -ον: ceaseless
ἀσέλγεια, ἡ: licentiousness
ἀσθενής, -ές: without strength, feeble
ἄσμενος, -η, -ον: well-pleased, glad
ἀσπάζομαι: to welcome, greet, bid farewell
ἀστράγαλος, ὁ: knuckle bone
ἄστυ, -εος, τό: a city, town
ἀσυνήθης, -ες, -εος: unaccustomed, inexperienced
ἀσφαλῶς: firmly, securely
ἀσχολέω: to engage, occupy
ἀτρέμα: gently, softly
ἀτρεμής, ές: unmoved
ἄτριπτος, -ον: not worn, unused
Ἀττικός, -ή, -όν: Attic, Athenian
αὖθις: back, again
αὐλή, ἡ: a courtyard
αὐλητής, -οῦ, ὁ: a flute-player
αὐτίκα: immediately, at once
αὐτός, -ή, -ό: he, she, it; self, same
αὐτοσχέδιος, -α, -ον: offhand, improvised
αὐχήν, -ενος, ὁ: the neck, throat
ἀφαιρέω: to take from, take away
ἀφανής, -ές: unseen, invisible, viewless
ἀφίημι: to send away, discharge, send forth
ἀφικνέομαι: to come to, arrive
ἄφνω: suddenly
ἀφοράω: to look away from
ἀφόρητος, -ον: intolerable, insufferable
ἀφροδίσιος, -α, -ον: belonging to Aphrodite; (subst.) lust, sex
ἄφωνος, -ον: speechless, silent
Ἀχαία, ἡ: Achaia
ἄχθομαι: to be loaded down
ἄχθος, -εος, τό: a weight, burden, load
ἀχθοφορέω: to bear burdens
ἀχθοφορία, ἡ: the bearing of burdens
ἀχρεῖος, -α, -ον: useless, good for nothing
ἄχρηστος, -ον: useless, unserviceable
ἀωρία, ἡ: the wrong time, dead of night

213

B β

βαδίζω: to go, walk
βαθύνω: to sink deep
βαθύς, -εῖα, -ύ: high, deep
βακτηρία, ἡ: a staff, cane
βαλανεῖον, τό: a bath
βάλλω: to throw, hurl, pelt, thrust
βαρύς, -εῖα, -ύ: heavy
βάσανος, ἡ: agony, torture
βασιλεύς, -εως, ὁ: a king
βάσκανος, -ον: envious, jealous,
   malicious
βαστάζω: to lift up, raise, carry off
βέλτιστος, -η, -ον: best
Βέροια, ἡ: Beroea
βιάζω: to force
βίος, ὁ: life
βλέπω: to see, look at
βλέφαρον, τό: an eyelid
βοάω: to cry, shout
βοή, ἡ: a cry, shout
βόσκω: to keep, tend
βουβών, -ῶνος, ὁ: the groin
βούλευμα, -ατος, τό: a purpose, design,
   plan
βουλεύω: to take counsel, plan
βούλομαι: to will, wish
βραδύς, -εῖα, -ύ: slow

Γ γ

γαμετή, ἡ: a married woman, wife
γαμέω: to marry, take as a lover
γάμος, ὁ: a wedding, marriage
γάρ: for
γάρος, ὁ: fish sauce
γαστήρ, γαστρός, ἡ: the belly, stomach
γε: especially
γείτων, -ον: neighboring
γελάω: to laugh
γέλως, -ωτος, ὁ: laughter
γεμίζω: to fill full
γενναῖος, -α, -ον: noble
γένος, -εος, τό: race, stock, family
γέρων, -οντος, ὁ: an old man
γεωργέω: to farm
γεωργός, ὁ: a farmer
γῆ, ἡ: earth

γίγνομαι: to become, happen, occur
γιγνώσκω: to know, perceive
γλυκύς, -εῖα, -ύ: sweet
γλῶσσα, -ης, ἡ: the tongue
γνώμη, ἡ: a thought, judgment, opinion
γονάτιον, τό: the knee
γονεύς, -έως, ὁ: a begetter, parent
γόνυ, τό: the knee
γοργός, -ή, -όν: fierce, terrible
γραῖα, ἡ: an old woman
γράμμα, -ατος, τό: something written,
   a letter
γραῦς, γραός, ἡ: an old woman
γρυπός, -ή, -όν: hooked, curved
γυμνάζω: to train naked, train in
   gymnastic exercise
γυμνός, -ή, -όν: naked, unclad
γυναικεῖος, -α, -ον: of or for a woman
γυνή, γυναικός, ἡ: a woman, wife
γύννις, -ιδος, ὁ: an effeminate man
γύψ, ἡ: a vulture

Δ δ

δαιμόνιον, τό: a spirit
δαίμων, -ονος, ὁ: divine spirit, god
δάκνω: to bite
δακρύω: to weep
δάκτυλος, ὁ: a finger
δαλός, ὁ: a fire-brand, piece of burning
   wood
δαπανάω: to spend, consume
δάφνη, ἡ: laurel
δαψιλής, -ές: abundant, plentiful
δέ: and, but, on the other hand (*preceded
   by μέν*)
δείδω: to fear
δείκνυμι: to show, display, exhibit, bring
   to light
δείλη, ἡ: afternoon
δειλός, -ή, -όν: cowardly, miserable
δεινός, -ή, -όν: fearful, terrible, dire
δεινῶς: terribly, dreadfully
δειπνέω: to dine, eat a meal
δεῖπνον, τό: a dinner, meal
δέκα: ten
δένδρον, τό: a tree
δεξιόομαι: to welcome, greet
δεξιός, -ά, -όν: on the right, fortunate

δέομαι: to need, ask
δέον, τό: a duty
δέος, δέους, τό: fear, alarm, affright
δέρμα, -ατος, τό: skin, hide, coat
δέρω: to skin, flay
δεσμεύω: to fetter, put in chains
δεσμός, ὁ: a band, bond, tie, noose
δεσμωτήριον, τό: a prison
δέσποινα, ἡ: a mistress, lady of the
   house
δεσπότης, -ου, ὁ: a master, lord
δεῦρο: hither, to this place
δέχομαι: to take, accept, receive
δή: now, of course
δημόσιος, -α, -ον: of the people, public
διά: through (+ gen.); with, by means of (+
   acc.)
διαγιγνώσκω: to distinguish, discern
διάγω: to lead across
διαδίδωμι: to pass on
διακαρτερέω: to endure to the end, last
   out
διακονέω: to serve
διάκονος, ὁ: a servant
διακύπτω: to peep through, look out
διαλέγω: to converse, speak to
διανέμω: to distribute, apportion
διαρπάζω: to tear in pieces
διασπάω: to tear apart
διαστέλλω: to part, open up
διάστημα, -ατος, τό: an interval, gap,
   space between
διασῴζω: to preserve, maintain
διατρίβω: to spend time
διαφθείρω: to destroy
διδάσκαλος, ὁ: a teacher, master
διδάσκω: to teach
δίδωμι: to give
δικάζω: to judge, to give judgment on
δίκαιος, -α, -ον: just, fair
δικαστής, -οῦ, ὁ: a judge
δική, ἡ: justice, law, custom, lawsuit
δινεύω: to twirl, roll, twist
δινόω: turn with a lathe
διοικητής, -οῦ, ὁ: an administrator
διορύττω: to dig through
δίφρος, ὁ: a seat, throne
δίχα: apart from, without (+ gen.)
διώκω: to pursue
δοκέω: to seem

δόλος, ὁ: a trick
δόξα, ἡ: a belief, notion, reputation
δουλεία, ἡ: servitude, slavery, bondage
δοῦλος, ὁ: a slave
δραπέτις, -ιδος, ἡ: a runaway
δράσσομαι: to grasp, reach
δραχμή, ἡ: a drachma
δρόμος, ὁ: a course, running, race
δύναμαι: to be able, capable, possible
δύναμις, -εως, ἡ: power, ability
δυνάστης, -ου, ὁ: a lord, master
δυνατός, -ή, -όν: able, strong, capable,
   possible
δύο: two
δυσσεβής, -ές: ungodly, impious,
   profane
δυστυχής, -ές: unlucky, unfortunate
δυσωπέω: to put to shame
δωμάτιον, τό: a bedchamber
δῶρον, τό: a gift, present

E ε

ἐάν: = εἰ + ἄν
ἐγγύς: near, close
ἐγείρω: to awaken, wake up
ἐγκαλέω: to call in, blame, accuse,
   charge with (+ dat.)
ἔγκατα, τά: the entrails, bowels,
   innards
ἐγκατοικίζω: to place in
ἔγκειμαι: to lie in
ἐγκεράννυμι: to mix
ἐγκρύπτω: to hide, conceal in
ἐγώ, μου: I, my
ἐδώδιμος, -η, -ον: eatable
ἐθέλω: to will, wish
εἰ: if, whether
εἴδομαι: to be visible, appear
εἴκοσι: twenty
εἰμί: to be
εἴπερ: if indeed
εἶπον: to say
εἰρκτή, ἡ: a prison
εἷς, μία, ἕν: one
εἰς: into, to (+ acc.)
εἰσάγω: to lead in
εἰσβάλλω: to throw into, fall upon
εἰσδέχομαι: to take in, admit, receive

215

Glossary

εἰσέρχομαι: to go in, enter
εἰσκομίζω: to carry into
εἰστρέχω: to run in
εἴσω: to within, inside
εἶτα: then, next
εἴτε... εἴτε: either...or
ἐκ, ἐξ: from, out of, after (+ *gen.*)
ἕκαστος, -η, -ον: every, each
ἑκάστοτε: each time, on each occasion
ἐκβάλλω: to throw out, cast out of
ἐκδύω: to take off, strip off
ἐκεῖθεν: from that place, thence
ἐκεῖνος, -η, -ο: that
ἐκμισθόω: to let out for hire, loan
ἐκπεριέρχομαι: to go around
ἐκπίπτω: to fall out
ἐκπλήσσω: to strike out of
ἐκτείνω: to stretch out, cast, lay out
ἐκτέμνω: to castrate
ἐκτομή, ἡ: castration
ἐκτρέχω: to run out
ἐκτρίβω: to rub out, wear out
ἐκφύω: to grow out
ἐκφωνέω: to pronounce
ἑκών, ἑκοῦσα, ἑκόν: willing, voluntarily
ἔλαιον, τό: olive oil
ἐλαύνω: to drive, set in motion
ἐλεγεῖον, τό: an elegy
ἔλεγος, ὁ: a song of mourning, a lament
ἔλεγχος, ὁ: a test, trial
ἐλέγχω: to disgrace
ἐλεύθερος, -α, -ον: free
ἐλέφας, -αντος, ὁ: an elephant
ἑλίσσω: to turn around, twist around
ἕλκος, -εος, τό: a wound
ἕλκω: to draw, drag
Ἕλλην: Hellen, Greek
ἐλπίζω: to hope, expect, look for
ἐλπίς, -ίδος, ἡ: hope, expectation
ἐμβαίνω: to step in, walk into
ἐμβάλλω: to throw in, put in
ἐμβάπτω: to dip in
ἐμπίμπλημι: to fill up
ἐμπίπτω: to fall upon
ἐμπλέω: to fill up (+ *gen.*)
ἐμπόδιος, τό: an impediment
ἐμπρησμός, ὁ: a burning down, conflagration
ἐν: in, at, among (+ *dat.*)
ἐναντίος, -α, -ον: opposite

ἐνδίδωμι: to give in
ἔνδον: in, within
ἔνδοξος, -ον: esteemed, honored
ἕνεκα: on account of, for the sake of (+ *gen.*)
ἔνθα: there
ἐνθάδε: here, in this place
ἔνθεν: from there, thence, then
ἔνθεος, -ον: inspired, possessed
ἐνίστημι: to be upon, present
ἐννοέω: to think, consider, reflect
ἐνσείω: to plunge in, dive into
ἐνσκευάζω: to get ready, prepare
ἐντεῦθεν: hence, thence
ἐντίθημι: to put into
ἐντυγχάνω: to fall in with, meet with, read
ἐξαιρέω: to take out, remove
ἐξαίσιος, -α, -ον: portentous
ἐξαίφνης: suddenly
ἐξάλλομαι: to leap up, swell
ἐξανίστημι: to raise up
ἐξαπίνης: suddenly
ἐξάπτω: to fasten from
ἐξελαύνω: to drive out, ride out
ἐξέλκω: to draw out, withdraw
ἐξεμέω: to expel, disgorge
ἐξέρχομαι: to come out, go out, leave
ἐξευρίσκω: to find out, discover
ἔξοχος, -ον: standing out
ἔξω: out, outside
ἔξωθεν: from without
ἐξωθέω: to thrust out, force out
ἔοικα: it seems good
ἐπάγω: to lead on, bring
ἐπαινέω: to approve, applaud, commend
ἐπαίρω: to lift up, raise
ἐπαιτέω: to ask besides, beg
ἐπακολουθέω: to follow after
ἐπαλείφω: to smear over, anoint
ἐπανάγω: to lead back
ἐπανθέω: to bloom, be bright
ἐπανίστημι: to set up again
ἐπαρχία, ἡ: a district, province
ἔπαυλις, -εως, ἡ: a farmhouse
ἐπαφρόδιτος, -ον: charming, romantic
ἐπεγείρω: to rouse up, raise
ἐπείγω: to urge on, hasten, press down, weigh down

216

Glossary

ἐπειδάν: whenever
ἐπεισέρχομαι: to come in (besides)
ἔπειτα: thereupon
ἐπέρχομαι: to come upon, approach
ἐπί: at (+ *gen.*); on, upon (+ *dat.*); on to, against (+ *acc.*)
ἐπιβαίνω: to go upon, mount
ἐπιβάλλω: to throw or cast upon
ἐπιγελάω: to laugh approvingly
ἐπιδείκνυμι: to show, exhibit, display
ἐπίδειξις, -εως, ἡ: a demonstration
ἐπιδέχομαι: to admit
ἐπιδίδωμι: to give besides, lend, hand over
ἐπιθορυβέω: to shout
ἐπιθυμέω: to set one's heart upon, desire
ἐπιθυμία, ἡ: desire, yearning, longing
ἐπικαθίζω: to set upon
ἐπικινέω: to move
ἐπικλίνω: to incline, tilt
ἐπικουρία, ἡ: aid, help
ἐπιλαμβάνω: to take hold of
ἐπίλοιπος, -ον: still left, remaining
ἐπιπίπτω: to fall upon, attack
ἐπιπολάζω: to come to the surface, rise up
ἐπιπρωθέω: to push forward (upon)
ἐπιρριπτέω: to throw, hurl
ἐπισάττω: to pile a load upon, load down, burden
ἐπίσταμαι: to know, be acquainted with
ἐπιστάτης, -ου, ὁ: an attendant, supervisor, overseer
ἐπιτάττω: to enjoin, order, put upon
ἐπιτέρπομαι: to rejoice, delight
ἐπιτήδευμα, -ατος, τό: a pursuit, practice
ἐπιτηδεύω: to pursue, practice
ἐπιτίθημι: to lay on, place upon
ἐπιτρέπω: to turn towards, attack
ἐπιφέρω: to set upon, attack
ἐπιχέω: to pour over
ἐπιχώριος, -α, -ον: of or from a place, native
ἕπομαι: to follow (mid. of ἕπω)
ἔραμαι: to love
ἐραστής, -οῦ, ὁ: a lover
ἐράω: to love, desire
ἐργάζομαι: to work, labor

ἐργαστήριον, τό: a workshop, gang
ἐργάτης, -ου, ὁ: a workman
ἔργον, τό: a deed, work, act
ἐρευνάω: to seek, search
ἐρῆμος, -ον: desolate, lonely, solitary
ἐρωτάω: to ask, enquire
ἐρώμενος, ὁ: beloved
ἔρως, -ωτος, ὁ: love, desire, passion
ἐρωτικός, -ή, -όν: amatory, passionate
ἐσθής, -ῆτος, ἡ: dress, clothing
ἐσθίω: to eat
ἑσπέρα, ἡ: evening
ἔστε: until
ἑστία, ἡ: a hearth, fireside, fire
ἔσχατος, -η, -ον: utmost, extreme
ἔσω: to the interior, inside
ἑταῖρος, ὁ: a comrade, companion
ἔτι: still
ἑτοῖμος, -ον: at hand, ready, prepared
ἔτος, -εος, τό: a year
εὖ: well
εὐαγγέλιον, τό: good news
εὐγενής, -ές: well-born, brave
εὐγνωμοσύνη, ἡ: considerateness, prudence
εὐγνώμων, -ον: of good feeling, kindhearted, considerate
εὐήκοος, -ον: hearing well, obedient
εὐθέως: immediately, straightaway
εὐθύς, -εῖα, -ύ: straight
εὐκαταφρόνητος, -ον: easily despised, contemptible
εὐνή, ἡ: a bed
εὐνοῦχος, ὁ: a eunuch
εὐπορέω: to prosper, thrive, be well off
εὕρημα, -ατος, τό: an invention, discovery
εὑρίσκω: to find
εὔρυθμος, -ον: rhythmical
εὔσαρκος, -ον: fleshy, plump
εὔτονος, -ον: well-strung, vigorous
εὐτρεπής, -ές: prepared, ready
εὐτρεπίζω, -ιῶ: to make ready, prepare
εὐτυχέω: to be well off
εὐτυχής, -ές: lucky, fortunate
εὔφημος, -ον: well-spoken
εὐφραίνω: to cheer, delight, gladden
εὐφροσύνη, ἡ: mirth, merriment
εὔφωνος, -ον: loud voiced
εὐχάριστος, -ον: grateful, thankful

Glossary

εὐχερής, -ές: easily handled, easy, ready
εὔχομαι: to pray
ἔφηβος, ὁ: one arrived at puberty
ἐφίστημι: to set or place upon
ἐχθρός, -ά, -όν: hated, enemy, hostile
ἔχθω: to hate
ἔχω: to have, be able
ἔωθεν: from morning, at dawn
ἕως: until, till

Z ζ

ζάω: to live
Ζεύς, Διός, ὁ: Zeus
ζηλοτυπία, ἡ: jealousy, rivalry
ζημία, ἡ: loss, damage
ζητέω: to seek, search for
ζήτημα, -ατος, τό: a search
ζωμός, ὁ: a broth, soup
ζῷον, τό: an animal

Η η

ἤ: or
ἡγεμών, -όνος, ἡ: a governor, ruler
ἥδομαι: to enjoy oneself, take delight, take one's pleasure
ἡδονή, ἡ: delight, enjoyment, pleasure
ἡδύς, -εῖα, -ύ: sweet, pleasant
ἥκω: to have come, be present
ἡλικία, ἡ: time of life, age
ἥλιος, ὁ: the sun
ἡμέρα, ἡ: a day
ἥμερος, -α, -ον: tame, tamed, reclaimed
ἡμέτερος, -α, -ον: our
ἡμίονος, ἡ: a mule
Ἡρακλῆς, ὁ: Heracles
ἡττάομαι: to give way, yield

Θ θ

θάλασσα, ἡ: the sea
θάνατος, ὁ: death
θαρσέω: to have courage, be bold
θάττων, -ον: quicker, swifter

θαυμάζω: to wonder, marvel, admire, be amazed
θέα, ἡ: a looking at, sight, view, spectacle
θεάομαι: to look on, view, behold, see
θεατής, -οῦ, ὁ: one who sees, a spectator
θέατρον, τό: a theater
θεός, ὁ/ἡ: a god, (fem.) a goddess
θεοφόρητος, -ον: carrying a god
θεράπαινα, ἡ: a female slave, handmaid
θεραπεία, ἡ: a treatment, cure
θεραπεύω: to be an attendant, do service; to heal, treat
θεράπων, -οντος, ὁ: an attendant, servant
θερμός, -ή, -όν: hot, warm
θέρμω: to heat, make hot
θέρος, -εος, τό: summer
θέω: to run
θήκη, ἡ: a grave, tomb
θηρίον, τό: a wild animal, beast
θνήσκω: to die
θόρυβος, ὁ: a noise, uproar, clamor
θρίδαξ, -ακος, ἡ: lettuce
θρίξ, τριχός, ἡ: hair
θύρα, ἡ: a door
θυρίς, -ίδος, ἡ: a window
θυσία, ἡ: an offering, sacrifice
θύω: to sacrifice

Ι ι

ἰάομαι: to heal, cure
ἰατρεία, ἡ: a medical procedure
ἰατρός, ὁ: a healer, physician
ἱδρύω: to make to sit down, to seat
ἵεμαι: to speed, rush
ἱερεύς, -έως, ὁ: a priest
ἱερόσυλος, -α, -ον: sacrilegious, impious
ἵζω: to make to sit, seat, place
ἵημι: to send forth, (mid.) to hasten
ἱκανός, -ή, -όν: becoming, befitting (+ dat.), sufficing, capable, adequate
ἱκετεύω: to beg
ἱκέτης, -ου, ὁ: one who comes to seek protection, a suppliant
ἱκνέομαι: to come
ἱμάς, ὁ: a leather strap
ἱμάτιον τό: an outer garment, a cloak

Ἰνδικός, -ή, -όν: Indian
ἰξύς, -ύος, ἡ: the waist
Ἵππαρχος, ὁ: Hipparchus
ἱππικός, -ή, -όν: of a horse, equine
ἵππος, ὁ/ἡ: a horse, mare
ἱπποφορβός, ὁ: a horse-keeper
ἴσος, -η, -ον: equal, the same
ἵστημι: to make to stand
ἱστορία, ἡ: a history
ἰσχάς, -άδος, ἡ: a dried fig
ἰσχύω: to be strong
Ἰταλός, ὁ: an Italian
ἰταμός, -ή, -όν: hasty, eager
ἰχθῦς, -ύος, ὁ: fish

Κ κ

κάδος, ὁ: a jar, vessel
καθαρισμός, ὁ: a cleansing, purification
καθέζομαι: to remain seated
καθεύδω: to lie down, sleep
καθέψω: to boil, roast
κάθημαι: to be seated, sit, abide
καθίζω: to make to sit down, seat
καί: and, also, even
καινός, -ή, -όν: new, fresh, novel
καιρός, ὁ: the proper time
Καῖσαρ, -αρος, ὁ: Caesar
καίω: to light, kindle
κακός, -ή, -όν: bad, evil, ill
κακόω: to treat ill, maltreat, afflict, distress
κακῶς: badly
καλέω: to call, summon
κάλλος, -εος, τό: beauty
κᾶλον, τό: wood
καλῴδιον, τό: a rope, cord
κάμηλος, ὁ: a camel
κάμνω: to work
καρδία, ἡ: the heart
καρηβαρέω: to be dizzy
κατά: down (+ acc.)
καταβαίνω: to go down
καταβάλλω: to throw down, overthrow
κατάβασις, -εως, ἡ: a way down, descent
καταγιγνώσκω: to remark, discover
κατάγομαι: to lodge, stay

κατάγω: to lead down, bring down
καταγώγιον, τό: a place of lodging
καταδέω: to bind down, tie up
καταδικάζω: to pass judgment against, condemn
κατακαίω: to burn
κατάκαυμα, -ατος, τό: a burn
κατάκειμαι: to lie down, lie outstretched
κατακλάω: to break down, crush
κατακλείω: to shut in, enclose
κατακλίνω: to lay down, put to bed
κατακοιμίζω: to put to bed
κατακόπτω: to cut up, cut in pieces
κατακρίνω: to give a sentence, condemn
καταλαλέω: to talk loudly
καταλαμβάνω: to seize upon, lay hold of, catch
καταλείπω: to leave behind
καταλύω: to put down, lodge (with + gen.)
καταμάττω: wipe off
καταμένω: to stay behind, remain
κατανεύω: to nod "yes"
καταπάσσω: to sprinkle, strew
καταπηδάω: to leap down
καταπίνω: to gulp down
καταπίπτω: to fall down, drop down
καταράομαι: to curse
κατασβέννυμι: to put out, quench
κατασκευάζω: to prepare fully
κατασπαράττω: to tear to pieces
κατατίθημι: to place, put down, store
κατατρώγω: to eat up
καταφρονέω: to think down upon
καταχέω: to pour down upon, pour over
καταχράομαι: to make full use of (+ dat.)
καταψεύδομαι: to lie, speak falsely of (+ gen.)
κατέρχομαι: to go down
κατεσθίω: to eat up, devour
κατέχω: to hold fast, hold back
κατηχέω: to instruct
κάτω: down, downwards
κάτωθεν: from below, from behind
κεῖμαι: to be laid, lie
κελεύω: to bid, command, order, urge
κενόω: to empty out, drain, loot

Glossary

κεράτινος, -η, -ον: of horn
κερδαίνω: to gain, earn
κέρδος, -εος, τό: gain, profit, advantage
κεφάλαιος, -α, -ον: chief, main, principle
κεφαλή, ἡ: a head
κῆπος, ὁ: a garden, orchard
κηπουρός, ὁ: a gardener
κῆρυξ, -υκος, ὁ: a herald, auctioneer
κηρύσσω: to proclaim, shout
κιβώτιον, τό: a small chest
κιβωτός, ἡ: a wooden box, chest
κίναιδος, ὁ: catamite
κινδυνεύω: to be in danger
κίνδυνος, ὁ: a danger, risk, hazard
κινέω: to set in motion, move
κιρνάω: to mix
κλάω: to break, tear
κλέμμα, -ατος, τό: a theft, loot
κλέπτης, -ου, ὁ: a thief
κλέπτω: to steal
κλῖμαξ, -ακος, ἡ: a ladder
κλίνη, ἡ: a couch, bed
κλινίδιον, τό: a couch
κλίνω: to lay down, lean, tilt, slope
κλονέω: to drive in confusion
κνῖσα, -ης, ἡ: smoke
κοιμάω: to lay down, put to sleep
κοιμίζω: to put to sleep
κοινός, -ή, -όν: common, shared
κοινωνέω: to have in common, share
κοινωνός, ὁ: a companion, partner
κοιτών, -ῶνος, ὁ: a bed-chamber
κολλάω: to glue, cement
κόλπος, ὁ: the bosom
κόμη, ἡ: hair
κομίζω: to carry, convey, lead, take care of
κομψός, -ή, -όν: smart, clever, ingenious
κοπίς, -ίδος, ἡ: a cleaver
κόπτω: to strike, hit, knock
κόραξ, -ακος, ὁ: a crow
κοράσιον, τό: a small girl, young maiden
κόρη, ἡ: a maiden, girl
κόρρη, ἡ: face, jaw
κόσμος, ὁ: fashion, ornament, decoration, order
κοῦφος, -η, -ον: light, nimble

κράτιστος, -η, -ον: strongest, mightiest, best
κρέας, τό: flesh, meat
κρεμάννυμι: to hang, hang up
κρημνός, ὁ: an overhang, cliff
κριθάω: to be barley-fed, to wax wanton
κριθή, ἡ: barley
κριθίδιον, τό: barley
κριθίον, τό: barley
κρίνω: to choose
κρότος, ὁ: a striking, clapping
κρούω: to strike
κρύπτω: to hide, cover
κρώξω: to crow
κτάομαι: to get, gain, acquire
κτείνω: to kill, slay
κτῆμα, -ατος, τό: a possession, attribute
κτῆνος, -εος, τό: a beast, animal
κύκλος, ὁ: a ring, circle
κυλίω: to roll along
κύπτω: to bend forward, stoop down
κύριος, ὁ: a lord, master
κυρτόω: to curve into an arch
κύων, ὁ: a dog
κώδων, -ωνος, ἡ: a bell
κώμη, ἡ: a village
κωμήτης, -ου, ὁ: a villager, countryman
κώπη, ἡ: a handle, spoke

Λ λ

λαγχάνω: to obtain by lot
λαθραίως: secretly
λαλέω: to talk
λαμβάνω: to take, receive
λαμπρός, -ά, -όν: bright, magnificent, radiant
λάμπω: to shine, beam, be bright
λανθάνω: to escape notice, be unseen
λάξ: with the foot, (subst.) a kick
λαφύσσω: to gulp down, devour
λάχανον, -ου, τό: vegetables, greens
λέβης, -ητος, ὁ: a kettle, caldron
λέγω: to speak, say
λείψανον, τό: a remnant, leftover
λεπτός, -ή, -όν: little, slight, thin
λέχος, -εος, τό: a couch, bed
λέων, -οντος, ὁ: a lion

220

Glossary

λήγω: to stay, abate, cease
ληστής, -οῦ, ὁ: a robber, plunderer
λίαν: very, exceedingly
λιβανωτός, ὁ: frankincense
λίθινος, -η, -ον: of stone, stony, craggy
λίθος, -ου, ὁ: a stone, rock
λιθόω: to turn to stone
λιμός, -οῦ, ἡ: hunger
λιτός, -ή, -όν: simple, inexpensive, frugal
λίχνος, -η, -ον: greedy, gluttonous
λογίζομαι: to count, reckon, think
λόγος, ὁ: a word, phrase, speech, story
λόγχη, ἡ: a spear
λοιπός, -ή, -όν: remaining, the rest
λοπάς, -άδος, ἡ: shellfish
Λούκιος, ὁ: Lucius
λουτρόν, τό: a bath
λούω: to wash
λύκος, ὁ: a wolf
λυττάω: to be raging, be mad
λυχνία, ἡ: lampstand
λύχνος, ὁ: a lamp
λύω: to loose, separate

M μ

μά: (swearing) by (+ acc.)
μαγγανεύω: to use charms, practice magic
μάγειρος, ὁ: a cook
μαγεύω: to conjure, practice magic, enchant
μάγος ὁ: a magician, sorcerer
μᾶζα, ἡ: a barley-cake
μαθητής, -οῦ, ὁ: a learner, pupil
μακάριος, -α, -ον: blessed, happy
Μακεδονία, ἡ: Macedonia
μακρός, -ά, -όν: long, far
μάλα: very, exceedingly
μαλακός, -ή, -όν: soft, weak, effeminate
μανθάνω: to learn
μάντις, -εως, ὁ: a seer, prophet
μάστιξ, -ιγος, ἡ: a whip, scourge
μάτην: in vain, fruitlessly, idly
μάχαιρα, -ης, ἡ: a sword
μάχη, ἡ: battle, fight, combat
μάχλος, -ον: lewd, lustful
μάχομαι: to fight

μέγας, μεγάλη, μέγα: big, great
μέγεθος, -εος, τό: greatness, magnitude, size
μέδιμνος, ὁ: a corn-measure, bushel
μειδιάω: to smile, laugh
μειράκιον, τό: a boy, lad, stripling
μεῖραξ, -ακος, ἡ: a young girl, lass
μελίπηκτον, τό: a honey-cake
μέλλω: to be about to, be going to
μέλος, -εος, τό: a tune, melody
μέμφομαι: to blame, censure
μέν: on the one hand (followed by δέ)
μένω: to stay, remain, await
μερίς, -ίδος, ἡ: a part, portion, share
μέρος, -εος, τό: a part, share
μέσος, -η, -ον: middle, in the middle
μεσόω: to be in the middle of (+ gen.)
μεστός, -ή, -όν: filled, full of (+ gen.)
μετά: with (+ gen.); after (+ acc.)
μεταβολή, ἡ: a change, transformation
μεταμορφόω: to transform
μεταξύ: between
μεταπίπτω: to fall differently, change
μετατίθημι: to change, alter, place among
μεταφέρω: to carry over, transfer
μετέωρος, -ον: raised from the ground
μετρέω: to measure in any way
μέτριος, -α, -ον: measured, moderate, within measure, reasonable
μέτρον, τό: a measure
μέχρι: to a point, even so far
μή: not
μηδαμῶς: in no way, not at all
μηδείς: and not one
μηδέποτε: never
μηκέτι: no more, no longer
μηνύω: to disclose, reveal, betray
μηρός, ὁ: a thigh, haunch, rump, ham
μήτηρ, μητερος, ἡ: a mother
μηχανή, ἡ: an instrument, contrivance, trick
μηχάνημα, -ατος, τό: machine
μιαρός, -ά, -όν: abominable, foul
μισθός, ὁ: pay, reward, a bribe, fee
μισοπόνηρος, -ον: hostile
μίτρα, ἡ: a head-dress
μνήμη, ἡ: a remembrance, memory
μνημονεύω: to call to mind, remember
μνηστεύω: to woo, court

Glossary

μοιχός, ὁ: an adulterer, paramour
μόλις: scarcely
μονομαχέω: to fight in single combat
μόνος, -η, -ον: alone, only
μουσικός, -ή, -όν: musical
μύλη, ἡ: a millstone
μυλών, -ῶνος, ὁ: a millhouse
μυρίζω: to rub with unguent, anoint
μύρον, τό: an unguent, sweet oil
μυστήριον, τό: a mystery, secret rite

N ν

ναός, ὁ: a temple
νᾶπυ, τό: mustard
ναῦς, ἡ: a ship
νεανίσκος, ὁ: a youth, young man
νεκρός, -ά, -όν: dead
νεκρός, ὁ: a dead body, corpse
νέμεσις, -εως, ἡ: retribution
νέμω: to pasture, graze
νεόνυμφος, -ον: newly married
νέος, νέα, νέον: young, youthful
νεύω: to decline, nod
νοέω: to think, intend
νομεύς, -έως, ὁ: a shepherd, herdsman
νομίζω: to believe, think
νόμος, ὁ: a custom, law
νομός, ὁ: a pasture
νουθετέω: to admonish, warn
νοῦς, νοῦ, ὁ: a mind
νυκτερινός, -ή, -όν: of night, nightly
νυμφίος, ὁ: a groom, newlywed
νῦν: now
νύξ, νυκτός, ἡ: night
νύττω: to prick, spur, pierce
νῶτον, τό: a back

Ξ ξ

ξένος, -η, -ον: foreign, strange
ξένος, ὁ: a foreigner, guest, stranger
ξίφος, -εος, τό: a sword
ξύλον, τό: wood, a stick

O o

ὁ, ἡ, τό: the (*definite article*)
ὀβολός, ὁ: an obol
ὀγκάομαι: to bray
ὀγκηθμός, ὁ: braying
ὁδεύω: to go, travel
ὁδοιπορέω: to travel, walk
ὁδός, ἡ: a way, path, journey, road
ὀδούς, -όντος, ὁ: tooth
ὀδύνη, ἡ: pain
ὄζος, ὁ: a stub, offshoot, twig
ὀθόνη, ἡ: a cloth
οἶδα: to know
οἴκαδε: home, homewards
οἰκεῖος, -α, -ον: domestic, of the house, related
οἰκέτης, -ου, ὁ: a house slave, servant
οἰκέω: to inhabit, live in, occupy
οἰκημάτιον, τό: a little room
οἰκία, ἡ: a house, home
οἰκίδιον, τό: a small house, cottage
οἴκοθεν: from one's house, from home
οἴκοι: at home, in the house
οἶκος, ὁ: a house
οἴκτιστος, -η, -ον: most pitiable, lamentable
οἰνοπότης, -ου, ὁ: wine-drinking
οἶνος, ὁ: wine
οἰνόχοος, ὁ: a cupbearer
οἴομαι: to suppose, think, imagine
οἶος, -α, -ον: such as
οἰστράω: to drive mad, arouse
οἶστρος, ὁ: madness, frenzy
οἴχομαι: to be gone, leave
οἰωνός, ὁ: an omen, token
ὀκνέω: to shrink
ὀκνηρός, -ά, -όν: shrinking, hesitating, timid
ὄλεθρος, ὁ: ruin, destruction
ὀλίγος, -η, -ον: few, little, scanty, small
ὁλόκληρος, -ον: complete in all parts, whole
ὅλος, -η, -ον: whole, entire, complete
ὁμιλέω: to be in company with
ὅμιλος, ὁ: a crowd, throng
ὄμμα, -ατος, τό: an eye
ὁμόδουλος, ὁ: a fellow-slave
ὅμοιος, -α, -ον: like, similar

Glossary

ὁμοιότης, -ητος, ἡ: a likeness, resemblance
ὁμοῦ: in the same place, together with (+ dat.)
ὄναρ, τό: a dream
ὄνειος, -ον: of an ass
ὀνηλάτης, -ου, ὁ: a donkey-driver
ὀνίνημι: to profit, benefit
ὄνομα, -ατος, τό: a name
ὄνος, ὁ: an ass
ὄνυξ, -υχος, ὁ: a nail
ὀξύς, -εῖα, -ύ: sharp, keen, steep
ὀπή, ἡ: an opening, hole, crack
ὄπη: by which way, in what direction
ὄπισθεν: behind, at the back
ὀπίσω: back, behind, backwards
ὁπλή, ἡ: a hoof
ὁπλίζω: to make ready
ὅπλον, τό: a tool, weapon
ὅποι: to which place, whither
ὁπότε: when
ὀπτάνιον, τό: a kitchen
ὀπτάω: to roast
ὁράω: to see
ὀργίζομαι: to be angry, rage
ὀρθός, -ή, -όν: straight, correct, sharp, steep
ὄρθρος, ὁ: daybreak, dawn
ὁρμή, ἡ: an attack, urge
ὄρνις, ὄρνιθος, ὁ: a bird
ὄρος, -εος, τό: a mountain, hill
ὀρχέομαι: to dance
ὄρχημα, -ατος, τό: dancing
ὅς, ἥ, ὅ: who, which (*relative pronoun*)
ὀσμή, ἡ: a smell
ὅστις, ὅτι: anyone who, anything which
ὀσφύς, ἡ: loins, waist
ὅτε: when
ὅτι: that, because
οὐ: not
οὐδαμός, -ή, -όν: not even one, no one
οὐδαμοῦ: nowhere
οὐδείς, οὐδεμία, οὐδέν: no one
οὐδέποτε: not ever, never
οὐκέτι: no more, no longer
οὖν: therefore
οὐρά, ἡ: the tail
οὖς, ὠτός, τό: an ear
οὔτε: and not
οὗτος, αὕτη, τοῦτο: this

οὕτως: this way
ὄφελος, τό: an advantage, help
ὀφθαλμός, ὁ: an eye
ὄχημα, -ατος, τό: a carriage, cart
ὄχλος, ὁ: a crowd, a throng, mob
ὄψιος, -α, -ον: late
ὄψις, -εως, ἡ: a look, appearance, view, aspect
ὄψον, τό: cooking, cooked food
ὀψοφαγία, ἡ: luxurious eating

Π π

πάγος, ὁ: a rock
παίγνιον, τό: a game, comic performance
παιδάριον, τό: a young, little boy
παιδιή, ἡ: childish play
παιδισκάριον, τό: a little maiden
παιδίσκη, ἡ: a young girl, maiden
παίζω: to play like a child, play a trick
παῖς, παιδός, ὁ/ἡ: a slave, boy, (fem.) girl
παίω: strike, hit, beat
πάλαι: long ago, for a long time
παλαιός, -ά, -όν: old, ancient
πάλαισμα, -ατος, τό: a bout of wrestling, wrestling maneuver, hold
παλαιστής, ὁ: a wrestler
παλαίω: to wrestle
πάλιν: back, again
παλινδρομέω: to run back
πανός, ὁ: a torch
παντάπασι: altogether, wholly
πανταχοῦ: everywhere
πάντως: altogether
πάνυ: altogether, entirely
παρά: from (+ *gen.*); beside (+ *dat.*); to (+ *acc.*)
παραβάλλω: to throw to
παράγω: to lead by
παραδέχομαι: to receive
παραδίδωμι: to hand over
παράδοξος, -ον: incredible, paradoxical, strange
παρακαλέω: to call to
παρακατακλίνω: to lay down beside
παράκειμαι: to lay before

Glossary

παρακρεμάννυμι: to hang beside
παράκυψις, -εως, ἡ: peeping
παραλαμβάνω: to receive, take up,
  take besides
παράπτω: to apply
παρασκευάζω: to get ready, prepare
παρασκευή, ἡ: preparation, training
παρατίθημι: to place before, place
  beside
παραφέρω: to bring to
παρεδρεύω: to attend, tend to, frequent
πάρειμι: to be present
παρεισέρχομαι: to come in beside, be
  inserted, come in secretly
παρελαύνω: to drive past
παρεμβολή, ἡ: an insertion
πάρεξις, -εως, ἡ: presenting
παρέρχομαι: to go beside, come to, pass
  by, go secretly
παρέχω: to furnish, provide, supply
παρθένος, ἡ: a maiden, girl
παρίστημι: to make to stand, place
  beside
παροδεύω: to pass by
παροξύνω: to urge, spur on
πᾶς, πᾶσα, πᾶν: all, every, whole
Πασιφάη, ἡ: Pasiphae
πάσχω: to experience, feel, suffer
πατέω: to tread, walk
πατήρ, ὁ: a father
Πάτραι, -ῶν, αἱ: Patras (a city)
πατρικός, -ή, -όν: of one's father,
  paternal, hereditary
πατρίς, -ίδος, ἡ: native land
παύομαι: to cease, stop
πείθω: to prevail upon, persuade, win
  over
πεινάω: to be hungry
πεῖρα, -ας, ἡ: a trial, attempt,
  experiment
πειράω: to attempt, endeavor, try
πέμπω: to send, dispatch
πένης, -ητος: poor
πέντε: five
περάω: to cross, traverse
περί: around, about (+ gen., dat., acc.)
περιβάλλω: to throw around, embrace
περιβόητος, -ον: much talked of,
  famous
περιβόσκω: to feed around

περιεργία, ἡ: curiosity
περίεργος, -ον: inquisitive, curious
περιέρχομαι: to go around, wander
περιίστημι: to place round
περιλαμβάνω: to seize around,
  embrace
περιμένω: to wait for, await
περιπατέω: to walk about, go around
περιπίπτω: to fall around, fall in with,
  encounter
περισκοπέω: to look round
περισπάω: to strip off
περισσός, -ή, -όν: too much, prodigious
περισφίγγω: to bind tight around
περιφέρω: to carry around, turn around
πετεινός, -ή, -όν: able to fly
πέτομαι: to fly
πέτρα, ἡ: a rock
πέττω: to bake
πήγνυμι: to fasten
πηλός, ὁ: clay, earth, mud
πῆχυς, ὁ: the forearm
πίθηκος, ὁ: an ape, monkey
πίθος, ὁ: a wine-jar
πικρός, -ά, -όν: pointed, sharp, bitter,
  painful
πίμπλημι: to fill
πίνω: to drink
πιπράσκω: to sell
πίπτω: to fall, fall down
πιστεύω: to trust, believe (+ dat.)
πίτυρον, τό: a husk
πίων, -ον: fat, plump
πλακοῦς, -οῦντος, ὁ: a cake
πλάτος, ὁ: breadth, width
πλεῖστος, -η, -ον: most, largest
πλευρόν, τό: a rib
πλέω: to sail
πλεών, -ον: more
πληγή, ἡ: a blow, stroke
πλῆθος, -εος, τό: a great number,
  crowd, multitude
πλησιάζω: to bring near
πλήσιος, α, ον: near, close to (+ gen.)
πλήττω: to strike, hit
πλούσιος, -α, -ον: rich, wealthy,
  opulent
πλουτέω: to be rich, have wealth
πλοῦτος, ὁ: riches, wealth
πνέω: to blow

224

Glossary

πόθεν: whence? from where?

ποθέω: to long for, yearn after

ποιέω: to make, do

ποιητής, -οῦ, ὁ: a poet

ποικίλλω: to work in embroidery, decorate

πολεμέω: to be at war, make war

πολέμιος, -α, -ον: of war, hostile, enemy

πόλεμος, ὁ: a fight, battle, war

πόλις, -εως, ἡ: a city

πολίτης, -ου, ὁ: a citizen

πόλιτις, -ιδος: belonging to one's city

πολλάκις: many times, often

πολυάνθρωπος, -ον: full of people, populous

πολυπρόσωπος, -ον: many-faced, with many acting roles

πολύς, πολλή, πολύ: many, much

πολυτελής, -ές: lavish, extravagant, expensive, very costly

πολυχρόνιος, -ον: long-existing

πονέω: to labor, suffer, toil

πορεία, ἡ: a march, journey

πορεύομαι: to be carried, go, walk

πόρρω: forwards, onwards, further (+ gen.)

πόρρωθεν: from afar

πορφύρεος, -η, -ον: purple

ποταμός, ὁ: a river, stream

ποτέ: at one time, once upon a time

ποτήριον, τό: a cup

ποτόν, τό: a drink

πότος, ὁ: a drink, drinking

πούς, ποδός, ὁ: a foot

πρᾶγμα, -ατος, τό: a deed, act, matter

πρᾶσις, -εως, ἡ: a selling, sale

πράττω: to do, act

πρίν: before

πρό: before

προβάτιον, τό: a little sheep, lamb

προδίδωμι: to give away, betray

πρόδομος, ὁ: vestibule, entryway

προέρχομαι: to come forward, advance, go forth

πρόθυμος, -ον: ready, willing, eager

πρόκειμαι: to be set before one, propose, prescribe

προογκάομαι: to bray before

προοράω: to foresee

προπίνω: to drink before

πρός: to (+ dat.)

προσαγορεύω: to address, greet

προσάγω: to bring to

προσβάλλω: to throw against, put to

προσβάλλω: to throw to

προσβολή, ἡ: an attack, strike, impact

προσδέω: to bind to, tie to, attach

προσδοκάω: to expect

πρόσειμι: to be present

προσέρχομαι: to go to

προσέχω: to hold to, offer

προσήκω: to come to, arrive at, be akin

προσίημι: to admit, submit

προσκαλέω: to call to, summon

προσκεφάλαιον, τό: a cushion, pillow

προσμειδιάω: to smile upon

προσμένω: to stay through, remain longer

πρόσοδος, ἡ: a income, profit

προσπαίζω: to play, joke

προσπαλαίω: to wrestle

προσπίπτω: to fall upon

προσποιέω: to pretend, affect

προσπταίω: to stumble

προσπτύω: to spit upon (+ dat.)

προστίθημι: to put to, place upon

προστρέχω: to run forward, run to

προσφέρω: to bring to

πρόσω: forwards, further

πρόσωθεν: from afar

πρόσωπον, τό: a face

πρότερος, -α, -ον: before, earlier

προφέρω: to bring forth

πρόχειρος, -ον: at hand, ready, accessible

προχέω: to pour forth

προωθέω: to push forward

πρωκτός, ὁ: a bottom, rear

πρῶτος, -η, -ον: first

πτερόν, τό: feathers

πτερόω: to feather, give feathers or wings

πυγή, -ῆς, ἡ: buttocks

πυκνός, ή, όν: thick-set, crowded

πυνθάνομαι: to learn

πυξίς, -ιδος, ἡ: a box

πῦρ, πυρός, τό: fire

πυρίκαυστος, ον: inflamed, caused by burning

πυρός, ὁ: wheat
πωλέω: to exchange, barter, sell
πῶλος, ὁ: a foal, young horse
πῶς: how? in what way?
πως: in some way, somehow

P ρ

ῥάβδος, ἡ: a rod, stick, switch
ῥᾴδιος, -α, -ον: easy, ready
ῥᾳθυμία, ἡ: laziness, carelessness
ῥαφανίς, -ῖδος, ἡ: a radish
ῥήγνυμι: to break
ῥίπτω: to throw, cast, hurl
ῥίς, ῥινός, ἡ: a nose
ῥοδοδάφνη, ἡ: rose-laurel
ῥόδον, τό: a rose
ῥύομαι: to rescue, save

Σ σ

σαρδάνιος, -α, -ον: bitter, scornful
σελήνη, ἡ: the moon
σέλινον, τό: parsley
σήπω: to rot
σιγή, ἡ: silence
σιωπή, ἡ: silence
σκάπτω: to dig
σκέλος, -εος, τό: the leg
σκεπάζω: to cover
σκέπτομαι: to look about, look for
σκευάζω: to prepare, make ready
σκεύη, τά: possessions, belongings
σκῆψις, -εως, ἡ: a pretext, excuse, pretense
σκιμπόδιον, τό: a small pallet
σκίρτημα, -ατος, τό: a leap, kick
σκληρός, -ά, -όν: hard
σκοπέω: to look, behold, consider, take care
σκοπός, ὁ: one that watches, a lookout
σκορπίζω: to scatter, disperse
σκώληξ, -ηκος, ὁ: a worm
σκώπτω: to mock, jeer, scoff at
σοφιστής, -οῦ, ὁ: a sophist, teacher
σοφός, -ή, -όν: skilled

σπαίρω: to gasp, pant
σπαράττω: to tear, rend
σπάω: to draw
σπεύδω: to hasten, hurry, quicken
σπλάγχνον, τό: the inner parts
σπουδή, ἡ: haste, speed, eagerness
στάζω: to drop, let fall, shed
στενός, -ή, -όν: narrow, strait
στένω: to moan, sigh, groan
στενωπός, ὁ: a narrow lane, ally
στέφανος, ὁ: a garland
στεφανόω: to crown, wreath, surround with garlands
στιβάς, -άδος, ἡ: a bed of straw
στολή, ἡ: an equipment, armament
στόμα, τό: the mouth
στρατιώτης, -ου, ὁ: a soldier, recruit
στρατός, ὁ: an army, troop
στρέφω: to turn
στρόμβος, ὁ: a top
στρῶμα, -ατος, τό: a bed, bedding, trappings
στυππεῖον, τό: flax
σύ, σου: you
συγγενής, -ές: born with, related
συγγραφεύς, -έως, ὁ: a writer
συγκαθεύδω: to lie down with, sleep with
συγκατακλείω: to shut in together
σύγκειμαι: to lie together, be agreed
συγκινδυνεύω: to incur danger along with, share danger
συγκλαίω: to weep with
συγκλείω: to shut, close up, enclose
συγκόπτω: to beat up, thrash
σύγκρισις, -εως, ἡ: a comparison
συγχωρέω: to come together, meet
συλλαμβάνω: to collect, gather together
συλλέγω: to collect, gather
συμβάλλω: to throw together, infer
συμβόλαιον, τό: a contract, engagement, transaction
σύμβολον, τό: a sign, mark, symbol
συμβουλεύω: to advise, counsel
σύμβουλος, ὁ: an adviser, counselor
συμπεριφέρω: to carry around x (acc.) along with y (dat.)
συμπίπτω: to fall together, attack

Glossary

συμπλέκω: to entangle, grapple, twine together

συμπόσιον, τό: a drinking-party, symposium

συμπότης, -ου, ὁ: a fellow-drinker

συμφέρω: to bring together, gather, collect

συμφορά, ἡ: an event, circumstance, chance

συναιχμάλωτος, ὁ: a fellow-prisoner

συναποδράω: to run away with, escape together

συναριστάω: to share a meal

συνάριστος, ὁ: a meal companion

σύνδουλος, ὁ: a fellow-slave

συνεκπέμπω: to send out together, send with

συνελαύνω: to drive together

συνεργός, -όν: working together, sharing in a trade

συνευνάζω: to lay down with

συνέχω: to hold together, secure

συνήθης, -ες: accustomed, customary, usual, acquainted

συνίημι: to bring together, understand, put together

σύννομος, -ον: grazing together

συνοδοίπορος, ὁ: a fellow traveler

συνοικέω: to dwell with

συνοικίζω: to make to live with, house with

συνουσία, ἡ: a being with, intercourse

συντάττω: to arrange, make ready

συντίθημι: to put together, arrange

συντρέχω: to run together with, coincide

συντρίβω: to grind, beat to a pulp

συνωθέω: to force one's way in

Σύριος, -α, -ον: of or from Syria

συρράπτω: to sew up, stitch together

σύρω: to draw, drag

σῦς, συός, ὁ: a pig, boar

σύσκηνος, ὁ: a messmate

συχνός, -ή, -όν: much, long, great, many

σφάζω: to slay, slaughter

σφηκόω: to bind tightly

σφίγγω: to bind tight, bind fast

σφόδρα: very, exceedingly

σφός, σφή, σφόν: their, their own

σχεδόν: close, near

σχέτλιος, -α, -ον: unwearying, cruel

σχῆμα, -ατος, τό: form, appearance, figure

σχίζω: to split, cleave, divide

σώζω: to save

σῶμα, -ατος, τό: a body

σωτήρ, -ῆρος, ὁ: a savior, deliverer

σωτηρία, ἡ: deliverance, safety

σώφρων, ὁ: temperate, moderate

Τ τ

ταλαίπωρος, -ον: suffering, miserable

τάλας, τάλαινα, τάλαν: suffering, wretched

ταχέως: quickly

τε: and

τείνω: to stretch

τέκνον, τό: a child, offspring

τέλεος, -α, -ον: finished, at the end

τελευταῖος, -α, -ον: last, final

τέλμα, -ατος, τό: a pond, marsh, swamp

τέλος, -εος, τό: an end, fulfillment, completion

τέμενος, -εος, τό: a sacred space

τέμνω: to cut

τερατεύομαι: to say monstrous things

τερατώδης, -ες: monstrous

τέρψις, -εως, ἡ: enjoyment, delight

τέσσαρες: four

τεύχω: to work, make, bring about

τέχνη, ἡ: art, skill, craft

τίθημι: to set, put, place

τίκτω: to bear, give birth

τιμάω: to honor

τιμή, ἡ: value, price, compensation

τίμιος, -ον: valued, valuable

τινάττω: to shake, brandish

τις, τι: someone, something (indefinite)

τίς, τί: who? which? (interrogative)

τιτρώσκω: to wound

τίω: to pay honor to

τοιοῦτος, -αύτη, -οῦτο: such as this

τοιοῦτος, -η, -ον: such as this

τοῖχος, ὁ: a wall

τολμάω: to take heart, dare

Glossary

τόλμημα, -ατος, τό: an adventure, enterprise, daring deed
τολμηρός, -ά, -όν: hardihood
τόμη, ἡ: a cutting, knife
τοσοῦτος, -αύτη, -οῦτο: so great, so much, so large
τράπεζα, -ης, ἡ: a table
τραῦμα, -ατος, τό: a wound, hurt, injury
τράχηλος, ὁ: a neck, throat
τραχύς, -εῖα, -ύ: rugged, rough
τρεῖς: three
τρέμω: to tremble in fear
τρέφω: to raise, maintain, support, care for
τρέχω: to run
τριάκοντα: thirty
τριπλόος, -η, -ον: triple, threefold
τροφή, ἡ: nourishment, food
τρυφάω: to live luxuriously
τρυφή, ἡ: softness, delicacy, luxuriousness, wantonness
τυγχάνω: to hit, happen upon, befall
τύπτω: to beat, hit, strike
τυρεύω: to create mischief, cause trouble
τυρός, ὁ: cheese
τύχη, ἡ: chance, fortune

Υ υ

ὑβρίζω: to run riot, insult
ὕβρις, -εως, ἡ: wantonness, insolence, hubris
ὑγιαίνω: to be healthy
ὑγρός, -ά, -όν: wet, damp, moist, fluid
ὕδωρ, ὕδατος, τό: water
υἱός, ὁ: a son
ὕλη, ἡ: a forest
ὑπαίθριος, -α, -ον: in the open air, outside
ὑπάκουσις, -εως, ἡ: sense
ὑπακούω: to listen, attend, obey, answer (a knock)
ὑπανοίγω: to open secretly
ὑπεξέρχομαι: to go out from under, escape
ὑπεραλγέω: to feel pain

ὑπερβάλλω: to throw beyond, stick out beyond
ὑπεροράω: to look down upon, disdain
ὑπερτρυφάω: to be excessively haughty
ὑπερῷον, τό: an upper room
ὑπερῷος, -α, -ον: above, upper
ὑπέχω: to undergo
ὑπηρετέω: to service
ὑπηρέτης, -ου, ὁ: a public slave, assistant, underling, attendant
ὑπισχνέομαι: to promise
ὕπνος, ὁ: sleep, slumber
ὑπό: from under, by (+ gen.); under (+ dat.); toward (+ acc.)
ὑποβάλλω: to throw down, put under, suggest
ὑποβεβρεγμένος, -η, -ον: somewhat drunk
ὑποβλέπω: to look up
ὑποδέχομαι: to receive (in one's home), host
ὑπόδημα, -ατος, τό: a shoe, sandal
ὑποζεύγνυμι: to put under the yoke
ὑπολακτίζω: to kick out
ὑπολείπω: to leave remaining
ὑπομένω: to stay, remain
ὑπόνοια, ἡ: a suspicion
ὑποπτεύω: to suspect, be suspicious
ὕποπτος, -ον: viewed with suspicion
ὑποσπάω: to draw off
ὑποστόρνυμι: to lay under, make a bed
ὑποτέμνω: to cut from under
ὑποχωρέω: to go back, withdraw
ὕπτιος, -α, -ον: backward, on one's back
ὕστατος, -η, -ον: latest, last
ὑστεραῖος, -α, -ον: the next day
ὕστερος, -α, -ον: later, afterward
ὑφέλκω: to withdraw
ὑφίστημι: to place under
ὑψηλός, -ή, -όν: high, lofty

Φ φ

φαίνομαι: to appear, seem
φαίνω: to show
φάρμακον, τό: a drug, medicine
φάρυγξ, φάρυγγος, ἡ: a throat
φάσκω: to say, affirm, assert

Glossary

φάτνη, ἡ: a manger, feeding-trough
φαῦλος, -η, -ον: easy, slight
φείδομαι: to spare
φειδώ, -οῦς, ἡ: a sparing, thrift
φέρω: to bear, bring, carry, endure
φεύγω: to flee, escape, run away
φημί: to say
φθείρω: to ruin, destroy
φιάλη, ἡ: a bowl
φιλάργυρος, -ον: fond of money, miserly
φιλέω: to love, kiss
φίλη, ἡ: a friend
Φίληβος, ὁ: Philebus
φίλημα, -ατος, τό: a kiss, embrace
φίλιος, -η, -ον: beloved, dear
φίλος, -η, -ον: beloved, dear
φίλος, ὁ: a friend
φιλοτιμία, ἡ: munificence
φίλτατος, -η, -ον: dearest, most beloved
φλύαρος, ὁ: one who talks nonsense, a babbler
φοβερός, -ά, -όν: fearful
φόβος, ὁ: fear
φονεύς, -έως, ὁ: a murderer
φορβειά, ἡ: a halter
φορτηγέω: to carry loads
φορτίον, τό: a load, burden
φρήν, φρενός, ἡ: a thought
φροντίζω: to think, consider, have a care
φρουρά, ἡ: a watch, guard
φρουρέω: to keep watch, guard
φρύγω: to roast
φυγή, ἡ: flight
φυλάζω: to divide up
φυλάττω: to keep watch, guard
φύλλον, τό: a leaf, petal
φύρω: to mix
φυσάω: to blow
φυτεύω: to plant
φυτόν, τό: a plant
φύω: to bring forth, produce, grow
φωνή, ἡ: a sound, tone, voice

X χ

χαίρω: to rejoice, be glad
χάλασμα, -ατος, τό: a relaxation, a gap

χαλάω: to slacken, loosen
χαλεπαίνω: to be sore, be grievous
χαλεπός, -ή, -όν: hard to bear, painful, heavy, difficult
χαλινός, ὁ: a bridle
χαμαί: on the ground
χαμεύνιον, τό: a small pallet bed
χαμόθεν: from the ground
χάρις, -ιτος, ἡ: favor, grace
χεῖλος, -εος, τό: a lip
χειμών, -ῶνος, ὁ: winter
χείρ, χειρός, ἡ: a hand
χελώνη, ἡ: a tortoise
χλωρός, ά, όν: fresh, blooming
χόνδρος, ὁ: a grain
χόρτος, ὁ: feed, hay
χράομαι: to use, enjoy (+ dat.)
χρεία, ἡ: use, advantage, need (+ gen.)
χρή: it is fated, necessary
χρῆμα, -ατος, τό: a thing that one uses, money
χρήσιμος, -η, -ον: useful, serviceable
χρῖσμα, -ατος, τό: an anointing, ointment
χρίω: to anoint
χρόνος, ὁ: time
χρύσεος, -η, -ον: golden, of gold
χρυσίον, τό: a golden object
χρυσός, ὁ: gold
χύτρα, ἡ: a pot
χωλεύω: to be lame, limp
χωλός, -ή, -όν: lame
χώρα, ἡ: a place, country, space, land
χωρέω: to make room, give way
χωρίον, τό: a place, spot

Ψ ψ

ψαύω: to touch
ψευδής, -ές: lying, false
ψεύδομαι: to lie, pretend
ψιλός, -ή, -όν: bare, uncovered, open
ψοφέω: to make a noise, sound
ψυχαγωγέω: to beguile, entertain, lead the soul
ψυχή, ἡ: soul, life
ψυχρός, -ά, -όν: cold, chill

Glossary

Ω ω

ᾠδή, ἡ: a song, incantation

ὠθέω: to thrust, push, shove

ὠκύς, -εῖα, -ύ: quick, swift, fleet

ὠμός, -ή, -όν: raw

ὦμος, ὁ: a shoulder

ὠνέομαι: to buy, purchase

ὥρα, -ας, ἡ: a period, season, time

ὡραῖος, -α, -ον: in season, ripe, young

ὡς: *adv.* as, so how; *conj.* that, in order that, since; *prep.* to (+ *acc.*); as if, as (+ *part.*); as _____ as possible (+ *superlative*)

NOTES:

NOTES:

NOTES:

NOTES:

NOTES:

CPSIA information can be obtained
at www.ICGtesting.com
Printed in the USA
LVHW011629091222
734911LV00005B/543